Feminists, Feminisms, and Advertising

Feminists, Feminisms, and Advertising

Some Restrictions Apply

Edited by
Kim Golombisky and Peggy J. Kreshel

LEXINGTON BOOKS
Lanham • Boulder • New York • London

Published by Lexington Books
An imprint of The Rowman & Littlefield Publishing Group, Inc.
4501 Forbes Boulevard, Suite 200, Lanham, Maryland 20706
www.rowman.com

Unit A, Whitacre Mews, 26-34 Stannary Street, London SE11 4AB

British Library Cataloguing in Publication Information Available

The hardback edition of this book was previously catalogued by the Library of Congress as follows:

Library of Congress Cataloging-in-Publication Data

Names: Golombisky, Kim, editor. | Kreshel, Peggy J. (Peggy Jean), 1953- editor.
Title: Feminists, feminisms, and advertising : some restrictions apply /
edited by Kim Golombisky and Peggy J. Kreshel.
Description: Lanham : Lexington Books, [2017] | Includes bibliographical references and index.
Identifiers: LCCN 2017037220 (print) | LCCN 2017040465 (ebook) |
ISBN 9781498528276 (electronic) | ISBN 9781498528269 (cloth)
Subjects: LCSH: Advertising—History. | Women in advertising—History.
Classification: LCC HQ1150 (ebook) | LCC HQ1150 .F463 2017 (print) |
DDC 305.420973—dc23
LC record available at https://lccn.loc.gov/2017037220

ISBN 978-1-4985-2826-9 (cloth)
ISBN 978-1-4985-2828-3 (pbk.)
ISBN 978-1-4985-2827-6 (electronic)

To our feminist mentors

Contents

Acknowledgments xi

1 Introductory Remarks on the Advertising Business and a Community of Feminist Scholars Making Advertising *Their* Business 1
Peggy J. Kreshel

PART I: HISTORIES OF FEMINISTS, FEMINISMS, AND ADVERTISING **27**

2 Women versus Brands: Sexist Advertising and Gender Stereotypes Motivate Transgenerational Feminist Critique 29
Jacqueline Lambiase, Carolyn Bronstein, and Catherine A. Coleman

3 The Entangled Politics of Feminists, Feminism, Advertising, and Beauty: A Historical Perspective 61
Dara Persis Murray

4 "Don't You Love Being a Woman?": Advertising, Empowerment, and the Women's Movement 85
Ann Marie Nicolosi

PART II: ENCODING: FEMINIST CRITIQUES OF ADVERTISING PROFESSIONALS AND PRACTICES **107**

5 Black Women and Advertising Ethics: A Womanist Perspective 109
Joanna L. Jenkins

6 "What's Wrong, You Can't Take a Joke?" Advertisers' Defenses of Images of Violence against Women in Their Ads, 1979–1989 133
Juliet Dee

7 Exceptional Exemplars: Practitioners' Perspectives on Ads that Communicate Effectively with Women and Men 155
Kasey Windels

8 The Creative Career Dilemma: No Wonder Ad Women Are Mad Women 177
Karen L. Mallia

9 Exporting Gender Bias: Anglo-American Echoes in Swedish Advertising Creative Departments 207
Jean M. Grow

PART III: DECODING: FEMINIST ANALYSES OF INTERSECTIONAL ADVERTISING AUDIENCES 229

10 Engaging in Consumer Citizenship: Latina Audiences and Advertising in Women's Ethnic Magazines 231
Jillian M. Báez

11 "You Get a Very Conflicting View": Postfeminism, Contradiction, and Women of Color's Responses to Representations of Women in Advertisements 251
Leandra H. Hernández

12 Social Exclusion and Gay Consumers' Boycott and Buycott Decisions 271
Wanhsiu Sunny Tsai and Xiaoqi Han

PART IV: PROFESSIONAL DEVELOPMENT: HISTORIOGRAPHY AND BIOGRAPHY 293

13 The Curious Story of Home Economics' Contribution to Women's Careers in Advertising 295
Kimberly Wilmot Voss

14 A Woman's Place: Career Success and Early Twentieth-Century Women's Advertising Clubs 313
Jeanie E. Wills

15 Closing Arguments: A Feminist Education for Advertising Students 337
Kim Golombisky

Index 369

About the Editors and Contributors 389

Acknowledgments

We are especially grateful for the skill and forbearance of our talented copy-editor Noelle Barrick and for the patience of our long-suffering Lexington acquisitions editor Nicolette Amstutz. We also are thrilled with Rebecca Hagen's ingenious cover art.

Chapter 1

Introductory Remarks on the Advertising Business and a Community of Feminist Scholars Making Advertising *Their* Business

Peggy J. Kreshel

After more than thirty years teaching advertising, you'd think I wouldn't have a problem coming up with a "hook" for this introduction. You know, the tease that leaves you wanting more, that gets your attention and lets you know you've done the right thing in picking up this book.

I didn't think that you'd be particularly interested in knowing how much money was spent on advertising each year (an estimated $184 billion in 2017). You might be intrigued by the fact that advertising helps consumers make $7 trillion in spending decisions annually (Rothenberg 2015), but then I thought, "No. This is a book about feminism and advertising." So I thought you might be unpleasantly startled to know that in a recent 3% Conference survey of six hundred women working in advertising, "The Elephant on Mad Ave" (3% 2016), 54 percent of the respondents indicated they had been subjected to an unwanted sexual advance during the course of the their careers. But then, you may already be aware of that.

So I flipped through (well, I clicked through) some of the trade publications looking for the "hook" and this headline in *Marketing Week* (Ritson 2017) caught my attention: "Heineken should remember marketing is about profit, not purpose." And in case all the advertising folks who read this trade didn't get the point, the subhead filled in the details: "Heineken's new purpose-driven ad might express all the right values, but marketers must remember if you don't use your budget to create sales, you've failed." It's a commentary on the four-minute Heineken ad "Open Your World." The ad includes viewpoints on transgender rights, feminism, and climate change; "created acres of coverage and tons of social media response"; and, according to Heineken's head of marketing, was meant to "inspire more people to focus on the things that unite us rather than divide us."

Personally, I liked the ad.

At that moment, I thought about something feminist historian Joan Wallach Scott (1999, 179) said: "The social practices of members of a profession are intimately related to the ways they interpret the meaning of their work." And I wondered, how *do* advertising professionals interpret the meaning of their work?

In advertising's efforts to achieve professional stature, the American Association of Advertising Agencies adopted the "Standards of Practice," essentially a code of ethics, in 1924. That document clearly stated in the opening line how the profession perceived its work: "We hold that a responsibility of advertising agencies is to *be a constructive force in business*" (emphasis added).

Now, a lot has happened in the media world since 1924: TV, the VCR, cell phones, smart phones, the internet, Facebook, Instagram, Twitter, ad-blocking technology, and . . . well, you get the idea. Today advertising is in the throes of a revolution. Elsewhere (Kreshel 2016, 357), I've identified some of the key characteristics of that revolution: a constant flow of new capabilities fueled by fast-paced technologies, exuberance for all things digital, optimistic vision of possibility and "ambitious entrepreneurship in a rarely questioned market economy and a complex global marketplace." Couple that with advertising becoming an active player in the ad-tech and analytic sectors, and *Voilà,* you've got a revolution.

Oh and did I mention there's been a lot of social changes since 1924? You know, civil rights, the women's movements, sixteen presidents, and we have millennials now.

What hasn't changed is the opening line of the "Standards of Practice" (revised twice, 1990 and most recently 2011). Nearly a century has passed and the advertising industry continues to view its role as being "a constructive force in business." That's something you need to know

Given the enormous amounts of money spent on advertising, and the ubiquity of advertising in our everyday lives, it is difficult to think of advertising as anything other than a business tool. Yet scholars invite consideration of what they view to be a more critical role, that of social communication, circulating meaning in culture. Canadian scholars Leiss, Kline, Jhally, and Botterill (2005, 5) suggest, "Advertising is not just a business expenditure undertaken in the hope of moving some merchandise off the store shelves, but it is rather an integral part of modern cultures." In fact, they suggest that perhaps "the least important aspect of advertising's significance for modern society is its role in influencing specific consumers . . . about purchasing products."

Still, the advertising industry remains singularly focused on its role in business, grounded in utilitarian marketplace concerns. "Within this focus, individuals are primarily viewed . . . as means to an economic end rather than as human beings, themselves worthy of being treated with dignity, honesty, and fairness" (Kreshel 2016, 360). The profession dismisses decades of consistent negative public opinion with little more than a metaphorical shoulder shrug. The industry and to some lesser degree advertising scholars have largely been unconcerned with the broader political, social, cultural, economic, and ideological concerns, and instead focus on "making advertising work better." Maybe that helps to explain the relationship between advertising and feminism. Consider this: Feminists' concerns with the hypersexualization and objectification of women's bodies are of little import to advertisers given the apparent advertising norm: "Sex sells."

And now, a word about me.

As I said, I've been teaching advertising for just over thirty years, in the same department (even the same office), with wonderful colleagues. Still, I think of myself as something of an outlier. Oh, I teach what we call "the skills courses." In fact, I often teach students how to get messages to the right people at the right time, efficiently and (I add) in a socially responsible way. Yes, I'm a "media" professor. But I also developed the advertising and society course (some twenty years ago) and courses on media culture and diversity, media literacy and social justice, and feminist media studies. I like to think of myself as the social conscience of the department, college, and, heck, the entire discipline. I'm the one whose research doesn't focus on how to make advertising *work* better, but on how to make *advertising* better. I don't get excited about new platforms or better metrics, and I admit to not being particularly enchanted by the commercial promise of "the Internet of Things." Instead, I wonder about the social justice dilemmas that might arise in the seemingly chaotic media–advertising ecosystem in which "we have the potential to make bad decisions far more quickly, efficiently, and with far greater impact than we did in the past" (Etlinger 2014).

I recognize and appreciate the global, social, and economic power of advertising. I applaud and frequently am amazed by its creativity and vision. That being said, I admit to being disheartened at times both by the industry's seeming inability to extend that vision beyond the confines of the business sphere and the persistence with which people are recognized solely as consumers valued differentially based on their ability and enthusiasm to "buy something," rather than as citizens and individuals. I understand and even appreciate the wonders, benefits, and possibilities brought about by technological innovations and data analytics. Still, I am troubled, as are many, by concerns over privacy and surveillance, and I worry that the determination, haste, and exuberance with which we seek the latest gadgetry and infinite possibilities divert attention from the moral dimensions of our work as advertising professionals, educators, and citizens. I am a feminist.

And now, a word about the book you're about to enjoy.

Kim and I have been creating this collection in our conversations for several years.

Our primary goal was to bring together feminist scholars doing research in advertising: feminist scholars who may not be (and more than likely aren't) in advertising departments; feminist scholars who may or may not know of each other's work; feminist scholars who share a desire to understand how advertising practices and representations create, nurture, and perpetuate patterns of social injustice and how we might intervene, perhaps even using advertising and advertising practices to challenge those injustices.

In doing that, we hoped to energize the ongoing conversations about feminism and advertising with new and innovative ideas, and foster the vigilance necessary in the rapidly changing matrices of our experiences. In some ways, maybe, my colleague Kim Golombisky and I wanted to encourage a "click" moment. Not a click of the mouse, but a moment when a group of feminist scholars realized that, indeed, they were a community.

The number of responses we received in response to our call was far greater than we anticipated. We were thrilled not only with the numbers but with the breadth of the research being done. Feminist scholars enter the discussion of feminism and advertising at any number of points. We saw all kinds of feminisms and all kinds of methodological approaches. To all of you we say, "Thanks." We couldn't have done it without you.

In the remainder of this chapter, I'll tell you a bit about what you'll find in these pages. But before I do that, I have a suggestion. You might like to *start* by reading the last chapter, Kim Golombisky's "Closing Arguments: A Feminist Education for Advertising Students."

Perhaps you are well-acquainted with feminist concepts and theories, controversies pulling at feminism's boundaries or pushing at its core, and the history of the movement. If so, you'll find Dr. Golombisky's discussion to be a welcome touch point, a reminder of why it's important to be a feminist scholar. Alternatively, if you are just starting to work your way through the complexities and nuances of feminism(s), her chapter is essentially a primer on feminism(s). It's a terrific way to begin or continue your feminist journey. You'll want to keep her roadmap close by and refer to it often.

We've divided the book into four sections. In the following pages, I take you through what you'll find in each, adding an occasional aside to clarify, provide context, or to relay something in which I think you might be interested.

The chapters in the first section provide historical accounts of the relationships between feminists, feminisms, and advertising. The researchers remind us that those relationships, grounded as they are in the material conditions of particular moments, have been both complicated and dynamic. No doubt, they will continue to be so.

PART I: HISTORIES OF FEMINISTS, FEMINISMS, AND ADVERTISING

In the May 2017 issue of *Vogue,* writer and Barnard professor Mary Gordon recounts her first moment of political engagement in antiwar protests of the 1960s, and her participation in the January 2017 Women's March. She writes, "So much of political effectiveness is a matter of endurance, of staying in for the long haul" (98). In "Women versus Brands: Sexist Advertising and Gender Stereotypes Motivate Transgenerational Feminist Critique," Jacque Lambiase, Carolyn Bronstein, and Catherine Coleman provide a primer on feminists' critiques of advertising, and the "creative, forceful, and persistent way that feminist activists have strategized to confront and reform a powerful image industry over the past half century." They identify key actors (from Betty Friedan's *Feminine Mystique* to advertising executive Madonna Badger's current #WomenNotObjects campaign to stop the objectification of women and girls), episodes (remember Brooke Shields and her Calvins?), academic research, and industry responses or lack thereof.

Strategies undertaken by feminist activists reflect changes in advertising, as well as differences in feminisms and transformations in feminist thought from a focus primarily on concerns of privileged white women to movement toward more inclusive intersectional understandings of feminisms and lived experiences (May 2012, 164). Technological innovations have provided advertisers with an array of opportunities to enter every nook and cranny of our lives, and, today, to create individualized and interactive consumer experiences. At the same time, these innovations offer new avenues of resistance that enable immediate global communication and organization, among them the creation of original content, social media, and meme diffusion.

Over the last half century, feminist activism has experienced "progress, stagnation, backlash, and even backsliding." Drs. Lambiase, Bronstein, and Coleman provide ample evidence that feminists are indeed "in it for the long haul."

Some of those feminists work in advertising.

In a polemical essay, "Market Feminism: The Case for a Paradigm Shift," Linda Scott (2000, 17) critiqued what she viewed to be an "anti-market prejudice" in contemporary feminist thought. She argued that this prejudice creates a dilemma for women in advertising: "How is one to act as a feminist while working for an advertising agency?"

In "The Entangled Politics of Feminists, Feminism, Advertising, and Beauty: A Historical Perspective," Dara Persis Murray begins to answer

Scott's question. She investigates the relationships between feminist politics, advertising, sex, beauty, and consumer culture through a discussion of *moments of entanglement,* those "moments in which women have navigated social conventions as well as institutional barriers in their efforts to change attitudes and representations of women and of feminism."

Her narrative begins with the suffrage and women's reform movements in which white, middle-class women created a political identity through appearance and merchandising, simultaneously defining themselves as activists and consumers. It concludes with a discussion of present-day postfeminism linking women's empowerment with hypersexuality, hyperconsumerism, narrow representations of beauty, and a grammar of individualism. Dr. Murray pauses to examine several other moments of entanglement along the way:

- Advertising copywriter Helen Resor and consumer specialist Christine Frederick, feminists both, undertook very earnest but dramatically different efforts to undo denigrating stereotypes of white women as consumers in the early years of the twentieth century, yet inadvertently reinforced traditional gender roles.
- Aspirational advertising during the interwar years portrayed the "modern" white woman liberated by labor-saving appliances in the home, and by her power to purchase goods and shape and dress her body to secure men's approval.
- Feminist Gloria Steinem attempted to draw a boundary between feminist values and beauty advertising in *Ms.* magazine, but was forced to make accommodations to meet economic imperatives of publishing.

Dr. Murray's account illustrates the complex negotiations involved as feminists in advertising struggled to communicate complex visions of women while balancing the economic goals of the industry and the political goals of feminism. One need only consider former advertising executive Cindy's Gallop's "If We Ran the World" (ifweranttheworld.com) or Kat Gordon's 2012 initiation of the 3% Conference to support women's creative leadership in advertising to realize that the balancing act is ongoing.

Feminist historian Ruth Rosen (2000, 311) noted that, starting as early as the 1970s, the "advertising industry scarcely missed a beat as they geared up to sell 'liberation' . . . some of the most popular pseudo-feminist ads appropriated the language of emancipation in order to sell women products." Today, this strategy of cooptation is commonly known and widely critiqued as *commodity feminism* (Goldman, Heath, and Smith 1991). In "'Don't You Love Being a Woman?' Advertising, Empowerment, and the Women's Movement," Ann Marie Nicolosi focuses on that pivotal historical moment in the women's movement. The advertising industry approached changes that had taken place with an optimism fueled by visions of enormous economic returns, but with significant uncertainty. Having long viewed white "women" to be a single market, advertisers recognized that "women now [came] in infinite varieties" (Cadwell 1971, 1). Women were trying on different identities and advertisers wanted and needed to reach them all. "Giants in washing machines and little men in boats who paddled around . . . toilet bowls" would no longer work (Bassin 1970). But they wondered, what would?

Dr. Nicolosi takes up advertisers' strategic use of commodity feminism, drawing on select advertisements from the 1970s as cultural artifacts. Advertisers targeted products once marketed only to men as "family breadwinners" to the "new woman" and the "workwife" using very different appeals, often of newly found "independence" (Mccall 1977, 55). As women gained financial independence and access to credit, realtors touted houses as sites of liberation. Retail advertising for products ranging from lingerie for the "feminist at home" to home appliances, as well as ads for household and beauty products long targeted to women incorporated feminist themes and language. Advertisers faced a dilemma of reaching out to the new woman while not offending their consumer base of traditional women. Dr. Nicolosi notes that shadows of long-held stereotypes—domestic bliss; reliance on men; and the importance, indeed, the necessity of beauty—often lingered behind advertiser celebrations of women's newly discovered "empowerment."

Moving beyond the now seemingly customary critique, Dr. Nicolosi argues that reducing advertisements to "mere instances of commodity feminism" overlooks the very real contribution these advertisements made to the women's movement. Advertisements designed to sell products to the "new woman" simultaneously, even if unintentionally, advertised the women's movement. Then, too, advertising provided support for commercial magazines that brought the movement into women's daily lives: "Millions of nonmovement women first learned about feminism . . . within the familiar pages of women's magazines" (Rosen 2000, 328), expanding the reach of the movement in ways feminists never could.

Critical scholars view communication not simply as the transmission of information, but as the circulation of meaning through culture. This circulation is conceptualized as a circuit in which meaning is constructed through ongoing cultural processes ("moments") rather than simply "found" in texts or things (du Gay et al. 1997, 14). Advertising texts are encoded with meaning in the production moment and decoded by audiences in what Hall (1980) termed the *consumption moment.* That is, to paraphrase du Gay (1997), meanings are not just "sent" by producers and "received" passively, by consumers; rather meanings are actively made in reception, through the use to which people put those texts in their everyday lives.

As noted (see Murray, Chapter 2), feminist activists have largely focused their critiques of advertising on representations of women. In the next two sections of this volume, feminist researchers focus on the construction of meaning in the lesser-investigated processes of encoding and decoding.

PART II: ENCODING: FEMINIST CRITIQUES OF ADVERTISING PROFESSIONALS AND PRACTICES

The production of advertising texts is shaped by a number of factors, among them routines and codes, professional values and norms, informal and formal knowledge, makeup and subjectivities of key practitioners, and workplace culture. The feminist researchers in Section II address three components of the encoding process: (1) the ethical norms of the profession, (2) the subjectivities of advertising creatives, and (3) workplace and gender cultures in advertising agency creative departments.

Since its earliest days, advertisers have sought to achieve recognition as a profession, establishing educational programs, trade publications, and ethical codes and interjecting "science" into decision making. Still, although ethics is an inherent part of our cultural understanding of what it means to be a professional, and advertising certainly possesses codes of ethics, the relationship between advertising and ethics might best be perceived as being "rather tenuous" (Kreshel 2016, 357). A recent study assessing advertising practitioners' views of ethics discovered that "ethical issues did not appear to be on the radar screens" of many of the informants; even when recognized, ethical issues were seldom discussed (Drumwright and Murphy 2004, 10). Today, a host of new advertising platforms and capabilities made possible by technological innovations and the inability of current legal frameworks to keep pace with those innovations have created a perfect storm in which to reexamine the role of ethics in advertising (Kreshel 2016). In "Black Women and Advertising Ethics: A Womanist Perspective," Joanna L. Jenkins advocates womanist ethics as a framework to contemplate complex intersectional ethical concerns visible in contemporary advertising ethics: the strategic use of indistinguishable advertising and the persistent lack of diversity in the advertising and media workforce.

Grounded in black feminist thought, three ideological strands frame Dr. Jenkins's discussion. The first is the political economy of our commercial media system, a system in which media create content to actively draw together "niche audiences" as commodities to be "sold" to advertisers who rank-order an audience's "desirability" based on its economic value. In this way, advertising indirectly creates the media landscape, and "entire segments of the population might be ignored if advertisers don't deem them 'desirable' as a target market" (Kreshel 2017, 203). The second strand is fast-paced technological innovation, which has resulted not only in pinpoint behavioral targeting, but in product placement, native advertising, brand storytelling, and other advertising formats often indistinguishable from other mediated forms. Because indistinguishable advertising is meant *not* to look like advertising, seemingly it is unethical by definition. The third strand framing the argument is the everyday reality of inequities based on intersectional lived experiences of racial, economic, sexual, and gender oppressions.

Dr. Jenkins cites the value of adopting a "particular ethical framework first for witnessing and second for parsing the problems, dilemmas, and injustices peculiar to black women." That framework is womanism. A discussion of womanist ethics and its emphases on intersectionality and the elimination of all forms of oppression, the importance of historical context, and the search for practical solutions for social justice change sets the stage for her womanist ethics analysis of two television series, *Scandal* (ABC) and *Empire* (Fox). Both series provide links to a "desirable" black millennial audience but are popular among mainstream audiences as well. Dr. Jenkins describes how tactics and strategies used in those programs contribute to and even promote economic oppression and prejudice. Although she makes her arguments "by way of black women, specifically, and race, gender, class, and sexuality more generally," womanist ethics and her concerns with indistinguishable advertising go beyond women of color. She concludes that "womanism urges advertising ethics to set a different standard that elevates the role of social justice in capitalist enterprise [advertising], thereby making 'social responsibility' less a euphemism and more a reality."

Lisbet van Zoonen (1994, 67) has called advertising "one of society's most disturbing cultural products. . . . As a cultural form, advertising displays a preoccupation with gender that is hardly matched in any other genre." Advertiser efforts reflect and construct particular understandings of women, of feminists, and of the feminist movement, and yet, those doing creative advertising work, their perceptions, norms, and subjectivities, have largely been neglected by both feminist and advertising scholars (Gurrieri, Brace-Govan, and Cherrier 2016; Nixon 2003; Nyilasy, Canniford, and Kreshel 2013; Soar 2000; Zayer and Coleman 2015). In the two chapters that follow, feminist researchers talk to practitioners to answer what may appear to be a simple question (but is not): *What were you thinking?*

Juliet Dee's chapter "'What's Wrong, You Can't Take a Joke?' Advertisers' Defenses of Images of Violence against Women in Their Ads, 1979–1989" is a retrospective look at advertisers' thoughts on the use of gender violence in advertising. At that time, "images of sadomasochism began creeping into advertising, fashion photography, and popular culture" more generally; "date rape" and "sexual harassment" had entered the American vernacular; anti-pornography activism had emerged; Kimberlé Crenshaw (1989) introduced the concept of intersectionality; and a "backlash" against advances of the women's movement was evident in social and legal setbacks (Faludi 1991).

Dr. Dee grounds her research in feminist dominance theory, which explains women's sexual subordination as an effect of men assuming their sex and gender dominance. Because structural barriers reinforcing male dominance are pervasive in many aspects of women's lives, women are perpetually vulnerable to violence, in this case, violence in advertising. In 1985 and 1989, Dr. Dee interviewed advertising professionals who had been involved in the production of violent advertising campaigns that had appeared between 1979 and 1989. Were they aware of the violence implied in their executions? Had market research informed those violent executions? How did professionals justify the use of violence? How did management respond to any negative public reaction that arose?

Only one respondent indicated that market research had been used in development of the campaign. This suggests the executions were based on what? Advertising norms? Stereotyped understandings of gender? The whims of the moment? None reported that the campaigns resulted in a drop in sales. The use of violent images appears to have been centered on managerial concerns such as creating awareness or increasing brand sales. Violent images grabbed consumers' attention in a cluttered marketplace; images that offended consumers would hurt sales. There was no acknowledgement of the possibility of any broader, long-term social consequences such as the normalization of violence or exploitation of women. These findings echo research that has shown that practitioners frequently display *moral myopia,* "a distortion of moral vision, ranging from shortsightedness to near blindness, which affects an individual's perception of an ethical dilemma" (Drumwright and Murphy 2004, 11). Moral myopia is often most acute at the societal level; practitioners seldom recognize their individual executions as contributing to any broader social injustice.

Respondents voiced a variety of rationalizations in distancing themselves from ethical concerns. Despite the passage of time and changes in social norms, the rationalizations provided by Dr. Dee's respondents nearly thirty years ago, are remarkably similar to those we hear today (see Gurrieri, Brace-Govan, and Cherrier 2016): "it's art," "it's satire," "it's meant to be funny, you can't take a joke?" The persistence of these rationalizations suggests they contribute to and reinforce the continued use of violence in advertising, raising the possibility that violent exploitation of women has become a strategy sometimes used almost casually, a norm of middle-class, white advertising culture.

In "Exceptional Exemplars: Practitioners' Perspectives on Ads that Communicate Effectively with Women and Men," Kasey Windels draws on feminist theory that argues that gender is constructed in discourse, texts and speeches of any kind, informal conversations, media texts, interviews, and so on. The idea that gender is a natural binary as well as the dominance of men and masculinity are constructed in discourse. As a part of this discourse, advertisers routinely incorporate stereotypes of gender, race, class, ability, and heteronormativity into their texts. The goal of Dr. Windels's research was to determine the dominant discourses that practitioners draw on to effectively communicate with men and women, and to explore how practitioner perceptions enter into the strategic creative process to become visible in advertising executions.

Advertising professionals (both men and women) were asked to identify ads they believed communicated effectively with men and ads that communicated effectively with women. This chapter is a discourse analysis of Dr. Windels's subsequent interviews with those professionals and their descriptions of the ads they selected.

Dr. Windels found little indication that respondents realized or questioned issues of race, gender, class, sexuality, disability, or power embedded in the discourses from which they drew. Instead, their focus was on incorporating symbolic meanings that resonate with consumers. Ads perceived to successfully communicate with women were those that challenged gender discourse, social norms, and advertising norms. "Empowerment ads" currently trending in advertising reflect the larger popular discourse of affirmation of women and girls. Despite earning widespread praise, outpourings of thanks, and substantial media attention, these ads are not without criticism and are frequently charged with commodifying feminism. For example, a *USA Today* article "Are women being played by 'feminist' ads?" (Ngabirano 2017) includes a comment from Andi Zeisler, author of *We Were Feminists Once* (2016) and founding editor of Bitch Media: "There are many more brands that are really grabbing onto feminism and being like, OK, this is a good way to sell products that have nothing to do with feminism or progress. Marketplace feminism comes to steal the show from more explicit active feminism." By contrast, ads believed to work for men were grounded in traditional gender norms and discussed in terms of power, control, authority, masculinity, and over-the-top humor.

Dr. Windels concludes, "the advertising professionals who participated in this study leave us with a gender narrative that urges women to push the boundaries of gender and urges men to reinforce those boundaries." Given that advertising representations are "key to the consolidation of . . . identities shaped through the world of commercially produced goods and services" (Nixon 2003, 6)—mirroring and shaping social understanding of gender; the binary nature of gender; and heteronormatvity; as well as race, class, and sexuality—this is not without significance.

Before reading the final chapters in Section II, consider the following:

At the April 2009 meeting of the American Association of Advertising Agencies, Dan Wieden, cofounder of Wieden and Kennedy, made an "impassioned diversity pitch" (McMains 2009), noting that "[The issue of diversity] continues to gnaw at me because, like it or not, in this business I essentially hire a bunch of white, middle-class kids, pay them enormous, enormous sums of money to do what? To create messages to the inner-city kids who create the culture the white kids are trying like hell to emulate. But if you go into the inner city, odds are these kids aren't even going to see advertising as a possibility, as an opportunity for them."

At the 2016 Cannes Festival of Creativity, Cindy Gallop, former president of a global agency BBH, and now advertising consultant and well-known advocate of advertising diversity, urgently called for advertising to "break the closed loop of white guys talking to white guys about other white guys" (Saner 2016).

In 2017, Carol H. Williams became only the second African-American woman named to the American Advertising Federation Hall of Fame since its inception in 1948.

Taken together, these observations tell the story of the advertising workplace today. Advertising has had a history of discrimination against African Americans for more than a half century; today African Americans represent only 5 percent of all professional and managerial positions in the industry (Dan 2016). In the next two chapters, two successful creatives, "ad women" who are now "ad professors," examine a second long-term, well-documented, widely acknowledged diversity problem in the advertising industry: women's under-representation in the creative departments of advertising agencies, and particularly the lack of women creative directors. Although women make up about half of the advertising workforce, only 11 percent of the creative directors are women (3% Conference).

Scott (1999, 179) suggested that the full meaning of occupational identities can be better understood "when we see not only who is included in them but how differences among practitioners are dealt with, which differences matter, how they are understood, and whether and how they change over time."

In his 2003 book *Advertising Cultures: Gender, Commerce, Creativity,* sociologist and in this case ethnographer Sean Nixon provided insight into the workplace culture of the creative department of advertising agencies, identifying it as a "masculine cult of creativity" (162). Today, discussions of advertising creative departments are peppered with descriptors that affirm Nixon's assessment: "a frat boy culture"; "locker room"; "playgrounds of privileged young men"; and, in a May 2017 *Advertising Age* cover story (Stein 2017, 14), a "dude fest."

In "The Creative Career Dilemma: No Wonder Ad Women Are Mad Women," Karen Mallia introduces the advertising creative department, a distinctive subculture where "anything goes," a subculture that she says is "similar from agency to agency, and even, from country to country" (see Grow, Chapter 9). After a successful twenty-year career in the advertising industry, Karen claims to be "mystified" by the gender disparity, and here, systematically explores the circumstances underlying the gender divide in advertising creative departments.

Framing her discussion in terms of three broad dimensions—the nature of creative work and working in a creative industry, traits of creative people, and work practices and cultural codes—Professor Mallia meticulously catalogs a widespread array of interlocking factors at play in the "irrefutable and tenacious" diversity problem in the creative department. Among these factors are structural barriers (e.g., lack of flexible work schedules), deliberate discrimination (e.g., gendering client assignments), encultured biases (e.g., favoring male humor), gender stereotyping (e.g., perceptions that mothers are less dedicated to work and careers), under-representation of women's creativity, a host of factors that make work–life balance for *all* creative people nearly impossible, and even women's systemic unwillingness to recognize that their experiences have anything to do with their gender. Professor Mallia attributes this reluctance to women's "internalization of the industry's discourse of meritocracy so thoroughly that they cannot or will not acknowledge that gender is a factor in their career growth."

Professor Mallia is heartened by progress being made in the industry, noting "people actually do care." The lack of women creative directors is "on the industry radar" in the trade and popular press, at conferences, and even at the Cannes Lions Festival of Creativity. Research has been commissioned and scholarly interest and research into the disparity has increased. Advocacy groups have been established and broad industry initiatives undertaken around the world. An increasing number of clients are demanding diversity in their agencies. Since the launch of the 3% Conference in 2012, the percentage of creative directors who are women has risen to 11 percent. Still, Cindy Gallop reminded attendees at the 2015 3% Conference, "The ultimate, the rarest unicorn in our industry is the black female ECD [executive creative director]."[1]

In "Exporting Gender Bias: Anglo-American Echoes in Swedish Advertising Creative Departments," Dr. Jean Grow, also a successful advertising career woman turned advertising professor, explores the global pervasiveness of the Western, heteropatriarchal gender subculture in advertising creative departments that Professor Mallia (Chapter 8) so vividly detailed. Dr. Grow draws on cultural feminism that views gender differences as grounded in socialization, and on feminist perspectives on organizational management that suggest that organizations are never gender neutral. In the workplace, women and men perform gender differently, reinforcing culturally constructed differences. Men may stress certain stereotyped notions of female gender in an effort to maintain particular privileges.

According to the European Institute for Gender Equality, Sweden is the most egalitarian country in the world. If the goal is to determine whether or not locally specific or indigenous cultural norms and values influence the cultural norms and values of advertising creative departments, it seems Sweden provides an ideal setting.

Dr. Grow interviews Swedish women creative directors about their perceptions and experiences working in advertising. She discovers that the women interviewed perceive structural and attitudinal barriers similar to those in Western-style advertising environments including hiring, promotional, and compensation inequities. The women spoke of gendered silos in which "[men] share the same humor and jokes. They build a culture that is very encouraging and nourishing for them. Women feel alienated; they don't really feel like they belong."

In Sweden then, Dr. Grow discovers a sexist culture that supports a "masculine cult of creativity" much like that in the United States, leading her to reflect: "If, as I believe, we are exporting the US culture of misogyny in the advertising industry's idealized myth of the creative department around the world, then we are also exporting our racism, homophobia, ageism, and ableism."

In light of Dr. Grow and Professor Mallia's findings, it is but one short step to essentialist thinking. Lest we take that step, both are careful to remind us that "In the end, women working in advertising creative departments are not less creative. They are simply stymied by a system defined and replicated by and for men."

PART III: DECODING: FEMINIST ANALYSES OF INTERSECTIONAL ADVERTISING AUDIENCES

Lisbet van Zoonen (1994, 105) has called attention to what she identifies as a "textual determinism" prevalent in many feminist studies of media representations. She suggests that often assumptions derived in those studies (e.g., audiences will be affected by sexist media content) are difficult to validate on an analysis of texts alone. Echoing critical scholar Stuart Hall's discussion (1980), she argues, "Audiences should be understood as producers of meaning instead of as mere consumers of meaning taking up prescribed textual audience positionings." She continues, "This production of meaning can only be understood in its everyday context which is, in turn, located within social and power relations that circumscribe the potential of audiences to make meaning." In the context we are discussing here, if we want to understand how advertisements work, *we need to understand advertising texts as they are understood by the audiences.*

The researchers in this section do exactly that. They investigate how audiences make sense of advertising, looking particularly at how intersectional audiences incorporate advertising and advertising messages into their lives and personal identities.

In "Engaging in Consumer Citizenship: Latina Audiences and Advertising in Women's Ethnic Magazines," Jillian M. Báez draws on feminist audience studies and Chicana and Latina feminisms. Dr. Báez adopts an intersectional understanding of Latinas' lived experience as "shaped by colonization, migration, and racialization."

Much like Steinem's (1990) "Sex, Lies, and Advertising," Dr. Báez's discussion, based on interviewee responses, provides a near-textbook example of how constructing and prioritizing target markets, a routine activity in the day-to-day practice of advertising, and the media system dependent on the financial support of advertising dollars work, and the ethical dilemmas inherent in those processes.

Latina/os were for the most part invisible, served by local advertisers until the late 1980s when entrepreneurial broadcasters seeking to establish a broadcast network in the United States constructed and set about "selling advertisers" on what they identified as a lucrative untapped market. By definition, targeting is stereotyping. Astroff (1988, 155) has noted that "existing stereotypes constrain and shape market recognition of minorities." In a textual analysis of *Advertising Age,* an industry trade publication, she found "the U.S. Latino population was transformed from an 'invisible market' into 'Spanish gold' through the redefinition, but not the elimination, of traditional stereotypes: though basic elements of the stereotypes persist, values useful to advertisers are now assigned to the stereotyped ascriptions and behaviors." To be "marketable," the Latino market needed to be large enough to be commercially valuable to advertisers and different enough to require separate media. As a result, Latinos, whatever their ethnicity, nationality, race, and so on, became the "Hispanic market," a Spanish-speaking "nation within a nation" (Dávila 2001).

Latina/os became visible in Spanish-language media, but remained underrepresented in mainstream English-language media; their bilingual language competencies and bicultural experiences were ignored. In 1996, Christy Haubegger, a Mexican-American woman, recognized that Latinas, particularly educated, professional Latinas were underrepresented in existing publications, and established *Latina,* a niche publication targeting English-speaking Latinas. Like Steinem's experience with *Ms.,* Haubegger initially struggled to find advertisers. She noted that, although she had data showing Latino buying power, when advertisers "close their eyes and picture Hispanic women, they picture someone who cleans up their office at night" (Weissman 1999, 37).

Dr. Báez interviewed Latinas to determine how they make sense of advertising targeting them in *Latina* magazine. Sophisticated in their understanding of the commercial imperatives involved, the Latina respondents recognized that the magazine content was constructed for them as consumers, not as citizens. They observed that *Latina* lacked substantive content, that content had shifted from a focus on social and cultural issues to articles on beauty and fashion, and that the publication had too much advertising. Again, these comments strongly suggest an awareness that *Latina* had been crafted and recrafted not to appeal to them, the readers, but to advertisers. Although the editorial content of *Latina* magazine emphasized educational, professional, and financial issues, advertising relied on stereotypical representations of objectified and exoticized Latina bodies. Respondents preferred more professional images and distanced themselves from the air-brushed hypersexualized images, which they associated with "poor, working-class, uneducated women." The Latinas interviewed indicated that they had become "accustomed" to seeing hypersexualized imagery in *Latina*'s pages. They believed those images appealed to advertisers. Respondents generally expressed frustration at essentially losing control of their image. They were frustrated by the fact that they were rarely included in market research; when they were, the focus of the discussion was more about targeting them as audiences than consulting them for reader input.

A number of ethical dilemmas are inherent in addressing niche markets through specialized media built on marketer-initiated imperatives. Although the media made possible by marketing efforts can provide entertainment and information on issues important to the community, it is often the case that even niche media fail to recognize the diversity in the community. That is, niche media in many instances target only the more "desirable" subsegments of a diverse minority market. In short, markets are given a voice, albeit a commercially driven voice.

In this case, Latina's relationship to advertising is shaped by what Dr. Báez calls *consumer citizenship,* the assumption that being "wooed" as potential consumers with buying power is itself an indication of power and belonging. She warns, however, that "having quantitatively more diverse images within a commercial media system must not be confused with equity." It is unrealistic to harbor any illusions that targeting and construction of niche markets will disappear. It is fundamental to advertising work, the media system, and the functioning of the marketplace (Kreshel 2017). However, it is vital that efforts be undertaken with ethical sensitivity, recognizing diverse groups without reifying difference as exceptional rather than ordinary, representing difference without exploiting it.

Much like the Latina market Báez discussed (Chapter 10), and indeed, like virtually any market, the gay and lesbian market Wanhsiu Sunny Tsai and Xiaoqi Han consider in "Social Exclusion and Gay Consumers' Boycott and Buycott Decisions" was "consciously constructed in service of our capitalist economy and commercial media system." In "Advertising and the Political Economy of Lesbian/Gay Identity," Fejes (2001) recounts the story of constructing the gay and lesbian market. Studies undertaken in an attempt to create a picture of a more "marketable" affluent gay market were often contradictory and revealed a gay population quite different from that constructed in the advertising mind. Thus, gays and lesbians live with an image that bears only slight resemblance to the realities of gay and lesbian life.

Drs. Tsai and Han draw on previous ethnographic work on gay and lesbian consumers (Tsai 2011) to suggest that, cognizant of their power as a "desirable" market, gays and lesbians view the free market as a "legitimate battlefield in which minority groups could demand market reform and social changes by exercising their consumer power." Boycotts have long been used as a form of protest. The Montgomery bus boycott in 1955 began the nonviolent protest movements in the civil rights struggle. Some view boycotts as being largely symbolic, a kind of statement having little real economic impact. Yet boycotting is becoming a more common phenomenon worldwide as citizens have turned to a more politicized marketplace, and social media have become useful communicating and organizing tools (see Chapter 2). Then, too, boycotting is becoming more costly for targeted corporations when factoring in terms for legal and public relations expenses, disruption of corporate operations, and reputational damage. Politically motivated purchases (buycotting) or withdrawal from purchases (boycotting) *are* an important form of political engagement.

In an experimental study, Drs. Tsai and Han highlight the nuances and complexities involved in gay and lesbian consumers' engagement in politically motivated market behavior based on ostracism and discrimination. They conclude that "social minorities can be a potentially powerful force in initiating, advocating, and publicizing boycotting campaigns, and thus can lead social trends."

The researchers in Section III focus on under-investigated marginalized audiences, but from different points of entry. As just discussed, Drs. Tsai and Han investigate how a niche market, gay and lesbian consumers, uses their status as "desirable" to marketers to engage in politically motivated market behavior. Dr. Báez examined how a niche group, Latinas, made sense of advertising targeting them in niche media, that is, media specifically targeted to them.

The issue of whether to use targeted media or mainstream media to reach minority audiences is a point of some debate. Frequently, advertisers choose not to spend advertising dollars in niche media, arguing that minority audiences are "capturable" in majority-targeted media. Yet there has been very little research on how minority audiences engage with advertising in mainstream media (advertising that contains few minority images; when included, minority images are often stereotypical).

In the third chapter in this section, "'You Get a Very Conflicting View': Postfeminism, Contradiction, and Women of Color's Responses to Representations of Women in Advertisements," Leandra H. Hernández interviewed twenty-five women of color to explore how they "decode, interpret, and evaluate representations of women in advertising." She focuses on the particularly controversial relationship between women, health, beauty, ethnicity, and self-image in *mainstream* magazines.

The relationship between women and girls, cultural norms, and what appears to be an advertising norm of "ideal" beauty is fraught with tension. For all the industry's pride in its "cutting edge creativity," the portrayal of women and girls in ads is "strikingly and alarmingly similar" (Kreshel 2017, 183). Persistent feminist critiques charge advertising images with maladies ranging from eating disorders, to anxiety and lack of self-esteem, among others. "Outing" celebrities for obvious photo manipulation (e.g., Beusman 2014) stands as testimonial to continued concern with body perfection.

There is evidence that the advertising (and fashion) industries have heard consumer and activist concerns. Advertisers and select magazines are pledging to use only "real" models. A recent surge in empowerment ads targeting women and girls are in some sense a response to feminist criticism, although they are frequently critiqued as commodifying feminism as a brand. Still, for all the discussion, our understanding of how audiences make sense of those portrayals of unattainable ideals is limited, and again, understanding of how women of color make sense of those images has rarely been studied.

Dr. Hernández's investigation is grounded in postfeminist advertising contradictions, particularly in health advertising. Among these contradictions are the conflation of health with beauty and appearance, dieting as an indication one cares about one's self, and the suggestion that pounds will disappear if women love their bodies as they are. These contradictions put women in a no-win situation. Advertising encourages women to work on their bodies under the guise of personal freedom and empowerment. Health becomes a matter of consumption or the right products.

Respondents identified negative ads to be those with an emphasis on the ideal body, and applauded what they viewed to be a new trend toward "normal" rather than "model bodies." Health claims connected to appearance were also identified to be negative.

Contradiction also characterized the responses to the advertising. Respondents acknowledged that they didn't relate to images in the ads that "keep showing white women who are super tall and super skinny," noting, "That's not common of normal people, and that's negative. Where is the Latina of average body size?" They also recognized the unattainability of the bodies pictured in ads. Still, they compared themselves to the representations. One respondent noted, "I know I can't relate to these women. I don't identify with them. It's hard not to want to look like them, though." Advertisements empowered respondents to feel confident about their appearance but simultaneously reinforced anxieties, inviting "constant corporeal surveillance."

Dr. Hernández's research suggests the importance of conducting reception studies to better understand points of resistance to advertising messages. Previous research suggested that Latinas use ethnic identity and cultural values and preferences to mediate the information in ads. Although that wasn't found to be the case among these respondents, many credited education with giving them strategies to resist advertisements (all respondents were college-educated; two-thirds were graduate students). This suggests media literacy efforts can be used as an intervention to temper reactions to advertising messages.

PART IV: PROFESSIONAL DEVELOPMENT: HISTORIOGRAPHY AND BIOGRAPHY

The advertising discipline, wedded as it is primarily to the pragmatic concerns of business, has shown little interest in the history of the profession. Those historical accounts that existed were largely devoid of women's voices and experiences or contributions of African Americans. It's been only recently that interest in history of women in advertising has drawn academic interest (Davis 2016; Scanlon 1995; Sivulka 2009; Sutton 2009). Jason Chambers (2008) provided a rich historical account of African Americans in advertising. More recently, in *Pioneering African-American Women in the Advertising Business: Biographies of MAD Black Women,* Jody Foster Davis (2016) introduced "trail-blazing African-American women" who launched careers in the 1960s and went on to prominent careers.

In *Occupations for Women,* temperance activist Frances Willard (1897, 149) noted that advertising was a business field that women were "exploring with success." She continued, "they are becoming advertising agents, taking the position in establishments in charge of the advertising department, and above all, are finding large remuneration in writing special advertisements for manufacturers' firms . . . hardly a manufacturer having goods toward which he wishes to attract attention, fails to avail himself of their [clever women's] ability."

The two chapters included here are a part of the same narrative, one that began in earnest in the early years of the twentieth century. Women came to be recognized as the country's primary consumers and middle-class businessmen and advertisers recognized the need for "the women's viewpoint." There is perhaps a certain irony in women seeking professional careers instructing, even constructing, women's modern role inside the home, while the advertising industry itself became a point of entry for white, middle-class women seeking careers outside the home. Those women touted an essentialist claim of feminine intuition as a professional skill.

Until recently, home economics largely had been written off by feminist historians as old-fashioned and irrelevant, viewed primarily as teaching the skills of homemaking and confining women to the domestic sphere (Goldstein 2012). When Robin Morgan, author of *Sisterhood Is Powerful* (1970), spoke to the national home economics convention in 1972, she addressed the home economists in the audience as the "enemy" and urged them to quit their jobs (Morgan 1973, 13).

As someone earning a home economics, advertising, and psychology degree attending college in the 1970s, I faced the "stigma" of being a home economics major. In my case this was exacerbated by the fact that University of Nebraska had two campuses; the East Campus housed home economics and agriculture. It was widely perceived that the East Campus was populated by the boys who wanted to go back to the farm and the girls who wanted to be their wives.

Kimberly Voss draws on an emerging reevaluation of home economics history and its role in the history of the women's movement to tell "The Curious Story of Home Economics' Contribution to Women's Careers in Advertising, 1940s to 1960s." Her narrative highlights the synergy of home economics and advertising in creating opportunities for women to enter a professional career throughout much of the twentieth century. Through careful review of texts, government reports, the internal dialogue of the discipline in academic journals and reports of conferences, and university curricula, Dr. Voss documents a story that stands in sharp contrast to Morgan's 1972 assessment. The goal of home economics education was not to teach homemaking skills nor to confine women to the home. It was career preparation.

Women were demanding more accurate, detailed, and technical information on the products they purchased, and advertisers believed women writers were more likely to understand the woman consumer, educate her about new technologies, and sell her products. Women educated in home economics were learning about writing copy, developing a "scientific grounding" of technologies in the home, and educating consumers, primarily a white, middle-class audience who did their own cooking and cleaning. That is, home economists were the ready-made experts sought by advertising agencies, advertisers and manufacturers, government, and trade associations.

In addition to working in advertising agencies as copywriters, selling advertising, and consultants, home economists undertook a broad range of activities outside of agencies including copywriting for manufacturers, the government, and trade associations; department store merchandising; test-kitchen management; and mail-order design. For example, *Advertising Careers for Women* (Claire and Dignam 1939) included a section on career possibilities in the food industry, pointing out that "In education, you want a well-rounded home economics course plus special training in a technical school or college" (Ebbott 1939, 115). Opportunities for home economists for consumer food products included among others: developing new recipes, overseeing cooking contests, running test kitchens, food photography, and answering letters about promoted products.

Jeanie Wills (Chapter 13) notes that, although women working in advertising agencies weren't overtly feminists, many were "feminists under the skin" (Blair 1980, 1): "The women who chose domestic science had no quarrel with women's rights, but neither did they have any desire to call themselves feminists. They wanted to have a career and they needed a cause, but they weren't interested in breaking very many rules, reordering society, or challenging men on their own turf" (Shapiro 1986, 9). Although the absence of detailed records makes it impossible to know, many of the women who helped professionalize the advertising industry may have been home economists. In truth, Dr. Voss writes, the women who chose home economics as a career were closer to their activist sisters as acquaintances than as enemies.

In "A Woman's Place: Career Success and Early Twentieth Century Women's Advertising Clubs," Jeanie E. Wills has drawn on a wide range of archival sources to piece together an account of women working in the largely male-dominated field of advertising. Grounded in standpoint feminism, Dr. Wills's narrative details how white, middle-class women, excluded from men's advertising clubs, established women's advertising clubs early in the twentieth century in their struggle to achieve professional recognition. These clubs supported individual careers, increased the influence of women in advertising, elevated the visibility of women as vital participants in the advertising industry, and shaped the professional dimensions of the industry.

Dr. Wills's narrative argues from feminist standpoint theory: "A standpoint is not merely a perspective that is occupied simply by dint of being a woman; . . . a standpoint is earned through the experience of collective political struggle" (Bowell n.d.). Advertising women surely recognized their marginalized position, and Dr. Wills's narrative outlines efforts and activities undertaken to overcome their subordinate status focusing on three separate women's advertising clubs: the Philadelphia Club of Advertising Women, the Women's Advertising Club of Chicago, and the League of Advertising Women of New York (later the Advertising Women of New York, and most recently She Runs It). Despite being established because of their exclusion from men's clubs, the white women who organized the women's clubs described here were themselves exclusionary, carefully policing racial and class boundaries. Thus, the club membership constructed and nurtured an "ideal" white, middle-class, professional advertising woman.

Dr. Wills explores the dynamics of the mutually beneficial relationship that developed between the clubs, the individual members, and the industry through a study of the life and career of a single advertising woman. That woman, Dorothy Dignam, was a member of all three advertising clubs. Documenting Dignam's career not only as a copywriter, but as a speaker, educator, author, and recognized advocate for women's success in advertising serves to illustrate not only the opportunities made possible by club membership but also the role club members played in elevating the recognition of the clubs and the status and importance of white women working in the advertising industry.

Added to all her accomplishments, one might wonder if Dignam was prescient. For all her optimism and enthusiasm, writing in *Advertising Careers for Women,* Dignam (1939, 9) noted some seventy-five years ago: "the advertising agency is and probably always will be a masculine stronghold." It appears, at the moment, that she was right. But we're working on it.

This volume demonstrates that a community of feminist scholars is actively conducting research on advertising. These scholars provide additional dimensions to an already-vibrant ongoing stream of research on advertising content (see Golombisky and Kreshel forthcoming). Collectively, the feminist researchers in this volume provide historical insights and findings related to two under-researched areas that are vital to our understanding of the advertising communication process. Those areas are the subjectivities and workplace culture in advertising creative departments, and how audiences make sense of advertising messages and incorporate their understandings into their everyday lives.

It is our hope that the research presented in this volume will encourage others to actively investigate advertising through feminist lenses to discover the role advertising plays in maintaining patterns of oppression and inequalities, remain vigilant as technological innovations provide ever-increasing numbers of formats and platforms by which advertising can reach into our daily lives, and continue to identify possible points of intervention and develop appropriate strategies of activism and resistance. In a 2014 documentary chronicling the birth of the second-wave feminist movement, "She's Beautiful When She's Angry," Virginia Whitehill, who gave oral arguments before the Supreme Court in *Roe v. Wade,* said, "You're not allowed to retire from feminist issues. You still have to pay attention cause someone is gonna try to yank the rug out from under you" ("She's Beautiful" 2014). Advertising plays a vital role in the smooth operation of our market economy. It's not going away anytime soon. We hope the community of feminist scholars studying advertising continues to grow. We are in it and *must be in it* for the long haul.

NOTE

1. Announcing the theme of its 2017 conference, the 3% Conference made the following statement: "We've become increasingly aware of the danger of agencies solving for the 'woman problem' and neglecting diversity in all its facets. So our fall [2017] agenda will explore and inspire on all fronts of diversity to make it crystal clear that our tagline—Diversity = Creativity = Profitability—is a rally cry that leaves no one behind and no one's needs back-burnered."

REFERENCES

Astroff, Roberta J. 1988. "Spanish Gold: Stereotypes, Ideology, and the Construction of a U.S. Latino Market." *Howard Journal of Communications* 1 (4): 155–73.

Bassin, Amelia. 1970. "The Picture of Women You Have in Your Mind is All Wrong." *Advertising Age* December 7.

Beusman, Callie. 2014. "The Enigmatic Mystery of Beyoncé's Golf Thighs," *Jezebel.* April 11. Retrieved June 14, 2017, from http://jezebel.com/the-enigmatic-mystery-of-beyonces-golf-thighs-1562154200.

Blair, Karen. 1980. *Clubwoman as Feminist: True Womanhood Redefined, 1868–1914.* New York: Holmes and Meier.

Bowell, Tracy. n.d. "Feminist Standpoint Theory." *Internet Encyclopedia of Philosophy* http://www.iep.utm.edu/fem-stan/.

Cadwell, Franchellie. 1971. "Shifting Women's Market Will Kill Some Products." *Advertising Age* August 16, 1, 71.

Chambers, Jason. 2008. *Madison Avenue and the Color Line: African Americans in the Advertising Industry.* Philadelphia: University of Pennsylvania Press.

Claire, Blanche, and Dorothy Dignam, eds. 1939. *Advertising Careers for Women.* New York: Harper and Brothers.

Crenshaw, Kimberlé. 1991. "Mapping the Margins: Intersectionality, Identity Politics, and Violence against Women of Color." *Stanford Law Review* 43: 1241–99.

Dan, Avi. 2016. "Women in Advertising, Particularly White Women, Are Still Doing Far Better Than Others." *Forbes,* March 21. Accessed June 8, 2016, from https://www.forbes.com/sites/avidan/2016/03/28/women-in-advertising-particularly-white-women-are-still-doing-far-better-than-others/#3bbe95c623c0.

Dávila, Arlene. 2001. *Latinos Inc.: The Making and Marketing of a People.* Berkeley: University of California Press.

Davis, Judy Foster. 2016. *Pioneering African-American Women in the Advertising Business: Biographies of MAD Black Women.* New York: Routledge.

Dignam, Dorothy. 1939. "Ideas and Copy." In *Advertising Careers for Women,* edited by Blanche Clair and Dorothy Dignam, 17–33. New York: Harper and Brothers.

Drumwright, Minette E., and Patrick E. Murphy. 2004. "How Advertising Practitioners View Ethics: Moral Muteness, Moral Myopia, and Moral Imagination." *Journal of Advertising* 33 (2): 7–24.

Du Gay, Paul, Stuart Hall, Linda Janes, Hugh McKay, and Keith Negus. 1997. *Doing Cultural Studies: The Story of the Sony Walkman.* London: Sage.

Ebbott, Dorothy. 1939. "The Home Economist in the Advertising Department." In *Advertising Careers for Women,* edited by Blanche Clair and Dorothy Dignam, 107–19. New York: Harper and Brothers.

Etlinger, Susan. 2014. "What do we do with all this big data?" TED, September. https://www.ted.com/talks/susan_etlinger_what_do_we_do_with_all_this_big_data. Accessed June 17, 2016

Faludi, Susan. 1991. *Backlash: The Undeclared War against American Women.* New York: Anchor/Doubleday.

Fejes, Fred. 2001. "Advertising and the Political Economy of Lesbian/Gay Identity." In *Sex and Money: Feminism and Political Economy in the Media,* edited by Eileen R. Meehan and Ellen Riordan Friedan, 212–29. Minneapolis: University of Minnesota Press.

Friedan, Betty. 1963. *The Feminine Mystique.* New York: W.W. Norton.

Goldman, Robert, Deborah Heath, and Sharon L. Smith. 1991. "Commodity Feminism." *Critical Studies in Mass Communication* 8: 333–51.

Goldstein, Carolyn M. 2012. *Creating Consumers: Home Economists in Twentieth-Century America.* Chapel Hill: The University of North Carolina Press.

Golombisky, Kim, and Peggy J. Kreshel. forthcoming. *What's the Big Idea: Feminist Perspectives on Advertising.* Lanham, MD: Lexington Press.

Gordon, Mary. 2017. "March with Me," *Vogue* May: 92+.

Gurrieri, Lauren, Jan Brace-Govan, and Helene Cherrier. 2016. "Controversial Advertising: Transgressing the Taboo of Gender-Based Violence." *European Journal of Marketing* 50 (7/8): 1448–69. doi: 10.1108/EJM-09-2014-0597

Hall, Stuart. 1980. "Encoding, Decoding." In *Culture, Media, Language,* edited by Stuart Hall, Dorothy Hobson, Andrew Lowe, and Paul Wills, 128–38. London: Hutchinson.

Kreshel, Peggy. 2016. "Ethical Advertising in Today's New Advertising Ecosystem." In *The New Advertising: Branding, Content, and Consumer Relationships in the Data-Driven Social Media Era,* edited by Ruth E. Brown, Valerie K. Jones, and Ming Wang, 353–73. Santa Barbara, CA: Praeger.

———. 2017. "Case 37. Niche Markets, Niche Media." In *Media Ethics: Cases and Moral Reasoning,* edited by Clifford G. Christians, Mark Fackler, Kathy Brittain Richardson, Peggy J. Kreshel, and Robert H. Woods, Jr., 10th ed., 231–37. New York: Routledge.

Leiss, William, Stephen Kline, Sut Jhally, and Jacqueline Botterill. 2005. *Social Communication in Advertising: Consumption in the Media Marketplace.* New York: Routledge.
May, Vivian. 2012. "Intersectionality." In *Rethinking Women's and Gender Studies,* edited by Catherine M. Orr, Ann Braithwaite, and Diane Lichtenstein, 155–72. New York: Routledge.
Mccall, Suzanne. 1977. "Meet the 'Workwife.'" *Journal of Marketing* 41 (3): 55–65.
McMains, Andrew. 2009. "Dan Wieden Makes Impassioned Diversity Pitch at 4As," *AdWeek,* April 29. Accessed May 28, 2017, from http://www.adweek.com/brand-marketing/dan-wieden-makes-impassioned-diversity-pitch-4as-99113/.
Morgan, Robin. 1970. *Sisterhood Is Powerful.* New York: Vintage.
———. 1973. "What Robin Morgan Said in Denver." *Journal of Home Economics* 65 (January): 13. Transcript of invited speech at American Home Economics Association Conference, 1973.
Ngabirano, Anne-Marcelle. 2017. "Are women being played by 'feminist' ads?" *USA Today,* March 14. Accessed June 17, 2017, from https://www.usatoday.com/story/money/2017/03/22/have-companies-taken-over-feminism/98706852/.
Nixon, Sean. 2003. *Advertising Cultures: Gender, Commerce, Creativity.* Thousand Oaks, CA: Sage.
Nyilasy, Gergely, Robin Canniford, and Peggy J. Kreshel. 2013. "Ad Agency Professionals' Mental Models of Advertising Creativity." *European Journal of Marketing* 47 (10): 1691–1710.
Ritson, Mark. 2017. "Heineken Should Remember Marketing Is about Profit, Not Purpose." *Marketing Week* May 10. Accessed June 7, 2017, from https://www.marketingweek.com/2017/05/10/heineken-marketing-purpose-profit/.
Rosen, Ruth. 2000. *The World Split Open: How the Modern Women's Movement Changed America.* New York: Penguin Books.
Rothenberg, Randall. 2016. "Ad-Blocking: Unnecessary Internet Apocalypse." *Advertising Age* September 22. Accessed June 8, 2017, from http://adage.com/article/digitalnext/ad-blocking-unnecessary-internet-apocalypse/300470/.
Saner, Emine. 2016. "Cindy Gallop: Advertising Is Dominated by White Guys Talking to White Guys." *The Guardian* June 26. https://www.theguardian.com/media/2016/jun/26/cindy-gallup-advertising-white-men-sex-tapes
Scanlon, Jennifer. 1995. *Inarticulate Longings: The Ladies' Home Journal, Gender, and the Promises of Consumer Culture.* New York: Routledge.
Scott, Joan Wallach. 1999. *Gender and the Politics of History.* New York: Columbia University Press.
Scott, Linda M. 2000. "Market Feminism: The Case for a Paradigm Shift." In *Marketing and Feminism: Current Issues and Research,* edited by Miriam Catteral, Pauline MacLaran, and Lorna Stevens, 16–38. London: Routledge.
Shapiro, Laura. 1986. *Perfection Salad: Women and Cooking at the Turn of the Century.* New York: Farrar, Straus and Giroux.
"She's Beautiful When She's Angry" (film). 2014. Directed by Mary Dore. Music Box Films.
Sivulka, Juliann. 2009. *Ad Women: How They Impact What We Need, Want, and Buy.* Amherst, NY: Prometheus Books.

Soar, Matthew. 2000. "Encoding Advertisements: Ideology and Meaning in Advertising Production." *Mass Communication & Society* 3 (4).
Stein, Lindsey. 2017. Advertising Is Still a Boy's Club. *Advertising Age* May 29, 12–14. http://adage.com/article/news/advertising-a-boy-s-club/309166/.
Steinem, Gloria. 1990. "Sex, Lies, and Advertising," *Ms.* July/August 1990, 18–28.
Sutton, Denise. 2009. *Globalizing Ideal Beauty: Women, Advertising, and the Power of Marketing*. New York: Palgrave McMillan.
3% Conference. "The Elephant on Mad Ave." http://www.3percentconf.com/sites/default/files/download-files/Elephant.pdf.
Tsai, Wanhsiu Sunny. 2011. "How Minority Consumers Use Targeted Advertising as Pathways to Self-Empowerment: Gay Men's and Lesbians' Reading of Out-of-Closet Advertising." *Journal of Advertising* 40 (3): 85–97.
van Zoonen, Lisbet. 1994. *Feminist Media Studies.* London: Sage.
Weissman, Rachel X. 1999. "Los Niños Go Shopping." *Advertising Age,* May 1, 37.
Willard, Frances E. 1897. *Occupations for Women.* Cooper Union, NY: The Success Company.
Zayer, Linda Tuncay, and Catherine A. Coleman. 2015. "Advertising Professionals' Perceptions of the Impact of Gender Portrayals on Men and Women: A Question of Ethics?" *Journal of Advertising* 44 (3): 1–12. DOI: 10.1080/00913367.2014.975878.
Zeisler, Andi. 2016. *We Were Feminists Once: From Riot Grrrl to Covergirl, the Buying and Selling of a Political Movement.* New York: Public Affairs.

Part I

HISTORIES OF FEMINISTS, FEMINISMS, AND ADVERTISING

Chapter 2

Women versus Brands

Sexist Advertising and Gender Stereotypes Motivate Transgenerational Feminist Critique

Jacqueline Lambiase, Carolyn Bronstein, and Catherine A. Coleman

Taking stock of feminists' interactions with the advertising industry—more than five decades of active contestation of mainstream representations of women's bodies and identities—we recognize progress, stagnation, backlash, and even backsliding, all of which underscore the importance of continued critique. Starting in the 1960s, feminists worked to raise public consciousness about the damage sexist images inflict on all people, especially in terms of reinforcing restrictive gender norms and reducing opportunities for women in the public sphere. Throughout the 1980s and 1990s, third-wave feminists added rich analyses of race and sexualities to this critique, exposing the ways that the advertising industry marginalized people of color in consumer ads, treating women of color as exotic, closely tied to nature, and highly sexualized (Cole and Daniel 2005). Over the past twenty-five years, as standards for women's bodies have increasingly emphasized thinness and distorted presentations have become the norm through digital manipulation, feminists have argued that such images may contribute to ailments such as low self-esteem, depression, and eating disorders (Harrison 2001; Harrison and Cantor 1997; Richins 1991).

In the past decade, some companies have responded with "femvertising," ad campaigns that contain commercially viable empowerment messages for girls and women; the term was coined in 2014 by SheKnows Media (Stampler 2014). These ad campaigns challenge gender norms and highlight the power, strength, and beauty of girls and women. Unilever (Dove), Procter & Gamble (Always), and Under Armour are currently at the forefront of this movement with Dove's Campaign for Real Beauty, #LikeAGirl, and the "I Will What I Want" campaign, respectively; these campaigns have garnered public attention and praise (Zmuda and Diaz 2014). A recent entrant in the "femvertising" space is Mattel, which debuted a 2015 advertising campaign promising parents that their daughters can be anything they imagine themselves to be when playing with Barbie dolls, including neuroscientists, veterinarians, and coaches for professional sports teams. Other corporations, including cosmetics giant Estée Lauder, General Mills (Yoplait), and athletic-wear brand Reebok, have aligned their advertising and marketing with woman-oriented issues and breast cancer awareness. Gucci has sponsored live events such as #ChimeForChange in London in 2013, which featured Beyoncé and Jennifer Lopez to raise awareness and money for women's education, justice, and global health issues. Nike's 2015 campaign, #betterforit, was the company's largest initiative to date to support and motivate women's athletic aspirations.

In each case, prowoman advertising reflects corporations' desires to connect with women as consumers and access their considerable spending power, probably more than a desire to deliver authentic feminist messages. As such, these practices have been criticized as "pinkwashing" that exploits women and feminism (Keane 2013; Lake 2015). Many brands using this strategy, such as Dove, have been called hypocritical for leveraging messages of women's worth to sell beauty products, for positioning problems of sexism in women's psyches and not sexist social structures, and for continued neglect of racial and ethnic diversity (Griner 2013). Dove's beauty-oriented advertising can be interpreted as antifeminist because it continues to define women's value and worth in terms of a lifelong project of consumer behavior designed to make oneself sexually attractive to heterosexual men. And in Dove's case, its parent company, Unilever, markets others products with contrary messages: One is Axe, a body spray for men that is marketed through sexist images of women; other Unilever products include skin-lightening creams marketed throughout India, where ad campaigns communicate the message that only fair-skinned women are beautiful and likely to be successful in romantic and professional pursuits (Parameswaran and Cardoza 2009).

Advertisers are also aware that women communicate with one another both interpersonally and in public discursive spaces, such as Facebook and Twitter, about brands and their advertising (L. Ford 2015; Perrin 2015). For decades, feminists have used communication tactics such as letter writing and defacing public ads to fight sexist campaigns. Today, women communicate immediately and globally via social media about ad campaigns perceived as demeaning and sexist, adding muscle to feminist attempts to raise public consciousness about media representation and its effects on gendered people.

More communication about advertising and good business practices with regard to representation has increased public expectation for corporate social responsibility (Duggan 2013). The Italian fashion designers Domenico Dolce and Stefano Gabbana learned this lesson in 2007, when they released a Dolce and Gabbana ad depicting what National Organization for Women (NOW) president Kim Gandy called "a stylized gang rape" (MacCurdy 2012, 266). The image of a woman lying in the prone position, forcibly restrained by one man with three other men hovering over her, generated outrage in Europe and the United States. Many people, mostly women, used Facebook and dozens of Internet sites such as Feministing.com and Jezebel.com to express their disgust at a glorified image of rape being used to sell clothing. Faced with global outrage and bans on the campaign in both Spain and Italy, the designers had little choice but to retract the image ("Dolce and Gabbana" 2007). The lesson is clear: Women pay attention to media representation and can respond—loudly and urgently—if advertisers depict them irresponsibly.

Yet the more positive trends have been hard won. The rape-scene ads created by Dolce and Gabbana, and then similarly by Calvin Klein in 2010, were only pulled after significant backlash and formal regulatory bans ("Controversy" 2010; "Dolce and Gabbana" 2007; Nudd 2010). Feminist activists and scholars have been analyzing advertisements and challenging the advertising industry since the 1960s, emphasizing the problems with sexist representations in the media, namely their real-world cognitive, attitudinal, and behavioral effects on viewers. Stimulated by the critical insights of women's liberation movements in the late 1960s and 1970s, along with a diversified mass communication environment, media became a central object of study for feminist researchers by the 1980s (van Zoonen 1994). At first, such investigations focused almost exclusively on heterosexual white women; researchers later expanded their analyses to include women of color and lesbians. Scholars sought to understand the ways in which all women had been relegated to secondary and unequal positions in the workplace and home, and how this subordination was actively created and maintained through media representations (Bronstein 2011; Coltrane and Messineo 2000; Gill 2007; Kang 1997; Lindner 2004; McKay and Covell 1997).

Advertising received a great deal of attention because of the limited roles available to women in commercial depictions, typically young sex goddess or blissfully domesticized wife and mother. Both served other people, ostensibly heterosexual, middle-class, white men, and existed primarily to meet their needs. Activists and scholars from the 1970s onward advocated for greater diversity in representation, noting that a wider spectrum of women of different races, ages, and body types should be featured to better reflect the real world (Goffman 1979; Green 1999; hooks 1984; Plous and Neptune 1997). In their analysis of the so-called Beauty Machine, Yang and Ragaza (1997, 12) tackled the white beauty yardstick used in American fashion advertising that preserves the status quo, even though the nation "is getting darker all the time." They noted both slow progress and regression: One 1991 content analysis found no models of color in the ads in three top women's fashion magazines in the 1960s, a small increase in the late 1970s, when 4.9 percent of models were women of color, and then a decrease to 1.6 percent in the late 1980s.

This chapter uses a cultural-historical approach to trace interactions in the United States between and among feminist activists, their organizations, and the advertising industry, as well as corporations and their leaders. For three periods since 1960, we:

- Provide background on feminist and intersectional activities, including key figures engaged in interactions about advertising.
- Give examples of key feminist critiques of advertising.
- Review social-scientific research related to sexism and advertising.
- Analyze case studies and industry responses.

FEMINIST WAVES[1]

We view this historical framework through the lenses of the second, third, and emerging fourth waves of feminism, and the modes of collective and connective activism that have characterized their organizing. Second-wave feminist activists in the liberal feminist tradition of the late 1960s and 1970s worked through vertical collective action marked by the establishment of bureaucratic organizations such as NOW, formal leadership, and the use of established legal and political pathways to move women into positions of power and pass prowoman legislation such as wage equity and no-fault divorce laws. Leading liberal feminists like Betty Friedan, the cofounder and first president of NOW in 1966, urged women to fight for equality, especially in the workplace; many believed that women (or at least white, middle-class women) could move closer to parity through ascension in the professions, government, and business. Whereas liberal feminists sought change through ratification of the Equal Rights Amendment to the Constitution and adoption of laws to ban workplace discrimination, their radical feminist counterparts in the women's liberation movement emphasized cultural and personal change, focusing on such issues as consciousness raising, sexuality, reproductive rights, sexism, and women's subordinate status in a patriarchal society. Radical feminists typically organized in less formal, smaller groups, often devoted to specific issues such as abortion rights or antiviolence activism (Echols 1989; Rosen 2000). Some of the key second-wave feminist leaders were Friedan; Gloria Steinem, a journalist and a founder of *Ms.* magazine; antirape activist and journalist Susan Brownmiller; poet Robin Morgan; journalist Ellen Willis; poet and lesbian-rights activist Adrienne Rich; Shirley Chisholm, who in 1968 became the first African-American woman elected to Congress; and attorney and US Representative Bella Abzug.

Third-wave feminism emerged in the early 1990s as a generational movement, composed of women too young to have experienced second-wave activity firsthand and women not emphasized by that movement. Third wavers espoused a new political commitment to combating intersectional oppressions stemming from multiple positionalities of gender, sexuality, race, ethnicity, ability, age, class, and nationality, among others. They built on late 1970s and early 1980s critiques of second-wave feminism and its exclusionary emphasis on the problems faced by white, middle-class, heterosexual women, a perspective developed and advanced by such prominent feminists of color as bell hooks (1984), Cherríe Moraga (Moraga and Anzaldúa 1981), Gloria Anzaldúa (Moraga and Anzaldúa 1981), Audre Lorde (1984), and Alice Walker (1984). Following these critiques, third wavers insisted that the sisterhood of the second wave poured energy into correcting such issues as barriers to women's professional career advancement, as opposed to issues like sterilization abuse, which only affected poor women and most often women of color. These critics (Collins 2000; Crenshaw 1989, 1991; Hull, Scott, and Smith 1982; Phelan 1989; Taylor and Rupp 1993; Williams 1991) and others argued that second-wave feminists had ignored and marginalized women of color, poor women, and queer women who experienced not just sexism, but also racism, homophobia, and economic inequality. Some theorists have characterized third-wave feminism as rejecting second-wave principles; yet others view the movement as interrogating and expanding prior forms of feminist thought to develop new modes of thinking that see oppression as multifaceted and connected to many different forms of identity (Hewitt 2010; Lotz 2003).

Fourth-wave feminism is an emerging movement closely associated with online activity, and involves the use of social media to promote gender equality and social justice. Fourth wavers connect with one another through technology, especially Instagram, Snapchat, YouTube, Facebook, and Twitter, to call out and challenge instances of sexism and other inequalities, and demand change (Cochrane 2013). Typically, individual actors mobilize through frequent digital actions and interactions that include creation of original content, meme diffusion, social media posting, hashtag advocacy, and loose digital networks. The fourth wave builds on the third wave's political agenda and more individual style of organizing, and has been credited for positively affecting media representation, especially concerning how companies market their products to women.

A significant difference that separates second-wave feminism from third- and now fourth-wave activism is the logic of collective versus connective action. This evolving theoretical framework developed by Bennett and

Segerberg (2012) describes the rise of "networked activism," a personalized, digitally networked politics in which individuals from a range of socioeconomic and political positions address contemporary problems such as sexism and rape culture. Their framework for connective action involves online communication as an organizational process that may replace or supplement traditional forms of collective action, such as the marches and demonstrations that were fundamental to second-wave activism. Today's fourth wavers engage in connective action as their primary means of political activity, and they have created a culture of awareness that can bring results quickly when problems with representation arise. Of course, charges of armchair activism or "slacktivism" abound, with some observers expressing concern that actions requiring little time or involvement, such as liking a feminist Facebook post or signing an online petition, are a far cry from the organized marches and demonstrations of the 1960s and 1970s that helped activists bring about radical social change.

In targeting offensive, especially sexist and racist forms of representation for connective action, fourth wavers call attention to the significance of media in shaping our collective perceptions. In this essay, we follow this lead and define *representation* as the attempt by media producers—especially corporate advertisers, marketers, and their agencies—to represent reality. They do so by choosing words, symbols, models (by age, race, ethnicity, nationality, gender, sexuality, standards of beauty and body size, abilities, and more), relationships among models, clothing, activity, stance, and settings to depict a context for selling products and services. As feminists engage with brands, some of the power of representation is redistributed to a more inclusive range of women, who begin to create and circulate their own images of beauty outside Madison Avenue, the corporate circle of power, and heteropatriarchal white culture.

Within the emerging fourth wave, the act of communication itself has become an organizing principle, as "individuals are tied together through their personal relationships and common interests, creating networks that are not necessarily bound by organizations" (McCluskey 2014, 679). Della Porta (2014, 270) calls this space "free of fences, [where] social beings are no longer defined by their place in the society." Operating inside connective networks allows content creators to enjoy a kind of "mental socialization that occurs in social media, where discourse is free . . . in effect practicing for their own projected futures" (Lambiase 2012, 538). The bloggers and activists currently operating in connective media spaces have greater potential to reach large audiences with their critiques of advertising and other popular media than most second wavers, who had less access to public discursive spaces. Journalists covering protests against sexist advertising in the early years used negative frames and terms such as "militant members of the National

Organization of Women" when the group picketed the offices of National Airlines and its advertising agency in 1971 (National Sundowners, n.d.; Schultz 2012). Collective action gave feminists their own chance at access to the public; during the second wave of feminist work in the 1970s, *Ms.* magazine provided a place without pejorative terms for feminists. Today's activists have more immediate and global means of critique through social media. In the 1960s, Friedan and novelist Margaret Atwood were among the few women who found traditional publishers willing to popularize their critiques of advertising and gender norms, but today's activists self-publish and contribute to thousands of online feminist publications and blogs.

ACTIVISM IN THE 1960s AND 1970s

The role of advertising captured the attention of foundational feminist authors, among them novelist Atwood and political organizer Friedan. In her landmark book *The Feminine Mystique* (1963), Friedan took advertisers to task for bombarding women with a suffocating ideology of white feminine domesticity that told women that their highest purpose lay in their roles as primary purchasers within consumer culture. These advertising "manipulators" took the brunt of Friedan's criticism; she described their "persuasive images" as responsible for perpetuating the problem that she named the "feminine mystique." To Friedan, consumer culture had duped women into abandoning any hope of political or intellectual engagement, as it relentlessly directed women's attention to shopping and durable goods purchasing to keep one's self, home, and family outfitted with the latest fashions, appliances, and other home products.

Friedan's book captivated national audiences, although its analysis was deeply exclusionary. The typical woman whom Friedan imagined as stuck at home, empty and unhappy, persuaded by advertisers to participate in a never-ending cycle of upscale consumption, was a white, heterosexual woman of privilege. Two decades after *The Feminine Mystique* was published, feminist theorist bell hooks (1984, 1–3) took Friedan to task for failing to address the needs of women living without men, without children, and without homes, and for ignoring the reality that wealthy, white women who worked outside of the home typically relied on women of color to perform their housework and childcare. hooks pointed out that many poor women working in service sector jobs as maids, babysitters, store clerks, and even prostitutes yearned to be housewives with the luxury of focusing on their families rather than working long hours to earn subsistence wages. The portrayal of all women as equally frustrated at home, longing to compete with white men in the professions, was a racist construction. Friedan also brought her longstanding discomfort with issues of racism and sexuality, especially lesbianism, to her account. She failed to analyze the oppressions that queer women faced, as the protected domestic life that she critiqued was unavailable to women who refused men. Without a male partner, lesbians were economically, socially, and physically vulnerable, threats far graver than the psychological malaise of the feminine mystique.

Despite the limitations of Friedan's book, its publication helped to generate a new surge of feminist creative and political work. Margaret Atwood created a powerful first-person novel depicting a white woman oppressed by the constraints of heterosexuality and consumer culture. In *The Edible Woman* (written in 1965 but not published until 1969), Atwood presents Marian, a young Canadian college graduate who works for a market research firm. In the novel, Marian realizes that expectations for her behavior and life path as a woman are carefully manipulated by society, including advertisers. She commutes to work on a city bus, passing time by taking quizzes in women's magazines and watching the panorama of ads outside the bus windows. Marian gazes at a girdle ad and realizes that the image of the young, slender woman is meant to make women suffering the dreaded "middle-aged spread" feel bad about themselves and seek self-improvement through consumption. "[P]erhaps the purchasers thought they were getting their own youth and slenderness back in the package," Marian thinks to herself as she looks at the image (Atwood 1969, 98). Through this description, Atwood critiques advertising directed to women. As Marian develops a greater feminist consciousness, she realizes women are exploited and treated as commodities for sale.

In the 1970s, social scientists began to formalize these feminist critiques through the systematic study of advertising representation, investigating the charges against advertising advanced by Friedan, Atwood, and others. Some of the first studies were conducted by scholars with direct connections to the mainstream women's movement. Lucy Komisar, a national vice president of NOW, analyzed advertising images in the late 1960s and early 1970s to conclude that viewers could never comprehend the true diversity of women's lives through them, because ads provided such a limited view. "A woman's place is not only in the home, according to most advertising copywriters and art directors; it is in the kitchen or the laundry room," she wrote (Komisar 1972, 301). Komisar described advertising's ideal woman as a combination sex object, wife, and mother who achieves fulfillment by looking beautiful for men. Women, she noted, were rarely, if ever, depicted as intelligent, but typically as submissive and subservient to men. Alice E. Courtney and Sarah Lockeretz published a 1971 study of images of women in general interest magazines that also revealed little diversity in women's roles. According to the authors, women were rarely shown working in professional out-of-the-home roles, and they were never depicted in public without a male escort.

Instead, advertisers showed women as subordinate to men, dependent on their protection, and primarily interested in cleaning products, home appliances, and fashion. Once again, it is important to note that these analyses did not attend specifically to the question of representation of women of color, but spoke more broadly about "women" in general, reproducing the white, middle-class bias evident in the women's movement at large.

Communication scholars Suzanne Pingree, Robert Hawkins, William Butler, and Matilda Paisley (1976) established a scale for sexism in magazine advertisements in the mid-1970s, finding that the majority of ads published in *Playboy, Time, Newsweek,* and even the feminist *Ms.* relied on sexist representations that either put women down or kept them in their place. Sociologist Erving Goffman published the landmark book *Gender Advertisements* in 1979, in which he identified six distinct categories of difference in the way that men and women were depicted in advertising, and the subtle, underlying messages about appropriate gender roles that these symbolic behaviors communicated. The symbolic behaviors worked together to communicate messages of feminine passivity, subordination, weakness, and excessive emotionality, whereas men were portrayed as strong, decisive, rational, powerful, and unemotional. The cumulative effect of these studies was significant. As their findings reached feminist activist circles, members of women's liberation determined that sexist ads needed to be publicly exposed. Women's organizations targeted corporate offenders with letter-writing campaigns and even boycotts. One of the most successful efforts was a 1977 national feminist boycott of the Warner Bros., Elektra, and Atlantic Records companies, which profited from the images of sexual violence against women used to advertise their albums (Bronstein 2011).

The advertising industry was slow to respond to feminist concerns. Advertisers were defensive in the face of assertions that they exploited women. For example, at the 1965 Advertising Federation of America convention, Jo Foxworth, an ad executive and future author of *Boss Lady: An Executive Woman Talks about Making It* (1979), called Betty Friedan's book a "mistaque" and challenged her to a debate. Nonetheless, Friedan's critical appraisals ultimately had some influence. NOW organized a Strike for Equality in August 1970, during which four major brands were targeted by protesters: Ivory Liquid soap, *Cosmopolitan* magazine, Silva Thins cigarettes, and Pristeen "feminine hygiene" spray (Siegel 2007). A Warner-Lambert company spokesperson asked how "can anyone be against" its product, Pristeen spray, which, he claimed, stood for "femininity, freshness and women's confidence" (K. Baker 2012). Feminists pointed to the sexist and body-shaming content of the Pristeen messages: One 1969 ad headline read, "Unfortunately, the trickiest deodorant problem a girl has isn't under her pretty little arms" (*Museum of Menstruation,* n.d.). Also targeted in 1970,

Procter and Gamble responded through a spokesperson who said the company "would not knowingly run advertisements that are offensive and demeaning to women—how could we since most of our products are sold to women?" (K. Baker 2012). The response from National Airlines after complaints about its sex role–dependent Fly Me campaign was also dismissive; flight attendants' names were linked to the company's tagline, as in, "I'm Cheryl. Fly me." The company said the format was "mere first-name friendliness," yet the sexual innuendo was obvious (*National Sundowners,* n.d.).

Despite these defensive and dismissive tactics, other women working as advertising executives confronted their own industry to advocate for women because it made good business sense. Agency owner Franchellie Cadwell of Cadwell Davis, a boutique agency associated with Compton Advertising, announced in a 1970 issue of *Advertising Age* that "the lady of the house was dead" (Craig 1997), perhaps hoping that sex role–dependent representations would finally disappear. That same year at an industry luncheon, Cadwell said "advertising makes women look as if they have the mentality of a 6-year-old" ("Franchellie Cadwell" 2003).

Over the next few years, some in the industry began acknowledging, at least tacitly, the findings of feminists, social scientists, and semioticians who demonstrated advertising's sexism. At their second annual meeting in 1972, members of the National Advertising Review Board (NARB) decided to enlarge the board's activities from monitoring truth and accuracy in advertising to also include matters of "taste and social responsibility" (Ewen 1975, i). In expanding industry oversight, board members sought to address public, and specifically feminist, outcry over the sexist portrayals of women that dominated contemporary advertising. In 1975, public pressure led the board to form an official panel charged with reviewing ads portraying or targeting women, noting that too many images remained "insensitive" to women. Women, the panel found, were disproportionately portrayed as housewives, mothers, and sex objects, images that could be interpreted as "negative and depreciatory," yet "accepted as true to life by many men, women, and children" (Ewen 1975, 1–2). The ads themselves were identified as media texts that actively shaped gender roles and expectations, as opposed to passively reflecting the status quo. With a direct nod to the vocal, powerful women's liberation movement in the 1970s and the centrality of this issue for feminists, the panel acknowledged that the "more vocal critics of advertising" who deemed it sexist propaganda tended to be "younger, better educated, more articulate women who often are opinion leaders" (Ewen 1975, 6). NARB further cautioned creatives in 1975 to avoid creating objectionable and sexist images of women, a directive that reflected their fear of alienating white, middle-class consumers as opposed to an authentic desire to create more inclusive representations of women of color and many other groups.

A few high-profile women within the advertising industry itself became involved in these debates, and advertising board leadership began to advise some corporations and agencies to take heed of limited gender roles for women and insensitive or sexist images within ads, although attention to issues of race, sexuality, age and other forms of difference was still minimal within industry circles. Second-wave feminist action in the 1960s and 1970s thus initiated an antagonistic, albeit sometimes cooperative and productive, dialogue between brands and women; this dialogue continues to the present day. Feminists' actions focused on the overall strategies of public consciousness raising, as well as exposure and pressure on advertisers. These strategies were coordinated by liberal and radical feminist groups using tactics such as street protests, boycotts, and letter-writing campaigns. At the same time, academic researchers began systematically categorizing types of representations of women found in mainstream advertising, as well as establishing a quantitative baseline through content analysis, which infused the debate with an empirical perspective.

RIDING THE WAVE: LATE 1970s THROUGH THE EARLY 1990s

Throughout the 1970s and 1980s, feminist groups in the United States and Europe kept a close watch on advertisers, using a range of consumer protest tactics—street theater, boycotts, and protests at company shareholder meetings—to call attention to campaigns they deemed sexist and antiwoman, such as Maidenform lingerie's "You Never Know Where She'll Turn Up," designed by the advertising agency Daniel and Charles in 1980. The ads featured women in public places and professional situations with their clothes thrown open to reveal lacy Maidenform bras and panties, which led critics to pan the campaign for sexualizing all women, everywhere ("Intimate Apparel" 2003). Feminists during this period also placed "This Ad Insults Women" stickers on billboards and posters, blacked out offensive images on ads in public places, and wrote new captions to turn the intended meaning of ads against themselves, calling attention to sexist elements (Sivulka 2011, 275). One powerful radical feminist group, the New York–based Women against Pornography (WAP), launched an annual advertising award event in the early 1980s to commend positive prowoman advertising with Miss Liberty awards (the "Libbies") and shame exploitative campaigns with WAP "ZAP" awards. In 1981, the organization slapped a "ZAP" on shoe manufacturer Joe Famolare, whose sexualized ads depicted women's bodies, typically naked except for the shoes (Bronstein 2011).

At a time when women's bodies and body parts were being objectified in advertising more than ever, another significant feminist critic emerged:

Jean Kilbourne. She specifically engaged the medium of advertising, and her 1979 film, *Killing Us Softly,* would be updated and reissued in each subsequent decade (Kilbourne 2000/1979, 1987; Jhally and Kilbourne 2000; Jhally, Kilbourne, and Rabinovitz 2010). In these videos and now TED talks, and through her books such as *Can't Buy My Love* (1999), Kilbourne critiques the persistent hypersexualized and other demeaning representations of women in advertising. These popular videos demonstrate both the ongoing need for consciousness raising among younger women, and the need to take advertisers to task as the industry uses even more extreme depictions of women, including violence and other symbols borrowed from pornography (Merskin 2006; Stern 1991). She also connected advertising culture to addiction and toxic relationships, developing language during this time for enlarging the conversation about eating disorders and other risks to physical and mental health (Kilbourne 1999). Through these arguments, Kilbourne continued to undermine "the industry's position that advertising is about brands" rather than the social reality that advertising provides strong cultural cues about gendered behavior (Boddewyn 1991).

Second-wave feminists continued working throughout the 1990s to evaluate and improve media images of women and to gain access to powerful organizations. Steinem ushered in the decade with a scathing critique of advertisers' control over women's magazine content in "Sex, Lies and Advertising," published in *Ms.* in 1990. In this essay, Steinem revealed how advertisers worked to uphold traditional values of romantic love, heterosexual marriage, and housewifery—often forbidding magazines to publish editorial material about divorce, lesbianism, illness, or disillusionment—by attaching these conditions to their contracts with women's magazines. She urged readers to take action by writing to editors, publishers, and advertisers to "put as much energy into breaking advertising's control over content as into changing the images in ads, or protesting ads for harmful products" and "support[ing] only those women's magazines and products that take us seriously as readers and consumers" (Steinem 1990, 4). The media literacy movement also got underway in the early 1990s through the work of Renee Hobbs, who asked whether media literacy should offer protectionist strategies for media viewers or should educate them about how to dissect and understand media and their ways of building representations (Lambiase et al. 2012). The Media Education Foundation, which distributes Kilbourne's DVDs, as well as the work of media critic Sut Jhally and others, was founded in 1992.

Friedan (2001, xxxi) reflected on feminist activities in the 1990s and the ways that the movement had expanded the conversation since the 1960s. Friedan (2001, xvii) acknowledged advertising, media, and film still show women as sex objects, but she asserted "it's no longer considered chic or even acceptable by much of America." Yet perhaps this was wishful thinking on her part. Novelist Atwood also reviewed her work later in life, calling *The Edible Woman* a protofeminist, rather than a feminist work; on the last page of Atwood's novel, its main character, Marian, is still labeled a consumer, and at the end of the second wave, the movement's goals "have still not been achieved," Atwood ([1969] 2013, x) wrote in 1979.

Although mainstream feminist thought was still focused on the voices of white, middle-class, well-educated women like Friedan, Steinem, Kilbourne, and other leading voices of the second-wave movement, undercurrents of future waves of feminism were building during the 1980s. Orr (1997, 30) traces the first references to a third wave of feminist thought to an unpublished anthology titled *The Third Wave: Feminist Perspectives on Racism,* which focused not on the generational divide that would soon become practice in defining the third wave, but "on multiracial alliances among women that grew out of political and theoretical discussions of the early eighties on race and sexuality," such as those found in the work of bell hooks. As discussed previously, hooks critiqued Friedan's work in 1984, and asserted that privileged feminists "have largely been unable to speak to, with, and for diverse groups of women because they either do not understand fully the inter-relatedness of sex, race, and class oppression or refuse to take this inter-relatedness seriously" (hooks [1984] 2000, 15). She charges that white women and black men have both "led liberation movements that favor their interests and support the continued oppression of other groups" (16). Others shared hooks' assessment, and many strains of thought involving class, gender, and race converged around 1990, when deconstruction, consumer-response research, and feminist literary criticism encountered postcolonialist work and sexuality studies (Stern and Schroeder 1994). These sophisticated analyses of overlapping forms of oppression would become identified as *intersectional theoretical approaches,* following the black legal scholar Kimberlé Crenshaw (1989), who coined this term.

With new theories and interdisciplinary work came a steady stream of advertising content and theme analyses, effects research, historical reclamation, theory building, and other important scholarly work. Researchers working in these areas affirmed that heterosexual content in advertising was widespread in the 1980s and was often attributed to sexual freedom and more liberal social mores after the sexual revolution of the previous decades (Soley and Reid 1988). Women featured in mainstream magazine ads were dressed more provocatively in 1984 than in 1964; in fact, men, to a lesser extent, were also dressed more suggestively (Soley and Kurzbard 1986). Another content analysis comparing 1983 magazine ads to 1993 revealed advertising was significantly more sexualized, with women about three times more likely than men in both 1983 and 1993 to be portrayed more explicitly (Reichert et al. 1999).

Many content analyses and much of the effects research could be seen as serving the industry more than feminist goals. For example, some effects research in the 1980s showed that advertising that used sexual content was less effective because of cognitive processing: Consumers distracted by sexual images were less able to recall the actual products being advertised (Judd and Alexander 1983; Severn, Belch, and Belch 1990). Alice Courtney continued advertising and stereotyping studies, working in 1977 with Thomas Whipple to create a bibliography of more than a thousand entries for research studies about sexual stereotyping in media conducted since the early 1970s (cited in van Zoonen 1994). In these same authors' 1983 study of sex stereotyping, they warned advertisers to "avoid overly seductive, nude, or partially clad models" (Courtney and Whipple 1983, 118). However, rather than emanating from a feminist standpoint, their recommendation pointed out that "sex in advertising could be offensive and distracting. More importantly, their caveat illustrates the concern for protecting advertisers' interests" (Reichert and Lambiase 2003, 3).

During this period, fashion photographer Richard Avedon caught feminists' attention with two campaigns. The first involved Calvin Klein's entry into the designer jeans market using the fifteen-year-old actress Brooke Shields. In an iconic 1980 television commercial, she asked in a sultry, come-hither voice, "You want to know what comes between me and my Calvins? Nothing." A *Vanity Fair* article called the ad "an early iteration of the fashion world's now perennial theme of the girl-woman, both innocent and sexual" (Sischy 2008). Yet despite criticism from feminists, conservative family values groups, child advocates, and pediatricians, the campaign continued to use both double entendre and the sexualized images of Shields (Sischy 2008). One year later, Avedon's work received the ZAP designation from WAP for the Famolare shoe advertising campaign, discussed earlier in this chapter. The negative public attention and antiwoman label motivated Joe Famolare to hire advertising expert Jane Trahey. She suggested a new campaign featuring smiling images of Famolare himself with his line of shoes, without using women or their bodies, shot by Avedon (Duka 1982). The creative public activism of the ZAP award, coupled with feminist critique, enabled activists to raise awareness of the symbolic environment and call attention to some advertising campaigns they saw as demeaning to women.

In the late 1980s, the International Chamber of Commerce produced the International Code of Advertising Principles, while the International Advertising Association addressed the difficulties of regulating and mitigating the types of advertising effects noticed by Kilbourne and academic scholars. In his study of these efforts worldwide, marketing scholar Jean Boddewyn found that both advertising industry governing bodies and practitioners themselves were improving their responses and becoming more open to critique. However, he recommended to practitioners operating in a global context to "pretest ads in terms of sex-and-decency reactions, and check them in advance with the media, self-regulatory bodies, and other relevant advisors" (Boddewyn 1991, 33). During the rise of the third wave, second-wave activists like Steinem continued their critique of the media machine that churned out stereotypical representations of women. However, the magazine that Steinem founded, *Ms.,* began including more sexualized images of women and resembled mainstream media in the 1980s (Ferguson, Kreshel, and Tinkham 1990). Also during this time, at least a few advertisers showed willingness to heed new guidelines set by advertising boards; however, the efforts were often undertaken to protect brands from criticism and backlash, and not to advance feminist goals.

FIGHTING FOR IMPROVED REPRESENTATIONS IN THE 1990s

The term *third wave* resurfaced in the mid-1990s in connection with activist networks focused on organizing young feminists, thereby fusing the movement with generational implications (Orr 1997). Advertisers throughout the 1990s continued to represent young, heterosexual, able-bodied, inordinately thin, white women, and to speak primarily to economically privileged and educated women, most of them white. Consumers on the margins—including lesbians, women of color, and poor women (Hurtado, 1996)—received little or no representation in advertising and little direct attention from marketers. In research about fashion advertising's use of black models between 1985 and 1994, Plous and Neptune (1997) found blacks to be underrepresented in white magazines and noted that black women were more likely to be shown in the jungle or on the plains, or otherwise tied to nature, often wearing animal-print fabrics. If present in advertising at all, African-American women often served as token, stereotyped minor characters or bystanders in both print and broadcast ads (Kern-Foxworth 1994; Licata and Biswas 1993; Mastro and Greenberg 2000; for review, see Green 1999). Women of color were typically marginalized in advertising images, functioning in a secondary "permission to buy" role to signal consumers that the product was not just for white people (Frith and Mueller 2010, 111). African Americans, Asians and Asian Americans, Native Americans, and Latina/os were secondary players, or wholly absent from advertising images in the 1990s, unless a cultural holiday was being celebrated (Sheehan 2004). Lesbian representations in mainstream advertising, sometimes called "lesbian chic," featured highly sexualized images of women that were meant to serve the male gaze (Reichert 2001; Reichert and Lambiase 2003) and "as a way of counterbalancing the risk of backlash from heterosexual consumers" (Oakenfull and Greenlee 2004, 1276). Transgender women were absent almost completely; when included, they were used for comic relief or "homoqueasy" responses (Tsai 2010; Wilke 2001). Using an intersectional lens for advertising history shows how far short the industry fell during this time.

Young feminists in the 1990s refused to endorse any single vision of feminism or feminist behavior, such as how a "proper" feminist might choose to behave, dress, or be sexual (Orr 1997). Instead, they embraced multiplicities of identity and reconstructed feminism in more diverse and inclusive ways. The advertising industry followed suit, to some extent, and during the 1990s, a few mainstream US advertisers began challenging contemporary social constructions of gender. For example, Grow's (2008) work on Nike's advertising to women during this period examines the challenges and successes of Wieden and Kennedy's atypical creative team composed of women who were working on the Nike women's account. Grow argues that, despite significant resistance from Nike executives, early Nike women's advertising created an "opening" for a new articulation of women's representation in advertising: "[N]o matter how contradictory the messages from the Nike executives—wanting the women's ads to remain hegemonically feminine, yet accusing the team of pinkifying the Nike parent brand—the creatives persevered as a collective unit, reflecting the actions of a feminist organization" (2008, 337–338). Thus advertising content in the 1990s allowed women some room to construct and reconstruct representations, likely agreeing with some elements of media representation but not others (Scott 1992).

Nike's ad campaigns targeted younger women, who were coming of age in an era when modest feminist gains had been achieved, and they benefitted from sustained second-wave critique against advertisers. This generation sought to reclaim the body and certain feminized practices, such as dressing fashionably and wearing cosmetics, as forms of personal empowerment—anathema to groups of second wavers who rejected these pursuits (Groeneveld 2010; Maclaran 2012; Riordan 2001). These new insights by scholars notwithstanding, one long-time observer saw no gains in advertising representations of women. Calling out Super Bowl advertising losers in the late 1990s, Bob Garfield wrote in *Advertising Age* (1999, 1):

> Now that the Super Bowl is over and the victory recorded for the ages, let's spend one quiet moment thinking about who lost: Gloria Steinem. Also Betty Friedan, Germaine Greer, your mother, your daughter. . . . After three decades of gradually weaning itself from naked objectification, advertising has apparently decided that the benefit of crudely impressing men trumps the disadvantages of honoring women. It's as if Madison Avenue sneaked into the nation's psyche and absconded with 30 years of feminist awareness.

Despite Garfield's lament, a new wave of feminists began to develop different ways to position contemporary empowerment by critiquing traditional collective action as oppressive to the diverse lifestyle choices of women (Orr 1997). Third-wave feminists turned to the grassroots punk Riot Grrrl movement and created a host of alternative 'zines and Internet sites in the late 1990s and early 2000s as a way to make feminism more personal and accessible (Bronstein 2005; Riordan 2001), rather than solely focusing on fighting mainstream media content such as Super Bowl ads produced by large brands. Instead, young feminists actively produced political texts deriding mainstream media, advertising, and fashion for their sexualized, infantilized, and photo-manipulated representations of women, and promoted an active and liberated sexuality as the right of all third-wave subjects (D'Enbeau 2011). Maclaran (2015) notes that the focus on individuality and a woman's right to pleasure—often realized through marketplace logic of individual expression and satisfaction through consumption—turned attention away from collective structural concerns of women's vulnerability and agency. Postfeminism and third-wave feminism are often conflated, especially for the shared focus on a neoliberal subject emphasizing personal choice, pursuits of pleasure, sexual agency, entitlement, and entrepreneurship (Lazar 2011). These themes seemed an easy fit for advertisers hoping to show women how to improve their lives by exercising individual preference through consumer practices. Although women's participation in important purchase decisions is not new, twenty-first-century advertisers increasingly recognize that women manage purchase decisions across a wide range of categories (e.g., technology, financial products, business travel) that extend well beyond the home (Dishman 2013). Advertising to women simply makes good business sense. Consumer-response studies during the 1990s and early 2000s, however, have shown that women were more likely to register more negative attitudes toward the brand and toward the ad, as well as exhibit lower purchase intention than men, when sexual objectification and other sexist images were used by advertisers (Ford and LaTour 1993, 1996; Lambiase et al. 2012; Reichert et al. 2007).

CONNECTIVE ACTION AND THE MOVE TOWARD BETTER REPRESENTATION FOR *ALL* WOMEN

Although mainstream media in the early 2000s continued to represent women in narrow ways, through sexist and highly sexualized images that featured young, able-bodied, mostly white, and mostly straight women, the advent of social media offered new tools and platforms for communication and activism. Women of all identities began to connect globally and immediately, engaging in active dialogues about representation via blogs, social media like Facebook, and hashtag activism, such as the 2016 #WomenNotObjects movement started by advertising executive Madonna Badger of the agency Badger and Winters to stand up against the objectification of women in advertising. Connective action tends to support positive representations and gives citizens an immediate, powerful means to condemn stereotypical and derogatory messages. Popular media have heralded these connective actions as indicative of emerging fourth-wave activities, developing through multi-platform communication unique in its use of technology and social media (Cochrane 2013; Solomon 2009). As Maclaran (2015, 1734) writes, "[T]here is a fresh feminist zeitgeist coming from young activists . . . who try to blend the micropolitics that characterised much of the third wave with an agenda that seeks change in political, social, and economic structures much like the second wave."

Against the twenty-first-century backdrop of women's empowerment messages discussed earlier in this chapter from brands such as Dove, the *Always* brand of feminine products launched its "Like a Girl" campaign in June 2014. This ad campaign tackled negative stereotypes associated with being a girl, such as lack of physical strength or athletic ability. When ad agency Leo Burnett placed the commercial during Super Bowl 2015, the campaign received increased media and consumer attention, spurring thousands of tweets with the hashtag #LikeAGirl. Shortly after, #LikeABoy emerged, reportedly as a response by some men who found #LikeAGirl to be "exclusionary and sexist" (Chittal 2014).

Digital technologies provide new spaces for consumers and brands to connect. Although some connection takes place through advertiser and agency-sponsored hashtag campaigns, other digital spaces provide forums for complaints, counter-representations, and even apologies by brands. One 2009 Ralph Lauren ad went viral after women noticed a model's waist had been reduced to be pencil-thin by Photoshop techniques; a spokesperson for Ralph Lauren apologized for the ad's "very distorted image of a woman's body" and promised to use high-quality artwork in the future to represent the brand "appropriately" (Sharp 2009). Following complaints about limited clothing sizes sold by Abercrombie and Fitch in 2013, the company posted a note on Facebook from CEO Mike Jeffries, which read that Jeffries regretted his "choice of words" used in a "resurrected quote . . . taken out of context" about the way the company chose its consumers: "We are completely opposed to . . . discrimination . . . or other anti-social behavior based on race, gender, body type" ("A Note from Mike" 2013). In 2006, Jeffries had remarked of sizing that "a lot of people don't belong (in our clothes), and they can't belong" (Denizet-Lewis 2006). Later in 2013, he was stripped of his job as board chair, and he stepped down as CEO in late 2014 (Team 2014).

Feminist blogger Jes Baker (2013, 2014) contributed to public pressure on Abercrombie and Fitch by modeling plus-sized clothing falsely labeled as belonging to the brand while standing alongside a shirtless male model. More recently, Baker started the #EmpowerAllBodies hashtag, accompanied by photographs containing diverse women who do not look like typical models to criticize plus-size fashion retailer Lane Bryant's too-white, too-perfect #ImNoAngel campaign (Bahadur 2015). Baker's countercampaign includes several races, body types, and a woman in a wheelchair. Her first-person account told through blog posts (and now a book) mirrors the first-person fictional work of Atwood in the 1960s; Jes Baker, like Marian in *The Edible Woman,* decides to abandon the sanctioned pathway for normative femininity in the Western world.

The fashion industry is not the only corporate target of digital campaigns by feminists and their allies. In late 2011, Denmark-based Lego introduced Lego Friends, pastel-colored kits featuring five skirt-wearing doll-like figures marketed exclusively to girls (Wittenberg-Cox 2014) and limited by heteronormative design. In response to Lego Friends, feminist activists created a petition through Change.org asking the retailer to create the same building sets for boys and girls and to market them without gender cues ("Gender Controversy" 2012). One organizer of the Change.org petition, Bailey Shoemaker Richards, represents the SPARK Movement, which stands for Sexualization Protest: Action, Resistance, Knowledge. It is described as "a girl-fueled, intergenerational activist organization working online to ignite an anti-racist gender justice movement" ("About Us" n.d.). In a radio interview, she called the new product "limiting" and said Lego had created "what we call a pink ghetto for girls" ("Gender Controversy" 2012). In response, Lego executive Mads Nipper (2012) said through the company's website, "We want to correct any misinterpretation that Lego Friends is our only offering for girls. . . . We know that many girls love to build and play with the wide variety of LEGO products already available." One year later, Lego created a magazine ad showing a girl with a one-of-a-kind structure created from basic Lego Friends pieces, with the tagline "It's as one of a kind as she is." SPARK Movement said the new ad was a step forward, "but it's an empty gesture when Lego's product lines and website continue to actively exclude girls"; the SPARK group conducted an analysis of all LEGO product lines, excluding Friends and any licensed characters such as Lord of the Rings, to find barely more than 10 percent of LEGO characters were girls or women (Richards 2013).

In 2014, using different digital tools, activists targeted a Mattel product released in 2010, the "Barbie: I Can Be a Computer Engineer" book, which was packaged with a Computer Engineer Barbie (Mlot 2014). The book depicts Barbie seeking help from two male programmers with writing code and dealing with a computer virus instead of doing the work herself. First, blogger Pamela Ribon wrote about the book she had found ("After Backlash" 2014), and soon #FeministHackerBarbie became a trending topic on Twitter, where some users created memes and at least one app so that people could create their own stories "using pages from the original book" (Lorenz 2014). One meme on Feministing.com showed the Barbie character asking, "Should I implement my visualization with P5.js, D3, Node.js, or Three.js with WebGL?" (Dusenbery 2014). On Facebook, Mattel addressed the controversy on its "Barbie" page by stating that "this specific story doesn't reflect the Brand's vision for what Barbie stands for. We believe girls should be empowered to understand that anything is possible. . . . We apologize that this book didn't reflect that belief." Within a few days of the start of the Twitter campaign, Mattel pulled the book from Amazon (Lorenz 2014). In 2015, Mattel showed its responsiveness again with a new campaign using its iconic Barbie doll to show nongendered career pathways for girls, such as engineering.

Third-wave feminists in the 1990s and early 2000s encountered many of the same challenges as the second wave, yet they began to think about these challenges in new ways with language and theory that was more inclusive of all women, no matter the race, age, ability, or sexual orientation. With the advent of social media in the early 2000s, feminists and their supporters built their own connective platforms for protest, critique, and discussion of advertising. However, large brands and corporations still retain incredible cultural power to shape people's consciousness about beauty and gender roles through advertising (Johnston and Taylor 2008).

CONCLUSIONS: LIMITED PROGRESS AND MORE WORK AHEAD

As we stated at the beginning of this chapter, we see signs of progress from the continuous work of feminists and their allies over the past half a century. Whether through the collective mindset of second-wave feminists, the evolving spirit of third-wave activists, or connections of an evolving fourth wave, advertisers have had to contend with critique by being responsive once feminists and their allies develop traction with the public at large.

In a few cases, celebrity women have been affirmed through the channel of the global brand and may display a kind of intersectional example of women's power; one example is the role of CoverGirl spokeswoman, which has been filled by Dania Ramirez, Sofia Vergara, Queen Latifah, Ellen DeGeneres, and Taylor Swift. It is this channel—brands and their marketplace—that scholar Linda Scott (2006) believes has been ignored by feminists for too long because of antimarket prejudice. She advocates use of market feminism to help women claim achievements in advertising and marketing to match those seen in other sectors of society; Scott admits this may be a difficult recommendation for many feminists to accept.

The social power of relentless and ubiquitous corporate advertising cannot be denied, but it is a power that has done more harm to women than good. It is this power that has thwarted much feminist activism since the 1960s; even the largest feminist coalition of collective-connection efforts hasn't been able to slow or stop sexist, objectifying, and violent representations of women in advertising. There is no doubt that these representations have become more extreme since the 1960s, when second-wave feminists were most concerned about women being depicted only in home settings; current-day concerns revolve around representations of gang rapes, stereotyped or hypersexualized girls, limited representations of racial minorities, and ever-thinner models. Efforts to halt these depictions continue to be important because effects research of the last twenty-five years is clear: Advertising images, replicated endlessly in print and in digital spaces, do affect the people who view them. It is also clear that advertising professionals working for companies or ad agencies do not always understand the influence of their work (Zayer and Coleman 2015). Studies show the presence of sexist, gendered, heterosexist, ableist, racist, violent, or objectifying images in advertising can cause people:

- to develop body-image distortions or dissatisfaction, especially among women and girls of all races (Goodman, 2002; Harrison and Cantor 1997; Haytko et al. 2014; Lavine, Sweeney, and Wagner 1999; Myers and Biocca 1992; Romo, Mireles-Rios and Hurtado 2016; Tiggemann and McGill 2004)
- to devalue their own attractiveness, as well as devalue a partner's attractiveness (Kendrick, Gutierres, and Goldberg 1989; McKay and Covell 1997; Richins 1991)
- to express more aggressiveness toward women (Gold 1995)
- to activate stereotypes and traditional gender-role socialization (Lafky et al. 1996; Signorielli 1993)

The worst offenders who replicate these images may be fashion advertisers, such as Dolce and Gabbana, Abercrombie and Fitch, and others. Unlike in the United States, advertising governing boards in other nations have been more vigilant in banning such violent or disturbing images; their regulations may bring awareness to these global brands in ways that connective or collective feminism in the United States cannot.

One long-held strategy for correcting corporate advertising images is still key—gaining the attention of large corporations by calling them out publicly to consumers and stockholders, and by showing them the incongruence between their professed values for women consumers and their advertising messages. Whether through picketing, boycotts, petitioning through Change.org, protests on digital platforms, or the new tools of market feminism, feminists and their allies must continue their pressure on these global brands, on advertising agencies that create campaigns, and on consumers who make choices in the transnational marketplace. The creative, forceful, and persistent ways that feminist activists have strategized to confront and reform a powerful image industry over the past half century are still relevant. And the work of feminists against problematic and harmful advertising practices, including distorted images of all kinds of women, is not finished.

NOTE

1. The metaphor of feminism occurring in "waves" has long been the dominant conceptual framework for identifying and explaining the rise and evolution of movements for women's rights in the United States. The first wave is generally understood to encompass the period from the 1848 Seneca Falls convention to the ratification of the Nineteenth Amendment to the US Constitution (women's suffrage) in 1920. The second wave began in the mid-1960s and ran through the mid-1980s and focused on analysis of the subordinate place of women in society as well as formal and informal challenges to institutions, through consciousness raising, public education, and legal reform, to achieve greater equality. The third wave emerged in the 1980s as a critique, mostly from women of color and lesbians, who saw second-wave goals and strategies as focused on the problems of white, privileged, heterosexual women, with little attention to the intersectional oppressions that structured the lives of nonwhite, poor, and queer women. Third-wave activists called attention to variables such as age, race, sexual preference, and class, and argued that the interaction of these identities created more nuanced forms of sexism and discrimination. The model of the waves, although still in common usage, has come under significant attack for positioning feminist activity as having fixed starting and ending dates, for suggesting that feminists in different waves are always working in opposition to one another, and for minimizing the contributions and perspectives of a diverse range of feminists working both inside and outside of the formal movements. For a full discussion of the limitations of the metaphor, see Laughlin et al. (2010).

REFERENCES

"About Us." n.d. *SPARK Movement.* Accessed July 6, 2015. http://www.sparksummit.com/about-us/.

"After Backlash, Computer Engineer Barbie Gets New Set of Skills." 2014. *National Public Radio.* Last modified November 22. http://www.npr.org/2014/11/22/365968465/after-backlash-computer-engineer-barbie-gets-new-set-of-skills.

Atwood, Margaret. 1969. *The Edible Woman.* New York: Little Brown.
Atwood, Margaret. (1969) 2013. Introduction (1979). In *The Edible Woman.* London: Virago.
Bahadur, Nina. 2015. "#EmpowerALLBodies is What a Truly Diverse Campaign Looks Like." *Huffington Post,* April 24. Accessed April 26, 2016. http://www.huffingtonpost.com/2015/04/23/empowerallbodies-jes-baker_n_7126500.html.
Baker, Jes. 2013. "To Mike Jeffries, c/o Abercrombie and Fitch." *The Militant Baker: Lose the Bullshit. Love Your Body* (blog), May 19. Accessed September 5, 2015. http://www.themilitantbaker.com/2013/05/to-mike-jeffries-co-abercrombie-fitch.html.
———. 2014. "Why We've Learned to Hate Our Bodies." *Everyday Feminism,* August 25. Accessed September 10, 2015. http://everydayfeminism.com/2014/08/learned-to-hate-ourselves/.
Baker, Katie J. M. 2012. "1970s Sexist Ads Depressingly Pretty Similar to Today's Sexist Ads." *Jezebel,* August 27. Accessed September 5, 2014. http://jezebel.com/5938122/1970s-sexist-ads-depressingly-pretty-similar-to-todays-sexist-ads.
Bennett, Lance, and Alexandra Segerberg. 2012. *The Logic of Connective Action: Digital Media and the Personalization of Contentious Politics.* Cambridge: Cambridge University Press.
Boddewyn, Jean. 1991. "Controlling Sex and Decency in Advertising around the World." *Journal of Advertising* 20 (4): 25–35.
Bronstein, Carolyn. 2005. "Representing the Third Wave: Mainstream Print Media Framing of a New Feminist Movement." *Journalism and Mass Communication Quarterly* 82 (4): 783–803.
———. 2011. *Battling Pornography: The American Feminist Anti-Pornography Movement, 1976–1986.* Cambridge: Cambridge University Press.
Chittal, Nisha. 2014. "#LikeABoy Responds to Always Super Bowl Ad." *MSNBC.com.* Accessed May 1, 2016. http://www.msnbc.com/msnbc/likeaboy-responds-always-super-bowl-ad.
Cochrane, Kira. 2013. "The Fourth Wave of Feminism: Meet the Rebel Women." *The Guardian,* December 10. Accessed September 15, 2015. http://www.theguardian.com/world/2013/dec/10/fourth-wave-feminism-rebel-women.
Cole, Ellen, and Jessica Henderson Daniel, editors. 2005. *Featuring Females: Feminist Analyses of Media.* Washington, DC: American Psychological Association.
Collins, Patricia Hill. 2000. *Black Feminist Thought: Knowledge, Consciousness, and the Politics of Empowerment.* New York: Routledge.
Coltrane, Scott, and Melinda Messineo. 2000. "The Perpetuation of Subtle Prejudice: Race and Gender Imagery in 1990s Television Advertising." *Sex Roles* 42 (5): 363–389.
"Controversy: Lara Stone for Calvin Klein 2010—Gang Rape or Fashion?" 2010. *Beautifully Invisible* (blog). Accessed October 31, 2015. http://www.beautifully-invisible.com/2010/10/controversy-lara-stone-for-calvin-klein-2010-gang-rape-or-fashion.html.
Courtney, Alice E., and Sarah Lockeretz. 1971. "A Woman's Place: An Analysis of the Roles Portrayed by Women in Magazine Advertisements." *Journal of Marketing Research* 8: 92–95.

Courtney, Alice E., and Thomas W. Whipple. 1983. *Sex Stereotyping in Advertising.* Lexington: D. C. Heath.

Craig, Steve. 1997. "Madison Avenue versus The Feminine Mystique: How the Advertising Industry Responded to the Onset of the Modern Women's Movement." Popular Culture Association conference, March 27. Accessed September 5, 2015. http://ruby.fgcu.edu/courses/tdugas/ids3301/acrobat/womensmovement.pdf.

Crenshaw, Kimberlé. 1989. "Demarginalizing the Intersection of Race and Sex: A Black Feminist Critique of Antidiscrimination Doctrine, Feminist Theory and Antiracist Politics." *University of Chicago Legal Forum* 140: 139–67.

———. 1991. "Mapping the Margins: Intersectionality, Identity Politics, and Violence against Women of Color." *Stanford Law Review* 43: 1241–99.

Della Porta, Donatella. 2014. "Comment on Organizing the Crowd." *Information, Communication and Society* 17 (2): 269–71.

D'Enbeau, Suzy. 2011. "Sex, Feminism, and Advertising: The Politics of Advertising Feminism in a Competitive Marketplace." *Journal of Communication Inquiry* 35 (1): 53–69.

Denizet-Lewis, Benoit. 2006. "The Man Behind Abercrombie and Fitch." *Salon,* January 24. Accessed September 10, 2015. http://www.salon.com/2006/01/24/jeffries/.

Dishman, Lydia. 2013. "Where Are All of the Women Creative Directors?" *Fast Company,* February 26. Accessed October 31, 2015. http://www.fastcompany.com/3006255/where-are-all-women-creative-directors.

"Dolce and Gabbana Bow to Criticism and Pull Ad." 2007. *Reuters,* March 6. Accessed October 8, 2015. http://www.reuters.com/article/industry-italy-dolcegabbana-advert-dc-idUSL0631454820070306.

Duggan, Maeve. 2013. "It's a Woman's (Social Media) World." *Pew Research Center Fact Tank,* October 7. Accessed October 21, 2015. http://www.pewresearch.org/fact-tank/2013/09/12/its-a-womans-social-media-world/.

Duka, John. 1982. "Notes on Fashions," *New York Times,* January 5. Accessed October 1, 2015. http://www.nytimes.com/1982/01/05/style/notes-on-fashions.html.

Dusenbery, Maya. 2014. "New Favorite Meme: Feminist Hacker Barbie." *Feministing* (blog). November 25. Accessed April 26, 2016. http://feministing.com/2014/11/25/new-favorite-meme-feminist-hacker-barbie/.

Echols, Alice. 1989. *Daring to Be Bad: Radical Feminism in America, 1967–1975.* Minneapolis: University of Minnesota Press.

Ewen, William H. 1975. Foreword. In *Advertising and Women: A Report on Advertising Portraying or Directed to Women.* New York: National Advertising Review Board.

Ferguson, Jill Hicks, Peggy J. Kreshel, and Spencer F. Tinkham. 1990. "In the Pages of Ms.: Sex-Role Portrayals of Women in Advertising." *Journal of Advertising* 19 (1): 40–51.

Ford, John B., and Michael S. LaTour. 1993. "Differing Reactions to Female Role Portrayals in Advertising." *Journal of Advertising Research* 33: 43–52.

———. 1996. "Contemporary Female Perspectives of Female Role Portrayals of Women in Advertising." *Journal of Current Issues and Research in Advertising* 16 (Spring): 81–95.

Ford, Liz. 2015. "Women's Rights Activists Use Social Media to Get Their Message Out." *Guardian,* March 18. Accessed March 6, 2016. http://www.theguardian.com/global-development/2015/mar/19/womens-rights-social-media-get-their-message-out.

Foxworth, Jo. 1979. *Boss Lady: An Executive Woman Talks about Making It.* New York: Warner.

"Franchellie Cadwell, Backer of New Image for Women in Ads, Dies at 70." *New York Times,* May 30, 2003. Accessed October 12, 2015. http://www.nytimes.com/2003/05/30/obituaries/30CADW.html.

Friedan, Betty. 1963. *The Feminine Mystique.* New York: W. W. Norton and Co.

———. [1963] 2001. *The Feminine Mystique* (reprint). New York: W. W. Norton and Co.

Frith, Katherine, and Barbara Mueller. 2010. *Advertising and Society: Global Issues.* New York: Peter Lang.

Garfield, Bob. 1999. "Chauvinist Pigskin: Ad Review: Super Bowl Advertisers Set the World Back 30 Years with Naked Appeals to Guys." *Advertising Age,* February 1 (1).

"Gender Controversy Stacks Up against 'Lego Friends.'" 2012. *National Public Radio.* Accessed July 6, 2015. http://www.npr.org/2012/01/18/145397007/gender-controversy-stacks-up-against-lego-friends.

Gill, Rosalind. 2007. *Gender and the Media.* Cambridge: Polity.

Goffman, Erving. 1979. *Gender Advertisements.* New York: Harper and Row.

Gold, Marion. 1995. "Portrayal in Ads Can Affect Harassment; Ad Images of Women, Pay Inequity Also Need Scrutiny by Industry." *Advertising Age,* May 1 (18).

Goodman, J. Robyn. 2002. "Flabless Is Fabulous: How Latina and Anglo Women Read and Incorporate the Excessively Thin Body Ideal into Everyday Experience." *Journalism and Mass Communication Quarterly* 79 (3): 712–27.

Green, Corliss. 1999. "Ethnic Evaluations of Advertising: Interaction Effects of Strength of Ethnic Identification, Media Placement, and Degree of Racial Composition." *Journal of Advertising* 28 (1): 49–64.

Groeneveld, Elizabeth. 2010. "'Join the Knitting Revolution': Third-Wave Feminist Magazines and the Politics of Domesticity." *Canadian Review of American Studies* 40 (2): 259–77.

Griner, David. 2013. "5 Reasons Why Some Critics Are Hating on Dove's Real Beauty Sketches Video." *Advertising Age,* April 19. Accessed March 5, 2016. http://www.adweek.com/adfreak/5-reasons-why-some-critics-are-hating-doves-real-beauty-sketches-video-148772.

Grow, Jean M. 2008. "The Gender of Branding: Early Nike Women's Advertising a Feminist Antenarrative," *Women's Studies in Communication* 31 (3): 337–38.

Harrison, Kristen. 2001. "Ourselves, Our Bodies: Thin-Ideal Media, Self-Discrepancies, and Eating Disorder Symptomatology in Adolescents." *Journal of Social and Clinical Psychology* 20: 289–323.

Harrison, Kristen, and Joanne Cantor. 1997. "The Relationship between Media Consumption and Eating Disorders," *Journal of Communication* 47 (1): 40–67.

Haytko, Diana L., R. Stephen Parker, Carol M. Motley, and Ivonne M. Torres. 2014. "Body Image and Ethnicity: A Qualitative Exploration." *Journal of Management and Marketing Research* 17 (October): 1–20.

Hewitt, Nancy A. 2010. *No Permanent Waves: Recasting Histories of U.S. Feminism.* New Brunswick, NJ: Rutgers University Press.

hooks, bell. 1984. *Feminist Theory from Margins to Center.* Cambridge, MA: South End.

———. [1984] 2000. *Feminist Theory from Margins to Center,* 2nd edition. Cambridge, MA: South End.

Hull, Gloria T., Patricia Bell Scott, and Barbara Smith. 1982. *But Some of Us Are Brave: Black Women's Studies.* Old Westbury, NY: The Feminist Press.

Hurtado, Aida. 1996. *The Color of Privilege: Three Blasphemies on Race and Feminism.* Ann Arbor, MI: The University of Michigan.

"Intimate Apparel." *Advertising Age,* September 15, 2003. Accessed April 25, 2016. http://adage.com/article/adage-encyclopedia/intimate-apparel/98724/.

Jhally, Sut, and Jean Kilbourne. 2000. *Killing Us Softly 3: Advertising's Image of Women.* Northampton, Mass.: Media Education Foundation.

Jhally, Sut, Jean Kilbourne, and David Rabinovitz. 2010. *Killing Us Softly 4: Advertising's Image of Women.* Northampton, Mass.: Media Education Foundation.

Johnston, Josee, and Judith Taylor. 2008. "Feminist Consumerism and Fat Activists: A Comparative Study of Activism and the Dove Real Beauty Campaign." *Signs* 33 (4): 941–66.

Judd, Benjamin B., and M. W. Alexander. 1983. "On the Reduced Effectiveness of Some Sexually Suggestive Ads." *Journal of the Academy of Marketing Science* 11 (Spring): 156–68.

Kang, Mee-Eun. 1997. "The Portrayal of Women's Images in Magazine Advertisements: Goffman's Gender Analysis Revisited." *Sex Roles* 37 (11/12): 979–97.

Keane, Erin. 2013. "Stop Posting That Dove Ad: 'Real Beauty' Campaign Is Not Feminist." *Salon,* April 18. Accessed April 12, 2016. http://www.salon.com/2013/04/18/stop_posting_that_dove_ad_real_beauty_campaign_is_not_feminist/.

Kendrick, Douglas T., Sara E. Gutierres, and Laurie L. Goldberg. 1989. "Influence of Popular Erotica on Judgments of Strangers and Mates." *Journal of Experimental Social Psychology* 25 (2): 159–67.

Kern-Foxworth, Marilyn. 1994. *Aunt Jemima, Uncle Ben, and Rastus: Blacks in Advertising, Yesterday, Today, and Tomorrow.* Westport, CT: Greenwood.

Kilbourne, Jean. 2000/1979. *Killing Us Softly: Advertising's Image of Women.* Cambridge, Mass: Cambridge Documentary Films.

———. 1987. *Still Killing Us Softly: Advertising's Image of Women.* Cambridge, Mass: Cambridge Documentary Films.

———. 1999. *Can't Buy My Love: How Advertising Changes the Way We Think and Feel.* New York: Simon & Schuster.

Komisar, Lucy. 1972. "The Image of Woman in Advertising." In *Woman in Sexist Society,* edited by Vivian Gornick and Barbara K. Moran. New York: New American Library.

Lafky, Sue, Margaret Duffy, Mary Steinmaus, and Dan Berkowitz. 1996. "Looking through Gendered Lenses: Female Stereotyping in Advertisements and Gender Role Expectations." *Journalism and Mass Communication Quarterly* 73 (2): 379–88.

Lake, Brittany. 2015. "'Femvertising': Empowering or Enraging?" *We Are Genuine* (blog). April 30. Accessed April 12, 2016. https://www.wearegenuine.com/blog/femvertising-empowering-enraging/.

Lambiase, Jacqueline. 2012. "Crisis and *Kairos*: Social Media Activists Exploit Timing to Support Anti-Government Protests." In *Case Studies in Crisis Communication: International Perspectives on Hits and Misses,* edited by Amiso George and Cornelius Pratt, 523–39. New York: Routledge.

Lambiase, Jacqueline, Tom Reichert, Mark Adkins, and Michael LaTour. 2012. "Gender and Media Literacy: Women and Men Try on Responses to Objectification in Fashion Advertising." *Gender, Culture and Consumer Behavior,* edited by Cele C. Otnes and Linda T. Zayer, 139–59. New York: Routledge, Taylor and Francis Group.

Laughlin, Kathleen A., Julie Gallagher, Dorothy Sue Cobble, Eileen Boris, Premilla Nadasen, Stephanie Gilmore, Leandra Zarnow. 2010. "Is It Time to Jump Ship? Historians Rethink the Waves Metaphor." *Feminist Formations* 22 (1): 76–135.

Lavine, Howard, Donna Sweeney, and Stephen Wagner. 1999. "Depicting Women as Sex Objects in Television Advertising: Effects on Body Dissatisfaction." *Personality and Social Psychology Bulletin* 25 (8): 1049–58.

Lazar, Michelle M. 2011. "The Right to Be Beautiful: Postfeminist Identity and Consumer Beauty Advertising." *New Femininities: Postfeminism, Neoliberalism and Subjectivity,* edited by Rosalind Gill and Christina Scharff, 37–51. Basingstoke: Palgrave Macmillan.

Licata, Jane, and Abhijit Biswas. 1993. Representation, Roles, and Occupational Status of Black Models in Television Advertisements. *Journalism Quarterly* 70, 868–82.

Lindner, Katharina. 2004. "Images of Women in General Interest and Fashion Magazine Advertisements from 1955 to 2002." *Sex Roles* 51 (7/8): 409–21.

Lorde, Audre. 1984. *Sister Outsider: Essays and Speeches*. Trumansburg, NY: Crossing Press.

Lorenz, Taylor. 2014. "Meet #FeministHackerBarbie, The Best Responses to Mattel's Sexist 'Barbie: I Can Be a Computer Engineer' Book." *Business Insider,* November 24. Accessed July 15, 2015. http://www.businessinsider.com/responses-mattels-sexist-barbie-i-can-be-a-computer-engineer-book-2014-11.

Lotz, Amanda D. (2003). "Communicating Third-Wave Feminism and New Social Movements: Challenges for the Next Century of Feminist Endeavor." *Women and Language* 26 (1): 2–9.

MacCurdy, Marian Mesrobian. 2012. "The Four Women of the Apocalypse: Utopia or Dystopia?" *Utopian Images and Narratives in Advertising: Dreams for Sale,* edited by Luigi Daniele Manca, Alessandra Manca, and Gail Pieper, 260–72. Lanham, MD: Lexington.

Maclaran, Pauline. 2012. "Marketing and Feminism in Historic Perspective." *Journal of Historical Research in Marketing* 4 (3): 462–69.

———. 2015. "Feminism's Fourth Wave: A Research Agenda for Marketing and Consumer Research." *Journal of Marketing Management* 31 (15–16): 1732–1738.

Mastro, Dana E., and Bradley S. Greenberg. 2000. "The Portrayal of Racial Minorities on Prime Time Television." *Journal of Broadcasting and Electronic Media,* Fall: 690–703.

McCluskey, Michael. 2014. "Book Review: The Logic of Connective Action." *Political Communication* 31 (4): 679.

McKay, Natalie J., and Katherine Covell. 1997. "The Impact of Women in Advertisements on Attitudes toward Women." *Sex Roles* 36 (9): 573–83.

Merskin, Debra. 2006. "Where Are the Clothes? The Pornographic Gaze in Mainstream American Fashion Advertising." *Sex in Consumer Culture: The Erotic Content of Media and Marketing,* edited by Tom Reichert and Jacqueline Lambiase, 199–218. Mahwah, NJ: Erlbaum.

Mlot, Stephanie. 2014. "Mattel Apologizes, Pulls Sexist Computer-Engineer Barbie Book." *PC Magazine,* November 21. Accessed April 26, 2016. http://www.pcmag.com/articlc2/0,2817,2472529,00.asp.

Moraga, Cherríe, and Gloria Anzaldúa, editors. 1981. *This Bridge Called My Back: Writings by Radical Women of Color.* Watertown, MA: Persephone.

Museum of Menstruation. n.d. "Pristeen 'Feminine Hygiene Deodorant' Ad, 1969." Accessed April 12, 2016. http://www.mum.org/pristeen.htm.

Myers, Philip N., and Frank A. Biocca. 1992. "The Elastic Body Image: The Effect of Television Advertising and Programming on Body Image Distortions in Young Women." *Journal of Communication* 42 (3): 108–33.

National Sundowners. n.d. "Parting Shots: An Airline's Ad Encounters Some Turbulence." Accessed September 5, 2015. http://www.nationalsundowners.com/images/70/parting_shots_large.jpg.

Nipper, Mads. 2012. "Lego Group Commentary on Attracting More Girls to Construction Play." *Lego,* January 12. Accessed July 19, 2015. http://www.lego.com/en-us/aboutus/news-room/2012/january/lego-group-commentary-on-attracting-more-girls-to-construction-play.

"A Note from Mike, Our CEO." 2013. Abercrombie and Fitch Facebook page. Accessed September 5, 2015. https://www.facebook.com/AbercrombieBrussels/posts/367316806702989.

Nudd, Tim. 2010. "Calvin Klein Ads Banned for Promoting Rape," *Adweek,* October 21. Accessed March 6, 2016. http://www.adweek.com/adfreak/calvin-klein-ads-banned-promoting-rape-12033.

Oakenfull, Gillian, and Timothy Greenlee. 2004. "The Three Rules of Crossing Over from Gay Media to Mainstream Media Advertising: Lesbians, Lesbians, Lesbians." *Journal of Business Research* 57 (11, November): 1276–85.

Orr, Catherine M. 1997. "Charting the Currents of the Third Wave." *Hypatia* 12 (2, Summer): 30.

Parameswaran, Radhika, and Kavitha Cardoza. 2009. "Melanin on the Margins: Advertising and the Cultural Politics of Fair/Light/White Beauty in India." *Journalism and Communication Monographs* 11 (3): 213–74.

Perrin, Andrew. 2015. "Social Networking Usage: 2005–2015." *Pew Research Center,* October. Accessed October 12, 2015. http://www.pewinternet.org/2015/10/08/social-networking-usage-2005-2015/.

Phelan, Shane. 1989. *Identity Politics: Lesbian Feminism and the Limits of Community*. Philadelphia: Temple University Press.
Pingree, Suzanne, Robert Parker Hawkins, Matilda Butler, and William Paisley. 1976. "A Scale for Sexism." *Journal of Communication* 26 (4, December): 193–200.
Plous, S., and Dominique Neptune. 1997. "Racial and Gender Biases in Magazine Advertising: A Content-Analytic Study." *Psychology of Women Quarterly* 21 (4): 627–44.
Reichert, Tom. 2001. "'Lesbian Chic' Imagery in Advertising: Interpretations and Insights of Female Same-Sex Eroticism." *Journal of Current Issues and Research in Advertising* 23 (2): 9–22.
Reichert, Tom, and Jacqueline Lambiase. 2003. *Sex in Advertising: Perspectives on the Erotic Appeal*. Mahwah, NJ: Erlbaum.
Reichert, Tom, Jacqueline Lambiase, Susan Morgan, Meta Carstarphen, and Susan Zavoina. 1999. "Cheesecake and Beefcake: No Matter How You Slice It, Sexual Explicitness in Advertising Continue to Increase." *Journalism and Mass Communication Quarterly* 76 (1, Spring): 7–20.
Reichert, Tom, Michael S. LaTour, Jacqueline Lambiase, and Mark Adkins. 2007. "A Test of Media Literacy Effects and Sexual Objectification in Advertising," *Journal of Current Issues and Research in Advertising* 29 (1): 81–92.
Richards, Bailey Shoemaker. 2013. "A Year Later, How's Lego Doing?" *SPARK Movement*. Last modified June 19. http://www.sparksummit.com/2013/06/19/a-year-later-hows-lego-doing/.
Richins, Marsha L. 1991. "Social Comparison and the Idealized Images of Advertising." *Journal of Consumer Research* 18 (1): 71–83.
Riordan, Ellen. 2001. "Commodified Agents and Empowered Girls: Consuming and Producing Feminism." *Journal of Communication Inquiry 25* (3): 279–97.
Romo, Laura F., Rebeca Mireles-Rios, and Aida Hurtado. 2016. "Cultural, Media, and Peer Influences on Body Beauty Perceptions of Mexican American Adolescent Girls." *Journal of Adolescent Research* 31 (4): 474–501.
Rosen, Ruth. 2000. *The World Split Open: How the Modern Women's Movement Changed America*. New York: Viking.
Schultz, E. J. 2012. "A Century of Women in Advertising: From 'I Wish I Were a Man' Cigarette Ads to 'My Butt is Big and That's Just Fine.'" *Advertising Age*, September 23. Accessed September 10, 2015. http://adage.com/article/special-report-100-most-influential-women-in-advertising/a-century-women-advertising/237137/.
Scott, Linda M. 1992. "Playing with Pictures: Postmodernism, Poststructuralism, and Advertising Visuals." *NA—Advances in Consumer Research 19*, edited by John F. Sherry, Jr., and Brian Sternthal, 596–612. Provo, UT: Association for Consumer Research.
———. 2006. "Market Feminism: The Case for a Paradigm Shift." *Advertising and Society Review* 7 (2): 1–16.
Severn, Jessica, George E. Belch, and Michael A. Belch. 1990. "The Effects of Sexual and Non-Sexual Advertising Appeals and Information Level on Cognitive Processing and Communication Effectiveness." *Journal of Advertising* 19 (1): 14–22.

Sharp, Gwen. 2009. "Ralph Lauren Apologizes for Super-Skinny Photo-shopped Model." *The Society Pages*. Accessed September 5, 2015. http://thesocietypages.org/socimages/2009/10/12/ralph-lauren-apologizes-for-super-skinny-photoshopped-model/.

Sheehan, Kim. 2004. *Controversies in Contemporary Advertising*. Thousand Oaks, CA: Sage.

Siegel, Deborah. 2007. *Sisterhood Interrupted: From Radical Women to Grrls Gone Wild.* New York: Palgrave.

Signorielli, Nancy. 1993. "Television, the Portrayals of Women, and Children's Attitudes." *Children and Television: Images in a Changing Sociocultural World,* edited by G. L. Berry and J. K. Asamen, 229–42. Newbury Park, CA: Sage.

Sischy, Ingrid. 2008. "Calvin to the Core," *Vanity Fair,* April.

Sivulka, Juliann. 2011. *Soap, Sex and Cigarettes: A Cultural History of American Advertising*. New York: Wadsworth.

Soley, Lawrence, and Gary Kurzbard. 1986. "Sex in Advertising: A Comparison of 1964 and 1984 Magazine Advertisements." *Journal of Advertising* 15 (3): 46–64.

Soley, Lawrence, and Leonard Reid. 1988. "Taking It Off: Are Models in Magazine Ads Wearing Less?" *Journalism and Mass Communication Quarterly* 65: 960–66.

Solomon, Deborah. 2009. "Fourth-Wave Feminism." *New York Times,* November 13. Accessed September 15, 2015. http://www.nytimes.com/2009/11/15/magazine/15fob-q4-t.html?_r=0.

Stampler, Laura. 2014. "Here's How Women Respond to All Those 'Female Empowerment' Ads. *Time,* October 14. Accessed April 12, 2016. http://time.com/3502904/heres-how-women-respond-to-all-those-female-empowerment-ads/.

Steinem, Gloria. 1990. "Sex, Lies and Advertising," *Ms*. (July/August): 18–28.

Stern, Barbara B. 1991. "Two Pornographies: A Feminist View of Sex in Advertising." *Advances in Consumer Research* 18: 384–391.

Stern, Barbara B., and Jonathan E. Schroeder. 1994. "Interpretive Methodology from Art and Literacy Criticism: A Humanistic Approach to Advertising Imagery," *European Journal of Marketing* 28: 114–132.

Taylor, Verta, and Leila J. Rupp. 1993. "Women's Culture and Lesbian Feminist Activism: A Reconsideration of Cultural Feminism." *Signs* 19 (1) 32–61.

Team, Trefis. 2014. "Abercrombie and Fitch's CEO Mike Jeffries to Step Down Immediately." *Forbes,* December 10. Accessed September 10, 2015. http://www.forbes.com/sites/greatspeculations/2014/12/10/abercrombie-and-fitchs-ceo-mike-jeffries-to-step-down-immediately/.

Tiggemann, Marika, and Belinda McGill. 2004. "The Role of Social Comparison in the Effect of Magazine Advertisements on Women's Mood and Body Dissatisfaction." *Journal of Social and Clinical Psychology* 23 (1): 23–44.

Tsai, Wah-Hsin Sunny. 2010. "Assimilating the Queers: Representations of Lesbians, Gay Men, Bisexual and Transgender People in Mainstream Advertising." *Advertising and Society Review,* 11 (1). Accessed October 16, 2016. http://muse.jhu.edu/journals/advertising_and_society_review/v011/11.1.tsai.html.

van Zoonen, Liesbet. 1994. *Feminist Media Studies*. London: Sage.

Walker, Alice. 1984. *In Search of Our Mothers' Gardens: Womanist Prose*. San Diego: Harcourt Brace Jovanovich.

Wilke, Michael. 2001. "Transgender Ads in Transition." *Commercial Closet: Ad Respect, Where Successful Advertising Meets LGBT Equality,* December 24. Accessed April 30, 2016. http://www.commercialcloset.org/common/news/reports/detail.cfm?Classification=report&QID=4495&ClientID=11064&TopicID=344.

Williams, Patricia J. 1991. *The Alchemy of Race and Rights: Diary of a Law Professor.* Boston: Harvard University Press.

Wittenberg-Cox, Avivah. 2014. "Lego's Girl Problem Starts with Management." *Harvard Business Review,* September 15. Accessed July 19, 2015. https://hbr.org/2014/09/legos-girl-problem-starts-with-management.

Yang, Jeff, and Angelo Ragaza. 1997. "The Beauty Machine." *Facing Difference: Race, Gender and Mass Media,* edited by Shirley Biagi and Marilyn Kern-Foxworth, 11–15. Thousand Oaks, CA: Pine Forge Press.

Zayer, Linda Tuncay, and Catherine A. Coleman. 2015. "Advertising Professionals' Perceptions of the Impact of Gender Portrayals on Men and Women: A Question of Ethics?" *Journal of Advertising* 44 (3): 1–12.

Zamuda, Natalie, and Ann-Christine Diaz. 2014. "Female Empowerment in Ads: Soft Feminism or Soft Soap?" *Advertising Age.* Accessed September 2, 2014. http://adage.com/article/cmo-strategy/marketers-soft-feminism/294740/.

Chapter 3

The Entangled Politics of Feminists, Feminism, Advertising, and Beauty

A Historical Perspective

Dara Persis Murray

In October 2003, the Advertising Educational Foundation held a symposium called "How Is Advertising Shaping the Image of Women?" to generate a conversation among feminists, feminist teachers and scholars, and women working in the advertising industry. A central point of dialogue was the nature of the feminist politics of women in advertising. The struggles in defining feminism by people inside and outside of advertising are not just twenty-first century woes.

The feminist movement is popularly understood as being composed of multiple "waves": "the first wave prior to women's winning the vote; the second wave, during the 1960s and 1970s; and the third wave, beginning in the 1980s" (Golombisky 2012, 92). In an effort to move beyond the wave metaphor, which homogenizes and compartmentalizes the values and actions of each major strand of the feminist movement, historian Hewitt (2010, 10–11) works to "think about other types of waves, such as radio waves, that offer new conceptualizations of the feminist past. . . . Radio waves allow us to think about movements in terms of different lengths and frequencies . . . signals co-exist, overlap, and intersect." Her conception of the feminist movement, one that I share, emphasizes the complex emotional and historical connections women have with one another. That is, forms of feminist thought and action are not limited to their designation within a specific "wave," but instead move across various times and spaces.

In this chapter, I present a historical perspective on women's efforts as media producers to cultivate positive representations of women, feminists, and feminism from the early 1900s to the present day. In particular, I explore tensions involved in defining and representing feminism in advertising, particularly in relation to images and meanings of beauty. The snapshots I discuss in this chapter, which I have identified as "moments of entanglement," are instances in which women, often feminists, have produced representations and meanings of feminism and beauty. The broader trajectory of advertising strategies promoting ideas of women's liberation, beauty, and feminism over the last century provides the context for my discussion.

The focus of this chapter, then, is the relationships among advertising, feminists, feminism, beauty, and consumer culture. It is important to make some clarifications at the outset. Feminism, a social movement, seeks to liberate women from structural inequalities related to politics, economics, and cultural expectations that are based on gender. Feminists are those men and women who support these values by creating awareness of them through various forms of activism, ranging from consciousness raising to protests. At feminism's core is the realization of equality in society: namely, for women and men to have access to the same opportunities and be treated equally. Feminist writers Baxandall and Gordon (2000, 2) noted that "feminism's fundamental ideas are still controversial—indeed, they are at the root of the hottest debates of our times: abortion rights, contraception for teenagers, women in the armed forces, gay marriage, affirmative action." During the past several decades, meanings associated with the words *feminism* and *feminists* have become complicated, often separated from politics, collective action, or social change in favor of "aggressive individualism" (McRobbie 2009, 5). As I'll discuss later, this neoliberal approach, which connects women's power to hypersexuality and hyperconsumerism, "seek[s] to reverse, or undo feminism, substituting it for the promise of seemingly more modern freedoms" (McRobbie 2009, 5).

Having addressed feminism and feminists, I turn to beauty and consumer culture. *Beauty* is understood here as a social construct that is anchored in a woman's appearance and physical characteristics. Understandings of beauty, like those of femininity, are dynamic and grounded in culture. In United States consumer culture, media and advertising have been charged with creating, nurturing, and sustaining an "ideal" unattainable to most women (van Zoonen 1994). In advertising, beauty is often linked to the consumption of goods for the body and face (Frith, Shaw, and Cheng 2005), such as fashionable clothing and cosmetics (Peiss 1998b). Language and images in consumer culture circulate and reinforce cultural understandings of beauty (Frith, Shaw, and Cheng 2005).

Within this dynamic of consumer culture, individuals create a personal identity through the consumption of commodities. That is, consumers construct an image of "who they are" through meanings and associations attached to products they consume. The internalization of commodities as part of a woman's subjectivity is particularly important when the meanings attached to those products relate to feminist politics, women's freedom, and women's power.

This history is about white, middle-class women who created advertising representations of and for women who were unlike themselves both ideologically and socioeconomically. These women worked in a business dominated by men who shared their race and socioeconomic background (Sutton 2009). Thus white men and women in advertising agencies wielded the power to construct representations, deciding who and how people would be visible. Notably, because advertisers did not view blacks as an economically viable market, they did not target them in advertising or hire them for their marketing and advertising expertise. Chambers (2008, 10) described the industry dynamic, noting: "for most of the twentieth century both advertisements and the advertising industry remained 'lily white.'"

In this chapter, I present a nuanced picture of feminists and feminism's fraught relationship with advertising and beauty, highlighting the challenges involved in cultivating positive popular representations of women for the past hundred years. I draw heavily on the work of advertising, media, and women's and gender studies historians (Farrell 1998; Finnegan 1999; Fox 1984; Leach 1989, 1993; Lears 1994; Marchand 1985; Peiss 1998a, 1998b; Scanlon 1995; Schudson 1986; Sutton 2009). From those accounts, I identify several key moments of entanglement, that is, moments in which women have navigated social conventions as well as institutional barriers in their efforts to change attitudes and representations of women and of feminism. I map the arc of several of those moments in the sections that follow, beginning with the suffrage movement, which was "at the forefront of an emerging, commercialized style of politics" (Finnegan 1999, 7).

MARKETING SUFFRAGE IN EARLY CONSUMER CULTURE

At the turn of the twentieth century, women, primarily white and middle class, participated in a series of efforts—suffrage, temperance, and the Purity Campaign—to bring about social change under the umbrella of the women's reform movement. For American women at this time, alcohol consumption and men's sexual liaisons, which raised the possibility of spreading venereal disease, were "real social problem[s] that brought [their] worst evils home to torture innocent housewives" (Collins 2003, 321). Suffrage, temperance, and the Purity Campaign were efforts undertaken by women to realize more power in society and also in their personal lives. Women participating in the temperance movement and the Purity Campaign believed these efforts would help to heighten women's control in the home and in their relationships with their husbands (Collins 2003). If the sale of alcohol were banned, it was believed that women and children would run a lower risk of abuse by drunken husbands and fathers (Finnegan 1999). Collins (2003, 315) notes that "many women wanted to vote just so they could use the ballot box to ban the sale of alcohol." Women supported the Purity Campaign in their effort to "forc[e] men to behave" by eliminating prostitution, whereby men would "stop using women as sex objects" (Collins 2003, 320–321). The suffrage movement fought for the women's right to vote and run for office, and worked to pass amendments to the United States Constitution and to individual state constitutions.

In *Selling Suffrage: Consumer Culture and Votes for Women,* Finnegan (1999) examined the ways in which feminists cultivated concepts of feminism, beauty, and appearance in early consumer culture. Beginning in the early 1900s, feminists "added their own slant to capitalism's consumerist thrust by reworking its basic assumptions" (Finnegan 1999, 2) to promote their political ideology to the public. Early suffragists paid careful attention to their self-presentation via appearance and attitude to generate a positive response to feminists and feminist values. Their use of advertising; carefully controlled parades; public-speaking events; well-orchestrated performances; and merchandising suffrage buttons, banners, hats, and other items via advertising, catalogs, and specialized "suffragist shops" might be interpreted as attempts to "sell the [feminist] movement like a modern commodity" (Finnegan 1999, 3). However, Finnegan (1999) offers an alternative interpretation: Feminists reworked "marketing" strategies to suit their own needs. So, for instance, when advertisers praised women's public presence in their advertising as a means to sell their commodities, suffragists reframed those claims as validation for women's expansion into the public space. Similarly, "suffragists redefined both 'voter' and 'shopper,' making both terms synonymous with responsible, rational, and empowering action" (Finnegan 1999, 2).

Perhaps in response to a barrage of antisuffragist rhetoric and derogatory stereotypes, suffragists were conscious of how they publicly represented themselves and the suffrage movement (Finnegan 1999). Suffragists used fashion to create and manage a public identity linked to political activism in much the same way as consumers used fashion to express personal identity, presenting themselves in a nonthreatening way via familiar feminine appearance and a friendly demeanor (Finnegan 1999). Women participating in parades often were required to adhere to a dress code that served to visually unify them as proponents of feminist values and signify them as an organized movement as well as part of mainstream culture. Suffragists sought to promote an image that would attract women supporters and the male voters who held the power to grant or deny suffrage by suggesting that suffragists "(and thus, potential women voters) were attractive, stylish, charming, dignified, and virtuous . . . personable, likable, and modern individuals" (Finnegan 1999, 81).

As reformers, suffragists circulated in public spaces (that is, outside the home) connecting political messages to women's appearance. Finnegan

(1999) notes that while a woman might wear a lapboard, sandwich board, or current fashion to advertise the cause and attract attention, this simultaneously translated into the use of her body as "a form of spectacle," making it "susceptible to the controlling gaze of the flâneur/male voter" (Finnegan 1999, 62–63). The emphasis on visual unity communicated a one-dimensional image of feminist identity through appearance, and at the same time an underlying message about class. Meeting parade dress code required financial resources, and thus served to effectively distance the middle-class reformers from "the working girls" and their attempts to "play the lady" (Enstad quoted in Finnegan 1999, 70).

Intentionally crafting an embodied political identity aligned feminism with consumer culture; to wit, suffragists "compared good voters to comparison shoppers, defined commodity-enhanced lifestyles as a right, [and] spoke in tribute to fashion and mass consumerism" (Finnegan 1999, 12). In this way, feminists encouraged a close relationship between the support of material consumption and the articulation of feminist politics. The suffragists' strategy raises questions about "what a feminist looks like," and how consumerism fits into a "feminist" appearance and ideology. These questions echoed across twentieth-century consumer culture, and often continue to do so today.

In sum, suffragists' use of strategies grounded in consumer culture to advance the feminist cause provides a starting point for considering the complicated relationship between meanings of feminism, advertising, and the portrayal of empowered women. Linking feminist identity with commercialized values and consumption, the suffragist became a commodity whose "identity as a woman citizen could be packaged, sold, and redesigned as necessary" (Finnegan 1999, 106–107). Whereas suffragists created an image that identified them as both political activists and as consumers, by contrast, early advertisers often overlooked the political, addressed women primarily as consumers, and frequently emphasized the importance of beauty in their appeals to sell products to women. The following section calls attention to how different understandings of feminism entered into the creation of advertising in the early years of the twentieth century. I examine the contributions of two women who played instrumental roles in the advertising business: Christine Frederick and Helen Lansdowne Resor.

WOMEN AS TWENTIETH CENTURY MEDIA PRODUCERS: VARIED PERSPECTIVES ON WORK AND BEAUTY

The following accounts of two women who worked as media producers in the early twentieth century illustrate differences in the conceptualization of gender roles during that period. The conflicting views of these two women—Christine Frederick and Helen Lansdowne Resor—centered on women's position in public versus private spheres, and their approach toward representing women in advertising. Both women had a lasting influence on the cultivation of women's attitudes relative to consumption, image construction, and notions of beauty. Taken together, Frederick's and Resor's work, perhaps inadvertently, reinforced problematic gender norms in advertising.

Christine Frederick completed her undergraduate education at Northwestern University in 1906 and later earned a PhD at a time when educational opportunities were severely limited for women. Frederick was influenced by the campaign for suffrage and "aware of the public discourse on women's place in early twentieth-century America" (Rutherford 2003, 32). She maintained progressive values, campaigning for women's labor laws and marching with suffragists; however, as Rutherford (2003, 32) notes, Frederick "skirted the subject [of marching with suffragists] in her writings."

It was against this shifting cultural background regarding women's right to political participation that Frederick "built a successful business career by promoting domesticity" through her role in the home economics movement (Sivulka 2009, 148). This movement was focused on professionalizing homemaking through the application of scientific concepts to the home. Frederick viewed the housewife as a worker and a domestic efficiency expert. She promoted this concept to a mass audience of American housewives via articles she wrote as a contributor to and consulting editor at *Ladies' Home Journal.* These pieces, later published in her book, *The New Housekeeping: Efficiency Studies in Home Management* (Frederick 1913), endorsed the value of housewives' labor, emphasizing the challenges of housework as well as her control of household finances. Frederick normalized women's work as unpaid and consciously sought to maintain traditional gender roles, declaring in 1914 that "Our greatest enemy . . . is the woman with the career" (quoted in Sivulka 2009, 148). She essentially reinforced the social order and reinscribed social value to the home, where a woman should be the best possible wife and mother.

Somewhat paradoxically, Frederick sought to expand the visual codes of women in advertising representations beyond beauty alone, even as she solidified women's role as a consumer, a buyer in the home. In her book, *Selling Mrs. Consumer,* Frederick (1929) emphasized the importance of studying the purchasing habits of "Mrs. Consumer," examined changes in American consumptions habits, and assessed the possible effects of those changes on future trends. She wrote "special advertising copy for food and household articles" (Frederick [1924] 2007, 221).

As an advertising consultant, Frederick tied women's power to material consumption and believed that to reach the "so-called Average Woman," advertisers needed to understand the myriad qualities that women possess.

She contended, "The cardinal principle by which to explain womankind is paradox . . . she is both kind and cruel, highly practical and other-worldly" (Frederick [1924] 2007, 226).

In advising male advertisers about how to construct representations of women, she rejected the existing "P.G." ("Pretty Girl") image, viewing it as overused and questioning why the image was perpetuated. She suggested it might be the result of men's narrow interpretations of women, or perhaps a lack of creativity: "Is it because men chiefly prepare and draw our advertising copy? Could it be because of the poverty of ideas on the part of the advertiser, who, because he can't think of anything else or build up a convincing argument, slaps on a P.G.?" (Frederick [1924] 2007, 231–32).

Despite her role as a consultant to male copywriters, Frederick and other women working in the advertising industry near the turn of the twentieth century were excluded from attending events at the Advertising Men's League of New York. When Mary Bronson of Macy's approached Frederick's husband, J. George Frederick, about attending a presentation at the club, he indicated it was impossible, but suggested advertising women form a club of their own (Frederick 1939). In response, the League of Advertising Women of New York was established in 1912, creating a community in which advertising women could share their experiences. Christine Frederick was never a dues-paying member of the League but attended meetings and frequently made educational presentations (Sivulka 2009).

In the 1920s, the leaders in the advertising business were primarily men educated in methods of mass production and distribution. In large agencies, about 3 percent of all professionals were women, and they rarely held positions that required face-to-face interaction outside the firm (Peiss 1998a). Still, at the urging of businessmen who recognized women to be the primary shoppers in the household, women copywriters were brought into the business to provide a "women's viewpoint." These women took on the roles of information brokers and tastemakers because of their perceived ability—based on their gender—to understand and communicate with women as consumers (Peiss 1998a). Thus, even when women made up only a small percentage of the advertising workforce, they held influential positions as copywriters on "women's accounts," such as cosmetics and skin care products. In that role, women working in advertising, many of whom were feminists, reinforced the role of women as consumers. Later, however, women would find themselves pigeonholed on "women's accounts" and were seldom assigned to work on larger general accounts or national campaigns.

Still, writing on "women's accounts" served as a point of entry into the profession for some women; advertisers "welcomed" white, primarily middle-class women into the business far earlier than did other businesses. Women also entered the advertising workplace far more easily than African

Americans: "[E]xecutives had little interest in upsetting the existing social fabric by hiring an African American for the intimate role of communicating with the white, middle-class women who were the targets of most advertising (or to work with the white women who crafted that advertising)" (Chambers 2008, 10).

Helen Lansdowne Resor, identified as "one of the most celebrated copywriters of her generation" (Keding 1994, 265), like Frederick, was a feminist and suffragist. Resor was something of a retiring woman who seldom took credit for her accomplishments (Keding 1994, 269). She once summarized her work merely as: "I added the feminine point of view. . . . I watched the advertising so that the idea, the wording, and the illustrating were effective for women" (Sivulka 2009, 127). In fact, Helen Resor was viewed to be the "driving, creative force at the [J. Walter Thompson] company" both by her peers at the company and in the industry (Peiss 1998a), and was "one of the main architects of JWT's growth" (*J. Walter Thompson Company News* 1964).

Helen Resor had established her presence in the advertising world even prior to her move to the J. Walter Thompson New York office in 1911. Helen Lansdowne (she had not yet married Stanley Resor) worked for Procter and Collier in Cincinnati, created retail advertising for a Cincinnati newspaper, and wrote copy for a firm that advertised for streetcar companies. When Stanley Resor, whom she had met while working at Procter and Collier, became head of JWT in Cincinnati in 1908, he offered Helen Lansdowne a job as the company's sole copywriter. She accepted. She wrote ads for "women's products," among them Yuban Coffee, Lux soap flakes, Cutex nail polish, and Crisco, a newly invented product, and was the first woman to write ads for national rather than retail campaigns (Scanlon 1995; Sutton 2009).

Helen Lansdowne sought to broaden the representation of women beyond the household and made her mark in the advertising world in 1910, when she created a national campaign for Woodbury soap. The ad, which tapped into JWT's emphasis on science, is often considered to be the first use of sex appeal in advertising (Scanlon 1995; Sutton 2009). Directed to women consumers using an engaging emotional appeal, and "couched in the myth of romance" (Sutton 2009, 100), the ad targeted white, middle- and upper-class readers of national women's magazines (Sivulka 2009). The ad depicted "a handsome couple in evening dress, the man embracing the woman from the side, the woman smiling and winsomely looking away" (Keding 1994, 265). The headline, "A skin you love to touch," was designed to draw readers into the ad copy, which was a mix of science ("Your skin is changing every day! As the old skin dies, new skin forms in its place.") and feminine appeal ("Proper treatment can keep this new skin so active that it cannot help taking on the greater loveliness you have longed for."). It is ironic, Scanlon

(1995, 176) notes, that this ad, which seeded the controversy over the sexual objectification of women in advertising, "was developed by a woman who most likely saw the recognition of women's sexuality as a step forward in an advertising world that had primarily portrayed women as asexual wives and mothers."

Lansdowne moved to JWT's headquarters in New York in 1911 and married Stanley Resor in 1917, shortly after he became president of JWT, then one of the largest, if not the largest, advertising agency in the world (Kreshel 1990). The equality in their professional relationship was widely acknowledged: "It was known that on an informal level, they discussed all aspects of the business. . . . Decisions typically emerged with no clear line of accountability to either" (Keding 1994, 264).

Openly identifying as a feminist, Resor was committed to employing and advancing women in an advertising world that remained largely dominated by men. The "woman's viewpoint" was, in many respects, a change in advertising style that required an intimacy with consumers and an understanding of how a product fit into their lives. In response, Helen Resor "assembled the greatest collection of women writers in the advertising business" to establish the Women's Editorial Department at JWT (*J. Walter Thompson News* 1964, 9). The all-women department represented the paradox of a woman's place in the advertising business. Although the copywriters were valued for their intuitive "woman's sense," they were segregated from the men in the company and rarely dealt directly with JWT clients (Sutton 2009).

Many of the copywriters in the Women's Editorial Department had worked in service industries, as well as in retail advertising, publishing, public relations, and teaching prior to coming to JWT. Many had connections to social reform work (Sutton 2009). These women were mostly white and middle- or upper-class, and often were highly educated with degrees from Ivy League universities and Seven Sisters Colleges, among them Smith, Barnard, Vassar, and Wellesley (Sivulka 2009). More than half of them "never lived below the average national income level (nor had they known anyone who did)," and 66 percent employed a housekeeper, a "luxury" only 5 percent of the households in the United States enjoyed (Sutton 2009, 20). Thus these women were far different from the "ordinary consumer" to whom most of the advertising they created was targeted.

Resor believed the job of feminists in advertising was to undo the denigrating stereotypes that surrounded the woman consumer by imbuing advertising texts targeting women with a sensibility derived from feminist politics (Sutton, 2009). Paradoxically, the women in the Women's Editorial Department, most of whom were socially progressive, "promoted the same stereotypical imagery of women that many of them fought against in former careers" (Sutton 2009, 1). Although copywriters' personal values no doubt entered into the ads they created, those ads were designed to influence audiences. Women's products—soap, food, cosmetics and other beauty aids—were, in some sense, the mainstay of JWT. In 1918, copy written by the Women's Editorial Department contributed 58 percent of the company's total revenue (Sutton 2009, 124). Although the women in the Women's Editorial Department wrote "wildly successful" advertising targeting the average woman, they often "grew frustrated with her, or at least with her limited and limiting image" and envisioned a "new woman" more like themselves (Scanlon 1995, 192).

Helen Resor and the Women's Editorial Department are credited with revolutionizing testimonial advertising, then identified as *endorsement advertising*. In 1924, Resor created a national advertising strategy for Pond's vanishing cream that transformed that product's image from an ungendered utility-and-cost product to a gendered product to enhance personal feminine beauty (Sutton 2009); "Well-known and respected women, from actresses to socialites to European royalty" (Sivulka 2009, 139) appeared in advertisements backing the product in a strategy seeking to enhance Pond's brand status and prestige by associating it with women of accomplishment (Peiss 1998a). Sutton (2009, 69) writes of those ads that "the use of class- and race-coded words [*aristocratic, exclusive, distinguished*] with an image of a white woman implies that white women are upper-class (effectively erasing any class distinctions among whites) and that Pond's is a product for those who have higher aspirations."

In the first of these ads, Helen Resor enlisted the testimonial of prominent feminist and socialite Alva Belmont to reinforce a political message in the text of the ad. Belmont had bankrolled the National Women's Party, an organization dedicated to realizing women's suffrage, and agreed to appear in the ad because of feminist ties in the Women's Editorial Department. She exacted a contribution to the National Women's Party in return for her participation. Although the copy acknowledged Belmont's feminist identity—"'Mrs. Belmont not only has given lavishly to women's causes from her colossal fortune, [but she] has been and is a tremendous worker'" (Peiss 1998b, 137)—Belmont refused to allow her picture to appear in the advertising, lest she be interpreted "as a shill" (Peiss 1998a). Even without her picture, the message clearly linked white women, feminism, social status, and the use of cosmetics.

As the experiences of Frederick and Resor illustrate, the participation of women in the advertising business reflected the conflict, now longstanding, between the economic goals of industry and the political goals of feminism. Frederick reinforced women's role in the domestic sphere, promoted modernization of the home, and professionalized homemaking; Resor opened up opportunities for women to work in the advertising industry and attempted to bring feminist values into representations of women. Furthermore, Frederick and Resor both attempted to complicate images of women while simultaneously positioning them as consumers. Frederick rejected the focus on a woman's appearance as the primary marketing message in favor of presenting a woman as a "paradox." Resor sought to portray women as sensual—rather than asexual—beings; in doing so, she participated, perhaps unintentionally, in the creation of an idealized, sexualized beauty that came to characterize many subsequent representations of women in advertising.

Helen Resor's experiences, and those of feminist copywriters, illustrate the complicated entanglements of feminism, advertising, sexuality, beauty, and consumer culture. As they created representations of and for women, feminist copywriters in JWT's Women's Editorial Department struggled to negotiate a balance between their feminist belief systems and their clients' demands. In the next section, I explore advertisers' construction of the "modern" woman.

SOCIAL TABLEAUX: DEPICTING "MODERN" WOMEN

Industrialization in the World War I "war years" led to urbanization; an accelerated pace of daily life; wider availability of new products ranging from household appliances, radios, phonographs, and electric razors, to frozen vegetables and Planters Peanuts; and the rise of consumer credit. A professional middle class with enough disposable income to consume emerged (Leach 1993). In addition, the Nineteenth Amendment to the United States Constitution, enfranchising women and granting them legal rights and responsibilities equal to those of men, was ratified in 1920. Perhaps in response to that milestone and the post–World War I shift from a society based on production to one fueled by consumption, advertisements presenting enticing portrayals of modernity began to appear around 1920, and representations of women in those advertisements began to change (Lears 1994; Marchand 1985).

Marchand (1985, 165) identified these advertisements as social tableaux "in which persons are depicted in such a way as to suggest their relationships to each other or to a larger social structure." Social tableaux advertising arose as advertising *men,* observers of popular culture, "recognized that consumers would rather identify with scenes of higher status than ponder reflections of their actual lives" (xvii). Social tableaux ads, thus, did not reflect the realities of people's lives, but instead, the social aspirations of their lives, employing pictorial conventions in which individuals could "comfortably and pleasurably place themselves" (Marchand 1985, 167).

In a thorough analysis of social tableaux ads of the 1920s and 1930s, Marchand (1985, 167) found that women were the "leading ladies," and the image of women that emerged was "striking in its complexity." The separation of workplace and home established in the previous century remained. The idea of modernity carried with it the dual connotations of business' efficiency and control, and fashion's extravagance and expressiveness. In advertising, women were portrayed as adapting to modernity in two ways: through their power to purchase goods and their power to shape and dress their bodies. The exercise of these powers became entwined with the representation of women's "American Dream." White women were acknowledged to be America's primary consumers; market research claimed that women made 85 percent of all consumer purchases (Schudson 1986). The emerging home economics movement was characterizing women as the "family G.P.A" (general purchasing agent), "Mrs. Consumer" (Marchand 1985, 167). Copywriters emphasized the advantages of bringing scientific approaches into the home and "constantly congratulated women for their presumed new capacities for management. Yet, the proper field for these managerial talents remained the home" (Marchand 1985, 168).

As such, the power granted to women by their position as the primary consumers did little to alter their subordinate role. Lears (1994, 120) offered this observation regarding the power of the modern woman in popular culture of the time: Mrs. Consumer's "ravenous appetite for goods would still be a stock gag in comic strips and vaudeville humor . . . corporate advertising sublimated women's imagined voracity into efficient household management." Equating woman's purchasing power primarily with items for the home, the familiar sphere of domesticity, further reinforced her traditional role as a housewife.

Social tableaux advertisements also linked the modern woman's leisure time to the modern pursuit of self-expression (read: her appearance) that would make her an admirable partner for her modern husband. A woman's mastery of laborsaving appliances and time-saving innovations improved her ability to manage the home and made it possible for her to devote herself to presenting a "modern" look that would secure men's approval. In short, women became part of an "ongoing 'beauty contest of life'" (Marchand 1985, 176). As copywriters or illustrators, men often created conscious links between womanhood and vanity. Positioning women in front of mirrors in ads "served as a reminder of an inescapable 'duty' beyond that of efficient homemaking—the duty 'to catch and hold the springtime of her beauty'" (Marchand 1985, 176). Scare tactics reinforced the idea that a modern woman needed to pay attention to her appearance. For example, in a series of ads, the soap company Camay warned women, "You against the Rest of Womankind; your Beauty . . . your Charm . . . your Skin"; asked women, "'What Do Men Think When They Look at You?"; and alerted women that "The Eyes of Men . . . the Eyes of Women Judge your Loveliness Every Day" (Marchand 1985, 176–78).

Social tableaux often prescribed a particular look for women, a body distinct from the older, rounder appearance of women that had been embraced by earlier generations. These new "grotesque moderne" bodies, as Marchand (1985, 181) called them, had fantastical and imposing proportions, elongated eyes, fingers, legs and necks such that they "approached the status of a geometric abstraction." These distorted representations, associated with white, high-fashion women, distinguished them from black women and women of lower social status. Although the modern body originated in fantasy, the slim image signaled that real women were freed from their traditional maternal role because no mother of four could maintain such a figure. Still, this image did little to "suggest [women's] commanding presence as new women of broader capacities and responsibilities" (Marchand 1985, 185). Instead, the fashionably attired young and elongated white woman suggested decorative potential and maintained the patriarchal domination–subordination relationship with the modern man.

Taken as a whole, beginning in the 1920s, the modern woman in advertisements was often portrayed as a white, middle-class consumer, presumably heterosexual and seemingly liberated through laborsaving appliances, materialism, and pursuit of beauty. Although it became acceptable for a woman to move outside the house as a shopper, her sphere of influence was limited in that her purchasing power remained tethered to the home. Then too, beauty, particularly the look of the skin and slimness of body represented in many social tableaux ads, encouraged a physical "ideal" and a specific aspirational appearance that anchored women in traditional gender norms and stereotypes, among them whiteness, heterosexuality, competitiveness, and social class. In the next section, I examine the challenges faced by *Ms.* magazine in its effort to negotiate a rapprochement between feminist ideals and the financial imperatives inherent in commercial media.

POPULARIZING FEMINISM AND REPRESENTING BEAUTY IN A FEMINIST MAGAZINE

Ms. magazine provides a compelling case study of how feminists represented feminism, particularly with regard to beauty and appearance. Here, I discuss a complex progression of entanglements of feminists, advertisers, and representations of beauty and appearance leading to the incorporation of beauty ads into this feminist text.

Gloria Steinem, *Ms.* cofounder and editor, became one of the most well-known spokespersons for the feminist movement in the 1960s. A graduate of Smith College, a journalist, political columnist, and activist, Steinem and her public visibility as a feminist figure were launched by her 1963 exposé of the Playboy Club, *Outrageous Acts and Everyday Rebellions* (1983). Her investigation was charged by feminist values: uncovering the demeaning patriarchal attitudes toward women in the Playboy Club, detailing the labor of beauty performed by Bunnies, and documenting their treatment as sexual objects by men. Steinem (1983, 69) subsequently noted that among the "long-term results" of her exposé was her realization that "all women are Bunnies."

When *Ms.* was launched in 1972, Steinem brought feminists and feminism into the workplace with the goal of bringing feminist thinking to popular culture audiences. Thom (1997, 45), one of the coeditors, recounts that the staff viewed the magazine as "both a publishing enterprise and a center for activism." *Ms.* sought to carve out a popular feminist enterprise in the patriarchal for-profit media culture; as such, "the history of *Ms.* is, in the end, about the possibilities and limitations of forging an oppositional politics within the context of commercial culture" (Farrell 1998, 2).

Steinem (1990) stated that *Ms.* never considered *not* taking ads. For *Ms.*, the value of advertising was to keep "the price of a feminist magazine low enough for most women to afford" (19). Additionally, the editors hoped that they could provide "a forum where women and advertisers could talk to each other and improve advertising itself" (Steinem 1990, 19).

Steinem's concerns about the power of advertising as a social institution and as an economic foundation for the magazine industry seemingly were at the core of the magazine's emergence (Ferguson, Kreshel, and Tinkham 1990). She had an explicit vision of what women's magazines and advertising to women should be. The "nothing-to-read feeling" of women's magazines, Steinem (1990, 21) wrote, "comes from editorial pages devoted to 'complimentary copy'; to text or photos that praise advertised categories, instruct in their use, or generally act as extensions of ads." At the time that *Ms.* was launched, its goals were a reflection of Steinem's vision that women media producers deserved more power in their relations with advertisers by being able to (1) maintain editorial control, (2) maintain a fair and aesthetically pleasing proportion of advertising to editorial content, (3) present advertising that accurately reflects the way women spend their hard-earned dollars, (4) present advertising that treats women as people, and (5) train advertising salespeople who themselves would be agents of change ("Personal Report from *Ms.*" 1974). These goals were reflected in the magazine's advertising policy: "Obviously, *Ms.* won't solicit or accept ads, whatever the product they're presenting, that are downright insulting to women. Nor will we accept product categories that might be harmful" (quoted in Ferguson, Kreshel, and Tinkham 1990, 41).

The fact that *Ms.* didn't provide "complimentary copy" made it difficult to attract advertisers who had become accustomed to the "supportive editorial atmosphere" that most magazines, particularly women's magazines, supplied

(Steinem 1990, 18–19). For example, in 1986, because of a decline in advertising pages, *Ms.* "started soliciting hair care, makeup and fragrance ads to benefit the 'whole' feminist woman" (Ferguson, Kreshel, and Tinkham 1990, 41). Steinem herself approached Leonard Lauder, president of Estée Lauder, but he stated that "*Ms.* readers are not *our* women. . . . They're not interested in things like fragrance and blush-on. If they were, *Ms.* would write articles about them" (Steinem 1990, 24). The implication was clear: There's no complementary copy. Furthermore, *Ms.* wouldn't be an appropriate advertising vehicle because, according to Lauder, "Estée Lauder is selling 'a kept-woman mentality'" (Steinem 1990, 24). In other instances, Clairol refused to advertise in the magazine "for the rest of its natural life" because of a *Ms.* report that linked chemicals and carcinogens in hair dye (Steinem 1990, 20); Revlon refused to advertise because Soviet women on the *Ms.* cover were not wearing makeup (Steinem 1990, 23).

At the outset, representatives armed with market research approached advertisers whose products were "used by both men and women but advertised mostly to men—cars, credit cards, insurance, sound equipment, financial services, and the like" (Steinem 1990, 19). The advertising sales reps suggested that advertising in *Ms.* would expand the market for goods that had previously not been advertised to women. Then, too, the advertisers were assured that, thanks to the magazine's selectivity, its pages would be less cluttered, thus diminishing the likelihood that a competitor's ads would appear in the same issue.

Still, even when provided with research showing that *Ms.* readers were more likely than readers of other publications to buy a particular product category, advertisers repeatedly refused to advertise in *Ms.*, often falling back on strongly held negative stereotypes of feminists. Their reasoning went something like this, as exemplified by an executive of an electronics company: "But women don't understand technology. . . . If women *do* buy it [technology] . . . they're asking their husband and boyfriends what to buy first" (Steinem 1990, 21).

Reflecting on the earlier years of *Ms.*, Steinem (1990, 24) wrote that even though *Ms.* did "refuse most of the ads that would look like a parody in our pages, we get so worn down that some slip through." *Ms.* began to accept cigarette ads because "few magazines could compete and survive without them"; however, she noted, "[T]he necessity of taking cigarette ads has become a kind of prison" (Steinem 1990, 22). The decision to align *Ms.* with traditional health and beauty companies in 1986 was motivated by a serious lack of funds needed to continue publication. Despite Steinem's and *Ms.* editors' efforts to include only advertisements that met their policy, an analysis of ads appearing in *Ms.* from 1973 through 1987 indicates that *Ms.* fell short of its goal (Ferguson, Kreshel, and Tinkham 1990). Ads reinforced problematic stereotypes of sexism, especially with regard to sexuality and women as sex objects.

Over time, the constant effort to reach broader audiences and attract advertising dollars resulted in a shift "in the way the magazine packaged itself, sold itself to readers and advertisers, and presented the ideology and issues of feminism" in the 1970s and 1980s (Farrell 1998, 114). These changes had implications for *Ms.*'s representations of beauty. A comparison of two cover images, the first in September 1977 and the other in May 1984, is suggestive. The September 1977 cover featured "a slim white woman's torso, with the words 'Why Women Hate Their Bodies' tattooed on her back" (Farrell 1998, 115); the editors felt that, through use of this depiction, "they had attempted to make a statement about the ways all women, even those with the most culturally perfect bodies, experienced self-hate about their bodies" (115). The image on the May 1984 cover portrayed the "back of a white woman's torso . . . no tattooed words forced the reader to question this representation of women; rather, the woman was pictured in the shower, with soap sensuously dripping down her naked back" (Farrell 1998, 115–116). Although likely inadvertent, without subheadlines as context, the image became the focus of the cover, and presented a simplistic, mainstream, sexualized view of the woman's body as object. The only words on the image were "The Beauty of Health." Farrell (1998, 116) suggests that the cover image "redirected attention from any 'feminist' articles contained in the issue and provided a perfect set-up for advertisers to sell their products." In 1984, the magazine's annual health issue morphed into a beauty issue, which "was much easier for the marketing staff to sell to advertisers with flyers such as 'Healthy, Wealthy and Wise,' which promoted [to] advertisers an 'environment tailor-made for them'" (Farrell 1998, 145). Linking implied feminist values, beauty images, and consumption, Steinem and her editors, in a sense, were forced to embrace the "sex sells" mentality of the beauty industry to sustain publication of the magazine.

Some of the tensions and ambiguities in the alliance between feminist activism, mainstream feminist media, and beauty advertising become visible in the behind-the-scenes story of how *Ms.* attempted to make a difference and survive as a popular feminist text. It also suggests the difficult situation that feminists and members of other social movements may face as a result of the economic demands of media institutions. Although Steinem attempted to draw a boundary between popularized feminist values and beauty advertising, she also seemed to understand the necessity of securing her position of power in consumer culture by making accommodations.

In the first "no-advertising" issue of *Ms.* in 1990, *Ms.* included one of the magazine's own ads in the "No Comment" section noting: "This feature in the old *Ms.* showcased other people's bad ads. Now we can include some of our own." A 1988 advertisement for *Ms.* in *New York Magazine* and *Advertising Age* aimed at attracting advertisers included the headline, "We're Not the *Ms.* We Used to Be." In the ad, images in a grid formation present one white woman wearing the same turtleneck in seven of the eight images. At first, she wears wire-rimmed glasses, no makeup and a beaded, bohemian-style forehead band. In the next five images the woman is transformed, purportedly into the new *Ms.* reader. She removes the forehead band and glasses, applies makeup (lipstick, blush, and eyebrow), and perms her previously straight hair to reveal the new—modern?—woman. The final image is a picture of a *Ms.* cover featuring pop singer Cyndi Lauper. The copy reads: "Times change. People change. And *Ms.*, the only general interest news magazine for women, reflects those changes. . . . The new *Ms.* As impressive as the woman who reads it." This depiction visually portrays the evolution of the *Ms.* reader, and perhaps even the magazine itself, as it adapted in an effort to attract funding, often at the expense of its feminist mission. That 1980s *Ms.* reader embraced beauty and popular culture; however, her feminist politics are far less visible.

The entanglement of feminists, advertising, femininity, and beauty becomes even more complex as advertisers attempt to incorporate the language of feminist ideology in commodity narratives. I discuss this "commodity feminism" in the next section.

ADVERTISERS SELLING FEMINISM AND BEAUTY: COMMODITY FEMINISM AND POSTFEMINISM

Frank (1997) wrote, "Feminism, as it was understood by the [advertising] industry in the late sixties and early seventies, was an almost perfect product pitch" (152). Feminists were perceived both as a new consumer market, open to products that reinforced and legitimatized their countercultural identity, and as a spur to the consumption of traditional products by women who feared the gender challenges activists posed (Craig 2003).

In an analysis of advertisements in a popular woman's magazine from the 1980s, Goldman, Heath, and Smith (1991) identified an emerging feminist discourse that they labeled "commodity feminism." They defined it as the process of "Turning feminism into a commodity value [that] fetishizes feminism. . . . Such sign-objects [e.g., brands and branded products] are thus made to stand for (or made equivalent to) feminist goals of independence and professional success. Personality can be expressed, and relationships achieved, through personal consumer choices" (Goldman, Heath, and Smith 1991, 336). Commodity feminism's co-optation of the feminist language reduces feminists' drive for social change, instead encouraging "women to activate a true inner self and overcome social forces that now block that deep self from realizing itself" (Goldman and Papson 1996, 172). An individual focused on her "true inner self" alone is not changing society. Commodity feminism uses signs that signify "independence, participation in the work force, individual freedom, and self-control" (Goldman, Heath, and Smith 1991, 337) and redefines them in terms of freedom to shop. According to Goldman, Heath, and Smith (1991), advertisers create links between feminism and femininity whereby choice and freedom are associated with sexual liberation.

This connection focuses on the body as the site for women's freedom and pleasure: "The commercial marriage of feminism and femininity plays off of a conception of personal freedom located in the visual construction of self-appearance" (Goldman, Heath, and Smith 1991, 338). Douglas (1994, 245) identifies the new emphasis on self: "narcissism as liberation."

Commodity feminism, then, is an advertising approach that co-opts the most radical ideas of the women's movements and feminisms and repurposes them for popular audiences in a palatable form of consumption. Advertisers develop messages that seemingly support feminist values, thus commandeering feminist discourse as a strategy to achieve audience identification (Goldman, Heath, and Smith 1991). Such appropriations devalue the meaning of feminist politics, remove the political context, and trivialize feminist social goals as "a lifestyle accessory" (Talbot 2000, 187). Commodity feminism raises an important discussion about how popular notions and practices of women's "resistance" and "liberation" are increasingly depoliticized and circulated in consumer culture as part of broader discourses of women's "empowerment."

A now-well-known illustration of commodity feminism was advertising agency Leo Burnett's 1968 campaign for Virginia Slims cigarettes, which carried the slogan "You've Come a Long Way, Baby." Craig (2003, 19) writes that "according to one marketing executive, [the campaign] 'set a new tone in women's products advertising.'" Virginia Slims, a Philip Morris company product targeted to women, drew on themes of the day such as "the oppressive cigarette establishment, nonconformity, self-determination, and the liberating power of the youth counterculture" (Frank 1997, 155). The ad referenced suffrage, with the voiceover of a man stating, "'It used to be, Lady, you had no rights. No right to vote, no right to property, no right to the wage you earned'" (Frank 1997, 155). The white woman in the ad cuts her "old-time" dress apart to reveal a stylish poncho, and then continues the self-beautification project, separating herself from the old and embracing the new. As described by Frank (1997, 156), the woman then "lets her hair down, dons earrings, and applies mascara. Similarly, the flute music is replaced by the brand's rock 'n' roll jingle, to which the woman begins to dance: 'You've come a long way, baby, to get where you've got to today.'" The woman who smoked Virginia Slims is portrayed as a feminist and is beautiful: She is white, fashionably dressed, complete with matching accessories, and wears makeup. She connects her liberation as a modern woman with her ability to choose to smoke cigarettes, and to choose this particular brand of cigarettes that is "made for women."

Scholars locate commodity feminism within the social–historical context of neoliberalism, which emerged in the 1980s under Ronald Reagan's administration in the United States and Margaret Thatcher's in the United Kingdom. Neoliberalism's policies, including deregulation, free markets, entrepreneurialism, and privatization have brought about significant political, social, and economic changes. McRobbie describes neoliberalism as prioritizing consumer citizenship "through notions of governing the self: looking after the self, the self as a task" at the expense of social welfare. She goes on to argue that "consumer culture, and the fashion and beauty complex, together with consumer culture—they're really inseparable, come to function as a kind of displaced substitute for old fashioned patriarchy" (Social Science Bites 2013). Neoliberal subjects view themselves as calculated entrepreneurs of their own lives with little concern for social welfare.

Postfeminism, located in the neoliberal context, emerged in the 1990s and began to inform popular culture in the United States and the United Kingdom (Lazar 2009; Tasker and Negra 2007). Gill and Scharff (2011) contend that there is a three-fold synergy between neoliberalism and postfeminism: (1) They both configure individualism as distinct from social or political control or forces. (2) There is a parallel between the "autonomous, calculating, self-regulating subject of neoliberalism . . . [and] the active, freely choosing, self-reinventing subject of postfeminism" (Gill and Scharff 2011, 7). (3) Neoliberal popular culture discourses that stress self-regulation, self-discipline, and self-transformation as self-directed values emphasize them more for women than for men.

Tasker and Negra (2007, 1) define postfeminism as "a set of assumptions, widely disseminated within popular media forms, having to do with the 'pastness' of feminism, whether that supposed pastness is merely noted, mourned, or celebrated." Gill and Scharff (2011) propose that postfeminism can be conceived of as a backlash against feminism itself; that is, postfeminism allies with the view that gender equality has been achieved in the public sphere and, subsequently, that feminist politics are no longer necessary. Given this, the focus of "empowerment" shifts from the collective to the individual. Postfeminist notions of women's freedom and choice are linked to the marketplace, whereby, McRobbie (2009) argues, "empowerment" occurs primarily through acts of consumerism rather than acts for advancement in the public sphere.

Postfeminism emphasizes the pursuit of beauty as a constructive value that supports self-improvement, personal responsibility, self-surveillance (especially of one's body), and self-governance for attaining social and economic mobility. This one-dimensional view of beauty seldom reflects diversity in class, race and ethnicity, sexual orientation, or ability. Postfeminist discourse and media representations of white, sexualized, and economically empowered women are the predominant images employed in consumer culture, thus aligning this "empowered" viewpoint with the Western ideal of beauty. Postfeminism, then, is a strategy of "empowerment" for the economically advantaged, and its proponents are, "by default," white and middle class (Tasker and Negra 2007, 2).

Postfeminist representations of beauty embody the current incarnation of entanglements between feminists, feminism, advertising, and beauty. Lazar's (2009, 371) work on beauty ads in the first decade of the 2000s from Singapore, Europe, Japan, and the United States identifies "entitled femininity" as central to the "postfeminist feminine identity." She writes that the postfeminist woman "is entitled to be pampered and pleasured, and to unapologetically embrace feminine practices and stereotypes" (Lazar 2009, 372). Postfeminist discourse in beauty ads emphasizes the viewpoint that "It's about me!" and stresses femininity as a positive aspect of womanhood. Douglas (1994, 246) notes, "Women's liberation metamorphosed into female narcissism unchained as political concepts, and goals like liberation and equality were collapsed into distinctly personal, private desires." In postfeminist representations of beauty, women are presented as "assertive, in control and autonomous, having a strong public presence, while confidently embracing feminine practices," but they are without any concern for feminist politics (Lazar 2009, 371).

My analysis of the branding campaign of the Dove Campaign for Real Beauty places it within the postfeminist context (Murray 2013). I contend that Dove situates itself as the site for women's activism about contemporary beauty norms. This strategy minimizes the powerful mentoring role that women play in girls' everyday lives, instead bolstering the role for corporations to be both personal and "feminist" change agents. Moreover, I suggest that this global branding campaign spreads postfeminist values and signals a problematic forecast for future meanings and practices of feminism, especially in relation to beauty. In the current context, media discourses of postfeminism continue to devalue feminist politics by linking women's empowerment with hypersexuality, hyperconsumerism, and narrow representations of beauty. The power of postfeminism illustrates the increasing cultural complexity surrounding the meanings and practices of feminism, beauty, and women's empowerment.

FINAL THOUGHTS

In this chapter, I have provided a historical view of several entanglements of feminism, feminists, advertising, and beauty. Looking at the participation of feminists within the advertising industry provides a snapshot of the century-long ambivalence surrounding feminist appearance and the meaning of feminism in relation to beauty. This history shows how women and feminists have struggled in their attempts to communicate complex visions of women, feminism, and feminists. The rise of neoliberal culture has continued to complicate practices and representations of feminism in early twenty-first-century consumer culture, raising concerns about future notions and images of resistance in a culture of appropriation that continues to minimize the value of feminist political and activist thought and practice. Currently, feminism is often promoted in consumer culture as being realized through acts of material consumption; it has thus made "inroads into mass culture, but it's still unclear what happens once it's there . . . marketplace feminism itself is not equality" (Zeisler 2016, 253). There is still work to be done to improve advertising and media depictions of women and to access political, economic, and social equality for all people, regardless of gender. Importantly, many people—within and outside of the media industries—continue to rise to the challenge.

REFERENCES

Baxandall, Rosalyn, and Linda Gordon. 2000. "Introduction." In *Dear Sisters: Dispatches from the Women's Liberation Movement,* edited by Rosalyn Baxandall and Linda Gordon, 1–18. New York: Basic Books.

Chambers, Jason. 2008. *Madison Avenue and the Color Line: African Americans in the Advertising Industry.* Philadelphia: University of Pennsylvania Press.

Craig, Steve. 2003. "Madison Avenue versus the Feminine Mystique: The Advertising Industry's Response to the Women's Movement." In *Disco Divas: Women and Popular Culture in the 1970s,* edited by Sherrie A. Inness, 13–23. Philadelphia: University of Pennsylvania Press.

Collins, Gail. 2003. *America's Women: 400 Years of Dolls, Drudges, Helpmates, and Heroines.* New York: HarperCollins.

Douglas, Susan J. 1994. *Where the Girls Are: Growing Up Female with the Mass Media.* New York: Three Rivers.

Farrell, Amy Erdman. 1998. *Yours in Sisterhood: Ms. Magazine and the Promise of Popular Feminism.* Chapel Hill: The University of North Carolina Press.

Ferguson, Jill Hicks, Peggy J. Kreshel, and Spencer F. Tinkham. 1990. "In the Pages of *Ms.*: Sex Role Portrayals of Women in Advertising." *Journal of Advertising* 19 (1): 40–51.

Finnegan, Margaret. 1999. *Selling Suffrage: Consumer Culture and Votes for Women.* New York: Columbia University Press.

Fox, Stephen. 1984. *The Mirror Makers: A History of American Advertising and Its Creators.* Urbana: University of Illinois Press.

Frank, Thomas. 1997. *The Conquest of Cool: Business Culture, Counterculture, and the Rise of Hip Consumerism.* Chicago: University of Chicago Press.

Frederick, Christine. 1913. *The New Housekeeping: Efficiency Studies in Home Management.* Garden City, NY: Doubleday, Page and Company.

———. (1924) 2007. "Advertising Copy and the So-Called 'Average Woman.'" In *Masters of Copywriting: A Complete Course on the Principles and Practice of Writing Advertising and Direct Mail Copy That Sells,* edited by J. George Frederick, 225–246. http://andybrocklehurst.com/wp-content/uploads/2012/11/masters-of-copywriting.pdf

———. 1929. *Selling Mrs. Consumer.* NY: The Business Bourse.

———. 1939. "Historical Introduction." In *Advertising Careers for Women,* edited by Blanche Clair and Dorothy Dignam, xiii–xi. New York: Harper and Brothers.

Frith, Katherine, Ping Shaw, and Hong Chen. 2005. "The Construction of Beauty: A Cross-Cultural Analysis of Women's Magazine Advertising." *Journal of Communication* 55 (1): 56–70.

Gill, Rosalind, and Christina Scharff. 2011. "Introduction." In *New Femininities: Postfeminism, Neoliberalism, and Subjectivity,* edited by Rosalind Gill and Christina Scharff, 1–17. New York: Palgrave Macmillan.

Goldman, Robert, Deborah Heath, and Sharon L. Smith. 1991. "Commodity Feminism." *Critical Studies in Mass Communication* 8: 333–351.

Goldman, Robert, and Stephen Papson. 1996. *Sign Wars: Cluttered Landscape of Advertising.* New York: Guilford.

Golombisky, Kim. 2012. "Feminism." In *Encyclopedia of Gender in Media,* edited by Mary Kosut, 90–95. Thousand Oaks, CA: Sage.

Hewitt, Nancy. 2010. "Introduction." In *No Permanent Waves: Recasting Histories of US Feminism,* edited by Nancy Hewitt, 1–12. Piscataway, NJ: Rutgers University Press.

J. Walter Thompson Company News. 1964. "Helen Lansdown Resor—1886–1964." January 10: 1, 9.

Keding, Ann Maxwell. 1994. "Helen Lansdowne Resor." In *The Ad Men and Women: A Biographical Dictionary of Advertising,* edited by Edd Applegate, 262–72. Westport, CT: Greenwood.

Kreshel, Peggy J. 1990. "The Culture of J. Walter Thompson: 1915–1925." *Public Relations Review* 16 (3): 48–71.

Lazar, Michelle M. 2009. "Entitled to Consume: Postfeminist Femininity and a Culture of Post-Critique." *Discourse and Communication* 3 (4): 371–400.

Leach, William. 1989. *True Love and Perfect Union: The Feminist Reform of Sex and Society.* Middletown, CT: Wesleyan University Press.

———. 1993. *Land of Desire: Merchants, Power, and the Rise of a New American Culture.* New York: Vintage Books.

Lears, Jackson. 1994. *Fables of Abundance: A Cultural History of Advertising in America.* New York: Basic Books.

Marchand, Roland. 1985. *Advertising and the American Dream: Making Way for Modernity, 1920–1940.* Berkeley, CA: University of California Press.

McRobbie, Angela. 2004. "Post-feminism and Popular Culture." *Feminist Media Studies 4,* 255-264.

———. 2009. *The Aftermath of Feminism: Gender, Culture, and Social Change.* Thousand Oaks, CA: Sage.

Murray, Dara Persis. 2013. "Branding 'Real' Social Change in Dove's Campaign for Real Beauty." *Feminist Media Studies* 13 (1): 83–101.
Peiss, Kathy. 1998a. "American Women and the Making of Modern Consumer Culture." *The Journal for Multimedia History* 1 (1). http://www.albany.edu/jmmh/vol1no1/peiss-text.html.
———. 1998b. *Hope in a Jar: The Making of America's Beauty Culture*. New York: Henry Holt and Company.
1974. "Personal Report From Ms.: Everything You Ever Wanted to Know About Advertising and Were Afraid to Ask." *Ms.* 3: 56–59
Rutherford, Janice Williams. 2003. *Selling Mrs. Consumer: Christine Frederick and the Rise of Household Efficiency*. Athens, GA: University of Georgia Press.
Scanlon, Jennifer. 1995. *Inarticulate Longings: The Ladies' Home Journal, Gender, and the Promises of Consumer Culture*. New York: Routledge.
Schudson, Michael. 1986. *Advertising, the Uneasy Persuasion: Its Dubious Impact on American Society*. New York: Basic.
Sivulka, Juliann. 2009. *Ad Women: How They Impact What We Need, Want, and Buy*. New York: Prometheus.
Social Science Bites. 2013. "Angela McRobbie on the Illusion of Equality for Women." *Social Science Space,* June 3. http://www.socialsciencespace.com/2013/06/angela-mcrobbie-on-the-illusion-of-equality-for-women/.
Steinem, Gloria. 1983. *Outrageous Acts and Everyday Rebellions*. New York: Plume.
———. 1990. "Sex, Lies, and Advertising." *Ms.* July/August, 18–28.
Sutton, Denise H. 2009. *Globalising Ideal Beauty: How Female Copywriters of the J. Walter Thompson Advertising Agency Redefined Beauty for the Twentieth Century*. New York: Palgrave Macmillan.
Talbot, Mary M. 2000. "Strange Bedfellows: Feminism in Advertising." In *All the World and Her Husband: Women in the 20th Century Consumer Culture,* edited by Maggie Andrews and Mary M. Talbot, 177–91. New York: Bloomsbury Academic.
Tasker, Yvonne, and Diane Negra. 2007. "Introduction: Feminist Politics and Post-feminist Culture." In *Interrogating Postfeminism: Gender and the Politics of Popular Culture,* edited by Yvonne Tasker and Diane Negra, 1–125. Durham, NC: Duke University Press.
Thom, Mary. 1997. *Inside Ms.: 25 Years of the Magazine and the Feminist Movement*. New York: Henry Holt and Company.
van Zoonen, Liesbet. 1994. *Feminist Media Studies*. London: Sage.
Zeisler, Andi. 2016. *We Were Feminists Once: From Riot Grrrl to CoverGirl®: the Buying and Selling of a Political Movement*. New York: Public Affairs.

Chapter 4

"Don't You Love Being a Woman?"

Advertising, Empowerment, and the Women's Movement

Ann Marie Nicolosi

When Peter Pan International, an undergarment manufacturer, ran a full-page advertisement in the *New York Times* in January 1970, it tapped into the political and social changes brought about by the women's movement and the new freedom of dress that was a hallmark of the late 1960s. A picture of a young woman holding up her bra as a political act was superimposed over a crowd of scornful onlookers, invoking what Rosen (2000, 160) calls "the most tenacious myth about the women's movement," the myth of bra burning that began in the 1969 Miss America Pageant protests. Peter Pan combined an appeal to a new attitude of women's independence with the familiar advertising technique of pandering to women's insecurities about their bodies. Telling women they needed to put their bras back on to be attractive was meant to undermine the radical subversion of unbound breasts, which Young (2003, 156) noted sarcastically, made a mockery of the "ideal of the perfect breast." Breasts freed of brassieres, she went on, do not remain the "firm and stable objects that phallocentric fetishism desires" (156).

The ad's copy addresses a young female consumer in a one-on-one conversational tone, maintaining an air of authority as it guides her through the complexities of deciding whether or not to wear a bra. The viewpoints of feminists as well as designers are presented so the reader might make an informed decision. According to Peter Pan, "[S]upporters of the women's liberation movement will tell you that the bra symbolizes everything that's anti-female in our male-dominated society. A shackle some man thought up to keep you in your place and under his thumb, a weapon used to exploit the female consumer." The designer will tell the young woman to either forgo the bra as it will "destroy the drape and look of his latest work of art," or at the very least "take off that bunchy-push-up and push-out bra." The copy continues, imploring the woman to listen to what her body is saying: "and

[it] is probably saying, 'unless you are among the lucky miniscule minority, and are like most girls, with a bustline you think is too big or too little, or if you're OK but your breasts and your muscles just aren't tight enough, and if you really don't think you look so hot, then you probably couldn't go bra-less.'" Peter Pan, of course, had the answer to the quandary—its new "Soft 'n Low bra." Still, according to Peter Pan, even the Soft 'n Low bra "will never satisfy the new feminists. Nothing we can come up with will."

In one page of copy, Peter Pan simultaneously acknowledged women's newfound empowerment; attempted to make them feel bad about their bodies, specifically their breasts; and disparaged feminists as a group of women who could never be pleased. This ad, and others like it, drew on the illusion of women's choice even as they sought to shape women's consumption and their bodies. One of the most important social movements of the century was reframed as a revolution granting women the freedom to shop.

In this essay, I provide a historical overview of how advertisers in the 1970s drew on the gains and goals of the women's movement in strategic efforts to reach new segments of the women's market. Advertisers did so amid faltering economic prosperity, debates about women's changing roles, uncertainties about women's aspirations, and an increasing feminist focus on advertising representations of women. In selling products to women, advertisers often coopted feminist language and ideals of women's political, social, and economic empowerment and recast them in the narrow confines of personal consumption choices (Lazar 2009). Today, this strategy is known and widely critiqued as "commodity feminism" (Goldman, Heath, and Smith 1991). Angela McRobbie (2008, 539) writes of contemporary forms of commodity feminism, "Indeed it is my claim that there is now, embedded within these forms of feminine popular culture, a tidal wave of invidious insurgent patriarchalism which is hidden beneath celebrations of female freedom." Here, I demonstrate advertisers' use of this strategy during the second-wave women's movement, but I argue that it would be unwise to reduce these advertisements to mere instances of commodity feminism. There is a larger story to tell. Although primarily viewed as business tools, advertisements are also cultural artifacts, reflecting (and constructing) political and social changes and understandings, sometimes subtly, and other times pointedly. Advertisements for products also advertised the women's movement. In this way, advertisers participated in efforts to realign women's demands for civil and economic rights in American capitalism and society. Then, too, advertisements provided the financial support for commercial magazines that expanded the reach of the movement in ways feminists never could have.

My argument is grounded in a number of related research areas, among them feminism and the women's movement, advertising history, women's history, and feminist history. While acknowledging the richness of that work, in the section that follows, I draw primarily on the literature most intimately related to my topic of interest here—feminism and the women's movement, and the histories of feminism and advertising.

FEMINIST CRITIQUES OF ADVERTISING

The relationship between feminism and advertising is fraught. Beginning in the late 1960s, feminists argued that advertising representations insulted and demeaned women, and failed to reflect the changing realities of women's lives, relying instead on outdated stereotypes. A 1972 study of television commercials conducted by the National Organization for Women found that women in advertising "played two stock roles—the housewife-mother or the sex object. In both they are viewed solely in their relation to men" (Hennessee and Nicholson 1972, 12).

In response to feminist criticism, advertising scholars developed a considerable body of literature, primarily using content analysis to inventory images of women in advertisements. Over the next twenty years, study after study confirmed the veracity of feminist critiques: Women were seldom shown outside the home, rarely made important decisions, were dependent on men, and often were used decoratively or as sex objects. In short, gender stereotypes persisted (see Courtney and Whipple 1983 and van Zoonen 1994 for summaries of this body of research). Kilbourne's work over a period of forty years (1987, 1999, [1979] 2000, 2012; see also Jhally and Kilbourne 2000; Jhally, Kilbourne and Rabinovitz 2010) has highlighted a persistent host of additional concerns with advertising images of women, among them eroticized violence, trivialization of women's concerns and social advancement, infantilization, objectification and sexualization, and idealized standards of white beauty.

So-called image studies are frequently challenged by feminist scholars who note that simply counting images provides little information on the cultural context in which sexism thrives (see, e.g., Macdonald 1995; Walters 1995). Suggesting that "[w]e can only understand what advertisements mean by finding out *how* they mean, and analyzing the way they work" (Williamson 1978, 17), several scholars outside the discipline of advertising, most notably Goffman (1979), Walters (1995), and Williamson (1978), were among the first to conduct semiotic analyses of advertisements as sign systems. These analyses suggest that advertisers draw on widely shared systems of knowledge and clusters of meaning often rooted in stereotypical understanding, to facilitate sense-making of advertising in particular ways.

Goldman, Heath, and Smith (1991), looking at advertisements from a 1987 issue of *Mademoiselle,* a popular lifestyle and beauty magazine, identified an advertising strategy that they labeled "commodity feminism." They argued that "rather than fighting the legitimacy of feminist discourse," advertisers attached key tenets of that discourse onto "commodity narratives" (335). Commodity feminism, grounded in a discourse of neoliberal ideals of individualism, freedom, and choice, has become a staple in recent discussions of postfeminism (Douglas 2000; Gill 2007, 2008; McRobbie 2004).

Douglas (2000), for example, suggests that the political influence and gains of the women's movement have been reduced to a form of narcissism masquerading as liberation. She concludes, "Women's liberation metamorphosed into female narcissism unchained as political concepts and goals such as liberation and equality were collapsed into disturbing, private desires" (267). The depoliticization of feminism "has become commonplace, with 'feminism'—or rather a feminist gloss, emptied of its political implications—being used to sell everything from sanitary towels to cars" (Gill 2007, 95). Gill (2008) interrogates the way in which "sexual agency" has become a form of regulation in contemporary advertising, and Gallagher (2014) argues that language of empowerment in contemporary advertising is a "neutered" version of empowerment, which equates it with sexual assertiveness and buying power.

Advertising histories (Fox 1984; Marchand 1985) sketch women's entry into the profession, roles played, and in broad strokes, trends in women's representations. These accounts rarely venture into the arenas of feminism or the feminist movement (Craig 1997 is the rare exception). Then, too, most histories of women, feminism, and the women's movement mention advertising only tangentially if at all (Collins 2003, 2009; Evans 2010; Rosen 2000). Several more focused historical accounts, such as Fields's (2007) study of intimate apparel and Parkin's (2006) analysis of food advertisements in the mid-twentieth century, provide historical glimpses into relationships between advertisers' perceptions of women consumers, advertisements, and gender roles. However, these accounts provide little insight into how the women's movement influenced advertisements. An exception is Howard's (2010) study of automobile advertising in the 1970s and 1980s. Howard notes the use of commodity feminism in ads "urg[ing] women to purchase their way to freedom" but concludes that those ads "reflected a partial victory for the women's movement, as women's viability as breadwinners became accepted and recognized" (154).

I enter into these conversations to add fuller historical dimension to the contemporary postfeminist focus on commodity feminism, filling gaps in the historical narrative to better understand the complex role advertising played in society's efforts to come to terms with the "tidal wave" of change brought about by the women's movement (Evans 2010). As a feminist historian, I examine how material culture—in this case, selected advertisements primarily from the 1970s—reveals the struggles of advertisers trying to "find their footing" in a social, political, and economic world that itself was only beginning to understand and integrate the profound changes that had taken place.

I begin with a brief historical prologue to provide context for my discussion. The cultural and ideological meanings of the women's movement and the ads I examine here are rooted in a very particular historical moment in the United States: the end of a post–World War II economic prosperity that itself had dramatically transformed US culture and altered expectations. I then examine advertisers' uncertainties as they faced the women's movement. That discussion is followed by an analysis of several advertising strategies visible in select ads targeting mostly white, middle-class women. These strategies illustrate how advertisers—primarily white and middle class, and often men but women as well—incorporated tenets of the women's movement and feminist ideals in their efforts to address the newly "empowered" woman, meet sales goals, and expand their consumer base. Finally, I conclude with a discussion of commercial women's magazines. Those publications, supported by advertising dollars, "captured the kaleidoscopic chaos of women's lives" and helped spread the feminist movement to "millions of nonmovement women [who] first learned about feminism . . . within [their] familiar pages" (Rosen 2000, 310).

Collins (2009, 105), writing in *When Everything Changed: The Amazing Journey of American Women from 1960 to the Present,* notes that the end of post–World War II prosperity "was, all in all, a benevolent version of the perfect storm" for the emergence of the women's movement. In the following section, I outline the dimensions of that period of prosperity as prologue to my discussion.

SETTING THE STAGE: A HISTORICAL PROLOGUE

World War II: A Redefinition of "Woman's Work"

The exigencies of World War II disrupted strongly held notions of femininity and "women's work" in the home. War industries and government recruited women to high-paying production jobs typically filled by men. Government recruitment ads, attempting to change strongly held attitudes that interfered with hiring women, asked women to "step into men's shoes," suggested that homemaking talents easily translated into skills required on the production line, encouraged public acceptance of women in new roles, constructed women as patriotic guardians of the home front, and provided reassurance that entering into "men's work" would neither destroy female "womanliness" nor disrupt the family structure (Honey 1985; May 1999). Policymakers, industry leaders, and war contractors assumed that the new workforce would be made up primarily of housewives without work experience. Any concern over what would happen when men returned from the war was countered with assurances that women provided only a temporary labor reserve and would be eager to return to the home, start a family, and resume their role of full-time homemaker when the war ended.

Yet most of the women who entered the wartime labor force were not middle-class housewives, but instead were working-class women for whom "wartime employment was not a venture into something new but rather a part of their continuing work experience." These women "needed to earn a wage in peacetime as well [as in times of war], either to supplement family income or to support themselves" (Honey 1985, 19–20). As men returned from the war, many women chose to remain employed, although they were often relegated to lower-paying, pink-collar jobs in service and trade positions, nursing, and teaching. Ultimately, the war had done little to advance women's secondary status within the labor force (Honey 1985).

An Inequitable Consumer Republic

Post–World War II America gave rise to what Cohen (2003, 121) has identified as a "Consumer Republic in which the general good would best be served not by frugality or even moderation, but by individuals pursuing personal wants in a flourishing mass consumption marketplace." Private consumption was believed to be the most promising route "not only [to] economic prosperity, but also loftier social and political ambitions for a more equal, free, and democratic nation" (13).

Government policies such as the Service Readjustment Act of 1944 (the GI Bill), were established to ease veterans' transition into a civilian life. Cohen (2003, 137) writes that "by its very structure, the bill favored some Americans [disproportionally white, middle-class, heterosexual men] over others." In providing men with subsistence funding while they sought employment, resources to pursue further education and training opportunities, and low-cost loans to purchase homes or start businesses, the GI Bill "buttressed a male-directed family economy" (137). Similarly, a tax code revision designed to increase consumer purchasing power and borrowing on credit (sales tax, interest, and installment payments were deductible) favored married couples where the wife didn't work by allowing the filing of a joint return.

For some American demographics, postwar prosperity meant a higher standard of living than their parents had enjoyed. Relatively high-paying blue-collar jobs provided white, working-class men financial remuneration that once had been the domain only of middle-class, white-collar workers.

The median income increased eighty-five percent between 1947 and 1961 (US Department of Commerce 1969).

New home construction and the availability of affordable mortgages to white families created a housing boom that provided the "bedrock" of the postwar mass consumption economy. New homes "motivated consumers to purchase things to put in them" (Cohen 2003, 122–123). A mythical "American way of life" characterized by affluent suburbs populated by white, middle-class, heteronormative nuclear families came to characterize much of the discourse and advertising of the era. Contrary to that narrative, however, working-class families and families of color largely were excluded from suburbia by federal policies such as redlining that institutionalized racist lending and housing practices that would have far-reaching social and economic consequences. The postwar suburban landscape was highly segregated by class and race.

The Return to Domesticity

According to May (1999, 129), "Postwar Americans turned to marriage and parenthood with enthusiasm and commitment." Marriage rates increased, the age of marriage dropped, and the birth rate "took on almost mythical proportions" (129). Feminist Betty Friedan (1963, 218–219) laid the blame for this "feminine mystique" squarely at the feet of consumer society and advertising, noting that "an observer of the American scene today accepts as fact that the great majority of American Women have no ambition other than to be housewives. If they [advertisers] are not responsible for sending women home, they are surely responsible for keeping them there."

Increased productivity as war industries reverted to domestic production and the expansion of American markets fueled in part by federal policies, the housing boom, and the return to domesticity made it possible for large segments of white households to "continually ratchet up their standard of living all on the income from a single salary. It was a phenomenon that couldn't be repeated by the generations that followed" (Collins 2009, 399). In the meantime, Michael Harrington published *The Other America: Poverty in the United States* in 1962, and by 1964 President Lyndon B. Johnson was championing the Great Society in an effort to combat what was described as an invisible US class of the poor and a poverty rate estimated to encompass roughly one-fifth of the nation.

The "Benevolent Perfect Storm"

In the 1970s, the postwar boom went bust. Inflation decreased the buying power of the dollar, creating an economic crisis, especially for working-class and poor families, whose precarious entry into the middle class had depended on the postwar prosperity. Highly paid working-class labor began to see their economic gains disappear. Despite the elevated incomes of white American workers, newly achieved higher standard-of-living and lifestyle expectations became progressively more difficult to maintain on one salary. The number of women in the labor force nearly doubled between 1950 and 1974. Forty-four percent of married women worked and in 1975 over half of all married women with school-age children were employed. Divorce rates grew faster than the rate of marriage, nearly doubling between 1967 and 1975, increasing the number of single women in the work force (Laser and Smallwood 1977; National Center for Health Statistics 1973; Smith and Ward 1985).

Forty-seven percent of households were dual-income in 1970 (Hodge and Lundeen 2013). Women's financial contributions to the family became a necessity, not only to buy a second car or television but often simply to maintain the family's standard of living and to replace the buying power husbands' incomes had lost. For those families who had not yet joined the ranks of dual-income households, the path to maintaining their standard of living was clear; they too would need an additional income.

An advertising woman (Mccall 1977, 64) called the changes accompanying the women's movement "a first for our country." She recognized the challenges the industry faced: "There are no guidelines from which we may draw insight from the past." In the next section, I examine the industry's "conversation."

Advertiser Uncertainty

Amid the social, economic, and political changes brought about by the second-wave women's movement, advertisers realized that economic gains lay in generating and then capitalizing on women's new lifestyle. Advertisers had long viewed white women, except for the very rich and the very poor, as one mass market. "That oversimplification worked well," an ad woman noted in *Advertising Age,* "as long as women had little choice" (Cadwell 1971, 1). She continued, "Little choice but to be a housewife, little control over family size, little alternative but to stick with a bad marriage, little freedom in what they could buy beyond basic necessities" (1). But those times had changed. There were options beyond "housewife." Birth control and legal abortion made children optional. Even husbands were optional as women found "they [didn't] need a man to have a meal ticket." Women had greater disposable income and "dazzling new options in how they are to spend money" (1).

Discussions in the advertising trade press reveal the industry's sense of urgency to address this "more complex" woman, as well as its uncertainty about *how* to do so (Cadwell 1971, 71). *Advertising Age* warned that the methods advertisers had come to rely on for reaching women consumers were no longer sufficient. Headlines read: "Shifting Women's Market Will Kill Some Products" (Cadwell 1971); "Admen Must Reinvent Woman: 'Old Fictions Flop,' Says Ad Woman" (*Advertising Age* 1970); and "Today's Woman Explodes Yesterday's Ad Dream World" (Santi 1974).

Studies in the academic journals introduced the new phenomenon of the "workwife" (Mccall 1977, 55). A special edition of the *Journal of Marketing* (Bartos 1977; Laser and Smallwood 1977; Mccall 1977; Reynolds, Crask, and Wells 1977) explored demographic changes and differences in the consumer behavior of women variously identified as "working women," "full-time housewives," "modern women," "traditional women," and "women with a feminist orientation." Women were "a moving target," even though working women were not monolithic (Bartos 1977, 37).

Women were no longer one market, but "come in infinite varieties" (Cadwell 1971, 1): single women, married women, divorced women, married working women, mothers, working mothers, women who were feminists, and women grounded in traditional gender roles. Advertisers developed segmentation strategies to speak to a woman who "didn't exist 10 years ago. . . . She could be working in an office or she could be a homemaker and mother who works at life, or she could be both" (Santi 1974, 49).

Advertising expert Rena Bartos—herself a "new woman" who worked, traveled, carried her own credit card, and made use of the "traditional masculine financial services such as insurance, loans, and investments"—warned advertisers seeking to reach women of the seventies that they needed to rethink the ways in which they portrayed women in advertisements (Bartos 1973). "Advertising will have to move away from some of the stereotyped images of women as breathlessly hanging over the kitchen sink or the dressing table" (Bartos 1972, 2).

In the sections that follow, I examine several strategies advertisers used in their efforts to reach the new, "more complex" woman who had emerged (Cadwell 1971, 71), among them creating and targeting new products to women, introducing new appeals, and incorporating feminist language. My analysis reveals that in these efforts advertisers acknowledged women's empowerment, but in doing so, often exploited the excitement many women felt about liberation and the woman's movement. Shadows of long-held gendered stereotypes remained. I turn now to an examination of several of these woman-centered advertising strategies.

ADVERTISER ATTEMPTS TO REACH "THE NEW WOMAN"

Targeting New Products to Women

Prior to the 1960s and 1970s, men and women were viewed as separate markets based on traditional gender roles; products were categorized according to who had primary responsibility for their purchase (Wolgast 1958). Women, viewed as the family's "purchasing agent," were targeted with household and domestic goods, cosmetics, fashion, and furnishings. Men, as the "breadwinners," were targeted as decision-makers for financial services, automobiles, housing, and high-ticket items. Women who worked outside the home assumed greater independence as a purchasing agent and took a more active role in joint purchase decisions (Reynolds, Crask, and Wells 1977). Advertisers began to target women with products used by both men and women but sold primarily to men. One of these products was life insurance.

Life insurance companies typically targeted the husband–father in his role of family breadwinner. Evocative images and emotional appeals reminded him of his responsibility to family: A father gazes reflectively at his wife and children ("How Would Mary and the Kids Get by without Me?"). An extreme close-up of a child's small hand wraps tightly around a father's finger ("She needs me"). A woman wistfully traces an inscription on a headstone ("If you died today, who would take care of your family?").

Insurance companies used very different appeals when they began to market life insurance to white, middle-class women in the 1970s. For example, an ad from the Prudential Life Insurance Company of America (1970) in *Look* magazine, one of the most popular general-interest magazines of the era, might easily have been mistaken for a fashion advertisement. The advertisement is dominated by an extreme close-up profile photo of an attractive young white woman gazing off the page. The focal point of the image is the woman's large earring crafted as the Prudential logo (the Prudential rock). The headline uses the language of fashion, calling attention to "One accessory every working woman should have." The copy notes that, although more than half of all working women were married, and husbands usually had insurance, "husband insurance doesn't protect the two incomes a working couple earns." The copy targets the married working woman, acknowledges the importance of "a second income," and raises the specter of loss of one of those incomes. Although women worked for a variety of reasons, Prudential seemingly assumed working women were necessary second earners. There is no soft image, no mention of children or family responsibilities. Instead Prudential insurance protects "two incomes" and whatever those incomes make possible, be it a luxury or a necessity.

Prudential offered its policy, Woman's Exclusive life insurance, both to white and African-American women. The company placed the same ad, featuring a young Black woman, in *Ebony,* a magazine targeting African-American readers. The effort to reach out to the African-American women's market is noteworthy, yet Prudential perhaps unwittingly revealed its own sexism in copy encouraging women to "ask [their] Prudential man" about the new insurance product.

JC Penney (1980) adopted a different strategy in marketing life insurance to women. Again, a close-up photograph of a white woman dressed in what appears to be business attire, a tailored white shirt under a sweater or jacket, fills approximately two-thirds of the page. She appears to be confident, has an aura of authority, and gazes not at some distant landmark, but looks directly at the reader. The slight smile on her face suggests she's ready to have a conversation. The company capitalizes on goodwill the company had established with women through its retail stores and mail-order catalogs. The headline asks: "Who else but JC Penney would give women a break on life insurance?" suggesting the value placed on its female customers. Seemingly targeting women as "shoppers," it offers lower premiums than other insurance companies on its new insurance product (pointing out that many companies don't).

The copy explains, "Whether you work or not, you and your husband both have a lot of responsibility." The reduction in premiums is "not because you're less important [than your husband] but because you live longer." With a nod to women's newfound social empowerment, the policy is identified as Women's Rights Life Insurance, and the advertisement's call to action signals JC Penney's understanding of women's new financial power, inviting women to come in and "see how special you are."

In a 1976 ad in *Ms.* magazine, another insurance company, Equitable, included a photo of nine suited men and one well-dressed woman in business attire apparently waiting for a train. The headline instructs readers to "find the $25,000 executive without life insurance" amid the group. "She's the working woman. And she needs life insurance as much as anyone else in the picture" (Cohen 2003, 317). The copy continues: "If you're single, life insurance is a solid, sensible way to get ready for the future. And if you're married, you also need life insurance to protect your contribution to your family's income and lifestyle." Equitable offered a booklet that talks "woman to woman" about life insurance, noting, "It's time you figured out how much your life is worth." In these advertising concepts for insurance products, advertisers advanced the idea of independent professional women, who, by the way, represent a new market segment for life insurance, while at the same time continued to depend on conventions about women's social roles as attractive wives, nurturing mothers, and dutiful housekeepers.

Speaking of Liberation and the Home

If housing decisions were joint decisions, home buying was the responsibility of the male "homeowner." Government policies of the second wave era were based on strongly held gender stereotypes that "virtually all women married, had children, left the work force, and met their financial obligations only through their provider husbands" (Cohen 2003, 148). The revised tax code provided couples the opportunity to file a joint return "without requiring husbands to share legal rights to income and property with their wives" (Cohen 2003, 145). Thus, women faced attitudinal as well as structural barriers to home ownership. Mortgage lenders, including the government, were reluctant to lend money to single women; loans were granted on the husband's wage-earning ability, rarely taking the income of married women into account.

In 1973, the National Committee on Consumer Finance found that women and racial minorities were being treated unfairly by banking and lending practices. Motivated in part by that report as well as by a rising chorus of complaints from single, separated, widowed, and divorced women unable to establish credit in their own name, the 1974 Equal Credit Opportunity Act prohibited creditor discrimination with respect to race, religion, sex, marital status, and age.

The following 1974 advertisement for a townhouse in Chicago illustrates one realtor's effort to reach out to the newly financially empowered woman by beckoning potential female homebuyers (or perhaps renters) with an all-cap headline:

> WOMEN'S LIBERATION: In this low maintenance, 3 bedroom townhouse with super layout, 1½ baths & garage! Central air, humidifier, all appls., [*sic*] carpeting, drapes, water softener. Loaded with extras. (Homefinders 1974, 16)

There is perhaps a touch of irony here. "Home" harbors a rich constellation of meanings. Home ownership might signal the attainment of the American Dream, a safe haven following the tragedies of war, the "domestic sphere" in which some women delight and from which others seek escape. For many, home is the terrain of the homemaker; as more women have entered the workforce, homemaker is perceived to be an undervalued role. As to the "WOMEN'S LIBERATION" ad, one might wonder where the path to liberation lay. Was it the promise of "low maintenance" or the "super layout"? Perhaps it was the carpeting, drapes, appliances, and "extras"? Perhaps it was only in the headline.

The housing boom was the "bedrock" of postwar prosperity for white working middle-class families. The home, itself an expensive commodity, stimulated demand for related commodities. "The purchase of a new single-family home generally obligated the buyer to acquire new household appliances and furnishings" (Cohen 2003, 122). In an ad from an appliance store in Bridgeport, Connecticut, a fortunate "liberated" Bridgeport woman with a dazzling smile displays her shiny new Maytag appliances. In the artist's rendering, she is white and middle class, almost a caricature of an economically comfortable housewife: slim; fashionably dressed; of an indeterminate age, neither young nor old; and well-coiffed. Her well-pressed, neatly tied apron indicates her role as someone who performs domestic duties; her brilliant smile indicates she is happy to do so. In fact, she bears an uncanny resemblance to Phyllis Schlafly, the iconic antifeminist activist of the 1960s through the 1980s, who opposed, among other things, the Equal Rights Amendment until its demise in 1982. The ad implies that purchasing Maytag washers and dryers offers women "liberation" "from washday worries." Here women's political and social aspirations are completely recuperated and trivialized back into the gendered housekeeping drudgery that white, liberal, second-wave feminists like Betty Friedan were railing against.

For those advertisers who marketed consumer packaged goods and products associated with the home, food products, beauty products, and clothing, striking a balance between the "liberated" new woman and the traditional housewife who had long been their targeted consumer was especially difficult. A General Foods campaign for its Jell-O Pudding advertisements appeared in women's magazines in the 1970s. Each ad featured a close-up of a woman's face, vivid with expression—mischievous, sly, coy. The models represented women of an "undiscernible" age, proudly offering the culinary masterpieces they had created using Jell-O Pudding mixes. Each ad included a kitschy tagline suggesting the scenario that led the woman to create and present the dessert (purportedly) to her unseen husband; each ad also featured the recipe for the dessert.

In one ad, a woman proudly presents her Jell-O Pudding chocolate cheesecake as "The 'Dear, don't you think I'd be a more interesting person if I went to work?' pudding." This Jell-O ad subtly reinforces and encourages stereotypical feminine persuasion, sometimes seen as dishonest, in gaining a husband's permission to be liberated to work outside the home. In deference to the frail male ego that might feel emasculated by his implied inability to provide for his family as sole breadwinner, the wife suggests working will make her more interesting. Such a rhetorical strategy also points to tensions between popular notions of sexy and even sexually available women in the workplace at a moment in history when sexual harassment had not been codified into federal law and policy, and unattractive, dowdy wives labored with housekeeping and kids at home. These kinds of ad messages leave intact the assumption of a woman's subordination to a man who must be cooked for, on whose behalf one ought to be interesting, and from whom permission must be granted before seeking employment. The entire Jell-O campaign assumed women belong in the kitchen, are dependent on their husbands, and are stereotypically manipulative. The campaign also builds on the adage that for women "the way to a man's heart is through his stomach."

Feminism and Femininity Collide

The relationships between "women's work," and femininity was a complicated one. World War II recruitment ads struggled with notions that women's work was in the home, and were filled with assurances that a woman who worked outside the home not only could maintain the household, but also remain "womanly." The relationship between feminism, femininity, and appearance was equally fraught. Collins (2009, 202) writes that "the sense that feminists were all homely had dogged every struggle for women's rights in American history." Betty Friedan (2000, 190) disagreed with the notion that "to be a liberated woman you had to make yourself ugly, to stop shaving under your arms, to stop wearing makeup or pretty dresses or any skirts at all." "Being pretty," she said, was "good for self-image and good for politics" (190).

But stereotypes of unattractive manly feminists dredged up images of militant, sign-carrying protesters. Did embracing feminism mean the masculinization of women? Could feminists remain feminine? Could feminists be attractive? In a 1968 *New York Times* ad for women's lingerie, Bonwit Teller (1968) not only identified the feminist, but provided a vision of "the feminist at home." In several panels, fashionably coiffed women posed languidly in advertised lingerie. The third panel, an advertisement for a lounging shirt, carried the headline: "The feminist at home." The illustration left little doubt that feminists could indeed be feminine and subtly suggested that they necessarily needed to be. "The feminist at home wears a shifty little shirt that's all ruffles and charm." Bonwit Teller's pretty and passively posed line art assured its readers that whatever her activities might be during the day in the streets of New York City, the feminist could still be all "ruffles and charm" while lounging in her home. The message was double-edged, acknowledging the women's movement even as the implication that women remained dependent on attracting men for their own sense of self-worth undermined the very tenets of the movement.

The Beauty Regime: An Individual Project

By the late 1970s and early 1980s, the language of liberation had become a part of the discourse in the United States. In 1979, the prominent New York advertising agency Wells, Rich, Greene, Inc. landed the account for cosmetics giant Max Factor. The campaign that Wells, Rich, Greene, Inc. created for

Max Factor is an exemplar of what media scholar Susan J. Douglas (2000, 267) calls "narcissism as liberation." The ads appropriated the rhetoric of the women's movement, "unchaining" it from larger political goals and collapsing it into "distinctly personal, private desires" (267). Max Factor's advertisements capitalized on women's movement, liberation, and empowerment discourses, especially in reference to women in the work force, to persuade consuming women that vague ideas about success somehow still depended on a woman's beauty, defined as youthful, white, and middle class. "Success" remained contingent on the ability to attract the professional or romantic support of heterosexual men.

The Max Factor ads appeared in women's magazines ranging from the high-toned fashion glossy *Vogue* to housekeeping magazines such as *McCalls* in fall 1979. The series of ads asked point blank: "Don't You Love Being a Woman?" Max Factor's copywriters found a way to tap into anxieties faced by women as it sold them cosmetics. "Why should you postpone success?" inquired Max Factor in an ad for its eye shadow. After all, the copy continued, "One of the most effective secrets of success is a pair of loaded eyes" (Max Factor 1979a). The ad featured a young, beautiful, white woman, dressed in fashionable clothing—not quite business attire but also not casual—looking directly into the camera. In her hand, she held the prop connoting a seriousness of purpose: a pair of eyeglasses. Body language is distinctive in this ad, as well as in the other ads in the same campaign. Unlike the languid, passive poses that defined most advertisements for beauty products at the time, the model appeared active, her body fully facing the camera, her hand on her hip in a manner denoting power and no-nonsense business savvy. This different body language is repeated in each advertisement in the campaign. When advertising lipstick (Max Factor 1979b), the model drinks from a glass of wine as she boldly stares directly at the camera: "Now that you've found a way to speak up, finally there's a lipstick to make it stick." The copy goes on to strategically allude to connections between using the product and women's enhanced power, liberation, and beauty. In another ad in the series, women learned that make-up and blush also could make them more powerful. While acknowledging that "brains and wit will get you where you want to go," Max Factor pointed out that "a little gorgeous skin won't hold you back either." Max Factor's "shrewd little fluid" could provide that gorgeous skin (Max Factor 1979c).

Max Factor's ads illustrate the complicated relationship between the advances wrought by the women's movement and the need to reinforce women's desire to be attractive to men. Thus linked to a commodity, women's "success," "empowerment," and "liberation" became an individual responsibility, instead of a social movement of millions. One's feminist politics began to be defined by individual purchase decisions and consumption. Historian

Ella Howard (2010, 138) notes that "by the 1980s, even as women's economic independence became increasingly accepted, the visual and textual markers of feminism in advertisements were increasingly eclipsed by those of femininity."

COMMERCIAL MEDIA: CIRCULATING ADS, SPREADING THE MOVEMENT

Kitch (2001, 191) reminds us that "mass media exist, not only to make money, but to make meaning." Media provided a marketplace for advertisers but also shaped women's lives and perceptions of their world. Although advertisers focused on selling products and repackaging feminism to increase sales and gain market share, they also advertised the movement in ways feminists never could have. Rosen (2000, xv), in what she calls "consumer feminism," argues that "feminism became palatable to American mainstream culture by addressing the individual woman rather than women as a group," enabling what began as a "small political movement to enter daily life." The women's movement entered women's daily life in television programs, news, and movies. News broadened the reach of the second-wave woman's movement; media coverage of acts of protest inspired additional acts of protest (Andrews and Biggs 2006). Then, too, "Millions of non-movement women first learned about feminism, as well as the new occupations and opportunities that had opened up to women during the seventies, within the familiar pages of women's magazines" (Rosen 2000, 328). Reaching women who were not on politicized college campuses where revolutionary ideas and discourse were part of college life was especially important (Rosen 2000).

In 1973, *Redbook* reported that two out of three women favored the women's liberation movement (Tavris and Jayarante 1973). Magazines included advertisements and articles that reflected women's struggles navigating the women's movement. Articles discussed the women's movement in explicit terms, speaking directly about its ideals and activities, but also examining the effect on readers' lives and exploring what the movement meant to individual readers. Depending on the particular magazine, readers could learn about the movement on the local, national, or regional level. The glossy pages of magazines introduced prominent feminists and leaders in the movement. Readers became acquainted with Betty Freidan and other movement figures through magazine articles and frequent interviews. In a study of changing women's roles in magazines between 1954 and 1982, Demarest and Garner (1992, 363) found that by the late 1960s, articles on Freidan and Simone de Beauvoir became the "central focus of specific issues" in women's magazines such as *Ladies Home Journal.* Demarest and Garner also found that themes and articles focusing on political and social awareness increased from approximately

3 percent between 1954 to 1962, to 10 percent between 1964 and 1972, and to 18 percent between 1972 and 1982 (361–362).

Depending on a magazine's editorial and ideological bent, readers could learn about the positive aspects of the movement or negative ones; how "women's lib" could enhance their lives or how it might harm them and their marriages and relationships. Whatever a magazine's political and ideological stance, several things were clear: the women's movement had entered media content, political discourse, and entertainment. Successful magazines and successful advertisers acted together to sell products and spread the women's movement.

CONCLUSION

The advertising industry tends to flatter itself by its attempts to exist "ahead of the curve," introducing the new, the latest, the up-and-coming; predicting trends and patterns; reflecting to consumers what they don't yet know about themselves. The representations of imagined social and cultural realities and ideal futures communicate rigid gender roles that nonetheless constantly change what it means to be a man, a woman, successful, empowered, and beautiful. Gallagher (2014, 27) writes that the co-optation of feminist ideas into media discourse obliges feminists "to confront the question of how, despite apparent changes, media images and representations entwine with political and social ideologies to reaffirm relatively stable gender positions in society." In the midst of the second-wave women's movement, advertisers understood that things had changed; a revolution had taken place, empowerment had occurred. And in that milieu, advertisers needed to sell their products to women who seemingly now came "in infinite varieties" (Cadwell 1971, 1). The ads I have described here reveal advertisers' attempts to be responsive to women's changing needs to keep brands viable during an evolving social context. The advertisers sutured the old known world of female consumers to a brave new one that opened up exciting possibilities for advertisers as much as for women. But equating social reform with purchasing decisions nonetheless did expand the reach and appeal of the white, liberal, feminist women's movement, even as it narrowed the collective action down to an individual purchase decision in what today we know as commodity feminism.

REFERENCES

Advertising Age. 1970. "Admen Must Reinvent Woman: Old Fictions Flop, Says Adwoman." *Advertising Age* January 12: 3, 42.

Andrews, Kenneth T., and Michael Biggs. 2006. "The Dynamics of Protest Diffusion: Movement, Organizations, Social Networks and News Media in the 1960s Sit-ins." *American Sociological Review* 71 (5): 752–77.

Bartos, Rena. 1972. "Trends in American Advertising." Rena Bartos Papers, Rare Book, Manuscript, and Special Collections Library, Duke University. Durham: North Carolina.

———. 1973. "A Woman's Place (and Yours): A Changing Market." Speech delivered at Package Designers Council Symposium, May 16. Rena Bartos Papers, Rare Book, Manuscript, and Special Collections Library, Duke University. Durham: North Carolina.

———. 1977. "The Moving Target." *Journal of Marketing* 41 (3): 31–37.

Bonwit Teller. 1968. *New York Times,* April 9: 16.

Cadwell, Franchellie. 1971. "Shifting Women's Market Will Kill Some Products." *Advertising Age* August 16: 1, 71.

Cohen, Lizabeth. 2003. *A Consumers' Republic: The Politics of Mass Consumption in Postwar America.* New York: Alfred A. Knopf.

Collins, Gail. 2003. *America's Women. 400 Years of Dolls, Drudges, Helpmates, and Heroines.* New York: HarperCollins.

———. 2009. *When Everything Changed. The Amazing Journey of American Women from 1960 to the Present.* New York: Little, Brown and Company

Courtney, Alice E., and Thomas W. Whipple. 1983. *Sex Stereotyping in Advertising.* Lexington, MA: Lexington Books.

Craig, Stephen. 1997. "Madison Avenue versus *The Feminine Mystique:* How the Advertising Industry Responded to the Onset of the Modern Women's Movement." Paper presented at Popular Culture Association Conference, San Antonio, TX. March 27.

Demarest, Jack, and Jeanette Garner. 1992. "The Representation of Women's Roles in Women's Magazines Over the Past Thirty Years." *The Journal of Psychology* 126 (4): 357–368.

Douglas, Susan J. 2000. "Narcissism as Liberation." In *The Gender and Consumer Culture Reader,* edited by Jennifer Scanlon, 267–82. New York: New York University Press.

Evans, Sara. 2010. *Tidal Wave: How Women Changed America at Century's End.* New York: Free Press.

Fields, Jill. 2007. *An Intimate Affair: Women, Lingerie, and Sexuality.* Berkeley: University of California Press.

Fox, Stephen. 1984. *The Mirror Makers: A History of American Advertising and Its Creators.* Urbana: University of Illinois Press.

Friedan, Betty. 1963. *The Feminine Mystique.* New York: W. W. Norton.

———. 2000. *Life So Far.* New York: Touchstone.

Gallagher, Margaret. 2014. "Media and the Representation of Gender." In *The Routledge Companion to Media and Gender,* edited by Cynthia Carter, Linda Steiner, and Lisa McLaughlin, 23–31. New York: Routledge.

General Foods. (ND). "The 'Dear Don't You Think I'd Be a More Interesting Person If I Went to Work?' Pudding." Advertisement for Jell-O Pudding. Roy Lightner

Collection of Antique Advertisements, Rare Book, Manuscript and Special Collections Library, Duke University. Durham: North Carolina.

Gill, Rosalind. 2007. *Gender and the Media*. Cambridge: Polity.

———.2008. "Empowerment/Sexism: Figuring Female Sexual Agency in Contemporary Advertising." *Feminism and Psychology* 18 (1): 35–60.

Goffman, Erving. *Gender Advertisements*. 1979. New York: Harper and Row.

Goldman, Robert, Deborah Heath, and Sharon L. Smith. 1991. "Commodity Feminism." *Critical Studies in Mass Communication* 8: 333–51.

Harrington, Michael. 1962. *The Other America: Poverty in the United States*. New York: MacMillan.

Hennessee, Judith Adler, and Joan Nicholson. 1972. "NOW Says: Commercials Insult Women." *New York Times Magazine* May 28.

Hodge, Scott, and Andrew Lundeen. 2013. "America Has Become a Nation of Dual-Income Working Couples." Tax Foundation. Accessed May 2, 2017. https://taxfoundation.org/america-has-become-nation-dual-income-working-couples/.

Homefinders Realtors. 1974. Chicago *Daily Herald,* October 31: 16.

Honey, Maureen. 1985. *Creating Rosie the Riveter: Class, Gender, and Propaganda During World War II*. Amherst: University of Massachusetts Press.

Howard, Ella. 2010. "Pink Truck Ads: Second-Wave Feminism and Gendered Marketing." *Journal of Women's History* 22 (4): 137–61.

JC Penney. "Women's Rights Life Insurance." Wells Rich Greene Inc. Records, Rare Book, Manuscript, and Special Collections Library, Duke University. Durham: North Carolina.

Jhally, Sut, and Jean Kilbourne. 2000. *Killing Us Softly 3: Advertising's Image of Women*. Northampton, MA: Media Education Foundation.

Jhally, Sut, Jean Kilbourne, and David Rabinovitz. 2010. *Killing Us Softly 4: Advertising's Image of Women*. Northampton, MA: Media Education Foundation.

Kilbourne, Jean. 1987. *Still Killing Us Softly: Advertising's Image of Women*. Cambridge, MA: Cambridge Documentary Films.

———. 1999. *Deadly Persuasion: Why Women and Girls Must Fight the Addictive Power of Advertising*. New York: Free Press.

———. [1979] 2000. *Killing Us Softly: Advertising's Image of Women*. Cambridge, MA: Cambridge Documentary Films.

———. 2012. *Can't Buy My Love: How Advertising Changes the Way We Think and Feel*. New York: Free Press.

Kitch, Carolyn L. 2001. *The Girl on the Magazine Cover: The Origins of Visual Stereotypes in American Mass Media*. Chapel Hill: University of North Carolina Press.

Laser, William, and John Smallwood. 1977. "The Changing Demographics of Women." *Journal of Marketing* 41 (3): 14–22.

Lazar, Michelle M. 2009. "Entitled to Consume: Postfeminist Femininity and a Culture of Post-Critique." *Discourse and Communication* 3 (4): 371–400.

Macdonald, Myra. 1995. *Representing Women: Myths of Femininity in the Popular Media*. New York: St. Martin's Press.

Marchand, Roland. 1985. *Advertising the American Dream: Making Way for Modernity 1920–1940*. Berkeley: University of California Press.
Max Factor. 1979a. "Don't You Love Being a Woman." Eye Shadow Advertisement. Wells Rich Greene Inc. Records, Rare Book, Manuscript, and Special Collections Library, Duke University. Durham: North Carolina.
_____. 1979b. "Don't You Love Being a Woman." Long Lasting Lipstick Advertisement. Wells Rich Greene Inc. Records, Rare Book, Manuscript, and Special Collections Library, Duke University. Durham: North Carolina.
_____. 1979c. "Don't You Love Being a Woman." Whipped Crème Fluid Make-up Advertisement. Wells Rich Greene Inc. Records, Rare Book, Manuscript, and Special Collections Library, Duke University. Durham: North Carolina.
May, Elaine Tyler. 1999. *Homeward Bound: American Families in the Cold War Era*. New York: Basic Books.
Mccall, Suzanne. 1977. "Meet the 'Workwife.'" *Journal of Marketing* 41 (3): 55–65.
McRobbie, Angela. 2004. "Post-feminism and Popular Culture." *Feminist Media Studies* 4: 255–64.
———. 2008. "Young Women and Consumer Culture: An Intervention." *Cultural Studies* 22 (5): 531–50.
National Center for Health Statistics. 1973. "100 Years of Marriage and Divorce Statistics." Department of Health Education and Welfare. Series 21 (24). Accessed May 2, 2017. https://www.cdc.gov/nchs/data/series/sr_21/sr21_024.pdf.
Parkin, Katherine J. 2006. *Food Is Love: Advertising and Gender Roles in Modern America*. Philadelphia: University of Pennsylvania Press.
Peter Pan International. 1970. *New York Times* January 25, 211.
Prudential Life Insurance Company of America, 1970. "One Accessory Every Working Women Should Have." In *Look*, 75. Roy Lightner Collection of Antique Advertisements, Rare Book, Manuscript and Special Collections Library, Duke University. Durham: North Carolina.
Reynolds, Frank, Melvin Crask, and William Wells. 1977. "The Modern Feminine Lifestyle." *Journal of Marketing* 41 (3): 38–45.
Rosen, Ruth. 2000. *The World Split Open: How the Modern Women's Movement Changed America*. New York: Penguin Books.
Santi, Tina. 1974. "Today's Woman Explodes Yesterday's Ad Dream World." *Advertising Age* March 18: 49–53.
Smith, James P., and Michael P. Ward. 1985. "Time-series growth in the female labor force." *Journal of Labor Economics* 3 (1), Part 2: S59–S90.
Tavris, Carol and Toby Jayarante. 1973. "What 120,000 Young Women Can Tell You About Sex, Motherhood, Menstruation, Housework—and Men." *Redbook* January: 67–69, 127–129, 169.
US Department of Commerce. 1969. "Consumer Income." *Current Population Reports* 63 (September 8): 1. Accessed May 2, 2017. http://www2.census.gov/prod2/popscan/p60-063.pdf.
van Zoonen, Liesbet. 1994. *Feminist Media Studies*. London: Sage.
Walters, Susanna Danuta. 1995. *Material Girls: Making Sense of Feminist Cultural Theory*. Berkeley: University of California Press.

Watson's Appliance Store. 1970. "Women's Liberation for Washday Worries." *Bridgeport Post,* September 22: 20.

Wells, Mary Lawrence. 2002. *A Big Life (in Advertising).* New York: Mary L Book Corp.

Williamson, Judith. 1978. *Decoding Advertisements.* London: Marion Boyars.

Wolgast, Elizabeth H. 1958. "Do Husbands or Wives Make the Purchasing Decisions?" *Journal of Marketing* 23 (2): 151–58.

Young, Iris. 2003. "Breasted Experience: The Look and the Feeling." In *The Politics of Women's Bodies: Sexuality, Appearance, and Behavior,* edited by Rose Weitz, 152–63. New York: Oxford University Press.

Part II

ENCODING: FEMINIST CRITIQUES OF ADVERTISING PROFESSIONALS AND PRACTICES

Chapter 5

Black Women and Advertising Ethics

A Womanist Perspective

Joanna L. Jenkins

Elsewhere I have described triadic convergence in the contemporary era as a dynamic synergy among media, technology, and culture, enabling radical innovation and the potential for radical redistribution of social, economic, and political power (J. Jenkins 2014, 2015). I also have warned that this synergy has permitted the proliferation of indistinguishable advertising that blurs the boundaries of traditional advertising forms such that there is hardly a distinction between consumer advertising, news, and popular culture. Indistinguishable advertising includes such things as branded and sponsored programming and content, native advertising and product placement, social media and microblogs, celebrity endorsements, and marketing tie-ins. The obvious ethical problem is that consumers, however savvy, might not discern whether they are engaging advertising, as opposed to entertainment, editorial, or documentary content. Indeed, increasingly it is difficult to tell the difference. At the same time, as the advertising industry directs indistinguishable advertising techniques toward, among other objectives, increasing its reach and influence among so-called "desirable" populations, such as black women and millennials, the industry continues to deflect criticism that diversification among executive practitioners and power brokers is not commensurate with the audience it seeks. Critiques of these ethical issues generally are not well received among advertising industry opinion leaders. Nor are these ethical problems well considered or researched in the academy.

I begin this chapter by introducing Womanist ethics and discussing indistinguishable advertising before laying out some of the ethical dilemmas inherent in indistinguishable advertising tactics that target black women. I then describe two television series as exemplars illustrating the ethical complexities: ABC's *Scandal,* which debuted in 2012, and Fox's *Empire,* which debuted in 2015. The ethics of indistinguishable advertising and the ethics of advertising inclusion and diversity are discrete and not by any means always related sets of problems. However, here I mine the intersection between black women and indistinguishable advertising as an exercise few have been willing to take on. Where black women meet indistinguishable advertising warrants a particular ethical framework first for witnessing and second for parsing the problems, dilemmas, and injustices peculiar to black women. Womanism is uniquely suited to this task given its emphasis on celebrating the specificity of US black women's raced, gendered, classed experiences as historically specific but individually diverse; its origins in critiquing and supporting the US women's movement, despite white feminisms' racism, homophobia, and class elitism; and its commitment to the African-American community and civil rights, despite black men's sexism and the community's homophobia (Collins 1996).

In most instances, I demonstrate my arguments by way of black women, specifically, and race, gender, class, and sexuality more generally. My concerns with indistinguishable advertising, however, extend beyond women of color. Black women in the United States (which is a more inclusive term because not all black women in the United States are African American) are not a homogenous group, despite advertising segmentation practices that might suggest otherwise. Womanist ethics are inherently intersectional, meaning they account for the experience of race as predicated on the experience of gender and socioeconomic status among other factors, and vice versa. Womanism illuminates the ways raced, classed, sexed, and gendered advertisers and advertising professionals target raced, classed, sexed, and gendered audiences as consumers with raced, classed, sexed, and gendered advertising content suggesting seemingly commonsense social scripts and prescriptions for attitudes and behaviors. Indistinguishable advertising, by definition and design, is not meant to be recognized as advertising, even as it sustains what hooks (2015) might label "imperialist white supremacist capitalist heterosexist patriarchy."

WOMANIST ETHICS

To begin this conversation, I offer Womanist ethics as a lens through which to view contemporary advertising practices with new eyes from a rarely accounted-for standpoint—that of multifaceted US black women. Womanism recognizes complicated intersections of racial, economic, sexual, and gender oppressions. Alice Walker (1983) coined the term *Womanist* as an affirmative expression of love in response to the elitism and racism of white heterosexist US second-wave feminism. Interpretations of feminism by women of color involve recognition of the specific historical legacy of US black women who were active in antiracist and antisexist struggles through the first- and second-wave US women's movements. Originally associated with the values, traditions, and activism of the African-American community, Womanism by some accounts represents the pivot from white second-wave liberal equality feminisms to the US third wave founded on recognizing differences among women based on race, ethnicity, sexuality, ability, nationality, and economic status, among others. Womanism today continues to advocate for and celebrate inclusion, global links, and interdisciplinarity. However, Womanists tend to engage in the examination and integration of black women's experience into dominant understandings of the social world to debunk myths that perpetuate privilege and oppression, to construct ethics and virtues, and to envision human liberation (Harris 2010). Womanists are distinctly aware of the need for simultaneous liberation from all oppressions. Although Collins (1996) makes some important distinctions between Womanism, generally aligned with the African-American community including men, and black feminism, generally aligned with white feminisms' interests in global gender oppressions, the two terms are often used interchangeably. Given the often overlooked but foundational contributions by women of color to feminist thought, "[f]or feminist theory it becomes a moral imperative to examine interlocking systems of oppressions" (Golombisky 2015, 391).

Theologian and ethicist Katie G. Cannon (1988) is credited with developing Womanism's foundations in love into Womanist ethics through her liberation studies. Cannon (1988) affirms that white supremacy and male superiority shape and pervade society. For masses of people, particularly black women, suffering and social marginalization are the normal state of affairs. As long as white male experiences dictate ethical norms, marginalized communities suffer unequivocal oppression. As moral agents, black women create coping mechanisms, make moral judgments, and exercise ethical choices that not only inform Womanist ethics, but also extend to all marginalized communities across changing US demographics and social landscapes (Cannon 1988). In this discussion of advertising, I focus on three principles of Womanist ethics: inclusion, historical context, and pragmatic solutions.

First, regarding Womanist inclusion, even as the advertising industry searches for lucrative and sometimes-elusive niche audiences, diversification among its workforce continues to lag as racist and misogynist representations are employed in efforts to engage the very populations they seek. Meanwhile, as Kreshel (2017) notes, the "desirability" of an audience is usually defined in terms of consumption potential; thus the media landscape is designed to attract the "haves," and "entire segments of the population might be ignored if advertisers don't deem them 'desirable' as a target market, if advertisers aren't interested in talking to them" (203). Thus any interest in diversity on the part of the advertising industry is predicated on "desirable" audiences in terms of affluence or at least market potential.

Second, if diversity is absent in the advertising workforce, misrepresented in advertising content, yet valuable as a commodity that the media sell to advertisers, then Womanist ethics ask: What gave rise to this situation? Certainly the history of US racism and systemic forces within the advertising industry not only produce a male-dominated, homogenized industry relative to the general population but also justify the status quo. This speaks to power relations that can deflect criticism of its practices in the name of creative license, commercial free speech, client preference, neoliberal individualism, and heteropatriarchal capitalism.

Last, Womanism urges practical solutions for social justice. Womanism accounts for different ways of thinking and knowing based on diverse experiences. These varied perspectives can provide valuable insights into influential product categories in advertising. Take, for example, the beauty industry. According to the Nielsen Report (2015), "94% of all US households buy beauty products," but total sales have been flat. Diverse US communities demonstrate different standards of beauty, media preferences, and purchasing habits. Yet the advertising industry routinely continues to suggest that to be beautiful is a woman's most important calling and defines beauty in racist, ageist, heterosexist, and ableist parameters. Understanding culture and experience through applications of Womanism, advertisers might increase relevance to and connections with consumer audiences. However, embracing inclusion and diversity because it is profitable to do so, while a rhetorically expedient advocacy, is not necessarily an ethical one. Womanist ethics in advertising position inclusion as the starting point, not the payoff or a postscript.

INDISTINGUISHABLE ADVERTISING

A key feature of the media landscape in the converged era, which I argue emerged in the 1980s, is that advertising messages increasingly are intermingled with and often indiscernible from other mediated forms (J. Jenkins 2014, 2015). *Advertising Age* columnist Jack Neff (2015) writes, "In fact, you could make the case that all advertising is content, and vice versa." What is more, consumers' general dislike of, indifference toward, and technological capability to avoid advertising have led advertisers to develop strategies to overcome consumer resistance, including among others, covert-masking and media linking. Pointing out that covert communication tactics predate the 1980s by decades if not by a century, Petty and Andrews (2008, 7) define *masked marketing* "as marketing communications that appear not to be marketing communications"; such messages may be "masked as to their commercial source, their commercial message, or both." Covert masking includes "posers" disguised as researchers, buzz and viral marketing, advertorials, "ad-sults" from search-engine queries, urgent "ad-formation" disguised as trusted sources of private or personal account information, and "advertainment" as product and advertising placement in entertainment venues (Petty and Andrews 2008, 8). The Federal Trade Commission's (FTC) list is more succinct: Deceptive advertising formats include "Advertisements Appearing in a News Format or That Otherwise Misrepresent Their Source or Nature" (22396), "Misleading Door Openers" (22598), and "Deceptive Endorsements That Do Not Disclose a Sponsoring Advertiser" (22599) ("Notices: Federal Trade Commission" 2016). Consumers may be deceived when they let down their guard against such deceptive pitches. Petty and Andrews (2008) argue that if these kinds of practices are not "deceptive advertising" in the strictest historical sense, they do nevertheless fall under the authority of the FTC. This is an opinion shared more recently by the FTC ("Notices: Federal Trade Commission" 2016).

Indistinguishable advertising practices are often accompanied by media-linking strategies that connect multiple media channels to create sequenced touch-points for consumers and positive outcomes for advertisers. Some advertisers encourage "desirable" consumers to join discussion forums in varied formats, notably branded contests, testimonials, chats, parties, and so on, regarding their favorite brands. Henry Jenkins (2010, 944) describes "transmedia storytelling" in which elements of a story are "dispersed systematically across multiple delivery channels for the purpose of creating a unified and coordinated entertainment experience." In this case, each medium adds something to the story. Consumer audiences are not passive in this process because influencers are key for providing relevant media content, identifying trends in subculture, and gathering loyal followers of the brand across platforms, including blogs and social media (J. Jenkins 2015). Advertisers, in turn, enjoy essentially free benefits, "earned media," if you will. Such practices become especially onerous if the consumer "communicator" is being remunerated to communicate or is self-marketing but has not disclosed that information (Petty and Andrews 2008). Advertisers leverage information gathered on these platforms for a number of purposeful endeavors, including developing consumer and media insights, building campaigns, compiling user demographics, creating audience profiles, and, of course, increasing profit. Advertisers also broker the information to third parties who then merge those data with other "big data" to create information useful for their own purposes. All these tactics also remain ethically questionable.

Uncertainty about the legalities of indistinguishable advertising persists, too. False advertising, that is, advertising that outright lies, is illegal on its face. Deceptive advertising, a representation or omission of information likely to mislead a reasonable consumer in a material way, is also illegal, according to the FTC. But indistinguishable advertising hardly resembles what consumers and government would recognize as traditional advertising, which is precisely the legal question. Are viewers being deceived if they are unaware that they are watching a promotional message? The truthfulness of persuasive claims is particularly important in messaging environments where audiences let down their guard as consumers to be entertained, to connect with social networks, to gather information, or to express themselves creatively and politically. Government agencies have sought to develop guidelines with regard to indistinguishable advertising. For example, in December 2015, the FTC issued the "Enforcement Policy Statement on Deceptively Formatted Advertising" and indicated the agency's intention to take action against advertising it determined to be deceptive (Fair 2015). But in 2016, the FTC settled with Warner Bros. Home Entertainment about a video game scandal in an industry notorious for its racism, homophobia, and misogyny. Warner Bros. was accused of covert masking, surreptitiously paying off well-known online gamers who were using YouTube to promote Warner Bros. games without the gamers disclosing the paid nature of their endorsements (Federal Trade Commission 2016). Meanwhile, the Federal Communications Commission has updated its guidelines and imposed fines to communicate the need for ethical and transparent practices among advertisers and businesses (Heine 2015). Part of the success of indistinguishable advertising is that it has flown under regulatory radar. However, indistinguishable advertising does warrant ethical attention, regardless of movement toward legal and regulatory scrutiny.

ETHICAL CONCERNS WITH INDISTINGUISHABLE ADVERTISING

Here I focus on two ethical concerns associated with indistinguishable advertising: diminished consumer choice and gender disparity. As to diminished consumer choice, simply put, advertising that does not announce itself as such misleads consumers. Research affirms that indistinguishable advertising impedes consumers' abilities to determine if they are receiving advertising messages (Bermajo 2013). If consumers don't know they are consuming advertising, they cannot reject the advertising message or create counterarguments (Dahlen and Edenius 2007). When information is not readily perceived as advertising messaging or delivered in a recognizable advertising format, information processing is different (Dahlen and Edenius 2007). Consumers who interact with indistinguishable advertising might fail to create counterarguments for or to reject ad messaging that they normally would.

Diminished choices reduce the ability of consumers to boycott companies or to abstain from purchasing. Diminished choices also decrease citizens' ability to create and mobilize independent economies and media that are more representative of gender and culturally specific needs and wants (Gandy 2012). For marginalized communities, this ability can be crucial for survival. Civil rights movements, thriving economies, critiques of the media, and alternative media representations have resulted from independent mobilization in opposition to the discriminatory practices and marginalizing efforts of advertisers, who in some cases knowingly promote products that harm and produce campaigns with stereotypical and injurious images. Precedents set by African Americans in the 1930s affirm the legacy of successful outcomes from boycotting. African Americans urged consumers not to purchase from retailers that refused to employ people of color. Results from consumer mobilization contributed to reform in racist business practices as well as political and economic gain (Gandy 2008). More recently, consumer mobilization was critical to the removal of online advertising content deemed offensive and stereotypical to female, black, and Hispanic audiences. The Richards Group in Dallas created *Hail to the "V"* for feminine hygiene brand Summer's Eve in which talking hand puppets representing women's vaginas spoke in inflated ethnic accents and dialects. Although the client and agency supported the campaign and affirmed their creative license, the offensive advertising content was eventually removed largely because of pressure created by consumer mobilization and criticism (Nudd 2011).

Segmentation strategies that often accompany indistinguishable advertising also contribute to diminished choices among audiences. Segmentation strategies help to reproduce inequality by privileging particular groups because of preferred consumption patterns, distribution channels, and geographic location (Gandy 2012). Segmenting strategies create polarizing effects for those who exist outside constructed norms because they reproduce systems of inequity and limit alternative opportunities (Gandy 2008).

In addition to diminished choice, indistinguishable advertising can exacerbate women's social and economic inequities. Gender concerns are intersectional by definition, meaning gender issues always intersect with and so are inseparable from issues of race, socioeconomic status, age, sexuality, ability, and so on, across traditionally *constructed* demographic categories as well as invisible and unmarked positionalities. Thus issues concerning gender in advertising ethics in a converged era are always already complex and multidimensional. Additionally, historically speaking, advertising has long been heavily criticized for producing and exploiting gender concerns. One of the most-cited contemporary examples is the critique that advertising creates desire for unattainable and unsustainable lifestyles. Another example, more specifically regarding gender, is that advertising naturalizes gender traits and binary gender roles that damage human lives and stifle human expression (Borgerson 2007). Furthermore, advertising-induced effects on body self-image can result in women's body-dissatisfaction, low self-esteem, eating disorders, and unnecessary plastic surgery (Sobol and Darke 2014).

Coping mechanisms are of particular concern for women of color, as most can never achieve the dominant gender norms, beginning with beauty ideals in terms of skin color, physique, and hair texture. Beyond the difficulties of living with the knowledge that one can never match the cultural ideal of white beauty while every advertisement hawks products that require one to buy and try, Harris-Perry (2011) offers the contemporary trope of the "Strong Black Woman," which can be used to demonstrate aspects of gender oppression in advertising. According to this construct, black women are expected to be strong, selfless, resilient, and to excel, regardless of resource disparity, social norms, or debilitating realities. This can be extremely damaging because infallible strength is humanly impossible to maintain. Attempts toward such impossible goals can cause grave physiological and psychological harm, including those associated with feelings of shame, inadequacy, and rejection. For example, black women are structurally positioned to experience prolonged shame and rejection at greater rates than others, which is associated with hyperactive release of the steroid hormone cortisol (Harris-Perry 2011). As Harris-Perry (2011) notes, elevated cortisol contributes to weight gain, heart disease, hardening of the arteries, and decreased immune function. Hence, the connection between black women's marginal social status and poor health is not hyperbole. Black women are overrepresented for a number of stigmatized identities that are perpetuated by stereotypes and lifestyles spurred by advertising. Despite significant progress, as a group, black women are more likely to be impoverished, in poor health, unmarried, overweight, undereducated, and underemployed (Harris-Perry 2011). Black women who do not fall into underprivileged circumstances such as these are still subject to the damaging racial and gender stereotypes not only associated with such circumstances but also perpetuated by advertising (Harris-Perry 2011).

Furthermore expectations of infallible strength are not ascribed to all women. Although seemingly celebratory, Womanist ethics implores further contemplation of the Strong Black Woman trope present in modern advertising. Returning to appeals to consider historical context in Womanist ethics, it's important to reiterate the relationship between Strong Black Woman stereotypes and black women's history of slavery, servitude, exploitation, and labor, not to mention the most horrendous and extreme forms of physical, psychological, and sexual victimization in the United States. Crenshaw (1989, 1991) invented intersectional analysis in her exegesis of the symbolic violence that the US legal system does to black women who have already experienced assault, rape, and domestic and workplace violence in greater numbers than other women.

The stereotype of the Strong Black Woman, among numbers of destructive and devastating stereotypes and tropes about black women, creates unrealistic, unhealthy expectations of achievement and endurance for black women. It obscures the realities surrounding the truth of their actual lived experiences. Without an accurate depiction of reality, many of the ills that affect black women are easily ignored or disregarded, thus remaining socially invisible. Even more compelling, advertising depictions of the Strong Black Woman are apparent in character narratives that *are developed to resonate with black women*. Some "segments" of well-educated white-collar black women have become a targeted demographic thanks to their ability to generate profit and influence. Adaptations of the Strong Black Woman stereotype in advertising are also integrated within leading and supporting roles, which feature black women in branded television programming, movies, and entertainment. The emphasis here is *branded*.

Additionally, Womanist ethics are needed to respond to the needs of millennial audiences. Generational shifts in consumer markets are necessitating wider social rethinking about taken-for-granted binaries in terms of strict female–male gender, gender expression and identity; heteronormative sexuality; and more. At the same time, in many cases, cultural shifts are embracing new racial forms, such as mixed, bi-, and inter-identifications (as well as sometimes reverting back to learned racisms). In advertising, some segments of millennials, like affluent black women, represent "desirable" groups to target with advertising. Yet millennials as a group remain one of the most skeptical ever toward advertising, fueling the search for ever more clever and sometimes ethically questionable indistinguishable advertising tactics. Today millennials are largely considered advertising's primary and most lucrative audience. As this generation matures, sectors of life, leisure, industry, and commerce are expected to transform in accordance with their distinct characteristics and preferences (Howe and Strauss 2000). Millennials have gained a reputation in advertising of withholding support and openly criticizing brands and advertisers that demonstrate racial, gender, and sexual intolerance and misrepresentation. Although it is white millennials whose data are often highlighted to represent all millennials, Harris (2014, 252) notes, black millennials exhibit distinct but generally ignored characteristics, including a belief "that racism continues to be a major social ill in American society" (252).

Distinct preferences among black millennials contribute to trendsetting use of social media and mobile devices (Nielsen Report 2016). Increasingly, black women and black millennials have used these technologies as platforms to raise awareness about issues in their community and to promote solidarity (Nielsen Report 2016). Millennial black women, notably Patrisse Cullors, Alicia Garza, Opal Tometi, Umaara Elliott, and Synead Nichols, are founders, activists, and leaders of grassroots movements such as #BlackLivesMatter (Jobin-Leeds et al. 2016). Contemporary black millennial movements use social media tactically to elevate national consciousness regarding police brutality, racism, and other social injustices facing the black community. #BlackLivesMatter began as a hashtag in 2012 after the murder of Trayvon Martin, an unarmed African-American teenager. Since then #BlackLives-Matter has blossomed into a movement with more than 4.5 million mentions since August 2015 (Nielsen Report 2016). #BlackLivesMatter is a powerful example of millennial black women's leadership, influence, and social media usage.

The influence of black women as well as the distinct preferences and social media behaviors of black millennials are evident in the media as well. According to Nielsen data, 62 percent of black millennials support media depictions of celebrities who share their ethnic background (Nielsen Report 2016). Consequently, the repeated failure to recognize the contributions of people of color and the lack of diversity among 2015 Oscar nominations spurred the boycott and social media hashtag #OscarsSoWhite (Nielsen Report 2016). African-American actress Jada Pinkett-Smith championed the boycott. On Dr. Martin Luther King Jr. Day, Pinkett-Smith, in a video post to her Facebook page, announced she would not support the Oscars because of the award event and organization's lack of diversity (Griggs 2016). The influence of black women, black millennials, and distinct social media usage spurred the Oscars' governing body to take steps toward improving diversity. After nearly a century of exclusion, the 2016 Oscars reflected better diversity among its invited guests with 46 percent women and 41 percent people of color, compared with 25 percent and 8 percent, respectively, in previous years (Nielsen Report 2016).

TELEVISION, INDISTINGUISHABLE ADVERTISING, AND AUDIENCES

Although a number of indistinguishable advertising formats and practices are accompanied by covert media strategies, in this discussion I highlight examples that employ television. I cannot overemphasize that repeated exposure via advertising to stereotypical depictions and imagery of women, communities of color, and other dispossessed people is problematic. Research indicates that repeated exposure to television portrayals of particular groups can lead to the adoption of distorted beliefs (Rubie-Davies, Liu, and Lee 2013). Beyond creating and perpetuating harmful myths about the subordinate group among the dominant group, this means adopting and internalizing lies about oneself as a member of the subordinate group. Thus, like advertising, television is a ubiquitous source of information about culture and society through which "appropriate" roles in society are conveyed. Viewers are bombarded with images and content on television that is generally fictional. However, for many viewers, television portrayals represent an unspoken reality that consistently affects some viewers' future behaviors and beliefs (Rubie-Davies, Liu, and Lee 2013).

Among advertisers, network and cable television have traditionally been the prestige advertising media. Historically, television has enabled brands to send messages, gain notoriety, and develop emotive relationships with mass audiences. Television also has facilitated simple methods for audience segmentation. Through television, advertisers can target audiences that are heterogeneous in their demographics, spending power, interests, and lifestyle, which makes it easy to craft messaging and strategies to resonate directly with target audiences (Schiffman and Wisenblit 2015). But television today is struggling to compete with newer web and mobile digital media platforms for consumer attention, which means television is struggling to compete for advertising allocations. Moreover, sophisticated recording, streaming, and time-shifting devices allow viewers to avoid commercials, television's traditional advertising tactic.

To counteract consumer avoidance, target "desirable" audiences, and resuscitate television, branded programming has increased. Many popular television shows are extended commercials. Whereas some viewers believe they are simply watching television programs, they are actually enthralled with lengthy branded content laden with embedded advertising messages, product placements, and sponsorships. Advertising has long since developed content and programming with the primary purpose of luring "desirable" audiences to spaces to connect with advertisers (Wilson, Gutiérrez, and Chao 2003). Television programming not only provides an effective vehicle to communicate indistinguishable advertising messages, but it also allows advertisers to engage and build relationships with "desirable" audiences.

Women remain a particularly "desirable" consumer advertising television audience. This audience is also demonstrative of shifts spurred by convergence. To contemporary advertisers, women are influential and affluent, and control discretionary income. Market research estimates that their total purchasing power ranges from $5 trillion to $15 trillion annually and is expected to soar in the years to come (Nielsen Report 2013b). In the United States alone, women account for over 50 percent of online purchasing and influence over 80 percent of car, new home, and vacation purchases (Barletta 2014). Women are loyal and enormously valuable consumers whose unique complexities warrant distinct attention (Schiffman and Wisenblit 2015). Additionally, powerful audiences of women represent a myriad of diversity, including black women.

Today, black women are more educated and economically successful and hold more executive positions than ever before, which is typically a reliable predictor of future wealth and influence (Nielsen Report 2016). More than any other ethnic culture, black women tend to head their households (Miller and Kemp 2005). Research affirms that 40 percent of black women consider themselves to be trendsetters (Nielsen Report 2014). Known as early adopters of new technologies and communication tools, black women provide a strong base for brands (Nielsen Report 2014). Key demographic segments, including 73 percent of whites and 67 percent of Hispanics, believe African Americans heavily influence mainstream American culture (Nielsen Report 2013a). Yet another factor in connecting with black female audiences stems from generational shifts. According to US Census data between 2004 and 2014, the number of African Americans ages 18 to 34 and 55 and older grew in number by 33 percent and 55 percent, respectively (Nielsen Report 2016). The complexities of black women as an audience or market group are further characterized by differences based on age and opportunities to nurture loyal relationships with millennials. Nielsen research (2014) states that black women offer an unparalleled opportunity for brands and urges advertisers to "get to know" "African-American" women: "(U)nderstand the key drivers of her purchasing habits, likes, and dislikes, her preferences, behaviors and her value of culture and community."

Undoubtedly, black women are a powerful audience and important to advertisers now, and in the future (J. Jenkins 2014, 2015). Trite, disingenuous advertising risks not only missed opportunities to connect brands and causes with this group, but also exploits a historically marginalized community. Black women represent increasingly diverse, educated, conscious, and affluent consumers who research companies and financially support brands that reflect their ethnicity, cultural identity, and values. Compared with the total market, African Americans are 38 percent more likely to make a purchase when advertisements reflect their heritage (Nielsen Report 2014).

Evidence of contemporary attempts to connect with these economically "desirable" audiences of women can be found in some television programming. Communities of color often demonstrate distinct preferences and media selections that debunk general market norms. In comparison with total markets, African Americans watch fourteen more hours of television each week (Nielsen Report 2014). In addition to a preference for television, African-American consumer reports reveal a preference for television programing that provides diversity in casts and strong characters that reflect black lifestyles and cultures (Nielsen Report 2014). The appeal of connecting with such desirable audiences has contributed to growth in television advertising. In 2013, $2.6 billion was spent on media-linking strategies focused on African-American audiences, which included cable, syndicated, and network television (Nielsen Report 2014). This represents 7 percent growth over 2012, compared with a 2 percent increase in overall advertising spending. However, this amount is merely 2.6 percent of the total $69.3 billion companies have typically spent advertising using similar media strategies in 2013 (Nielsen Report 2014). In 2015, television captured the largest share of black advertising budgets. In the four-year period between 2011 and 2015, broadcast television advertising buys that focused on black audiences increased 255 percent (Nielsen Report 2016). Television programming that delivers these preferences receives both the highest ratings and most advertiser attention. This is where our discussion of the ethics of indistinguishable advertising intersects with Womanist ethics' interest in marginalized groups, in this case black women. Programs that attract black women as audiences are a magnet for indistinguishable advertising practices.

SCANDAL: POSTRACISM AND MEDIA-LINKING STRATEGIES

One program where black women and indistinguishable practices meet is the popular ABC network television program *Scandal,* which debuted in 2012. Part of *Scandal*'s popularity is the appeal of the program's lead character, Olivia Pope, played by Kerry Washington, the first African-American woman in a leading role in a network dramatic series in four decades (Wright 2014). Pope is inspired by Judy Smith, the DC-based black public relations crisis communication manager and powerbroker whose resume includes working with Monica Lewinsky, Wesley Snipes, and the George H. W. Bush administration regarding Clarence Thomas's confirmation hearings. In 2015, *Scandal* averaged "a 2.94 rating in the 18–49 demographic with 9.33 million viewers" (Kimball 2015). In advertising, that is formidable. In 2013, Nielsen consumer research (2013a) ranked *Scandal* as the highest rated scripted drama among African Americans, although *Empire* smashed that achievement in 2015. Nevertheless, with an audience of 37 percent black viewers, *Scandal* did break records (Pallotta and Steiter 2015). In 2016, Scandal remained the second highest-ranking network television program among black millennials, behind *Empire* (Nielsen, 2016).

However, *Scandal* is popular among mainstream audiences as well, according to advertising industry insiders (Stilson 2015). Contributing to *Scandal*'s mainstream success, 68 percent of its audience in 2016 was not African American (Nielsen Report 2016). This fact speaks to Franklin's (2014, 260) argument that advertising efforts and budgets once used to target

US black consumers specifically are increasingly "folded into total-market efficiencies." African-American advertising mogul Tom Burrell affirms many of these claims. Burrell challenges total market initiatives not to treat culturally diverse black audiences as if they are dark-skinned white people (Burrell 2010). This is assimilation aligned with what Warner (2015, 633) describes as "a colorblind agenda," which is advanced "by rarely addressing the cultural differences that marked social stratification lines that forced people of color into subordinate positions." If people are treated as individuals, rather than as members of a racial group, for example, then these individuals are also separated from their "historical trajectory of disenfranchisement" (Warner 2015, 637). Hence, colorblindness today under this guise of a postrace society poses no threat to white privilege (Peller 1990; Warner 2015).

Shonda Rhimes, *Scandal*'s creator, is credited for the series' racial sensibility, which is to cast people of color across the board for their talent, a practice called "blindcasting," in contrast to an entrenched practice of casting actors of color into tokenized roles scripted on the basis of the character's race. Despite progress, *Scandal* has been charged with the "erasure of race" and promulgating "US imperialist politics" so that "the supposed 'feminism' of the program is at first very upper class and career-oriented, and in the end very conservative and very traditional" ("*Scandal:* A Color-Blind Fairy Tale" 2015).

Allowing racism to persist under the guise of white colorblindness, postrace logic suggests that if a television series includes powerful, successful black stars, both as executives behind the program's production and as onscreen talent playing lead roles, then the narratives need not deal with race per se *because we are past all that and can turn our attention to issues pertaining to "everyone."* Racism, thus race, prior to postracial times, is assumed to be an issue only to those who are not white, as if whites don't have race and so need not concern themselves with white privilege. Rather, in a postracial series, the arc of the drama can focus on "mainstream" rather than racial or ethnic storylines and perspectives.

Joseph (2011) describes the rhetorical sleight of hand that postidentity discourses such as postrace and postfeminism achieve by operating as if the civil rights and women's movements have already achieved the goals of ending racism and sexism. In this delusion, mentioning racism or sexism is tantamount to unpatriotic. However, Joseph (2011, 67) also demonstrates the way "postidentity tactics" can be appropriated to be used against the racism and misogyny of postidentity. This can be accomplished by recoding claims about race and gender into less contentious, more palatable symbols, such as disguising race as class-based meritocracy and giving feminist goals a "stylistic mask" (Joseph 2011, 67) of postfeminist femininity. Rhimes understands that her ability to treat black audiences with TV they relate to in large part depends on her ability to simultaneously attract mainstream audiences that also ensure advertisers' interest. TV ratings for black women cost more than TV ratings for adults 18–49.

In addition to its cultural appeal, *Scandal* is influential because of its media-linking strategies, which effectively herd viewers back to network television, mitigate time shifting, and help collect valuable data for advertisers. Social media have been a vital component of *Scandal*'s strategic success since its launch. "During broadcasts cast members live-tweet about each episode," wrote Vega, who noted in 2013 that *Scandal* had "generated 2,838 tweets per minute and a total of 157,601 tweets" in an episode.

Social media platforms, notably Twitter, help advertisers maximize exposure among users already exposed to brand integrations, sponsorships, and tie-ins to achieve brand lift and message expansion. Twitter offers TV-conversation targeting, which allows advertisers to display their advertisements to users who are tweeting about a television program before, during, and after it airs. Twitter also offers keyword targeting tools, which advertisers can use to display promoted tweets to users who have tweeted specific and related phrases purchased by advertisers (Fleischman 2013). Additionally, *Scandal* watch parties—face-to-face and virtually through Facebook—encourage audiences to interact as interpretive communities to also advertise content (Elliot 2014). Hence, viewed through Womanist ethics, we find an exemplar where targeted branded advertising content intersects with high concentrations of "desirable" black women, who are eager to participate in media that seems to address them with empowering, aspirational messages, even commercial ones.

SCANDAL AND *EMPIRE*: BRANDED PROGRAMMING AND INDISTINGUISHABLE ADVERTISING

Branded programming not only facilitates methods to create and count viewers, but also provides covert pathways for advertisers to integrate products, lifestyles, and behaviors. Many audience-generated conversations about *Scandal* focus on clothing and fashion. Kerry Washington and the cast's stylized looks have been described as *gladiators in suits,* a riff-turned-catchphrase on the show's now-famous scripted lines describing Olivia Pope's staff as "gladiators in suits" and "warriors in suits." Clothing retailer The Limited leveraged *Scandal*'s popularity in a licensing deal with ABC to implement indistinguishable advertising practices. According to Elliot (2014), The Limited, hoping to reinvigorate its brand, launched a multimedia campaign featuring the tagline "Fearless fashion for ladies who lead." A coopted white upper-class feminist play on the trivializing cliché "ladies who lunch," The

Limited tagline also then invites critiques of race and class. Advertising executions featured spreadable video content, print advertisements, and product endorsements from *Scandal*'s creator and cast members, as well as the logos of the television series and ABC network. "The *Scandal* collection at The Limited contained more than 70 clothing items, with prices that range from $49 to $250" (Elliot 2014). The collection, advertised as designed by Kerry Washington, was meant to be "aspirational" yet "accessible" for "confident women everywhere," according to a story in *Target Market News: The Black Consumer Market Authority* ("Scandal Inspires Fashion Line" 2014). The $12 million campaign included social media brands Facebook, Instagram, Pinterest, and Twitter using the hashtag #scandalstylethelimited (Elliot 2014). Later The Limited incorporated its original *Scandal* campaign into a new iteration asking, "What does Leading Look Like?" Promoting The Limited's 2015 fashion collection as the "New Look of Leadership," the new campaign featured "over 60 diverse women who are leaders in their fields—business, education, government, tech and beyond" (Ciambriello 2015).

In addition to strategic alliances created through television programming, opportunities for advertisers to fuse messages directly into program scripts occur as well. As technology continues to provide ways to avoid commercials, networks are compelled to develop methods to deliver value to advertisers, not to mention shore up the future of the medium. Fox executive Gary Newman affirms existing partnerships with advertisers and encourages advertisers and networks to be open to finding new ways for brands to see the value in embedding brands and products within network programming (Flint 2015). Let us recall that native advertising is the chameleon that disguises itself to blend into its nonadvertising environment for the purpose of advertising. An example of such opportunities with branded programming is demonstrated through the relationship between Pepsi and the television program *Empire,* Fox's popular US dramatic series. In January 2015, after just three weeks on the air, 61 percent of *Empire*'s audience was black, an all-time US record high for that demographic (Pallotta and Steiter 2015). In 2016, *Empire* was the top-rated network television program among black millennials and ranked among the top ten network television programs among both black millennials and older black generations (Nielsen Report 2016). With 37 percent nonblack viewers, *Empire* is well on its way to mainstream success (Nielsen Report 2016).

Like *Scandal, Empire* represents what media pundits have referred to as a *postracial network television series* in the same way that the United States became a so-called postracial nation after Barack Obama became the forty-fourth US president (Wright 2014). Like *Scandal, Empire* features an ethnically diverse cast in complex leading roles aired during primetime slots. Much of *Empire*'s success is attributed to its leading woman character played by the black actress Taraji P. Henson. *Empire* also features fresh storylines that are of interest to those "elusive" audiences, notably communities of color, which include significant numbers of women and millennials. Whereas *Scandal*'s drama is set amid Washington DC's federal politics, *Empire*'s drama is set amid the corporate culture of hip-hop music and the entertainment industry. Lee Daniels—of *Monster Ball, Precious,* and *The Butler* Hollywood fame—cocreated, produces, and directs *Empire* with executive producer Danny Strong. *Empire* has averaged a 6.4 rating among total markets. Moreover, *Empire* has demonstrated consistent growth among its core audience, women ages 18 to 34, with ratings reaching 7.6. Overall, *Empire* has averaged 13.5 million viewers during live broadcasts and 9.2 million on digital and Internet platforms (Stilson 2015). Among black millennials, *Empire* received an average rating of 25.6 percent in 2016 (Nielsen Report 2016). *Empire* is also a social media dynamo, garnering up to 2.4 million tweets during live broadcasts and 15.8 million likes, comments, and shares on Facebook (Stilson 2015).

Empire's success provided unprecedented opportunity for advertisers to connect with what a Pepsi marketing vice president described as the "hottest show on TV, attractive to all demographics," but particularly "the all-important 18-to-49 demo" (Schultz and Poggi 2015). In a $2 million deal that exemplifies an unprecedented level of advertising integration, Pepsi in 2015 became a player within a three-episode subplot in *Empire* (Flint 2015). Described as a "meta-integration" (Schultz and Poggi 2015), the deal might have been more accurately described as a *mega*-integration. The details are as complex as the ethical concerns it represents: In an *Empire* storyline, a fictional pop star is contracted by Pepsi to write and perform a song for and star in a Pepsi TV commercial. The Pepsi commercial, part of *Empire*'s narrative drama, not only debuted during *Empire* in a commercial break that could have been part of the *Empire* episode, but also subsequently ran as regular commercial advertising on the Fox network. Lee Daniels not only appeared playing himself in a cameo role as the director of the Pepsi commercial in an *Empire* episode, he also directed the Pepsi commercial as it aired as bona fide advertising. Finally, the fictional *Empire* star performing "his song" in the commercial did *not* actually write the song, but the *Empire* character, Jamal Lyon, and the actor who plays the character, Jussie Smollet, now join the pantheon of real pop stars like Michael Jackson and Brittney Spears who did star in Pepsi commercials (Schultz and Poggi 2015). Meanwhile, the artist who did write the song, Tyrone Reginald Johnson, remains mostly obscure. Moreover, although it would not be relevant except for the present discussion of millennial attitudes toward diversity, Smollet is an out gay black man.

The 2014 television program season featured nearly five thousand in-program placements leveraging well over one hundred brands (Flint 2015). The success of branded content, such as Fox's *Empire* deal with Pepsi, is irresistible to advertisers ready to mimic successful practices. Strategies that link so-called multicultural demographics through multicultural casting and facilitate conversations through social media were projected to dominate the 2015–2016 television seasons (Stilson 2015). Also, television spinoff programs and increased so-called multicultural and female-driven programming are expected to become prevalent as television networks attempt to rebrand themselves. Considering the historical void and caricatured representations of communities of color on network television, increased multicultural representation might be refreshing. However, let us remember that contemporary multicultural representation also corresponds with the preferences of "desirable" audiences with buying power and influence.

CONCLUSION

Womanism requires contemplating ethical concerns regarding race, gender, sexuality, and class spurred by indistinguishable advertising. Increased awareness, knowledge, and media literacy education concerning indistinguishable advertising might mitigate potential harms to consumers and citizens, but traditional advertising ethical frameworks do not adequately account for contemporary intersectional diversity or indistinguishable practices, let alone in instances where the two converge. Advertising ethics tend to align with what is least likely to draw legal trouble.

Benefits of indistinguishable advertising—namely opportunities to connect with "elusive" and "desirable" consumer audiences, to lower costs, and to limit regulation—appeal to advertisers and contribute to its proliferation. Although appealing, indistinguishable advertising popularizes strategies and tactics that can promote, and set precedents for, economic oppression and prejudice (Gandy 2012). These ethical concerns are easy to ignore without an ethical framework that makes apparent what is generally invisible and ignored. Furthermore, citizens who buy more, and are perceived to have the potential to buy more, are privileged over those who do not. Although some may argue that such practices are inherently logical in the marketplace, Womanism urges advertising ethics to set a different standard that elevates the role of social justice in capitalist enterprise, thereby making "social responsibility" less a euphemism and more a reality. Excellent advertising practices accurately reflect "the society it emerges from and represents" (Golombisky 2003, 21).

Inclusive advertising ethics are needed as advertising transitions from producing work that primarily reflects the tastes and preferences of older white heterosexual men to work that targets and includes the preferences of women and communities of color, who represent a variety of lifestyles and a spectrum of diversity. Centrally locating Womanism within advertising ethics discourse might contribute to mutual respect and stronger relationships between consumers and advertisers. Moreover, the inclusion of Womanist ethics might improve self-regulation and cultural sensitivity, which could reduce litigation, advertising blunders, and private lawsuits.

In addition to complex racial issues, Womanist ethics are beneficial to understanding gender concerns spurred by indistinguishable advertising. Womanism is committed to the survival, liberation, and well-being of people before profit. Womanism compels intersectional critiques of antiquated and covert gender norms perpetuated through indistinguishable advertising. For example, as *Scandal* engages its seven million viewers (Nielsen Report 2015), Womanism asks why dominant cultural conversations structured around women remain focused on the consumption of fashion and why women continue to be valued primarily for their appearance rather than their character or achievement. Womanism questions why depictions of women of color in the twenty-first century remain tied to stereotypes and tropes that date back to early American justifications for slavery and servitude. Womanist ethics remind us to ask why we have to work so hard to have these discussions about racism and (hetero)sexism in the first place. Womanist ethics implores advertisers to commit to influencing relevant and resonant issues among audiences, rather than perpetuating dominant narratives that reinforce male hierarchy and white supremacy. Cannon (1988) identifies wisdom, dignity, grace, and courage as virtues intrinsically connected to black women in the United States because of their shared history. Moreover, Womanist ethics offers a body of human experience, literature, artistry, and historical narratives to inspire new and different ideals and values. Cannon's (1988) work also offers advertisers a method to reveal ethics and virtues unique to contemporary consumer audiences. These ethics and virtues can be applied to create empowering advertising that satisfies marketplace logic but remains culturally sensitive and successful (Harris 2010).

As an institution, advertising represents far more than the executions it produces. Its conditioning and practices promote ideal behavior and social organization. Advertising shapes the economy and labor practices, along with what we widely accept as ordinary social life. Through Womanist ethics it is hoped that what is produced in advertising, taught within its curriculum, experienced in its workplace, and consumed by citizens pushes us all toward a more complete pluralist democratic reality.

REFERENCES

Barletta, Marti. 2014. *Marketing to Prime Time Women: How to Attract, Convert, and Keep Boomer Big Spenders*. New York: Paramount Market.

Bermajo, Jesus. 2013. "Masking as a Persuasive Strategy in Advertising for Young." *Comunicar* 21: 157–165.

Borgerson, Janet L. 2007. "On the Harmony of Feminist Ethics and Business Ethics." *Business and Society Review* 112 (4): 477–509.

Burrell, Tom. 2010. *Brainwashed: Challenging the Myth of Black Inferiority*. New York: Smiley.

Cannon, Katie. 1988. *Black Womanist Ethics*. Georgia: Scholars.

Ciambriello, Roo. 2015. "Dozens of Women Leaders Star in The Limited's Fall Fashion Campaign." *Adweek,* September 22. Accessed September 16, 2016. http://www.adweek.com/adfreak/dozens-women-leaders-star-limiteds-fall-fashion-campaign-167088.

Collins, Patricia Hill. 1996. "What's in a Name? Womanism, Black Feminism, and Beyond." *The Black Scholar* 26 (1): 9–17.

Crenshaw, Kimberlé. 1989. "Demarginalizing the Intersection of Race and Sex: A Black Feminist Critique of Antidiscrimination Doctrine, Feminist Theory and Antiracist Politics." *University of Chicago Legal Forum* 139–67.

———. 1991. "Mapping the Margins: Intersectionality, Identity Politics, and Violence against Women of Color." *Stanford Law Review* 43 (July): 1241–99.

Dahlen, Michael, and Mats Edenius. 2007. "When Is Advertising, Advertising? Comparing Responses to Non-Traditional and Traditional Advertising Media." *Journal of Current Issues and Research in Advertising* 29 (1): 33–42.

Elliot, Stuart. 2014. "Scandal Inspires Clothing Line at The Limited." *The New York Times,* September 14. Accessed October 17, 2016. http://www.nytimes.com/2014/09/15/business/media/scandal-inspires-clothing-line-at-the-limited.html?_r=0.

Fair, Lesley. 2015. "FTC Issues Enforcement Policy Statement and Business Guidance on Native Advertising." Federal Trade Commission, December 22. Accessed October 17, 2016. https://www.ftc.gov/news-events/blogs/business-blog/2015/12/ftc-issues-enforcement-policy-statement-business-guidance.

Federal Trade Commission. 2016. "Warner Bros. Settles FTC Charges It Failed to Adequately Disclose It Paid Online Influencers to Post Gameplay Videos." News Release, July 11. Accessed October 17, 2016. https://www.ftc.gov/news-events/press-releases/2016/07/warner-bros-settles-ftc-charges-it-failed-adequately-disclose-it.

Fleischman, Michael. 2013. "T.V. Ad Targeting Now Generally Available; Lifts Brands Metrics and Engagement." *Twitter,* July 23. Accessed October 17, 2016: https://blog.twitter.com/2013/tv-ad-targeting-now-generally-available-lifts-brand-metrics-and-engagement.

Flint, Joe. 2015. "Pepsi Gets Taste of *Empire* Drama." *The Wall Street Journal,* November 19. Accessed October 17, 2016. http://www.wsj.com/articles/pepsi-gets-taste-of-empire-drama-1447902181.

Franklin, Esther T. 2014. "Are You Reaching the Black American Consumer? How the Rise of US Multiculturalism Ended Up Sending Mixed Marketing Messages." *Journal of Advertising Research* 54 (3): 259–62.

Gandy, Oscar. 2008. "Media Concentration and Democracy: Why Ownership Matters." *Journalism and Mass Communication Quarterly* 85 (2): 457–58.

———. 2012. “Privatization and Identity: The Formation of a Racial Class.” In *Media in the Age of Marketization*, edited by Graham Murdock and Janet Wasko, 109–28. Cresskill, NJ: Hampton.

Golombisky, Kim. 2003. “Locating Diversity within Advertising Excellence.” *Journal of Advertising Education* 7: 20–23.

———. 2015. “Renewing the Commitments of Feminist Public Relations Theory from Velvet Ghetto to Social Justice.” *Journal of Public Relations Research* 27 (5): 389–415.

Griggs, Brandon. 2016. “Jada Pinkett Smith, Spike Lee to Boycott Oscars Ceremony.” *CNN*, January 18. Accessed December 1, 2016. http://www.cnn.com/2016/01/18/entertainment/oscars-boycott-spike-lee-jada-pinkett-smith-feat/index.html.

Harris, Alexa A. 2014. “Black Millennial Women as Digital Entrepreneurs: A New Lane on the Information Superhighway.” In *Black Women and Popular Culture: The Conversation Continues*, edited by Adria Y. Goldman, Vanatta S. Ford, Alexa A. Harris, and Natasha R. Howard, 247–71. Lanham, MD: Lexington.

Harris, Melanie. 2010. *Gifts of Virtue, Alice Walker, and Womanist Ethics*. New York: Palgrave Macmillan.

Harris-Perry, Melissa. 2011. *Sister Citizen: Shame, Stereotypes, and Black Women in America*. New Haven: Yale University Press.

Heine, Christopher. 2015. “FCC Hits AT&T with $100 Million Fine for Its ‘Unlimited Data’ Ads.” *Adweek*, June 17. Accessed October 17, 2016: http://www.adweek.com/news/technology/fcc-hits-att-100-million-fine-its-deceptive-unlimited-data-ads-165391.

hooks, bell. 2015. *Feminism Is for Everyone: Passionate Politics*. New York: Routledge.

Howe, Neil, and William Strauss. 2000. *Millennials Rising: The Next Great Generation*. New York: Vintage Books.

Jenkins, Henry. 2010. “Transmedia Storytelling and Entertainment: An Annotated Syllabus.” *Continuum: Journal of Media and Cultural Studies* 24 (6): 943–958.

Jenkins, Joanna L. 2014. “Apparitions of the Past and Obscure Vision for the Future: Stereotypes of Black Women and Advertising during a Paradigm Shift.” In *Black Women and Popular Culture: The Conversation Continues*, edited by Adria Y. Goldman, Vanatta S. Ford, Alexa A. Harris, and Natasha R. Howard, 199–224. Lanham, MD: Lexington.

———. 2015. *The Convergence Crisis: An Impending Paradigm Shift in Advertising*. New York: Peter Lang.

Jobin-Leeds, Greg, Agit Arte, Rinku Sen, and Antonia Darder. 2016. *When We Fight, We Win: Twenty-First-Century Social Movements and the Activists That Are Transforming Our World*. New York: The New Press.

Joseph, Ralina L. 2011. “‘Hope Is Finally Making a Comeback’: First Lady Reframed.” *Communication, Culture and Critique* 4 (1): 56–77.

Kimball, Trevor. 2015. “Scandal: Season Five Renewal from ABC.” *TV Series Finale: Cancelled and Renewed TV Shows*, May 8. Accessed October 17, 2016. http://tvseriesfinale.com/tv-show/scandal-season-five-renewal-from-abc-36507/.

Kreshel, Peggy J. 2017. “The Media Are Commercial.” In *Media Ethics: Cases and Moral Reasoning*, by Clifford G. Christians, Mark Fackler, Kathy Brittain

Richardson, Peggy J. Kreshel, and Robert H. Woods, Jr., 202–04. New York: Routledge.
Miller, Pepper, and Herb Kemp. 2005. *What's Black About It: Insights to Increase Your Share of a Changing African-American Market.* New York: Paramount Market.
Neff, Jack. 2015. "Is It Content or Is It Advertising?" *Advertising Age,* October 12. Accessed September 14, 2016. http://adage.com/article/ad-age-research/content-advertising/300858/.
Nielsen Report. 2013a. "Resilient, Receptive and Relevant: The African American Consumer." *Nielsen Consumer Research,* September 19, Accessed October 17, 2016. http://www.nielsen.com/us/en/insights/reports/2013/resilient--receptive-and-relevant.html.
———. 2013b. "US Women Control the Purse Strings." *Nielsen Consumer Research,* April 2. Accessed December 1, 2016. http://www.nielsen.com/us/en/insights/news/2013/u-s--women-control-the-purse-strings.html.
———. 2014. "Powerful. Growing. Influential. The African-American Consumer." *Nielsen Consumer Research,* September 25. Accessed October 17, 2106. http://www.nielsen.com/us/en/insights/reports/2014/powerful-growing-influential-the-african-american-consumer.html.
———. 2015. "Age before Beauty: Treating Generations with a Personal Touch in Beauty Advertising." *Nielsen Consumer Research,* February 5. Accessed October 17, 2016. http://www.nielsen.com/us/en/insights/news/2015/age-before-beauty-treating-generations-with-a-personal-touch-in-beauty-advertising.html.
———. 2016. "Young, Connected and Black: African American Millennials Are Driving Social Change and Leading Digital Advancement." *Nielsen Consumer Research,* October 17, 2016. Accessed October 19, 2106. http://www.nielsen.com/us/en/insights/reports/2016/young-connected-and-black.html.
"Notices: Federal Trade Commission: Enforcement Policy Statement on Deceptively Formatted Advertisements." April 18, 2016. *Federal Register* 81 (74): 22396–601.
Nudd, Tim. 2011. "Summer's Eve Pulls Controversial Talking Vagina Videos." *Adweek,* July 27. Accessed December 3, 2016. http://www.adweek.com/news/advertising-branding/summers-eve-pulls-controversial-talking-vagina-videos-133714.
Pallotta, Frank, and Brian Steiter. 2015. "African-Americans Propel Prime Time TV Hits Like 'Empire.'" *CNN Money,* January 28. Accessed October 17, 2016: http://money.cnn.com/2015/01/28/media/empire-blackish-murder/.
Peller, Gary. 1990. "Race Consciousness." *Duke Law Journal* 4: 758–847.
Petty, Ross D., and J. Craig Andrews. 2008. "Covert Marketing Unmasked: A Legal and Regulatory Guide for Practices That Mask Marketing Messages." *Journal of Public Policy and Marketing* 27 (1): 7–18.
Rubie-Davies, Christine M., Sabrina Liu, and Kai-Chi Katie Lee. 2013. "Watching Each Other: Portrayals of Gender and Ethnicity in Television Advertisements." *The Journal of Social Psychology* 153: 175–195.
"*Scandal*: A Color-Blind Fairy Tale Promoting Corporate Feminism?" 2015. *Telesur,* November 1. Accessed September 16, 2016. http://www.telesurtv.net/english/news/

Scandal-A-Color-Blind-Fairy-Tale-Promoting-Corporate-Feminism-20151101-0019.html.

"*Scandal* Inspires Fashion Line Designed by Kerry Washington for The Limited." 2014. *Target Market News: The Black Consumer Market Authority,* October 5. Accessed May 11, 2017. http://targetmarketnews.com/storyid09161401.htm

Schiffman, Leon G., and Joseph Wisenblit. 2015. *Consumer avior.* Boston: Pearson.

Schultz, E. J., and Jeanine Poggi. 2015. "Behind Pepsi's 'Meta' Integration into Fox's 'Empire.'" *Advertising Age,* November 19. Accessed October 5, 2016. http://adage.com/article/media/pepsi-s-meta-integration-fox-s-empire/301420/.

Sobol, Kamila, and Peter R. Darke. 2014. "'I'd Like to Be That Attractive, But at Least I'm Smart': How Exposure to Ideal Advertising Models Motivates Improved Decision-Making." *Journal of Consumer Psychology* 24: 533–540.

Stilson, Janet. 2015. "Multicultural Talent Is Surging on TV and Winning Mainstream Audiences: A Long Awaited Shift." *Adweek,* May 18. Accessed October 17, 2016. http://www.adweek.com/news/television/multicultural-talent-surging-tv-and-winning-mainstream-audiences-164826.

Vega, Tanzina. 2013. "A Show Makes Friends and History." *New York Times,* January 16. Accessed October 17, 2016. http://www.nytimes.com/2013/01/17/arts/television/scandal-on-abc-is-breaking-barriers.html?_r=0.

Walker, Alice. 1983. *In Search of Our Mothers' Gardens: Womanist Prose.* San Diego: Harcourt Brace Jovanovich.

Warner, Kristen J. 2015. "The Racial Logic of *Grey's Anatomy*: Shonda Rhimes and Her 'Post-Civil Rights, Post-Feminist' Series." *Television and New Media* 16: 631–47.

Wilson, Clint C., Félix Gutiérrez, and Lena M. Chao. 2003. *Racism, Sexism, and the Media: The Rise of Class Communication in Multicultural America.* California: Sage.

Wright, Joshua K. 2014. "Scandalous: Olivia Pope and Black Women in Primetime History." In *Black Women and Popular Culture: The Conversation Continues,* edited by Adria Y. Goldman, Vanatta S. Ford, Alexa A. Harris, and Natasha R. Howard, 15–32. Lanham, MD: Lexington.

Chapter 6

"What's Wrong, You Can't Take a Joke?"

Advertisers' Defenses of Images of Violence against Women in Their Ads, 1979–1989

Juliet Dee

In this chapter I share telephone interviews I conducted in 1985 and 1989 with spokespersons for fourteen brands that depicted or suggested violence against women in advertisements between 1979 and 1989. Spokespersons who admitted that their ads used images of violence usually defended their ads by saying that the images were supposed to be funny, artistic, or shocking. Advertisers' responses to public criticism of their ads included apologizing, firing the agency, or defending the ads.

When I was twenty-seven years old, while teaching an introductory mass media course at Rutgers, I showed Jean Kilbourne's (2000/1979) *Killing Us Softly: Advertising's Image of Women* to my class of one hundred students. It electrified me. Kilbourne identified the toxic environment of advertising images surrounding women and men every day. It dawned on me that incessant exposure to these images was like breathing polluted air; we might not be conscious that the air we breathe is poison, but it harms us nonetheless. I wanted to know who was creating these images of women and why.

Here I use feminist dominance theory to contextualize my interviews. At the time I began collecting ads, I wondered to what extent the advertisers were aware of the violence against women their ads implied. I wondered about the creative rationales justifying such imagery. I define *violence* as rough or injurious physical force, although I'm aware that psychological and emotional violence are no less traumatic. For the present purpose, I include both explicit violence, such as a wife with a black eye and broken arm, and implicit violence, such as a man about to smack a woman's backside with his tennis racket. Violence might emphasize fear by featuring models in dangerous situations or even pose models as glamorous corpses, as *America's Next Top Model* did in March 2007. Violence is usually portrayed as erotic, with men as the aggressors. As Merskin (2011, 92) writes, "Equating masculinity with violence as a normal expression of manliness supports a social system built on acceptance of violence as a 'natural' male trait." Feminist dominance theory connects the dots to posit that it is impossible for women to be safe, let alone equal, or to develop healthy sexuality in a culture that equates men's performance of heterosexual masculinity with violent, often sexual, domination of women.

It is my hope that this historical work will be helpful to students and scholars of both advertising and feminist theory. As I revisit these interviews, I am struck by how little has changed. Yet now, as in the 1980s, the literature on querying advertisers about their creative decisions is thin. We know little about creatives in terms of why they choose to portray women or men as vulnerable or powerful, for example. We do know, however, that the gender dynamics of ad agencies represent "a cult of masculine hedonism" and homosocial relationships (Nixon and Crewe 2004, 139). In such an advertising environment, women have little influence on men as gatekeepers (Windels and Lee 2012).

HISTORICAL CONTEXT

Four decades ago, images of sadomasochism began creeping into advertising, fashion photography, and popular culture in general. The May 1975 issue of *Vogue* featured photographer Helmut Newton's "The Story of Ohhh," based on the 1954 French novel, *The Story of O,* chronicling a woman's submission as a sex slave. In 1976, the Rolling Stones advertised their *Black and Blue* album with a billboard on Sunset Boulevard in Hollywood; the image featured a woman in a ripped bodice with her hands tied in ropes above her head and her bruised legs spread apart under text that read, "I'm black and blue from the Rolling Stones—and I love it!" The feminist groups Women against Violence against Women (WAVAW) and Women against Violence in Pornography and Media (WAVPM) protested against the offensive billboard, which was later removed (Feshbach and Malamuth 1978, 111). Second-wave feminists suggested that images of violence against women on record album jackets could be seen "as a violent reaction on the part of men who are feeling guilty and sexually threatened by the women's new-found awareness and militancy" (London 1977–1978, 510). An example of such violence on television occurred on the soap opera *General Hospital,* when, in the fall of 1980, the character Luke raped the character Laura; later, however, Laura fell in love with Luke and married him (Van Stone 2015). The idea that a woman could fall in love with and marry a man who raped her is not just improbable. It is obscene. But, as Brownmiller (1975) pointed out, the myth that women enjoy sexual abuse is often reinforced in the mass media, particularly in pornography. In the 1970s and 1980s, there were few academic articles on images of violence against women, and trade publications were equally reticent. A 1983 *Advertising Age* article commented on abusive images of women in Europe and South Africa, but not in the United States (Cote, Kilalea, and Bacot 1983).

SECOND-WAVE FEMINISM AND DOMINANCE THEORY

Second-wave US feminism expanded discussion of women's rights to issues such as reproductive choice, domestic violence, and marital rape. Second-wave feminists established the first rape crisis centers and battered women's shelters and succeeded in naming sexual violence as violence, rather than as a private matter of passion. No one had heard of "date rape" or "acquaintance rape" until the 1980s. Susan Brownmiller's (1975) history of rape explained that heterosexual men use rape as a means of perpetuating men's dominance by keeping all women in a state of fear, although Brownmiller was criticized for glossing over white women's role in the US history of slave owners abusing, torturing, and raping their slaves. Feminists asserted that we live in a culture of violence against women, and this culture perpetuates a systemic tolerance of violent acts such as rape (Yodanis 2004). Radical feminists in the 1970s coined the expression *rape culture* to make the connection between rape as an act of violence and a society that not only makes women vulnerable to sexual violence but also blames them for their victimization.

Law professor Catherine MacKinnon argued that sexual harassment, a new term in the 1970s, constituted gender discrimination under Title VII of the 1964 Civil Rights Act. MacKinnon also worked with antipornography activist Andrea Dworkin to draft ultimately unsuccessful legislation against pornography. Some radical feminists argued that pornography harms women because it encourages men to treat women as sexual objects of men's erotic desire rather than as subjects of women's own erotic desires, and so pornography promotes rape culture. MacKinnon's (1989) dominance theory made sexuality central to men's cultural and social dominance. She argued that women's sexuality was socially constructed by male dominance, and men's sexual domination of women is a primary source of women's social subordination. Radical feminist dominance theory explains that women's sexual subordination is the result of men assuming their gender dominance, which renders women perpetually vulnerable to violence in every aspect of their lives, from how advertisers portray women to the way in which the legal system treats victims of violence.

In the 1970s, women of color filed the first sexual harassment lawsuits, most of which were not successful, a fact little remembered because history records it as a gender issue rather than as a matter of race (Golombisky 2012a, 2012b). By 1980, Eleanor Holmes Norton, as head of the Equal Opportunity Commission, had written hostile environment sexual harassment into federal employment policy. During the 1980s, Kimberlé Crenshaw (1989, 1991), another law professor, was developing the concept of intersectionality to make visible why women of color couldn't get either gender or racial legal justice. Crenshaw "applied the word *intersectionality* to express the specific marginalized and invisible social locations of African-American women based on race, gender, class, sexuality, and nationality in relation to not only violence against women but also social and legal responses to violence against women" (Golombisky 2015, 403).

Meanwhile, during the 1980s women also faced social obstacles and legal setbacks as a kind of "backlash" against the women's movement (Faludi 1991). The 1980s, under neoconservatism attributed to the Reagan era, included the defeat of the Equal Rights Amendment and witnessed attempts to roll back feminist momentum along with social and legal gains of the second wave. Conservatives responded to feminism with anger and a desire to resume the status quo. Stern (2012, 217) describes this as the "first wave of resistance," in which rage against "liberated" women led to "anti-feminism" and calls to return to traditional gender roles.

FOUNDATIONAL FEMINIST MEDIA THEORY

Kilbourne's (2000/1979, 1987; see also Jhally and Kilbourne 2000, Jhally, Kilbourne, and Rabinovitz 2010) *Killing Us Softly* films provided alarming examples of images of violence against women, as did a number of slide collections by groups such as WAVAW, WAVPM, and Women against Pornography (WAP). Kilbourne (1999, 26–27) linked the objectification of women in advertising to violence against women:

> Most of us know by now that advertising often turns people into objects. Women's bodies . . . are dismembered, packaged, and used to sell everything from chainsaws to chewing gum. But many people do not fully realize that there are terrible consequences when people become things. . . . Boys learn that masculinity requires a kind of ruthlessness, even brutality. Violence becomes inevitable.

Bronstein (2011, 2) argues that media that combine heteronormative ideas about women's sexuality with violence "function like training manuals for young men growing up in a patriarchal society based on the domination and oppression of women." She writes:

> Women protested against the use of sexually violent images to sell products, arguing that this commercial exploitation fueled rape and battering in real life. Feminist activists interpreted mediated violence against women as a powerful tool of patriarchal control. (2)

Kilbourne, however, was not the only scholar in the 1970s contemplating sexual objectification of women in the media. In 1972, John Berger observed of Western representational art conventions that "most relations between men and women" are determined by the fact that "men act and women appear" ([1972] 1977, 47). He wrote, "Men look at women. Women watch themselves being looked at." Others contributed to what would become foundational theory in feminist media studies. Laura Mulvey (1975) described the "male gaze" in cinema as a symbolic technology that not only turns women onscreen into feminine objects to be looked at through the eye of the camera's conventions but also positions audiences to see through the director's eyes as masculine voyeurs. Gaye Tuchman (1978) defined the absence, condemnation, and trivialization of women in mediated representations as "symbolic annihilation" (1978). Erving Goffman ([1976] 1979) developed a typology that demonstrated the "ritualization of subordination" in advertising's representational conventions of women.

MEDIATED VIOLENCE

During the same period some scholars were studying possible links between media violence and audience attitudes and behaviors. Turow (1984, 111) wrote that "advertisers and their agencies have found that certain forms of programs—violence-oriented action shows, for example—induce higher viewer recall of commercials than do more placid shows." With regard to ads featuring sexualized violence against women, one study found that men had more positive responses than women, including more positive attitudes toward the sponsor and more positive intentions to purchase (Capella et al. 2010). Experiments indicate that ads that combine violence and perceived humor are more effective with men than with women (Swani, Weinberger, and Gulas 2013; Yoon and Kim 2014).

Researchers also found links between viewing pornography and attitudes supporting violence against women, including rape, and actual aggression against women (Donnerstein 1984, 1987; Donnerstein and Berkowitz 1981; Linz, Donnerstein, and Penrod 1987; Malamuth 1983). Researchers found a similar relationship among viewers of R-rated slasher films that portray gruesome violence against women (Linz, Donnerstein, and Penrod 1984). Others found a relationship between watching television soap operas and acceptance of rape myths among both men and women (Kahlor and Eastin

2011). Some studied the representation of sexual violence toward women in music television (Kalis and Neuendorf 1989; Sherman and Dominick 1986). Others found links between such violence in music television and viewers' increasing acceptance of such violence in real life (Hansen and Hansen 1990).

THE INTERVIEWS

Although research has focused on violent content in advertising and the media more generally, along with audience responses to it, few have thought to query the professionals who produce such material. So when I began collecting advertising portraying implicit and explicit violence against women, I concluded that one way to find out why advertisers would sponsor such ads would be to ask them.

Between 1979 and 1989, I collected print advertisements portraying violence against women from popular women's magazines such as *Vogue, Cosmopolitan,* and *Seventeen*. In the present case, I also include one television commercial for Stroh's beer from 1984. The other brands I write about here include Henri-Charles Colsenet (HCC) tennis wear, Virginia Slims cigarettes, Jägermeister liqueur, Nunn Bush Brass Boot shoes, Bort Carleton shoes, Famolare shoes, Zodiac shoes, The Club strawberry daiquiri by Heublein/Spirits, Swept Away store, Guess jeans, Yves St. Laurent Opium perfume, Sebastian International Hair Gloss, and Smyth Brothers Garolini shoes. Among the ads, most of the models were white, except for one men's shoe ad that featured a woman and man who appeared to be Asian in addition to two white men. As to heteronormativity, even ads suggestive of lesbian images were filtered through a heteronormative perception of lesbianism as an object of heterosexual men's desires.

I then set up telephone interviews with spokespeople who worked with or for companies that sponsored the ads in my collection of images. These included people with titles such as director of marketing communication, director of corporate communication, communication director, assistant vice president of advertising, director of public relations, assistant to the director of public relations, and simply "spokesperson." On the agency side, I spoke with a creative director, a designer, a freelance photographer, and an assistant account executive. Other interviewees include a store proprietor, a sales manager, a sales representative, a director of retail, a brand manager, and a division director. Only rarely did I get as far as the creative who actually conceived of and produced the ads. In each case I asked about target audience; use of market research; the ad's impact on sales; the interviewees' interpretations of the ad in question, including perceptions of violent content; and consumer or public responses to the violent content, if any.

Responses revealed that more than twice as many ads (nine) targeted women as men (three), and only three targeted both genders, as is evident from the products advertised. Only one interviewee admitted to using market research, and, in that instance, the research was focus groups. None of the people I interviewed said the ad in question had hurt sales. With regard to advertisers' responses to questions about implied violence against women in their ads, advertisers said they did not want to offend their target audiences because this could potentially hurt their sales. Yet the competition among advertisers simply to get people to look at their ads was so intense that some of them used an outrageous image to try to tread a fine line between shocking or amusing consumers and offending them. If advertisers agreed that an ad could be interpreted as insinuating violence against a model, they generally explained the scene as meant to be tongue-in-cheek, taken as a joke, or artistic. Answers to queries about public responses suggest a continuum ranging from lighthearted ads that the public apparently liked to failed attempts at humor or art.

When I asked advertisers to justify the use of abusive images of women for either the sake of art or humor, their responses depended on the degree of public furor. For ads that triggered little or no negative feedback, advertisers rejected any form of censorship. Others offered embarrassed public apologies for ads that set off angry letters.

Interviewees' reasons for using such images fell into five categories:

1. We don't believe in censorship of any sort.
2. We're not just implying violence; it's overt, but it's just a joke, not to be taken seriously. What's wrong, you can't take a joke?
3. We may or may not have been implying violence against women. How you interpret it is your problem. We were just being artistic.
4. I didn't personally see anything offensive about the ad, but we discontinued it when it became clear that potential customers found it offensive.
5. We admit that our ad contained an image abusive to women. It was a terrible mistake that we will never make again.

Next I share the stories of my interviews. In most cases, I refrain from using people's names.

WHAT'S WRONG, YOU CAN'T TAKE A JOKE?

When I asked advertising professionals why their ads contained images of violence against women, a common response was, "What's wrong, you can't take a joke?" The interviewees made no apologies for their ads; they suggested instead that I needed to lighten up and expand my sense of humor.

In the April 1981 issue of *Vogue,* an ad ran for HCC tennis outfits made by Descente America. The ad pictured a self-assured woman who has just beaten a man at tennis. The caption reads, "When you've got the advantage on court and off, there's only one name: HCC." But the woman does not see that just behind her, the man is threatening to hit her with his racket, ostensibly out of his frustration at losing the tennis match. In 1985, when I asked the sales manager for Descente America about this ad, he said, "It was our intention to show the man about to hit her. She is strutting like a peacock; she's a liberated woman with a haughty air. We wanted to show, in a playful way, a woman looking attractive and winning." Of the man in the ad, he said, "The man is a typical macho-male. It is true he wants to hit her with the racket; no man can take getting beaten by a woman lightly. If men are honest, they'll admit that they can't stand losing to a woman in any sport." He said the ad targeted women tennis players and tried "to make men look silly." He also said the ad was well received by women who thought it was funny.

The public apparently also accepted a Phillip Morris Virginia Slims campaign that began in 1968. In the 1980s, the campaign began to use background images of turn-of-the-century women in the "Old West" as victims of violence for the apparent purpose of humor. A 1982 ad featured "Montana Myrt," a plump, feisty, middle-aged woman who asked "one of the boys" for a drag. In the second frame "one of the boys" has tied her up and is dragging her along the ground behind his horse. Another 1982 ad showed an Army wife sneaking a cigarette outside a fort. In the second frame, her husband has tied her to a post. The caption reads, "After her husband discovered her, she never left the post." A 1984 ad showed a young blonde smoking at "The Great Northern Lumber Camp." We next see her tied to a log floating downstream while five men watch with approval. A 1985 ad showed a husband so infuriated by his wife sneaking a cigarette that he strung her up on the backyard clothesline.

There is no indication that these ads met with any resistance from the public. In 1985, the brand manager of Virginia Slims at Phillip Morris told me, "We have received very few negative letters." She added that "99 percent of our consumer mail is positive."

Phillip Morris employed the Leo Burnett advertising agency to produce the Virginia Slims ads. So I also contacted the creative director of the Virginia Slims account, who refused to talk to me and insisted that I should speak with the director of marketing communication at Phillip Morris. The director of marketing communication, a man, said, "All the Virginia Slims ads are completely tongue-in-cheek; they're an attempt to highlight the plight of women at the turn of the century. I don't think anyone would ever think of taking them seriously."

I said, "Then you're saying that we shouldn't be disturbed at seeing all these women tied up because it's just a joke?"

He responded, "Humor is very subjective. What might be one person's hilarity might be another's disgust. A lot of folks feel very positive about our campaign being a feminist ad campaign."

Hanmer (1978, 219) observed that "at its most covert, the threat of force or force itself may proceed from behavior which on the surface may appear friendly or joking." She explained that joking can take the subtle form of veiled threats, which may serve to control women's behavior. In the Virginia Slims ads, modern-day women were expected to laugh at an earlier fictional situation where one woman is tied up, sometimes while three to five men gloat over her punishment. But if all print ads were gathered in a giant photo album of "the American family," an alien anthropologist might conclude that our society is often amused by fictional intimidation or abuse of women.

Philip Morris representatives argued that the background images of violence against women were tongue-in-cheek; after all, they were satirizing the way women were treated a century ago, and meanwhile were congratulating a contemporary woman hailed as "Baby" for having "come a long way."

Like the background scenes of the Old West in the Virginia Slims ads, the Stroh Brewery Company set a 1985 television commercial in the Old West. In Stroh's case, however, the company made the mistake of assuming that people would laugh at seeing a woman thrown out of a stagecoach. The commercial begins with a middle-aged woman and two men in a stagecoach. Outlaws are chasing them so, to lighten the load, the men realize that they might have to throw all their cases of beer off the coach. But they think twice, remembering that it is Stroh's beer, and decide to force the woman out of the coach instead.

The Stroh Brewery Company was barraged with letters objecting to the commercial. The manager of corporate communications for Stroh Brewery, R. Sue Denny, responded to the outcry with an official reply in which she explained that the stagecoach commercial "was a spoof of the Old West and of exaggerated values which we believe no longer hold a place in contemporary society. We certainly did not mean for the ad to be taken seriously, and we sincerely apologize to you if the ad offended you in any way."

When I asked her about the commercial in a 1985 telephone interview, she said, "The commercial was pretested in focus groups of both men and women before we aired it, and they seemed to like it. We generally don't get any criticism of our ads, but in this case, when it was broadcast, we had many complaints from women, and men complained about it, too." When I asked about Stroh's target audience, she said, "Well, 88 percent of all beer is sold to men. The female audience that drinks beer is so small that it couldn't even support one brand. If you did a beer commercial targeting the female audience, the men would cross that beer off. They wouldn't touch it." When I asked if she thought that men beer drinkers liked seeing the woman forced off the stagecoach, she said, "I'd prefer to say that the woman was kindly helped from the stagecoach. . . . Well, yes, I think the commercial may have appealed to a certain male mentality. Maybe some men are unhappy in their relationships with women, and they think, 'Why should I have problems with people? I have power. I have the ability to get this person out of my life,' which is exactly what the two men did—they got the woman out of the stagecoach."

The stagecoach commercial was produced by the Marschalk ad agency, where, in 1985, I called the assistant account executive for the Stroh's account. He admitted that there had been "a lot of flak" over this commercial and joked about making a second commercial with the same plot but reversing the sexes: "We were thinking of putting two women on a stagecoach drinking Stroh's Light, and throwing the man out when the bad guys attacked."

Of course, reversing the gender does not mitigate the violence.

Another 1980s ad that attempted humor was interpreted by many readers to be making light of a battered wife. This ad for Jägermeister liqueur showed a woman with puffy red eyes and one arm in a cast and sling. In her other hand she holds a cordial glass of Jägermeister. The copy reads from her point of view: "I'm drinking Jägermeister because you ought to see him!" The picture with the copy implies that she is a battered wife who batters back.

Jägermeister is marketed in the United States by the Sidney Frank Importing Company. Its sales representative commented, "That ad was one of a series of 175 slogans which began with 'I'm drinking Jägermeister because. . . .' Some of them were award-winning ads. For example, we had one where a man with a huge bald forehead says, 'I'm drinking Jägermeister because I'd rather have a bottle in front of me than a frontal lobotomy.' We just meant to be funny." He also said the ads were geared toward men. When I asked him if men would have found the "battered wife" ad amusing, he said, "Oh, no, that 'abusive ad' was a mistake. I can't think of any reason why my superiors thought it was funny. I feel embarrassed to even talk about it. It's obvious that it has generated a lot of bad will against us. It was not real sound thinking to run that ad." He also said, "We've hired a new ad agency now, in any case."

A point worth noting in the mechanics of humor is the difference between the target and the butt of a joke: The target is the one being criticized, but the butt is the one the joke is on; the target and the butt might not be the same (Golombisky, 1999). For example, in the Virginia Slims ads, the men who are torturing women are being criticized as the target of the humor; however, the women being tortured are the butt of the humor. Moreover, women are meant to laugh. Thus the power of making an example of the target of the joke—in this case the men as the people in power—is undermined by throwing away the people without power—in this case the women being tortured—as the butt of the joke.

BUT IT'S ART

In addition to the "just joking" defense, another frequent response to my questions about violence against women was that the photography was intended to be "artistic." For example, in an ad for Nunn Bush Brass Boot shoes, a woman is running away from two men. One might interpret her expression to be frightened. Like Cinderella, she loses one of her shoes as she is running, as we can see from three inset frames beneath the main visual. Each frame shows the shoes of one of the three characters. The sexually suggestive headline reads, "Do It with Your Shoes On." Fashion photographer Deborah Turbeville took the photo. Commenting on the photo, the director of the Brass Boot Division said, "We were running this series of ads using photographs by world-famous photographers such Deborah Turbeville." About the ad's sales success, he said, "More people said, 'Who did the ad?' But they didn't want the shoes. Well, I guess we got more interest in the shoes under Turbeville's photograph. The ad didn't necessarily get people in to buy our merchandise, but it was fairly successful as a conceptual ad, to get people familiar with our name." He also said, "We had all kinds of people calling in, asking what was going on between the woman and the two men. They're just good friends romping around, having fun on an autumn afternoon." When I asked why the woman looks so frightened and intimidated, he said, "Everyone reads what he or she wants into any picture. We only had three letters objecting to the picture; that's not bad out of the whole United States."

Another ad for a pair of shoes called "Nudes," made by the Bort Carleton Division of the Anwelt Corporation, was also defended as "artistic." This ad showed two women's legs from just above the knee down. The legs are intertwined and appear to be dangling, giving the impression that the women are hanging from above. Using a bit of Gestalt to fill in the rest of the picture, one realizes that the two models are hanging back-to-back, and possibly "nude" if one takes the cue from the bold-faced name of the shoes, which both women are wearing.

In 1985, I chatted with the communications director for the Bort Carleton Division. She said of the ad: "We were aiming at 17-year-olds with the 'Nudes' ad. We didn't want any background in the picture; our purpose was to focus on the shoes so they wouldn't be cluttered with other things. The only purpose we had in making the ad was to display our product fully." When I asked why they would show two women hanging back-to-back to sell shoes, the director said, "I would more think they were dancing rather than hanging. I would have put more emphasis on it if they were facing each other—that might imply lesbianism. I just don't see what your concern is. We were just being artistic."

CANCELING THE AD CAMPAIGN OR (IN A FEW CASES) FIRING THE AGENCY

In some cases, the general public was offended or outraged, whether or not an ad was considered "artistic." A series of 1985 Famolare shoe ads provoked an incensed public reaction. In one of the ads, a woman appears to be running away from a man operating a jackhammer. She seems to be bare from the waist down, but she is wearing Famolare shoes. We see only her hips and legs, although it's not clear why she is nude on a city street. In a similar ad, we again see only a woman's legs, but this time it appears she might be clad in a swimsuit. One foot is on a starting block for a race, and we see a man's hand about to fire a gun behind her.

For these ads, in 1985, I spoke with a Famolare family member working as the director of retail. She said that the ads had not offended her personally, although she quickly added that her company had completely changed its campaign: "Personally, I thought the model in those ads had nice legs, and the ads didn't offend me at all." However, she said, "Joe Famolare certainly did not intend to offend anyone with the ads." But WAP in New York and the National Organization for Women (NOW) were very upset about the ads. The director of retail said, "[WAP and NOW] said the model was being cut in half, and the jackhammer and the gun were phallic symbols that suggested violence. What wild things they brought into it!" She said that as a result, when Joe Famolare saw how much furor the ads were creating, he was one of the first to change his entire ad campaign. "In fact, WAP and other women's groups were so happy with him, they gave him the Ms. Liberty Award. He was the first man to get it. All the women started loving him because we changed our ad campaign to 'Footloose and Famolare,' with his face in the ad." She added, "We're using a different ad agency now, too." WAP had begun its Annual Advertising Awards in 1982; its Ms. Liberty Award celebrated "non-sexist advertisements that promoted women's dignity" (Bronstein 2011, 249).

Like the Famolare ads, the Encore Shoe Corporation, for its line of Zodiac shoes, sponsored an ad intended to be artistic but that resulted in public outcry. The ad pictures an Asian woman lying on the floor for a photo shoot. A crouching blond man is holding a light meter at her cheek, an Asian man straddles her, and another white man stands at her feet pointing a camera down at her. WAP singled out this ad as an example of the "woman-hating, sexually violent mainstream ads women are constantly bombarded with" (Women against Pornography 1983, 14). Zodiac's 1983 "Shoe Shot" advertisement is eerily similar to the 2007 Dolce and Gabbana gang rape image, which I will return to later. But the Zodiac image precedes the Dolce and Gabbana image by twenty-four years.

In 1985, when I asked Zodiac's assistant vice president of advertising about the ad, she said, "We came out with a new line of Zodiac shoes for men in 1981. Most men had never heard of Zodiac. The line was only known for women's boots. It's really hard to sell shoes. You compete against so many other ads out there. If you just do a close-up of the shoe, no one will look at it. People are interested in ads with people, in a lifestyle statement." She said their objective was name recognition among "the urban, upscale yuppie who wants daring fashion footwear." She explained, "The reason it came out as it did was that originally, we had planned for the woman to be the photographer taking pictures of the men's shoes—sort of a shoot within a shoot—but it didn't showcase the shoes well enough. In order to focus attention on the men's shoes, we ended up having her lie on the floor to draw people's eyes to the men's shoes."

When I asked her what kind of response the ad generated, she said, "*Gentleman's Quarterly* sent us a list of several hundred people who wrote objecting to the ad. We meant for it to be provocative, but we never intended for it to suggest violence toward women." The Zodiac VP said she attended the photo shoot that produced the ad's image. "It just never occurred to me that it looked like the men were threatening the woman. I wouldn't have allowed it if I had realized what it really looked like. As a woman, I just wouldn't have allowed it." She also said that when they started getting letters of complaint, she felt terrible about it. "I took the time to respond to every single letter individually," she said.

Whereas the Famolare and Zodiac shoe ads visually suggested violence, an ad for "The Club" strawberry daiquiri sponsored by the Heublein Spirits Group seemed to verbally suggest violence. A frumpy middle-aged woman becomes the butt of the joke when she says, "Hit me with a club." In 1980, *Ms.* magazine publisher Pat Carbine and more than a thousand other women objected to the ad, citing the copy as an invitation to physical abuse. The vice president of marketing for Heublein responded to Carbine's objections, saying that he was "stunned" by the negative reaction to the ad because it had never occurred to him that the ad encouraged or condoned physical abuse. He did concede that Heublein would cancel the ad, however (Corr 1980).

Another ad that was immediately withdrawn following a storm of protest was for a store called Swept Away in Santa Barbara, California. In December 1982, the morning edition of the *Santa Barbara News-Press* ran a Swept Away advertisement featuring a picture of a woman tied up in a carwash. The copy read, "All tied up? Christmas shopping got you in a bind? You'll find the most unusual gifts . . . at Swept Away." Readers were so enraged by the ad that it did not run in the afternoon edition of the paper. When I interviewed Swept Away's proprietor in 1985, he said, "I had hoped it would be funny. It was supposed to be a play on words—you know—all tied up for Christmas?"

The proprietor described himself as a "maverick" and "offbeat," and said, "Sex is sex; sex is always a big selling point." But then he said: "I wish you wouldn't ask me about that ad; I feel like we're beating a dead horse. I wish I had had a man tied up in the carwash and not a woman. We were ignorant." After admitting the ad was a mistake, he shifted blame by telling me he had fired the man who designed the ad for him.

In contrast to companies such as Joe Famolare, Zodiac, Heublein, and the retail store Swept Away, which canceled their ad campaigns and in a couple of cases fired their ad agencies, a spokesperson for Guess clothing made no apologies for its images of women. A number of ads for Guess comprised a disturbing ambiguity. Guess's director of advertising, Paul Marciano, hired photographer Wayne Maser who took one series of photographs with a man and woman in a swamp and another series of photographs with a man and woman in a corral.

In one photo from the 1987 ad for Guess jeans set in the swamp, a man dressed in a black suit and black hat is either replacing or removing the clothing of a young woman whose arms are at her sides in a passive pose. The scene raises some questions: Are they lovers having a little romance in the swamp? If so, why is she turning away from him and looking down with what might be interpreted as resignation? She is barely clothed; is it possible she has just been assaulted? Has he assaulted her, or has he found her this way and is trying to help? The corral scene is equally ambiguous: A young woman with her bra showing is either dancing or struggling with a cowboy in a corral with cattle in the background. Is she trying to stop him from taking off her shirt, or is she enjoying the encounter?

In 1989, when I asked about readers' reactions to the scene in the swamp, a Guess spokeswoman said, "Some people were offended by it, but that's advertising in the 1980s. Those people who were offended shouldn't be reading magazines; they have no idea what fashion is all about." She abruptly ended the conversation when I asked about the corral scene: "I'm not at liberty to discuss individual responses from the public."

DESIRE FOR "SHOCK VALUE"

Other interviewees defended their ads on the basis of "shock value," presumably to increase recall. Like the swamp and corral scenes in the Guess ads, a 1987 ad for Yves Saint Laurent's Opium perfume does not show overt violence against the woman in the ad but is somewhat ambiguous in that it shows a woman lying in repose, suggesting that she is asleep, drugged, or perhaps even dead. There are white flowers at her side; behind the flowers is the suggestion of varnished wood, which might call to mind a polished coffin.

When I asked about this ad, an assistant to the vice president for public relations for Yves Saint Laurent did not say whether there had been any negative public reaction to the ad. But she explained that the ad had been discontinued: "The ad was created in France, but it was discontinued here because of the sensitivity to drug abuse in the United States." Given the name of the perfume, Opium, she said, "It's easy to see how someone could imagine that the woman has been drugged or has overdosed, but it's kind of extreme to think she is in a coffin. She's just in a deep sleep; in our television commercial for Opium perfume, she is dreaming that a Prince Charming is coming to waken her. Maybe she is Sleeping Beauty or a Snow White waiting for her Prince Charming." Then she said, "There is a little bit of shock factor. It's an image that you don't normally see. It's to attract your attention so you'll never forget this ad. But the decision was made by management here that it was a little too shocking."

A 1986 ad for Sebastian International's Hair Gloss sparked an angry public reaction. In this ad, three white women styled to evoke "orientalism" are wearing tangles of thin ropes or very revealing string dresses. One woman seems to be kissing another as the third looks on. In a 1989 interview, the director of public relations for Sebastian International admitted that public reaction to the ad was less than positive: "I was new on the job, and with this ad, we had a crisis public relations situation. We were flooded with letters and calls, especially from the Midwest. We got quite a response to our 800-number, about four hundred calls a day. There are some people who will say, 'Response is response,' whether it's negative or positive, but I'm not so sure." She said they received letters "saying that the ad suggested sadomasochism, lesbianism, and bondage." She attributed the ad's creative rationale to shock value. "At the time, Sebastian International was interested in shock value and in taking risks; they thought that art needed shock and risk." She explained the cultural moment and the creative director's thinking: "The ad was meant to be minimalistic, to be avant-garde, to be unusual, and to be strange. At that time, the avant-garde was all the rage, but now it's passé. . . . If anything, our creative director was influenced by the art shows she was going to when she designed this ad. I admit that the ad did shock me quite a bit at the time, but nothing shocks me anymore."

But if an ad such as the Sebastian Hair Gloss ad receives extensive attention from news media because of its shock value, its sponsors may not mind because even negative publicity may be better than none. Such was the case with a 1984 ad for Garolini shoes, sold by the Smyth Brothers in Chicago. In this ad, a woman is lying unconscious on a bathroom floor. She is still clutching a goblet from which her drink has spilled, but she has dropped a hand mirror, reflecting the menacing face of a man standing over her. In 1989, I interviewed the freelance photographer in Chicago who took the photo. He said, "Yeah, some people were upset by that—They call us [creative people] a bunch of sick people—Well, I think Jean Kilbourne is sick. Fashion has always had the freedom to express all kinds of emotions." He defended the image: "The woman in the picture is laid out very elegantly." Then he shifted his attack to the agency that hired him for the ad: "I wanted to have more drama in the picture—to have the wine glass shattered, but the ad agency wouldn't let me. People in ad agencies are all scared; they're all covering their backsides. They should fire the art directors and let us take pictures. I design my pictures through gut feelings." Regarding the narrative of the photograph, he said:

> Maybe the woman is about to be seduced—I never looked upon it as rape. If the expression on the man's face looks malicious, the malice is in your mind. The picture was done to shake the mind, to rattle you. Sex has always been used in advertising, whether male or female. When it's subtle, it's much more interesting. If women say they feel threatened by this picture, they're probably sexually frustrated. There's so much crap that goes on in the world—people should get upset about real violence—to get upset about ads is ridiculous.

Then he defended his art again: "This ad targeted a very sophisticated clientele. My motives in doing the photograph were to copy Helmut Newton. The ad was very popular among advertisers; I got a lot of good accounts when people found out I had done the photography." Helmut Newton, sometimes referred to as the "King of Kink," is the iconic fashion photographer famous for black and white photography depicting women in sadomasochistic scenes.

The freelance photographer was candid about creating the ad for "shock value." Since then researchers have found that the creative directors at advertising agencies "believe that their most important creative mandate is to break through this resistance with ever-fresh creative work" (Nyilasy, Canniford, and Kreshel 2013, 1704). Furthermore, agency creatives can tend to create for other ad creatives instead of for their clients (Soar 2000). The freelancer said it clearly: "My motives in doing the photograph were to copy [photographer] Helmut Newton."

In 1985, I also discussed this woman-on-bathroom-floor ad with a designer at the agency that had employed the freelancer. She said, "That ad got a lot of bad publicity. After I obtained the account, I tried to turn things around. The ad got so much bad publicity—it was even on network television." She said that no one who worked on the ad was upset. She disagreed, however, with the "any publicity is good publicity" philosophy. She said, "The ad shouldn't have run. There is more violence against women in women's magazines; fashion editorials are the worst." Of the advertising industry and gender, she said, "Advertising is antifamily and antiwomen. Men are threatened by liberated women. They're less threatened by child-women, which is why you see so many sixteen-year-old girls selling everything. Most fashion photographers are male. . . . Now more and more women are offended by these ads and are taking measures to avoid certain things." At the end of our conversation, she said she had quit the account.

CONCLUSION

London (1977–1978, 520) commented that "romanticized, sensationalized and glorified media violence against women perpetuates those myths and stereotypes surrounding women's victimization that facilitate and legitimize the commission of crimes." Cortese (2008, 89) explains that the feminist critique of advertising "is a coherent indictment of advertising with a political following":

> Negative responses to advertising have undergone a remarkable transformation. At first, people merely complained about ads that offended them. Then consumers became braver; they started to deface ads, writing on them, for example, "That ad is sexist!" Now consumers are creating their own ads using companies' recognizable logos and symbols to ridicule them. (Cortese 2008, 89)

If members of the public found ads to be offensive in the 1980s, they could write letters or make telephone calls, but there was generally a delayed response between an ad's initial appearance and the public's reaction. With the advent of Facebook, Twitter, blogs, and other social networks, however, the public's reaction to an offensive ad can be instantaneous. For example, the website Tumblr, which David Karp founded in 2007, has become "an excellent vehicle for the expression of cyberfeminism" (Brandt and Kizer 2015, 122). Thus, when people see disturbing or offensive ads, they might blog or microblog to call for a boycott of the product and brand.

Back in 1980 when I began teaching, I was sure that all the racism and all the sexism in our culture would disappear before 1990. I never could have anticipated Dolce and Gabbana's 2007 ad in *Esquire* showing a man pinning a woman down on the ground by her wrists while four other men look on, in an image that strongly suggests gang rape. Nor could I have anticipated Duncan Quinn's 2008 ad featuring a dead woman in lingerie lying on the hood of a Corvette; a man is dragging her body across the car with a necktie around her throat. With regard to Dolce and Gabbana, Bronstein (2011, 331) writes that they "defended the ad as the representation of an erotic dream or a sexual game." She observes, "This explanation failed to quell protests. In response, the fashion house canceled the campaign and pulled the ad from its scheduled global print run" (331). In 2013 the feminist activist group UltraViolet organized both online and in-person protests outside a New York City Reebok store until, under intense pressure, Reebok finally dropped rapper Rick Ross as its celebrity spokesman. Ross had rapped about raping a woman whom he had drugged; the lyrics were "Put molly all in her champagne, she ain't even know it / I took her home and I enjoyed that, she ain't even know it." UltraViolet's petition demanding that Ross be dropped garnered nearly 100,000 signatures (Kennedy 2013).

In his discussion of wealthy patrons who hired artists to paint nude women during the Italian Renaissance, Berger (1972, 63) noted that "the painters and [patrons] were usually men and the persons treated as objects [models], usually women." Berger continued, "This unequal relationship is so deeply embedded in our culture that it still structures the consciousness of many women. They do to themselves what men do to them. They survey, like men, their own femininity" (63). Just as wealthy patrons during the Renaissance could commission paintings of nude women (symbolizing ownership of the models), men who own beauty pageants in 2016 may express "ownership" of the contestants in the sense that the pageant owner may engage in "fat-shaming" if the pageant winner had gained too much weight, for example. Examining the ads of the 1970s and 1980s through the lens of MacKinnon's (1989) dominance theory, we see far too many ads, at best, perpetuating the status quo of male dominance and female subordination, and, at worst, fulfilling twisted fantasies of men's violence against women. All along, Kilbourne has maintained that violent images in advertising both reflect and affect the way in which men treat women in the real world: "Advertising helps to create a climate in which certain attitudes and values flourish, such as the attitude that women are valuable only as objects of men's desire, that real men are always sexually aggressive, that violence is erotic, and that women who are the victims of sexual assault 'asked for it'" (Kilbourne 1999, 290–91). Nearly four decades have passed since MacKinnon, Kilbourne, and other feminists applied their critical inquiry to society's acceptance of subordinate roles for women; yet the pace of change has been glacial. In consumer societies such as ours, we "vote" with our dollars; thus we reward corporations (and advertisers) by purchasing their products. It is time for us to teach our students, colleagues, and children *never* to buy brands that use images of violence in their ads. Perhaps when consumers speak loudly enough, advertisers will listen.

REFERENCES

Berger, John. (1972) 1977. *Ways of Seeing*. London: Penguin.

Brandt, Jenn, and Sam Kizer. 2015. "From Street to Tweet: Popular Culture and Feminist Activism." In *Feminist Theory and Pop Culture,* edited by Adrienne Trier-Bieniek, 115–27. Rotterdam: Sense.

Bronstein, Carolyn. 2011. *Battling Pornography: The American Feminist Anti-Pornography Movement, 1976–1986*. New York: Cambridge University Press.

Brownmiller, Susan. 1975. *Against Our Will: Men, Women and Rape*. New York: Simon & Schuster.

Capella, Michael, Ronald Paul Hill, Justine M. Rapp, and Jeremy Kees. 2010. "The Impact of Violence against Women in Advertisements." *Journal of Advertising* 39 (4): 37–51.

Corr, J. E. 1980. "A Toast to the Readers of *Ms.* from an Advertiser Moved by Your Conviction." *Ms.,* August 8.

Cortese, A. J. 2008. *Provocateur: Images of Women and Minorities in Advertising,* 3rd ed. Lanham, MD: Rowman & Littlefield.

Cote, Kevin, Phil Hill, Des Kilalea, and Eugene Bacot. 1983. "Breaches of Taste Label Some Overseas Jeans Ads." *Advertising Age* 54 (42): M-40.

Crenshaw, Kimberlé. 1989. "Demarginalizing the Intersection of Race and Sex: A Black Feminist Critique of Antidiscrimination Doctrine, Feminist Theory and Antiracist Politics." *University of Chicago Legal Forum,* 1989 (1): 139–67.

———. 1991. "Mapping the Margins: Intersectionality, Identity Politics, and Violence against Women of Color." *Stanford Law Review* 43, 1241–99.

Donnerstein, Edward. 1984. "Pornography: Its Effect on Violence against Women." In *Pornography and Sexual Aggression,* edited by Neil Malamuth and Edward Donnerstein, 53–81. Orlando, FL: Academic.

———. 1987. *The Question of Pornography: Research Findings and Policy Implications*. New York: Free Press.

Donnerstein, Edward, and Leonard Berkowitz. 1981. "Victim Reactions in Aggressive Erotic Films as a Factor in Violence against Women." *Journal of Personality and Social Psychology* 41, 710–24.

Faludi, Susan. 1991. *Backlash: The Undeclared War against American Women.* New York: Crown.

Feshbach, Seymour, and Neal Malamuth. 1978. "Sex and Aggression: Proving the Link." *Psychology Today* (November): 111–22.

Goffman, Erving. [1976] 1979. *Gender Advertisements*. New York: Harper and Row.

Golombisky, Kim. 1999. "Getting a Sense of Humor: On Sex Scandal and Women Joking in Journalism." Paper presented at the annual meeting of the Association for Education in Journalism and Mass Communication, New Orleans, LA, August.

———. 2012a. "Feminism." *Encyclopedia of Gender in Media,* edited by Mary Kosut, 90–96. Los Angeles: Sage.

———. 2012b. "Feminist Thought for Advancing Women in the Academy." In *Women in Higher Education: The Struggle for Equity,* edited by Marian Meyers, 19–38. New York: Hampton.

———. 2015. "Renewing the Commitments of Feminist Public Relations Theory from Velvet Ghetto to Social Justice." *Journal of Public Relations Research* 75 (5): 389–415.

Hanmer, Jalna. 1978. "Violence and the Social Control of Women." *In Power and the State,* edited by G. Littlejohn, B. Smart, J. Wakeford, and N. Yuval-Davis. New York: St. Martin's.

Hansen, Christine, and Ranald Hansen. 1990. "The Influence of Sex and Violence on the Appeal of Rock Music Videos." *Communication Research* 17 (2): 212–34.

Jhally, Sut, and Jean Kilbourne. 2000. *Killing Us Softly 3: Advertising's Image of Women.* Northampton, Mass.: Media Education Foundation.

Jhally, Sut, Jean Kilbourne, and David Rabinovitz. 2010. *Killing Us Softly 4: Advertising's Image of Women.* Northampton, Mass.: Media Education Foundation.

Kahlor, LeeAnn, and Matthew S. Eastin. 2011. "Television's Role in the Culture of Violence toward Women: A Study of Television Viewing and the Cultivation of Rape Myth Acceptance in the United States." *Journal of Broadcasting and Electronic Media* 55 (2): 215–31.

Kalis, Pamela, and Kimberly Neuendorf. 1989. "Aggressive Cue Prominence and Gender Participation in MTV." *Journalism Quarterly* 66 (1): 148–54.

Kennedy, Gerrick D. 2013. "Reebok Drops Rick Ross over Controversial Lyrics." *Los Angeles Times,* April 11. Accessed June 21, 2016. http://articles.latimes.com/2013/apr/11/entertainment/la-et-ms-reebok-drops-rick-ross-over-controversial-lyrics-20130411.

Kilbourne, Jean. 1987. *Still Killing Us Softly: Advertising's Image of Women.* Cambridge, MA: Cambridge Documentary Films.

_____ . 1999. *Can't Buy My Love: How Advertising Changes the Way We Think and Feel.* New York: Simon & Schuster.

_____ . 2000/1979. *Killing Us Softly: Advertising Images of Women.* Cambridge, MA: Cambridge Documentary Films.

Linz, Daniel, Edward Donnerstein, and Steven Penrod. 1984. "The Effects of Multiple Exposures to Filmed Violence against Women." *Journal of Communication* 34 (3): 130–47.

Linz, Daniel, Edward Donnerstein, and Steven Penrod. 1987. "The Findings and Recommendations of the Attorney General's Commission on Pornography." *American Psychologist* 42 (10): 946–53.

London, Julia. 1977–1978. "Images of Violence against Women." *Victimology* 2 (3–4): 510–524.

MacKinnon, Catherine. 1989. *Toward a Feminist Theory of the State.* Cambridge, MA: Harvard University Press.

Malamuth, Neil. 1983. "Factors Associated with Rape as Predictors of Laboratory Aggression against Women." *Journal of Personality and Social Psychology* 45: 432–442.

Merskin, Debra. 2011. *Media, Minorities and Meaning: A Critical Introduction.* New York: Peter Lang.

Mulvey, Laura. 1975. "Visual Pleasure and Narrative Cinema." *Screen* 16 (3): 6–18.

Nixon, Sean, and Ben Crewe. 2004. "Pleasure at Work? Gender Consumption and Work-Based Identities in the Creative Industries." *Consumption, Markets and Culture* 7 (2): 129–47.

Nyilasy, Gergely, Robin Canniford, and Peggy J. Kreshel. 2013. "Ad Agency Professionals' Mental Models of Advertising Creativity." *European Journal of Marketing* 47 (10): 1691–710.

Sherman, Barry, and Joseph Dominick. 1986. "Violence and Sex in Music Videos: TV and Rock 'n' Roll." *Journal of Communication* 36 (1): 79–93.

Soar, Matthew. 2000. "Encoding Advertisements: Ideology and Meaning in Advertising Production." *Mass Communication and Society* 3 (4): 415–37.

Stern, Barbara B. 2012. "Masculinism(s) and the Male Image: What Does It Mean to Be a Man?" In *Sex in Advertising: Perspectives on the Erotic Appeal,* edited by Tom Reichert and Jacqueline Lambiase. New York: Routledge.

Swani, Kunal, Marc G. Weinberger, and Charles S. Gulas. 2013. "The Impact of Violent Humor on Advertising Success: A Gender Perspective." *Journal of Advertising* 42 (4): 308–19.

Tuchman, Gaye. 1978. "Introduction: The Symbolic Annihilation of Women by the Mass Media." In *Hearth and Home: Images of Women in the Mass Media,* edited by Gaye Tuchman, Arlene Kaplan Daniels, and James Benet, 3–38. New York: Oxford University Press.

Turow, Joseph. 1984. *Media Industries: The Production of News and Entertainment.* New York: Longman.

Van Stone Jr., William.2015. "General Hospital's Fail: How Rape Became Seduction." Blog post. Accessed May 11, 2017. http://rachelintheoc.com/?s=van+stone+general+hospital

Windels, Kasey, and Wei-Na Lee. 2012. "The Construction of Gender and Creativity in Advertising Creative Departments." *Gender in Management: An International Journal* 27 (8): 502–519.

Women against Pornography. 1983. "Send Us the Ads You Hate." *Newsreport* (Fall/Winter): 2, 14.

Yodanis, Carrie. 2004. "Gender Inequality, Violence against Women and Fear: A Cross-National Test of the Feminist Theory of Violence against Women." *Journal of Interpersonal Violence* 19 (6): 655–75.

Yoon, Hye Jin, and Yeuseung Kim. 2014. "The Moderating Role of Gender Identity in Responses to Comedic Violence Advertising." *Journal of Advertising* 43 (4): 382–96.

Chapter 7

Exceptional Exemplars

Practitioners' Perspectives on Ads that Communicate Effectively with Women and Men

Kasey Windels

As John Berger (1973, 47) famously observed of Western European *Ways of Seeing*, "*men act* and *women appear*." In this chapter I share my feminist discourse analysis of a study that queried thirty-nine advertising practitioners about their views on advertising messages that communicate effectively with women and men on the basis of gender. The participants, women and men, aligned women's messages with a critique of *to-be-looked-at-ness* while aligning men's messages with the power to *act* on their own behalf. According to participants, effective ads for men reinforce the kind of power and privilege that scholars have associated with white, hegemonic masculinity; effective ads for women challenge unattainable standards of feminine beauty and highlight women who demonstrate resilience in the face of adversity.

When asked to recall advertising they believed communicated especially well with women, participant practitioners described advertising that fell into three categories: (1) love-your-body discourses; (2) challenges to the idealized feminine body in advertising; and (3) challenges to society's prohibition against women having strong, athletic bodies. All three categories, although resisting traditional ideas about feminine bodies, nonetheless define gender for women mostly in terms of embodiment. When asked to recall advertising they believed communicated especially well with men, participant practitioners described advertising that seemed to shore up a waning masculinity based on (1) having power and control over their lives, (2) demonstrating macho masculinity, and (3) appreciating "over-the-top" humor that excuses sexism. Thus the advertising professionals who participated in this study leave us with a gender narrative that urges women to push the boundaries of gender and urges men to reinforce those boundaries.

ADVERTISING AS A CULTURE INDUSTRY AND COMMUNITY OF PRACTICE

Advertisers are in the business of developing communication that resonates with the target audience, so it makes sense to play on the characteristics of the audience when developing advertisements. Advertising practitioners act as cultural intermediaries (Kelly, Lawlor, and O'Donohoe 2005). They voraciously consume culture and popular media as the raw material needed in the creation of effective advertisements, and practitioners draw from values in the cultural system to create symbolic meaning for goods to communicate with intended audiences of potential consumers (Csikszentmihályi 1999; Kelly, Lawlor, and O'Donohoe 2005; McCracken 1989).

Hall (1980) wrote that both professional encoding and audience decoding of mediated messages is limited by dominant rules and available discourses. During encoding and production, institutional structures and professional norms, such as advertising conventions, for example, influence decision making, along with wider sociocultural norms. Hall argued that the professional encoder's concerns with avoiding miscommunication to audiences don't account for either the encoders' own professional insider practices or active audiences willfully resisting messages with more or less success. Yet effective communication with particular audiences is precisely the mission of advertising professionals.

The advertising creative must think about not only the transfer of meaning to a product or service in a way that speaks to the audience, but also demonstrate the norms and codes of the advertising business, a community of practice with its own conventions (Giaccardi 1995; McLeod, O'Donohoe, and Townley 2011; Stuhlfaut 2011). These conventions include creative codes for advertising stylistics and aesthetics, including what is and is not creative and how advertisements should look and be produced (Stuhlfaut 2011). Once developed, the work of advertising creatives is judged by gatekeepers such as creative directors, account executives, and clients in the community of practice (Csikszentmihályi 1999). Only creative endeavors sanctioned by the community are adopted. To succeed as a creative, an individual must have "a very strong internal representation of which ideas are good and which are bad, a representation that matches closely the one accepted by the field" (Csikszentmihályi 1999, 332).

Moreover, the creative department's norms are masculine, meaning it is a culture of men by men for men. Although women are well represented in most departments in the advertising agency, 73 percent of US advertising creatives are men (Grow and Deng 2014). Creative departments in advertising agencies have been called a "fraternity culture" where the personality is masculine, tough, and competitive (Grow and Broyles 2011; Mallia 2009).

Gregory (2009) used the term "locker room" to describe a place of men's power and identity maintained through informal and formal communication, socializing, and men's bonding. Existing power structures restrict women's access to material for forming a positive work identity and becoming full members of the advertising creative community (Windels and Mallia 2015). Creative directors, perhaps unconsciously, tend to prefer work with a traditional masculine sensibility and sense of humor, which gives an occupational advantage to men working in advertising creative departments (Gregory 2009; Nixon 2003; Windels and Lee 2012).

Practitioners also routinely incorporate gender stereotypes into advertisements. One study of US practitioners found they conceptualized gender in ways that largely mirrored societal discourses of men as stoic, powerful, and resistant to pain, and women as sensitive and vulnerable (Zayer and Coleman 2014). Research on gender stereotypes in advertising has shown that practitioners are not reflexive about their role as creators of popular culture and don't believe that the gendered messages they create can be problematic (Shao, Desmarias, and Weaver 2014; Zayer and Coleman 2014). This has been described as an ethical dilemma, in that practitioners avoid accepting that stereotypical representations are negative, and instead blame social norms for the existence of stereotypes, which, for advertisers, become shorthand for telegraphing shared meaning effectively and quickly (Windels 2016). Although research has examined how practitioners conceptualize gender when creating advertisements, there has been no research to deconstruct the dominant gender discourses practitioners draw on to effectively communicate with men or women. This study adopts a critical-interpretive feminist approach to examine this phenomenon.

FEMINIST DISCOURSE ANALYSIS

The material effects of discourse literally constitute the contours of society, including social relations and institutions (Foucault 1980). According to Fischer and Bristor (1994, 321), "The term *discourse* refers to the particular historical, social, and political situatedness of language and hence of subjectivity." Poststructuralist feminism deconstructs the discourse of gender to reveal power relations that disadvantage women (Fischer and Bristor 1994; Weedon 1997). "Gender," van Zoonen (1994, 33) writes, "can thus be thought of as a particular discourse, that is, a set of overlapping and often contradictory cultural descriptions and prescriptions referring to sexual differences." The idea that gender is a natural binary in the first place is constructed through discourse (Kelan 2010). Rejecting the dominance of men and the masculine in the gender binary, poststructuralist feminist thought exposes the fact that the dominant gender cannot be defined without a subordinate counterpart; thus the existence of the dominant gender depends on that subordinate counterpart. So gender represents a continuous discursive struggle influenced by existing power relations such that what is defined as masculine is not only more highly valued than that defined as feminine but is also given power over the feminine. But, if gender is discursively constructed, then it also can be resisted and subverted (van Zoonen 1994).

THE STUDY

Here, I am interested in the reasoning behind practitioners' choices for campaigns they believed communicated effectively with men or women. I conducted in-depth interviews with thirty-nine US advertising agency practitioners, twenty women and nineteen men, to elicit their perspectives. In terms of ethnicity, one practitioner was African American, one was of Middle Eastern descent, and one practitioner emigrated from India. All other participants were white Americans, a fact indicative of the state of diversity in the advertising industry. Participant practitioners represented a variety of roles within the advertising agency, including presidents and partners, creative directors, art directors, copywriters, designers, account executives, digital strategists, account planners, and media planners.

I conducted two rounds of interviews, one with agencies located in the Gulf Coast region and one with agencies in large US metro centers of advertising. For round one, I used *Advertising Redbooks,* a directory of advertising agencies, to develop a sample of agencies. I selected only agencies with thirty or more employees within 3.5 hours' driving distance from Baton Rouge. Of the eight agencies that met the criteria, five agreed to participate, and I worked with each agency to schedule a half to full day of employee interviews in conference rooms and offices. Round one included interviews with nineteen women and thirteen men, and skewed toward small- to mid-sized agencies. The interviews ranged from twenty-one to sixty-six minutes in length. The second set of interviews included five men and two women recruited from among my industry contacts working in large agencies in New York, Chicago, and Los Angeles. Round two interviews averaged forty-one minutes. All participants and their agencies and clients were ensured confidentiality.

Participants entered the interview knowing only that it was a discussion of gender representation in advertisements. To begin the conversation, participants were asked how they got their start in the industry. The first group of questions concerned if and how gender of target audience influences strategic and creative processes. A second group of questions concerned assumptions and rules of thumb participants believed to be true with regard to communicating specifically with women and with men on the basis of the target audience's gender. Finally, to examine specific advertising exemplars, participants were asked to recall recent advertisements they had seen that they believed communicated especially well with men (or some segment of men) and why. They were asked the same question for women. This meant that the ads discussed by participants were not prompted or cued, but offered by participants based on unaided recall.

Analysis focused on each practitioner's description of exemplar advertisements along with the practitioner's rationale for why she or he believed it communicated effectively. From a poststructuralist perspective, it was important to look at how participants' reflections were expressions of larger social discourses. From a feminist perspective, it was important to examine how gender was constructed and encoded, not only in the texts of the advertising under discussion, but also in the transcripts as participants provided clues regarding their own understandings of gender.

My analysis revealed that ads believed to communicate well with women incorporated love-your-body discourses, challenged gender conventions for women typical to advertising, and challenged societal gender norms. When detailing ads that communicated with men, practitioners discussed advertisements that incorporated themes of power and control, used hegemonic notions of masculinity as a selling feature, and employed "over-the-top" humor.

THEMES FOR ADS THAT COMMUNICATE WITH WOMEN

Regarding responses to questions about advertisements that communicate effectively with women, emergent themes centered on challenging the gender discourses. Participant practitioners discussed advertisements that celebrated women of diverse sizes through love-your-body discourses. They discussed ads that challenged stringent rules of beauty typical in advertising. They chose advertisements that challenged society's definition of women as weak and instead celebrated women's strength.

Love-Your-Body Discourse

Love-your-body discourse refers to positive, affirmative, feminist messages targeted to girls and women that tell them to love their bodies, remember they are incredible, and redefine values of femininity (Gill and Elias 2014). Whereas other ads tell women to improve themselves, love-your-body ads tell women they are beautiful as they are. Dove's ongoing Real Beauty campaign represents the exemplar for love-your-body discourses (Gill and Elias 2014; Murray 2013). Unilever's twenty-first-century advertising for its Dove-brand skin care products has employed unconventional models in terms of race, age, and body size to expand the definition of beauty for women.

Although love-your-body ads "appear to interrupt the almost entirely normalized hostile judgment and surveillance of women's bodies in contemporary media culture," they have been criticized as "pernicious forms of power that engender a shift from bodily to psychic regulation" (Gill and Elias 2014, 180). These messages imply that fixing negative body image is as easy as "remembering" that you are beautiful. In advertising, love-your-body themes sometimes employ the same conventions as typical beauty ads, such as digital reshaping and retouching, flawless skin, and similar body poses (Gill and Elias 2014). Such ads have been criticized for co-opting feminism in the name of institutional power (Murray 2013). Gill and Elias (2014) argue that such ads do not reject patriarchal appearance standards for women; instead they expand to include psychic labor. Women are urged to "embrace an affirmative confident disposition, no matter how they actually feel" (Gill and Elias 2014, 185). Additionally, such discourses continue to tie women's social worth to their bodies as objects of beauty, regardless of how broadly *beauty* is defined.

When talking to participant practitioners about campaigns that effectively communicated with women, Dove was the most frequently cited advertisement. Participant practitioners believed the Dove ads empathized with women's perspectives, spoke to women on a personal level, and accepted women for who they are. Practitioners said this is a powerful message for women, one that signifies respect.

A woman strategy vice president talked about how the Dove campaign started a conversation about women's love-hate relationship with beauty products. She said women "love the beauty category because it is a playground, but you never feel you will measure up to it." This practitioner believed Dove was positioned against beauty ads that made women feel "less than" or that they would "never measure up." In this practitioner's opinion, the Dove campaign highlights the unrealistic perfection showcased in other advertisements and provides an alternative to it. She elaborated: "[Dove said] it's okay to be natural, and you are an individual. . . . They just speak to them in a very personal level and that sparks, I think, something in women that makes them love that brand for accepting them for who they are." She felt the brand is saying Dove "understands you; we get you."

The Dove campaign has been criticized for using the same conventions as other beauty ads, such as flawless skin and retouched photographs while suggesting the reverse, that Dove models are "real" (Gill and Elias 2014). However, participant practitioners did not see this as purposeful deception. In contrast, participants felt the advertisements stood in contrast to typical beauty advertisements and "Photoshopped" representations. A woman group account director felt the Dove ads communicated, "I'm speaking to you, Woman, as a normal woman, not by holding up a silkscreened version of who you need to be."

A woman digital strategist believed the campaign succeeded because it encouraged women to believe they are "beautiful in all shapes and sizes." She could see that the Dove campaign was shot professionally, but she believed "those were real people." She said: "You could tell just because of the way it was edited. They took the real conversations and put them in the ad." She believed Dove communicated that all women were beautiful, regardless of age, skin color, or size.

Challenging Gender Conventions in Advertising

Participant practitioners believed the Dove campaign paved the way for other campaigns that challenged advertising norms for women. Other brands have started to adopt love-your-body discourse to demystify some of the gender-based norms of advertising. For example, the Victoria's Secret Angels position ideal women's bodies as young, thin, tall, beautiful, shapely, and mostly white. Practitioners pointed to newer kinds of advertising messages that challenge this convention. An African-American woman who was a vice president in the digital space said the Lane Bryant "I'm No Angel" campaign resonated with women. Positioned against the Victoria's Secret Angels, Lane Bryant's "I'm No Angel" featured full-sized brown, black, and ethnically ambiguous women modeling underwear as they talk about what makes them feel sexy. Toward the end of the advertisement, the women say, "I'm no angel; I'm all kinds of sexy." The vice president believed the advertisement was successful because it played on "the recent increasing female backlash against very stringent standards of beauty." The Lane Bryant campaign, like the Dove campaign, challenged the messages typically transmitted through marketing communication, in this case through the Victoria's Secret Angels. The campaign was an example of advertising as "social commentary" to "shatter" stereotypes of the advertising industry, according to the vice president. The plus-sized women in the advertisement were declaring and enacting "sexiness" while rejecting the small-sized definition of beauty and sex appeal showcased in Victoria's Secret ads. The Lane Bryant campaign also expanded the definition of beauty to include more women of color, although the practitioner did not mention race specifically in her description.

Nevertheless, the Lane Bryant "I'm No Angel" models are cast as beautiful and sexy, meaning they are defined by their (hetero)sex appeal, despite their realistic body sizes. The underwear-clad women in the ad resemble a harem, assembled for the pleasure of the male gaze. In fact, women's movement in the ad is aligned with the freedom to be sexual, a limiting and limited recuperation of women's emancipation threaded through their availability and appetites for sex with men (Boosalis and Golombisky 2010). Even the possibility of an oppositional lesbian gaze here is subverted as heterosexual girl-on-girl porn (Tsai 2010). The models also employ the "hyper-ritualized" "gender display" of advertising that Goffman (1976) documented decades ago, including feminine touch (touching themselves and others preciously) and the ritualization of subordination (infantilizing bodily gestures such as head and body cant). The frames and cuts in "I'm No Angel" also employ objectifying and fetishizing extreme close-ups of women's eroticized headless body parts, which Kilbourne (2000/1979) argued, dehumanizes. As Goffman (1976) observed, such advertising images should, but do not, seem ludicrous to us; all we have to do is imagine such scenes in everyday life or performed by men to realize how unnatural they are. Thus even the professionals responsible for producing such gender conventions seem unable to recognize them as such.

Challenging Gendered Social Norms

Participants also discussed advertisements that they believed challenged wider gender discourses. One example discussed by several participants was the Always feminine hygiene products' "Like a Girl" campaign, which includes a multiracial cast of adults, teens, and children. Focusing on preadolescent girls poised to begin menstruating, and thus buy and use Always products, an Always commercial video opens on a behind-the-camera director asking "real" women and men in a studio to act out what it means to "run like a girl" and "throw like a girl." The adults act out nonathletic and overly frivolous running and throwing motions. Next, a ten-year-old girl is asked the same question. She proceeds to provide a serious effort to run and throw to the best of her athletic abilities. The commercial ends by pointing out that in society, it's typically an insult to do things "like a girl." The ad then says people should be proud to act "like a girl." The tagline of the campaign is "rewrite the rules," presumably about girlhood and by extension womanhood.

A woman graphic designer said the Always ad demonstrated and challenged "how people perceive women." She said the ad critiqued the traditional image of a girl as "weak" and the "negative connotation" of "throwing like a girl." She said the video "flipped that terminology on its head." An account executive felt that "throwing like a girl should be empowering now. It should create a strong image instead of a weak one." Among participants, there was an acknowledgment that girls' athletic abilities historically have been positioned as weak, but that the present social moment demands a new interpretation. A male associate creative director felt the Always campaign challenged "this cultural notion or cultural insight, of why do you use this language" of "like a girl." In this way, practitioners, women and men, said they believed that the Always campaign genuinely aimed to update the language that denigrates girls' and women's sports competence.

It is worth mentioning that Always is not a product line for athletes or athletics. Nor did participant discussion of the Always campaign recognize either this fact or the fact that the Always product line *is* for feminine hygiene (i.e., menstruation). In fact, Always is a highly gendered product line intended for a gendered bodily function, which is discursively taboo. The Always "Like a Girl" campaign, however, comes across more like a public service announcement for boosting adolescent girls' athletic self-esteem than a sales message for pantiliners and tampons. Participant practitioners never mentioned this slippage. Similarly, the Dove and Lane Bryant campaigns communicate less about products—soaps and underwear—than prescriptions for how women should think about their bodies.

Referencing another brand, which is precisely about athletics, a woman account executive discussed the Under Armour commercial featuring ballet dancer Misty Copeland. In the commercial, a young voiceover reads snippets from ballet academy letters rejecting Copeland as an adolescent student because she lacked the correct body to be a ballerina: wrong feet, Achilles tendons, body type, and torso length. The commercial's visuals show Copeland, a woman of color, succeeding as a prima ballerina, along with the tagline "I will what I want." Once again, a participant advertising practitioner recalled a commercial that questioned narrow definitions of body type. The account executive felt the ad said: "Look what I am. Don't define me by your standards." As with the other exemplars for women audiences, in the Under Armour case, the participant did not reference Under Armour's product line, "workout clothes, shoes, and gear for women," according to the company website, which might be because the Misty Copeland ad did not advertise workout clothes, shoes, or gear for women, but rather focused on embodiment for a ballerina.

The traditional ballerina princess has been a pink-aisle fantasy marketed to little girls for decades as the epitome of feminine form. In the Under Armour ad, it is possible to read Copeland's black body, initially positioned as the wrong kind of body for a ballerina, as nonetheless being recuperated and, in the end, restricted back into the regressive feminine ballerina princess *en pointe*. In other words, in the Under Armour ad, is Copeland expanding and opening up the gender norm of the pink ballerina? Or is the gender norm of the pink ballerina containing the potentially subversive gender message that Copeland's "wrong" body communicates about women and gender? Visual analogies are open-ended in ways the syntax of verbal analogies are not, and that ambiguity of direction in visual analogy is precisely what makes them valuable in advertising creative departments.

Additionally, since Title IX of the Civil Rights Act in 1972, athletics for women institutionally, culturally, and commercially has emphasized "working out," a mostly individual effort, to achieve and maintain feminine beauty, including smaller body size in the form of weight loss. Functioning to ensure the gender binary, athletics for girls and women is constructed in opposition to athletics for men, which emphasizes "sports," including teamwork, increased body size, strength and stamina, and personal achievement through competition. For example, Under Armour for men is a product line of "workout clothes, gym and athletic wear for men," representing a small but telling rhetorical difference that denotes the "gym" and the "athletic" for men, compared with Under Armour's "workout clothes, shoes, and gear for women."

Finally, a male executive creative director believed the Nike ads with Serena Williams represented a site of struggle to expand athleticism to women. For him, the ads featured Serena Williams in a typically masculine role. He said the ads communicated, "You like to sweat; you are allowed to have visible muscles; you're allowed to grunt; you're allowed to be angry when you lose; and it's as gender-neutralized I think as we're capable of right now." This executive creative director's best advertising example for women "allowed" women to be like men. He said, "If I close my eyes, I think it's a guy." This description had a woman athlete taking on masculine characteristics. Thus, rather than reacting against the norms of typical advertising campaigns for women, as was the case for Dove and Lane Bryant, this advertisement portrays a woman who takes on social characteristics typically reserved for men. This participant's assessment of the advertisement drew on the discourse of traditional masculinity, yet it applied that masculinity to a woman athlete, perhaps the most celebrated woman athlete of all time. So Nike's "gender-neutralized" commercial actually privileges the masculine, while the creative professional who recalled the commercial revealed his assumption that masculinity is the dominant natural state. The executive creative director noted that Serena Williams's actions "not too long ago [were] disapproved of by some." This points to a socially and historically situated disapproval of women acting in a manner associated with dominance, which is seen as the prerogative of men, especially in sports. Moreover, much of the disapproval that the Williams sisters have endured, despite their elite athletic prowess, has been thinly veiled classist racism aimed at protecting tennis conventions of a white, upper-class, heteronormative femininity that the Williams' powerful brown bodies transgress. Indeed, this was the very racism that the Misty Copeland Under Armour ad critiqued, at least denotatively, by celebrating an African-American ballerina. What is more, assessing Serena Williams as a strong, perspiring athlete came uncomfortably close to the "strong black woman" trope (Harris-Perry 2011), a contemporary descendent of stereotypes about the physical endurance of African-American slave women. None of the white participants in this study contextualized their understanding of gender in terms of race, including whiteness.

These ads that participants named and the discourses surrounding them revealed how femininity has been historically and contextually situated within advertising, which both mirrors and drives the society it serves. Words take on meaning through conventions of use. The advertisements cited as effective for communicating with women were thought to challenge narrow definitions of women's worth that typically revolve around skin, youth, and body shape—in other words, white, heteronormative sex appeal. The advertisements that participants named in this thematic category were thought to reframe women as strong, powerful, and overcoming adversity. However, women's body politics remain intact across the exemplar ads because women are still defined by their bodies and to-be-looked-at-ness. The Under Armour and Nike advertisements presented women as active, self-interested, and self-assured. So it becomes clearer why the participant practitioners believed the love-your-body discourse works so well. Through these examples, one is taught what women are presumed to be "fighting against." According to the participants, women are fighting against stringent standards of what it means to be a woman. Women are fighting against unrealistic ideals of the slender feminine body types that are acceptable, even for tennis players or ballerinas, despite the fact that muscular bodies are appropriate for professional athletes and dancers. Participants spoke as if women in general—the presumed target audiences of the ads they described—are fighting against being seen as weak, especially compared with men. However, all of the ads in similar ways make individual women's bodies sites of struggle, rather than identifying the social institutions such as advertising that control gender discourse.

The Under Armour ad with Misty Copeland, a woman of color, tells women to embrace a passionate pursuit of personal bests, even if circumstances or others stand in their way. The Nike ad with Serena Williams, a woman of color, allows women to be masculine. The girls in "Throw Like a Girl" also include a greater number of nonwhite actors than are usually found in advertising. The advertisements showcase women who persisted and prevailed. The ads tell women to believe in themselves even when others don't; hold up women of color as examples of how to do femininity "differently"; and expand the modes of femininity available to women to include strength, power, and resilience.

Although the ads for women that participants discussed seemed to advance a quasifeminist agenda, the gender discourses they drew from perpetuate the idea that women are defined by their bodies, which should be beautiful, however beauty is redefined and regardless of age, size, or race. What is more, the exemplars characterize women's bodies as lifelong, individualized projects to be worked on by way of consuming brands. Thus this gender discourse revealed itself as bootstrapping neoliberal capitalism by constructing ideal gendered selves as self-motivated, self-policing bodies. In this discourse, one is entirely responsible for her own success or failure. So it is not surprising that the advertising professionals in the present study drew on but never recognized this discourse because it is merely commonsense to their careers in advertising. At the same time, participants' choices of branded ads that address women consumers effectively relied on messages that, for the most part, never advertised products. Instead these commercial messages sold highly gendered scripts for women's bodies.

THEMES FOR ADS THAT COMMUNICATE WITH MEN

When selecting advertisements that communicate well with men, practitioners—women and men—did not choose advertisements that challenge gender regarding manhood and masculinity. Instead, the ads that participants believed communicate with men emphasized the kind of traditional gender roles that these same participants believed to be challenged in ads communicating effectively with women. Participant practitioners believed that men as consumers desire a feeling of power or control over their own destinies. In thinking about effective advertising for men as target audiences, participants liked brands associated with masculinity, responded to masculine authority figures or celebrities, and preferred over-the-top humor.

(Restoring) Power and Control

Participant practitioners said that ads that sold well to men made men feel powerful and strong. They described advertisements that showcased men who were successful, confident, capable, and in charge. The ads in this theme played on a desire to feel "powerful" and "in control" in the face of unacknowledged threats to traditional masculinity.

This theme is evident in a description of a hot dog commercial discussed by a female vice president of strategy. She found through research that campfires and the culture of outdoor grilling were "sacred grounds for men." She said that grilling hot dogs "reinforces the feeling that, 'Yeah I'm in control. I'm a guy, and I can do this. And this is my memory of my dad.'" According to the participant, this gendered insight informs the campaign, which emphasizes eating "like a man" as opposed to shopping *like a girl.* The ad opens with a man sitting on a sofa near a dressing room in the mall. The man is holding a woman's purse. "And he was just sort of sitting there, looking humiliated, with her purse. And so a voiceover was like, 'You may have to do a lot of things, but at least you can eat like a man.'" According to the ad, grilling and eating hotdogs gives men control, which is contrasted against a situation in which a man had ceded control to a woman, who, significantly, is not winning tennis matches, for example, but shopping for clothing, a femininely gendered activity.

The words the participant used to describe the hot dog experience included "meat and men" as a "sacred ground." Through consuming hot dogs, presented as a manly food, men are assuming control over their own routines, their own weekends, their own lives. The humor of the storytelling deflects an underlying message of the ad, which is that men need to take back something already lost. Connoted is a message about who has taken the power away: women. Further, positioning subservience to women as a loss suggests that men's dominance is the natural order (Hooper 2001). Manly consumption—both buying and eating—is positioned as a way to regain power, in the hotdog ad's case, *from women.*

In another example, a male agency partner who was a white Baby Boomer discussed a Viagra advertisement as an example that effectively communicates with men in their fifties and sixties, a time when men can perceive diminishing sexual as well as social power as they face retirement. The participant referred to a Viagra ad that featured a white man repairing his car and fixing his sailboat. In each of the visuals, the man solves his own problems, independently. The participant said Boomer men like to make their own choices and don't like being told what to do. He felt the ad communicates, "You're a problem solver; you know, you've got a wealth of experience." He continued: "They like to be addressed in that tone. They don't like to be patronized. They like to be spoken to as intelligent, functioning, and not blown any kind of smoke at. So you look for images that show you're somebody who's, 'Yeah that's me' or 'I want to be like that.'"

The pharmaceutical Viagra represents an instance in which masculinity might particularly be on a man's mind because it is related to sexual performance. At the same time, the Viagra ads that the participant noted do not feature women, and thus might be interpreted as targeting either straight or gay men. The agency partner felt that the Viagra ad showed a man who was confident, active, self-sufficient, and in control of his own life, all semantically related to men or the masculine (Fischer and Bristor 1994). The participant's reference to the Viagra advertising men as demonstrating competence, experience, and problem-solving abilities corresponds to Schroeder and Zwick's (2004) description of traditional white masculinity tied to men who are active and self-assured decision-makers. Such characteristics of masculinity accrue to the gender privilege of white men, even gay white men if they can pass as straight (Stamps and Golombisky 2013). Men are sexy by what they do; women are sexy by how they look.

Selling Masculinity

Similar to the theme of power and control, participants tended to describe masculinity as a selling feature in advertising to men. Participants, women and men, used words such as *macho* and *manly* when describing why a particular ad communicated with men. For example, a male creative director discussed why he believed Porsche advertising resonated with men: "Porsche has always done a pretty good job of speaking to men. A rite of macho passage. A testosterone-driven performance vibe." *Macho* is a word associated with noticeable or exaggerated masculinity and testosterone is sometimes assumed to be a hormone exclusive to men. Both machismo and testosterone were thought to be selling features used by Porsche advertising.

Participants further described brands that used masculine celebrities and authority figures to represent and emphasize traditional masculinity. Participants also referred to the masculinity of the authority figures used in advertising as reasons why campaigns were successful in their attempt to persuade men. An example came from a woman account director who talked about a campaign for the power company to promote safety around power lines. The campaign portrayed the linemen who work with the power cables as masculine authority figures warning citizens, possibly do-it-yourselfer men with chainsaws who might be tempted to remove debris around downed power lines after severe weather. "If I try to put myself in a guy situation, these are guys [linemen] who come across as authoritative to me," said the account director. The lineman in the commercial said: "I work with this every day, and I'm going to tell you flat-out that you will be dead. You will be dead if you touch this stuff. Do not!" She continued, "So it was just very direct, and it was very much big manly men who were speaking to them; and that has been, I think, an effective campaign for men." Trying to empathize with her target audience, the account director thought about who would be "authoritative" to the target audience of men who felt they were "awesome with a power saw." Thus a credible authority on the matter, the lineman, was employed. The participant said linemen were authoritative because they are "big, manly men." Here physical stature—large, burly men—and forthrightness served as a proxy for expertise and authority. The rationale suggested that this masculinity was a reason men should listen to and be persuaded by the message. In this instance, manly men as physically active, skilled, blue-collar labor come across as more "manly" than, for example, a white-collar power company executive or even public communication officer (statistically likely to be a woman). Furthermore, the manly man lineman's masculine authority among men is communicated by embodied physicality, instead of cerebral repartee or argumentation.

Celebrities and athletes also were cited as effective in advertising that must convey masculine credibility. A woman strategist felt an effective ad for men was the Dove for Men campaign that used professional baseball player Albert Pujols. The practitioner believed Dove was unique in that it was typically branded for women. "And then they introduced a men's product. What they did was they promoted it through celebrity endorsement of sports figures who were using their product." She felt men might think it was inappropriate, unmanly, to use Dove, historically a brand for women. So, she imagined, Dove "used macho dudes, sports figures like Albert Pujols and people, using their men's products. And, kind of making it cool to dig skincare." She felt the credible sports figure would persuade men. "And so, once men saw that, 'Okay, well, this big tough guy can do it, I should care about my skin, too.'" She continued, "They made it cool and acceptable for men to care about their skin." Here, the practitioner believed Dove for Men associated its brand with machismo and coolness to overcome Dove's association with women, because only women care about their skin as a feminine function of beauty. Moreover, there is the implication that products become gendered in association with their uses and users, even if the product has no intrinsic quality of gender.

The Dove campaign for men mentioned by this participant featured athletes of color against backdrops of family life with wife and children. Several points are worth noting here then. First, the campaign's tagline, "Journey to comfort," communicated that using Dove for men products literally makes their users more comfortable in their own skin. However, men of color communicating that they are comfortable in their own skins takes on racial implications here. Second, at another level of consumer insight, Unilever targeted an older man in his thirties "who's reached a point in his life when he's very comfortable with who he is as a man" (Newman 2011). Regarding homophobia, such a claim leaves sexuality open to interpretation. The athlete's family in the commercial functions to signal heterosexuality in a "metrosexual" consumer advertising context where, as Stamps and Golombisky (2013) argue, using a feminized or effeminate product might be construed as otherwise. Third, like the blue-collar linemen, athletes of color who earn a living with their bodies, make for another uncomfortable logic by extension that positions being white, then, with white-collar work and the cerebral.

The campaigns discussed in the "selling masculinity" category drew on symbolic meanings by using masculine figures, and participant practitioners did not appear to realize or question race, gender, class, and sexuality discourses or the power relations inherent in them. Nor did they notice a contradiction between ads that encourage women to tear down gendered double standards for women and those that reinforce the gendered double standard that encourages men to embody and enact their male privilege. Instead, participants' emphasis was on the pragmatics of communicating effectively with men, presumably white, heterosexual, cisgendered men because neither race nor sexuality, let alone gender identity and gender expression, was discussed.

Over-the-Top Humor

Humor was another feature of the exemplar advertisements believed to communicate effectively with men. However, power and masculinity often crept into the descriptions of the humor and why it worked. For example, a male CEO categorized this kind of humor as the "over-the-top dude kind of bro stuff" that appears on *Monday Night Football,* yet another reference to the sports arena where women challenge and men reinforce gender norms.

Bringing up yet another exemplar reverting to white, male privilege, a male executive creative director felt the Dollar Shave Club did a good job of communicating with "a certain segment of men." "They also don't take themselves too seriously. It's kind of a manly product, and they're making you feel smart for using it." In this case, the Dollar Shave Club relies on that white, white-collar, thinking-man's masculinity in its use of exaggerated humor. In one of the company's viral commercials, "Our Blades are F***ing Great," "Mike," the young, white "founder of DollarShaveClub.com" not only wears a shirt and tie, but also infantilizes a young, brown-skinned, formerly unemployed employee named "Alejandro," who owes his factory job to Mike's business acumen and the Dollar Shave Club's success among consumers. This kind of manly humor assumes the privilege of not taking one's self seriously because there is no risk that others, such as Alejandro, will not take him seriously. Mike and his target market can make fun of the consumer product accoutrements of personal-grooming masculinity, such as razors, while encouraging the target audience of men to continue consuming the very same product. It might be worthwhile to contrast this kind of manly humor to the seriousness with which women are encouraged to take their body work in women's advertising such as Dove, Lane Bryant, Always, Under Armour, and Nike, as well as love-your-body discourse in general.

Perhaps the most revealing example of why ads that showcase masculinity and over-the-top humor are thought to be successful came from a male creative director, who discussed the Axe Effect campaign, another Unilever product line, this time targeting younger men. In Axe commercials, the "Axe Effect" is that attractive young women can't help but throw themselves at young men who wear Axe. Women in the ads are made helpless by the effect of the product on the Axe's wearer's heterosexual attractiveness. The creative director said, "Axe did an admirable job talking to teenage males, very well executed." He felt Axe exaggerated the benefits of using the product: "It managed to wink at, broadly enough that even teenage boys would get it, the power of the magical sauce." This participant said, "It was unapologetically, unashamedly sexist and brutal in its way, with a big wink—that we are just kidding . . . aren't we? They carried it off well. It appealed to that audience."

"Just kidding," nonetheless, can be a disguise for "not kidding at all" among what has been described as the metrosexual consumer, young men who are concerned about sex appeal through consumption and perhaps are not as confident in their sexual performance. Stamps and Golombisky (2013, 4–5) write, "At the same time, deploying sexist heteronormative gender, sexuality, and sex with humor and irony in men's media . . . disguises a resurgence of regressive forms of masculinity and sexism as 'just kidding' to short-circuit charges of misogyny and homophobia" (Benwell, 2004; Lindgren and LeLievre, 2009; Wisneski, 2007).

Humorous ads often include "benign violations" of social and cultural norms (McGraw and Warren 2010) that include "play signals" that communicate that an ad is not to be taken seriously (McGhee 1979). A longitudinal content analysis of outdoor advertisements revealed that in the last two decades, "more aggressive, slapstick, tendentious nonsense humor emerged" more frequently, alongside trends for advertisements with more aggression, sexual themes, and vulgarity (Weinberger, Gulas, and Weinberger 2015, 467). Through examples such as the Axe Effect campaign and the Dollar Shave Club, we can see that, although over-the-top humor is revered, it is often connected with regressive, even misogynist, masculinity that seems to be shoring itself up in the face of a changing social discourse that makes racism, sexism, and homophobia unacceptable. The ad humor isn't just over the top; it's over the top for "dudes" and "bros." It is not an accident that such an ironic hipster humor sensibility targets the very demographic that produces most advertising creatives—young urban metrosexual men. A woman senior account executive called the humor of Axe and its ilk "man cave boy stuff," but she thought it was effective. The Axe ad is exaggerated, but it exaggerates its benefits in a way that is "unashamedly sexist."

Even though the Axe campaign was described as "unashamedly sexist," it escaped the kind of ridicule typically associated with sexist advertising campaigns. The very fact that the ads were clearly and self-consciously exaggerated (Hooper 2001), that they included a "big wink," resulted in acceptance of the messages and a big sales boost for the brand. "As readers, if we are willing to accept the exaggerated realist conventions at face value, and are prepared to take on board the heavily signaled masculinity without even noticing it, then so much the better, as it is the naturalization of gender that gives it a great deal of its force" (Hooper 2001, 137). If by chance one chooses to object to the "unashamedly sexist" humor, one risks charges of lacking a sense of humor and being unable to take a joke, which are stereotypically associated with feminists and "political correctness" police (Golombisky, 1999).

CONCLUSION

Among advertising practitioners interviewed here, traditional ideas about heteronormative masculinity were revered in the advertisements assumed to communicate effectively with men. Participant practitioners' ideas about "exemplary" advertising for men employed themes of (restoring) power and control over one's life, selling masculinity via macho authority figures and manly men, and using "dude" and "bro" humor to get away with sexism, racism, and homophobia. Participant practitioners' ideas about "exemplary" advertising for women admonished women to love their imperfect bodies, to think of themselves as sexy even if they are "no angel" by Victoria's Secret standards, and to regard being "like a girl" as a strength. Participants interpreted all their preferred ads for women as meant for women to fight for their rights to expand definitions of feminine bodies.

Yet both genders of advertising professionals failed to notice the contradictions between, for one thing, so-called effective advertising that glorified men's greater power than women's and advertising that encourages women to fight for their rights. For another thing, so-called effective—feminist even—ads for women were those that equated women with a pleasing appearance, however broadly *pleasing* was defined, and so "fighting" for one's rights becomes synonymous with accepting the status quo. "Like a girl" not only infantilized but also gendered specific ways of being that reinforced the illusion of two genders that have significant irreconcilable differences. At the same time, participants might as well have framed their discussions of effective campaigns for men in terms of a public cultural pedagogy that taught the other gender how to behave "like a man."

Thus practitioners assumed that men respond to ads that sell masculinity, whereas women respond to ads that challenge stereotypical femininity. According to the advertising professionals interviewed, men find success in regaining or maintaining their power and status, and women find success in opposing and expanding the limits of feminine embodiment. Viewed from the perspective of power relations, it only makes sense that to create advertising that resonates with audiences who have power, advertisers would reinforce that sense of power, or at least avoid threatening it. At the same time, advertising designed to resonate with audiences who lack power would resonate with messages that empower, or at least critique power. What happens, however, when embodied women who are challenging gender norms encounter physically powerful men empowered with authority to control their worlds? Stamps and Golombisky (2013, 21) argue, "The potential for abuse in promoting such a narrative should be apparent, even as we gloss over its daily manifestations in the flow of news about brutality, exploitation, neglect, and violence."

Practitioner participants saw improvement in the way that advertisers hail gendered audiences with gendered representations; they saw fewer negative stereotypes now than in the past. Participating practitioners saw a message of empowerment that resonates with women as consumers. Feminists, however, argue that the advertising industry appropriates "the language of empowerment and feminism" for the benefit of institutions (LaWare and Moutsatsos 2013, 190) and drains feminism of its values, meanings, and political content (Goldman 1992; Lazar 2006). In the end, the discourse of gender in advertising still creates a world in which men act and women appear.

REFERENCES

Advertising Redbooks. 2014. "Directory of Advertising Agencies." http://www.redbooks.com.

Benwell, Bethan. 2004. "Ironic Discourse: Evasive Masculinity in Men's Lifestyle Magazines." *Men and Masculinities* 7 (1): 3–21.

Berger, John. 1972. *Ways of Seeing*. London: BBC and Penguin.

Boosalis, Elizabeth, and Kim Golombisky. 2010. "Women's Interpretations of Music Videos Featuring Women Artists." *Journal of Research on Women and Gender* 1 (1): 22–44. https://journals.tdl.org/jrwg/index.php/jrwg/article/view/60.

Csikszentmihályi, Mihaly. 1999. "Implications of a Systems Perspective for the Study of Creativity." In *Handbook of Creativity,* edited by Robert J. Sternberg, 313–35. Cambridge, UK: Cambridge University Press.

Fischer, Eileen, and Julia Bristor. 1994. "A Feminist Poststructuralist Analysis of the Rhetoric of Marketing Relationships." *International Journal of Research in Marketing* 11 (4): 317–31.

Foucault, Michel. 1980. *Power/Knowledge,* Brighton: Harvester.

Giaccardi, Chiara. 1995. "Television Advertising and the Representation of Social Reality: A Comparative Study." *Theory, Culture and Society* 12 (February): 109–31.

Gill, Rosalind, and Ana Sofia Elias. 2014. "'Awaken Your Incredible': Love-Your-Body Discourses and Postfeminist Contradictions." *International Journal of Media and Cultural Politics* 10 (2): 179–88.

Goffman, Erving. 1976. "Gender Advertisements." *Studies in the Anthropology of Visual Communication* 3 (2): 69–154.

Goldman, Robert. 1992. *Reading Ads Socially*. New York: Routledge.

Golombisky, Kim. 1999. "Getting a Sense of Humor: On Sex Scandal and Women Joking in Journalism." Paper presented at the annual meeting of the Association for Education in Journalism and Mass Communication, New Orleans, LA, August.

Gregory, Michele R. 2009. "Inside the Locker Room: Male Homosociability in the Advertising Industry." *Gender, Work and Organization* 16 (3): 323–47.

Grow, Jean M., and Sheri J. Broyles. 2011. "Unspoken Rules of the Creative Game: Insights to Shape the Next Generation from Top Advertising Creative Women." *Advertising and Society Review* 12 (1). DOI: 10.1353/asr.2011.0009

Grow, Jean M., and Tao Deng. 2014. "Sex Segregation in Advertising Creative Departments Across the Globe." *Advertising and Society Review* 14 (4). DOI: 10.1353/asr.2014.0003.

Hall, Stuart. 1980. "Encoding/Decoding." In *Culture, Media, Language: Working Papers in Cultural Studies 1972–79,* edited by Stuart Hall, Dorothy Hobson, Andrew Lowe, and Paul Willis, 128–38. London: Hutchinson.

Harris-Perry, Melissa. 2011. *Sister Citizen: Shame, Stereotypes, and Black Women in America.* New Haven: Yale University Press.
Hooper, Charlotte. 2001. *Manly States: Masculinities, International Relations and Gender Politics.* New York, Columbia University Press.
Kelan, Elisabeth K. 2010. "Gender Logic and (Un)Doing Gender at Work." *Gender, Work and Organization* 17 (2): 174–94.
Kelly, Aidan, Katrina Lawlor, and Stephanie O'Donohoe. 2005. "Encoding Advertisements: The Creative Perspective." *Journal of Marketing Management* 21 (5–6): 505–28.
Kilbourne, Jean. 2000/1979. *Killing Us Softly: Advertising's Image of Women.* Northampton, Mass.: Cambridge Documentary Films.
LaWare, Margaret R., and Chrisy Moutsatsos. 2013. "'For Skin That's Us, Authentically Us': Celebrity, Empowerment and the Allure of Antiaging Advertisements." *Women's Studies in Communication* 36 (2): 189–208.
Lazar, Michelle M. 2006. "'Discover the Power of Femininity!' Analyzing Global 'Power Femininity' in Local Advertising." *Feminist Media Studies* 6 (4): 505–17.
Lindgren, Simon, and Maxime LeLievre. 2009. "In the Laboratory of Masculinity: Renegotiating Gender Subjectivities in MTV's 'Jackass.'" *Critical Studies in Media Communication* 26 (5): 393–410.
Mallia, Karen L. 2009. "Rare Birds: Why So Few Women Become Ad Agency Creative Directors." *Advertising and Society Review* 10 (3). doi:10.1353/asr.0.0032
McCracken, Grant. 1989. "Who Is the Celebrity Endorser? Cultural Foundations of the Endorsement Process." *Journal of Consumer Research* 16 (December): 310–21.
McGhee, Paul E. 1979. *Humor.* San Francisco: W. H. Freeman and Co.
McGraw, A. Peter, and Caleb Warren. 2010. "Benign Violations: Making Immoral Behavior Funny." *Psychological Science* 37 (8): 1141–49.
McLeod, Charlotte, Stephanie O'Donohoe, and Barbara Townley. 2011. "Pot Noodles, Placements and Peer Regard: Creative Career Trajectories and Communities of Practice in the British Advertising Industry." *British Journal of Management* 22 (1): 114–31.
Murray, Dara Persis. 2013. "Branding 'Real' Social Change in Dove's Campaign for Real Beauty." *Feminist Media Studies* 13 (1): 83–101.
Newman, Andrew Adam. 2011. "Dove Shows Athletes Off the Court." *New York Times,* March 6. http://www.nytimes.com/2011/03/07/business/media/07adco.html?_r=0.
Nixon, Sean. 2003. *Advertising Cultures.* London: Sage.
Schroeder, Jonathan E., and Detlev Zwick. 2004. "Mirrors of Masculinity: Representation and Identity in Advertising Images." *Consumption, Markets and Culture* 7 (1): 21–52.
Shao, Yun, Fabrice Desmarais, and C. Kay Weaver. 2014. "Chinese Advertising Practitioners' Conceptualisation of Gender Representation." *International Journal of Advertising* 33 (2): 329–50.
Stamps, Jennifer Ford, and Kim Golombisky. 2013. "Woman as Product Stand-in: Branding Straight Metrosexuality in Men's Magazine Fashion Advertising." *Journal of Research on Women and Gender* 6 (March): 1–29. http://jrwg.mcgs.txstate.edu/archives/TOC-2013-Spring-Vol/untitled.html.

Stuhlfaut, Mark W. 2011. "The Creative Code: An Organisational Influence on the Creative Process in Advertising." *International Journal of Advertising* 30 (2): 283–304.

Tsai, Wan-Hsui Sunny. 2010. "Assimilating the Queers: Representations of Lesbians, Gay Men, Bisexual, and Transgender People in Mainstream Advertising." *Advertising and Society Review* 11. DOI: 10.1353/asr.0.0042.

van Zoonen, Liesbet. 1994. *Feminist Media Studies.* London: Sage.

Weedon, Chris 1997. *Feminist Practice and Poststructuralist Theory,* 2nd ed. Cambridge, MA: Blackwell.

Weinberger, Marc G., Charles S. Gulas, and Michelle F. Weinberger. 2015. "Looking in through Outdoor: A Socio-Cultural and Historical Perspective on the Evolution of Advertising Humour." *International Journal of Advertising* 34 (3): 447–72.

Windels, Kasey. 2016. "Stereotypical or Just Typical: How Do US Practitioners View the Role and Function of Gender Stereotypes in Advertisements?" *International Journal of Advertising* 35 (5): 864–87.

Windels, Kasey, and Wei-Na Lee. 2012. "The Construction of Gender and Creativity in Advertising Creative Departments." *Gender in Management: An International Journal* 27 (8): 502–19.

Windels, Kasey, and Karen L. Mallia. 2015. "How Being Female Impacts Learning and Career Growth in Advertising Creative Departments." *Employee Relations* 37 (1): 122–40.

Wisneski, Kirsten. 2007. "Maximizing Masculinity: a Textual Analysis of *Maxim* Magazine." Master's thesis, University of Massachusetts, Amherst, MA.

Zayer, Linda T., and Catherine A. Coleman. 2014. "Advertising Professionals' Perceptions of the Impact of Gender Portrayals on Men and Women: A Question of Ethics?" *Journal of Advertising* 44 (3): 1–12.

Chapter 8

The Creative Career Dilemma

No Wonder Ad Women Are Mad Women

Karen L. Mallia

Twenty years ago, trade press headlines noted, "Women Target Boys Club of Ad Creative" (Cuneo and Petrecca 1997), and asked, "So What's with the Dearth, Still, of Women Creatives?" (Kestin 1998). Ten years later, another *Advertising Age* headline asked, "Where Are All the Women in this Biz?" (Olson 2007). Such headlines are as apropos today as when they were written. Although shiny Macs and open seating may have replaced IBM Selectric typewriters and offices with doors, the advertising creative department remains the playground of privileged young men, just as Weisberg and Robbs (1997b) wrote for *Advertising Age* 20 years ago: "Creative Department Still Boys' Playground."

An irrefutable and tenacious diversity problem persists in agency creative departments across the globe, especially in senior leadership (Boulton 2013; Grow and Deng 2014; Grow, Roca, and Broyles 2012; Mallia 2008, 2009b; Mallia and Windels 2011; Martín Llaguno 2007; Pueyo Ayhan 2010; Weisberg and Robbs 1997a; Windels 2011; Windels, Mallia, and Broyles 2013). Despite feminist protest, equal rights and equal pay legislation, and class-action lawsuits, women remain underrepresented in creative positions such as copywriters, art directors, and creative directors (CDs)—in an industry where women constitute half the overall workforce (Grow and Deng 2014; Klein 2000; Mallia 2009a; Mallia and Windels 2015; Windels, Lee, and Yeh 2010). An ever-growing majority of women graduate from college and university advertising programs (National Center for Education Statistics 2012), and fairly even numbers of women and men finish portfolio schools (Mallia 2009a). Yet the number of women creatives in the United States today is actually *smaller* than it was a decade ago (Grow and Deng 2014). The ad industry loses talented, experienced, creative women almost as rapidly as ambitious new ones enter the business, accounting for this net zero. Like women in journalism, tech, and other male-dominated industries, numerous creative women exit advertising before achieving leadership positions—leaving women perpetually shy of the critical mass or proportional representation needed to effect systemic change (Dahlerup 2006; Kanter 1977).

In the past two decades, a stream of research on women and advertising creative departments has emerged that suggests that barriers to diversity and creative leadership persist, that they are global in scope, and that the only contributing factors that can be ruled out are a lack of ambition and creative talent among women. This research identifies numerous factors at play, among them effects of the dominant masculine culture in creative departments, unconscious biases, perceptions of gender stereotyping, negative effects of minority status and under-representation of women's creativity, and systemic factors that make work–life balance for *all* creative people nearly impossible.

The advertising business is notorious for its lack of diversity and has been the subject of litigation and Equal Employment Opportunity Commission investigation in the United States (Bendick and Egan 2009; Bruell 2015; Rossini v Ogilvy and Mather 1978). Regardless of their ethnicity, 89 percent of ad professionals agree that diversity needs improvement (Watson 2011). Industry trade groups, such as the American Advertising Federation (AAF) and the American Association of Advertising Agencies (4A's), have decades-old programs as well as newer ones designed to connect the very best minority graduates with advertising agencies, such as the AAF Most Promising Multicultural Student program and 4A's Multicultural Advertising Internship Program. These have helped minority recruitment and hiring ("About Us" 2016; "Education Services" 2016). Yet, just as women of all races and ethnicities do, racial and ethnic minorities of all genders exhibit high attrition, leaving advertising for other pursuits (Mallia 2009b; Target Market News 2012). African Americans and Hispanics are more likely than whites to cite the lack of diversity in the industry as a reason for leaving, illustrating the unease of being an outsider in this business (Target Market News 2012). Across the creative industries, both women and racial and ethnic minorities experienced a disproportionate decline during the economic fallout following the 2008 recession (Conor, Gill, and Taylor 2015).

When Jane Maas, a former president and CD of Earle Palmer Brown, launched *Mad Women: The Other Side of Life on Madison Avenue in the 1960s* with a fifty-four-city book tour in 2012, everywhere she went she heard women saying exactly what they had said sixty years earlier (Mallia et al. 2012; Jane Maas, pers. comm.). That is hardly surprising. Until recently, little industry or academy attention was given to the status of women in advertising leadership, or the curious anomaly that the proportion of women in creative departments is far lower than it is in other agency departments (Mallia 2008). Other than anecdotal reports, there was no real evidence to support the existence of a problem. Today, that is no longer the case.

In this chapter, I first review contemporary research on women as advertising creatives, including my own work and that of others who have tackled this understudied area. Next, I offer some reasons why women remain underrepresented in ad creative departments, including deliberate and unconscious biases, systemic factors such as industry practices that disadvantage women creatives, and the characteristics of creative work. I write as a "second-career" academic who has been mystified by the gender divide in the creative department I experienced firsthand for more than twenty years. My academic research agenda was launched in 2005 by the outrageous sexist comments of an internationally recognized global creative chief who ignited a media firestorm (Bosman 2005; Cadwalladr 2005; Mallia 2008). Although the "boys' club" was widely recognized, no one had ever explained *why* advertising creative departments lagged the rest of the business world in diversity, while we were seeing modest gains in women's leadership globally. I wanted to know why. My goal is to help explain—and solve—the creative woman's unusual dilemma by bringing the perspective of a seasoned practitioner to scholarship—important when business realities and ethics are often at odds.

IN ADLAND, IT'S *REALLY* COMPLICATED

Although shared by many creative industries, the culture, codes, and practices of the advertising industry are unlike those found in more traditional businesses. Thus it is important to understand the character of the industry before exploring the role of women in it. Ad legend Jerry Della Femina famously described the advertising business as "the most fun you can have with your clothes on" (Della Femina and Sopkin 1970). Working in the ad business is fun, stimulating, and possesses the glamour of cultural production. It is also highly competitive, fast-paced, and rapidly, constantly changing. It is client and deadline driven. Its long hours are fabled, and they have become worse with 24/7 connectivity and escalating client demands.

And then there's the advertising creative department.

Here, you find skateboards, Ping-Pong, foosball tables, drums, electronic games, beer-filled refrigerators, and espresso machines. The place is typically a ghost town early in the morning, a hotbed of activity after dark. The advertising creative department is recognized as a distinct subculture even within the larger agency culture, and this creative culture is similar from agency to agency and country to country. Therefore, in addition to encountering gender stereotypes and universal barriers to women's success, ad women confront additional dynamics that make creative careers more complex and problematic. These dynamics are found in three areas: the distinctive nature of doing creative work and working in creative industries, the traits of people who gravitate to the creative industries, and the work practices and cultural codes peculiar to the advertising industry.

Creative People Are Different. Creative Work Is, Too.

Researchers have discovered that, indeed, there *is* a creative personality. Since it was described by Guilford (1970), a stream of research has followed, identifying distinct characteristics and behaviors associated with creative personalities (Csikszentmihályi 1988, 1996; Guilford 1970; Runco 2007; Sternberg 2006; West 1993). Creative people are intrinsically motivated, capable of being wholly consumed in their work, described as "flow" by Csikszentmihályi (1988), and often perfectionists. Creative personalities can also include traits such as curiosity, openness to experience, autonomy, attraction to complexity, androgyny in thinking, emotional sensitivity, playfulness, risk taking, and great personal energy. The possession of creative personality traits helps explain how so many strong creative women have defied the odds in advertising, especially androgyny in thinking, attraction to complexity, and resilience.

Although it is interesting, fun, and personally rewarding, doing creative work is hard. One of the most successful creative women in advertising, Susan Credle, chief creative officer of BBDO New York, once told me, "Creative isn't just a job, it's a way of life. The reality: This job is really, really hard. Grueling. Consuming." She identifies characteristics inherent in creative work that make work–life balance more challenging than in other fields, and disproportionately affect those with family responsibilities. First, the creative process is an iterative one, and the brain doesn't always deliver ideas predictably (Amabile et al. 1996; Guilford 1970; Lubart 1994; Osborn 1957; Van der Pool 2002; Wallas 1926). Further, time spent generating ideas doesn't always yield presentation-worthy concepts within the business day—meaning, first, that creatives are "always on," and, second, creatives don't stop working until they've got something great—or the clock runs out. The intense, unpredictable nature of creative work is among the reasons many creative women cite for going freelance or leaving the industry after having children; others say that the job is only sustainable with a partner or nanny at home (Mallia 2009b). It is why Credle, one of a handful of women to make it to the chief creative officer pinnacle, says she "never got around to having kids" (Susan Credle pers. comm.).

Welcome to the "Boys' Club": Creative Culture 101

The masculine culture of the advertising creative department is well known and is widely described as the boys' club or the locker room (Alvesson 1998; Gregory 2009). This culture is extremely competitive and recognizable in the language that reinforces masculinity: Teams compete for an assignment in "gang bangs"; project rooms are dubbed "war rooms." In fact, just using the language of rape, as in "gang bangs," goes beyond merely offensive to constitute hostile environment sexual harassment, an illegal and thus actionable offense under Title VII employment law.

For those who work there, the atmosphere in the creative department is spirited and open. That is both a byproduct of the personality of creatives and a requisite environment for creativity (Amabile et al. 1996; Csikszentmihályi 1988; Ewing, Napoli, and West 2001; Hirschman 1989; Kover 1995). In the creative "locker room," conversation and behavior can range from playful to ribald. A Chicago woman copywriter said:

> I get told that I'm "like one of the guys." I roll with the punches and can dish it out as well as the best of them. . . . Of course, what goes along with this is hearing the stuff they would only say in front of "the guys." This can include sexual comments (favorable or unfavorable) about female co-workers, extremely lewd jokes, and harsh critiques of female superiors. (Anonymous pers. comm.)

This sexual language not only mirrors men's use of language meant to denigrate women but also might be construed to constitute hostile environment sexual harassment should anyone care to press the point.

The Chicago copywriter's story is PG-rated compared with others I have heard. Anyone who has not worked in an advertising agency can scarcely imagine the tenor of most creative departments. Literally *anything* goes. With few filters or constraints, some men go too far. In 2012, *Digiday* published an anonymous "Confessions of a Female Ad Exec" (2012), in which an anonymous author reflected on why the industry continued to struggle with gender diversity. Following an unprecedented social media response, *Digiday* republished the essay with a paragraph the editor had originally deleted, and identified the author as Colleen DeCourcy, now global chief creative officer at Wieden and Kennedy. These are her deleted words:

> There are, of course, crudely sexist moments. Here are two special quotes from my career that never fail to materialize when I close my eyes to fall asleep in whatever far-flung hotel I'm sleeping in tonight. "I like that necklace, I could choke you with it while I fuck you from behind," I was told. After a none-too-pleased response came the capper from this guy: "You're not offended are you?! We only say those things because we forget you're not one of us. It's a compliment!" (Edwards 2012)

Think there's a problem here beyond the obvious hostile environment? Let's review what research tells us.

WHAT THE RESEARCH TELLS US

Research exploring the dearth of women in creative departments has been hampered by lack of industry or government data identifying gender and positions or salaries, and a resultant lack of quantitative research. Finally, the number of women working in advertising creative departments has been calculated: Women are 20.3 percent of advertising creatives, and only 14.6 percent of the CDs, according to data gathered from fifty countries in the *Standard Directory of Advertising Agencies,* the agency "Redbook" (Grow and Deng 2014). CDs are experienced copywriters or art directors who have been promoted to supervise creative teams in advertising creative departments. Other research measuring the achievement of women suggests the proportion of female CDs is lower, 9 percent (Mallia and Windels 2015) or 11 percent ("History and Highlights" 2015). The Redbook is a useful tool for global studies, but the data include primarily large agencies. A recent examination of Advertising Halls of Fame shows that women represent only 11 percent of One Club Hall of Famers, 12 percent of those in the Art Directors Club, and 8.6 percent of AAF Hall of Fame members (Mallia and Windels 2015). Among the advertising creative elite, women are scarce.

Thus, although women control 85 percent of consumer spending and more than 20 trillion consumer dollars worldwide (Fiddner 2015), women do not control the majority of the messages being crafted in advertising creative departments. They cannot (Burke and McKeen 1996; Ely 1994; Ibarra 1992; Kanter 1977). Kanter's (1977) theory of proportional representation holds that a group cannot exert pressure on the dominant culture until it reaches at least 35 percent, or proportional representation. With representation of less than 15 percent, or tokenism, comes a host of negative consequences for minority groups (Kanter 1977). Although women constitute about half the total advertising workforce, they are predominantly found in the lower ranks across all departments (Grow and Deng 2014) and are unable to exert influence because of their minority representation and low status. Women creatives face both horizontal and vertical segregation, experiencing a glass ceiling as well as a glass wall, blocked from leadership and access to lateral opportunities (Grow and Deng 2014; Martin Llaguno 2007).

The cultural, systemic, and psychological barriers confronting women in most agency creative departments have changed little since the *Mad Men* era (Grow and Broyles 2011; Maas 2012; Mallia 2008, 2009b; Weisberg and Robbs 1997a; Windels and Lee 2012). Perhaps the most glaring and problematic of these barriers is the intensely competitive, hypermasculine culture that still pervades creative departments throughout the industry, and throughout the world (Alvesson 1998; Gregory 2009; Grow, Roca, and Broyles 2012; Klein 2000; Mallia 2014; Mallia and Windels 2015; Martín Llaguno 2007; Nixon 2003; Nixon and Crewe 2004; Pueyo Ayhan 2010; Williams, Muller, and Kilanski 2012; Windels 2011), with the exception of China (Mallia, unpublished data). In this kind of masculine environment, women are at a serious disadvantage and must work much harder to create and compete (Schwartz 2014; Windels 2011; Windels and Lee 2012). Environment is a key component affecting the creative process and creativity (Amabile et al. 1996; Csikszentmihályi 1988, 1996; Friedman and Forster 2001, 2005), as well as a factor in the career success of women (Gregory 2009; Kanter 1977; Nixon and Crewe 2004; Schwartz 2014; Tsui and Gutek 1984; Windels and Mallia 2015).

This masculine culture is sometimes evidenced in deliberate discrimination, such as gendering client assignments, giving creative women projects for feminine and baby products and men automotive and beverage brands (Grow, Roca, and Broyles 2012; Mallia 2008; Pueyo Ayhan 2010). Unconscious bias is at play when male CDs favor their "buddies" or favorite teams (most likely other men) with plum assignments and the kinds of brands more likely to win accolades (Mallia 2008, 2009b; Windels 2011). Men CDs judge subordinates' work through an enculturated bias favoring masculine humor, undermining the careers of women who fail to adopt that voice in their work and also influencing the nature of the work that ultimately gets produced. The predominance of men as judges of industry award shows is recognized to affect the type of work receiving international recognition ("Why Getting More Women" 2015), which in turn has a direct effect on the career trajectory of the individuals who created it (Mallia 2008, 2009b). This may also be why women consumers report that much advertising doesn't resonate with them (Vagnoni 2005; Van der Pool 2002).

Work Processes and Unwritten Codes

Masculine work processes and codes are deeply imbedded in creative departments, most notably in agencies that routinely pit creative teams against one another in internal competition for assignments, a practice that in and of itself disproportionately favors men (Schwartz 2014; Windels 2011; Windels and Lee 2012). Presenteeism, the mandate that one must be seen working in the office, remains the official agency work standard, and flexible arrangements are typically negotiated case by case rather than as standard practice (Mallia 2009b, 2014). This is a vestige of the dominant model of work, a model built on male standards and behaviors—one that is recognized to undermine the career success of women (Hewlett 2007). Yet when flexibility policies are implemented, they can and do work. Nancy Kestin and Janet Vonk took the job as co-CDs of Ogilvy Toronto as a team, which was not the way it was offered. They were responsible for a litany of award-winning and profitable work for their clients and the agency (Vonk and Kestin 2005). Still, agencies often cite the nature of client-service business needs, like tight deadlines and last-minute demands, as arguments against adopting formal flexible work policies.

Standard creative recruitment and hiring practices serve to sustain the status quo and impede diversity. Ibarra (1992) identified the implications of homophily in hiring, that is, hiring in one's own image. Hiring "someone I'd like to have a drink with" or someone who would "fit in here" continues to be cited as leading criteria for creative hires, right after a great portfolio (Mallia 2009b, 2014). The ephemeral nature of defining and measuring "great" among creative talent makes candidate evaluation inherently subjective; it also makes it nearly impossible to judge the fairness of hiring practices. Especially in middle- and higher-level positions, an influential personal network provides information and access to jobs. Men have the advantage here, as their networks tend to be more extensive and better developed as a result of controlling the agency structure and process that they invented for themselves.

The Codes of the Creative Department

Competitiveness is a defining characteristic of the creative personality and the creative department. Even with an outstanding portfolio, getting a creative advertising job is a keenly competitive process. Another contributor to the competitive climate comes from rivalry for ownership of a campaign, although many participate and collaborate in the process (Hackley 2003). Creative credit is important to career success, and it derives from internal acknowledgment of work and having authorship noted in industry award shows (Mallia 2008). Thus creative people routinely vie for prestige assignments and compete with their peers in the same agency, often leading them to "operate within a climate of mutual suspicion" (Hackley and Kover 2007, 71).

Workaholism is also common in advertising, compounded in the past two decades by increased demands from 24/7 client contact and a leaner postrecession workforce expected to do more work in less time (Barlow 2012). The creative department bears the brunt of fulfilling those demands. Along with constant change, a relentless pace makes it difficult to reenter the profession after taking leave (Nudd 2015). When agencies offer men paternity leave, few take it, and fewer still take all of it. They cite fear that they will be perceived as "not dedicated" and that they will return to find they have lost ground in terms of brand assignments and career momentum (Mallia, unpublished research). This is another byproduct of masculine industry codes built on strength and endurance, which serve to disadvantage those with a "second shift."

Creatives who are mothers report facing prejudiced perceptions that they are less dedicated to their work and careers and experiencing peer resentment when they leave work on time, regardless of their productivity (Mallia 2009b). Research suggests there is indeed prejudice against parents in the workplace, especially mothers (Fuegen et al. 2004; Heilman and Okimoto 2008).

The Ways of Creative Work

The brain's creative process itself conspires against anyone who desires a life outside work. Ideation requires that one's brain is "always on," either consciously or subconsciously mulling the problem to be solved (Csikszentmihályi 1988; Osborn 1957). This is compounded by the creative personality—a perfectionist, passionate about her work, consumed by "flow" in the creative process—and it is difficult to let go (Csikszentmihályi 1999). A CD said, "My last full-time job I worked 80 hours a week. It wasn't expected of me. It wasn't even frowned upon if I didn't do it, but it was often required to get the work done to the bar I personally set" (Mallia et al. 2012). Even when away from the office, this can be problematic for women, as their "share of mind" can be more divided than men's. Both married and single women typically bear a disproportionate share of family and household responsibilities, along with career pressures, and are more likely to report suffering from role conflict resulting from multiple competing demands (Aryee et al. 1999). Most seasoned, successful creative women in advertising identify as career-primary and consider this perspective essential to success (Mallia 2009b).

Despite the existence of some objective principles for what makes "great" advertising, subjectivity is part of the creative development and approval process (Ewing, Napoli, and West 2001; Stuhlfaut and Yoo 2011). In evaluating what work goes forward and what work dies, the CD plays a gatekeeping role, one currently dominated by white men throughout the world. Men's aesthetics for judging agency work and men stacking juries with men to judge awards explains why masculine humor dominates the worldwide advertising award show winners, making women's voices in advertising rare (Prakash and Flores 1985; Rare Birds of Cannes 2014; Stuhlfaut 2011). Groundbreaking campaigns developed by women, with or without a different sensibility or aesthetic, only occasionally break through to win awards. Take, for example, award-winners like the original Nike women's campaign, the Dove "Campaign for Real Beauty," or the more recent Always "Like a Girl" campaign. Creative awards are not merely a nicety; they are a catalyst for successful creative careers (Mallia 2008, 2009b).

Gender bias in the creative department is neither new nor localized. With few exceptions, women report similar experiences around the world. However, men's culture and its concomitant issues appear to be magnified in Latin countries, and elsewhere, where women's representation in advertising creative falls below the worldwide average (Alvesson 1998; Bird 1996; García-González and Piñeiro-Otero 2011; Grow and Deng 2014; Mallia 2009b; Martín Llaguno 2007; Pueyo Ayhan 2010; Rohrback 2003).

WHAT'S THE PROBLEM? WHAT PROBLEM?

Vast literatures are available on the glass ceiling, tokenism, and workplace discrimination. Advertising scholars and professionals have contributed additional knowledge, validating the under-representation of women in creative departments and helping to explain the many contributing factors. So why does the problem persist? And what can we do about it? Why are we even talking about this issue?

First, without data, a problem doesn't exist. Until very recently, lack of awareness of the under-representation problem was likely due, in part, to a lack of substantive data documenting its severity. Now statistics support the reality of women's under-representation. Next, we must provide concrete evidence that the system, and not women, is at fault. As *The Female Advantage* (Helgesen 1990) author Sally Helgesen (2015) states, change is only possible with "a serious effort to identify cultural and structural barriers to women's advancement *and* a commitment to helping senior leaders recognize how their own unconscious assumptions may undermine their support for women."

Second, the academy has a role to play in advocating change. This begins with forging relationships with industry advocates. Some of us have begun that work. Industry leaders can share knowledge among their peers with professional credibility, larger platforms, bigger budgets, and more powerful connections than advertising professors have. Combine professional and academic synergy with social and online media, and the rate of change could accelerate.

Culture Clings

In her work on the creative industries, Gill (2002) identified a "postfeminism problem," a reluctance of workers to understand their experiences as having anything to do with their gender. Advertising women can exhibit this unwillingness, having internalized the industry's discourse of meritocracy so thoroughly that they cannot or will not acknowledge that gender is a factor in their career growth. For example, a thirty-year veteran executive CD said she considered tension and disagreement healthy and essential to creativity: "I have never encountered what I consider sexual harassment. You can render guys speechless with a well-timed 'Eat my bush'" (pers. comm.). An inability or unwillingness to recognize systemic barriers is another culture-bound issue affecting ad women. Industry leaders have long used exceptionalism to dispel arguments that sexism and discrimination exist in creative departments, holding up an exemplary woman CD as "proof" of equality (despite her rarity). Some women have even echoed industry men in attributing female under-representation to explanations like "women don't work hard enough." Such claims are analogous to victim blaming (Slaughter 2013). That reasoning, and discounting the seriousness of a gender problem in advertising, are themselves demonstrations of the existence of larger cultural and systemic barriers to the success of women. Sheryl Sandberg (2013) initially dismissed systemic barriers to women becoming leaders by arguing that women should "lean in," and "fix" their own limiting behaviors. Now her McKinsey-Lean In Foundation research finds systemic barriers play a large role in impeding women's career achievements ("2015 Women in the Workplace").

A masculine environment disadvantages women, thwarts their progress, and in fact can constitute a toxic environment for women (Acker 1990, Hendryx 2012). In advertising, this climate negatively affects women's creativity and productivity, forcing women to work harder to succeed or to become risk-averse (Mallia and Windels 2015; Windels 2011; Windels and Lee 2012). Research also suggests that token women in male-dominated workplaces exhibit high stress and erratic cortisol levels, which can have serious health consequences (Manago and Taylor 2015).

Some women are simply unaware; others are unable to label what they see. Alison Beattie (pers. comm.), founder of the Minneapolis-based group MPLS MadWomen, had an epiphany after having a child and subsequently became an activist: "All of a sudden my eyes opened up to some of these issues that a lot of women were experiencing or I was seeing, but I didn't really have words or ways to describe what I now know is gender inequality." Young women frequently find no discrimination because increased competition comes only with promotion and years of experience. After claiming to have not experienced bias as part of the class in a lawsuit, one CD deeply regretted it years later. Though she was unaffected by bias as a junior, she saw a gaping gender gap when the men who were her peers began surpassing her (Alison Beattie, pers. comm.).

Bias Abounds: Deliberate, Accidental, and Unconscious

Bias, even if unwitting, is a powerful impediment to change. Opportunity for bias exists throughout the entire system of work within the creative department, a system in which CDs function as gatekeepers (Mallia, Windels, and Broyles 2013; Roca et al. 2016). Every decision, from forming creative teams to the timing of meetings and the selection of which ideas move forward, offers an opportunity for bias to intervene. Sometimes workplace bias arises in conflict between working mothers and childless women (Fuegen et al. 2004). Successful childless creatives, "queen bees," may resent family leave accommodations, especially when they are called to step in (Mallia et al. 2012). Then, too, bias is seen among men refusing to acknowledge the existence of gender disparities and among senior women who don't step up to sponsor or mentor younger women colleagues. Yet minority mentoring places undue burden on a very few "token" women or women of color, for example, who suddenly become responsible for not only overcoming "their people's" discrimination at the hands of others but also spending time mentoring that they might instead spend on guaranteeing the success of their own careers without mentors themselves.

Research on gendered double standards finds that women are perceived differently, typically more negatively, for behaviors regularly demonstrated by men (Fuegen et al. 2004; Heilman et al. 2004; Heilman and Haynes 2005), especially when they rise to leadership (Rhode 2003; Rudman and Kilianski 2000) and are judged against a masculine standard of leadership (Hendryx 2012). Women creatives are further constrained by prevailing assumptions of male creative superiority (Nixon and Crewe 2004). As a result, women's work faces steeper standards every time it is evaluated by a CD or client (Volpi 1998). However, neuroscientists find no brain differences between the genders that significantly affect creativity and no differences between measurements of creativity (Baer and Kaufman 2008). Good ideas are genderless. Notions of men's creative superiority are likely attributable to the greater creative *accomplishments* of men (Baer and Kaufman 2008; Windels and Mallia 2015). In other words, men are not innately more creative; they are just more likely to *succeed* at being creative, as is evident in their dominant role in advertising creative departments. Generally, women are less likely to be recognized for their accomplishments than are men (Henry 2009). As former BBH NY president and industry provocateur Cindy Gallop has frequently noted, "Men are hired and promoted on potential; women are hired and promoted on proof. As women, we are subject to a whole different set of standards" (Saner 2016).

Perhaps the strongest and most powerful evidence of the effect of gender bias in the creative department was presented by transgender CD Chris

Edwards (2015), who began his career as a woman but has stated that he only achieved success after transitioning to a man. Unconscious biases and gender stereotypes run far deeper than most people realize. "Female" computer voices have been judged less competent than "male" ones, and hurricanes given female names are perceived as weaker and less threatening than hurricanes with male names (Jung et al. 2014). A study of orchestra auditions found gender bias when candidates were visible, and equitable results in the blind experimental condition (Goldin and Rouse 1997). Rooms full of psychologists gasped at the findings of the Yale study that sent identical resumes for hypothetical job candidates, only varying the applicant's name as John or Jennifer (Rudman et al. 2012). *Every* respondent rated "John" higher than "Jennifer" on every hiring measure except likeability. "John" was offered a starting salary nearly $4,000 higher than "Jennifer." Women were as biased as men. No one is immune to bias, and subverting its influence requires conscientious and diligent effort.

Meritocracy and Other Advertising Myths

Advertising has its own inspiring versions of the Horatio Alger story, wherein anyone can succeed with talent and hard work. In the ad business, the creative department is widely believed to be a meritocracy, a place where success is "all about the work" (Eichler 2012; Mallia 2008, 2009b; Windels and Lee 2012). Search "It's all about the work" online and note its ubiquity: There are hundreds of agencies featuring this refrain, or some variation, in their mission statements or on their websites. (At BBDO, it is "The work. The work. The work.") The fact that a portfolio of work is a prerequisite to creative employment helps reinforce the belief that the quality of the work is the sole basis for hiring and promotion (Mallia 2014). However, no one is hired without an interview, an assessment of likeability ("someone I'd like to have a drink with"), and perceived fit with the agency and group culture (Ibarra 1992; Mallia 2009b; Mallia and Windels 2011). This hiring in one's own image undermines diversity, because young, white, male CDs perpetuate themselves, and creative hiring occurs outside regular human resources departments, as both industry firebrands like Cindy Gallop and academic researchers have noted (Boulton 2013; Mallia 2009b; Mallia and Windels 2011; and Saner 2016).

The widespread belief in meritocracy fails to acknowledge abundant research on the system of creativity demonstrating that process—the *way* creative work is done—influences creativity and the work (Amabile et al. 1996; Csikszentmihályi 1988, 1999). In advertising, this, in turn, influences the success of its creators (Mallia 2008; Mallia and Windels 2015; Windels and Lee 2012). Every stage of the creative process provides an opportunity for privileging white men, knowingly or inadvertently, when a CD (cum gatekeeper) judges work, forms teams, or makes account or project assignments (Hackley and Kover 2007; Mallia, Windels, and Broyles 2013; Windels and Mallia 2015). Bias even seeps into industry rituals and group socializing (Gregory 2009). When CDs assign creative people to high-status accounts, they give those creatives an imbedded opportunity. Or not. Women are frequently sidelined to the "pink ghetto," work on "feminine" products like baby care, personal hygiene, and diet plans (Gregory 2009; McLeod, O'Donohoe, and Townley 2011; Pueyo Ayhan 2010). Even if a "pink" position carries an equivalent CD title, the job is unlikely to carry the status, remuneration, or opportunity that come with working on coveted prestigious and "manly" brands like beer or cars (Gregory 2009; Mallia 2008; McLeod, O'Donohoe, and Townley 2011; Pueyo Ayhan 2010). The categories that win most industry awards—recognition that in turn leads to raises and promotions—are the ones typically assigned to men (Grow, Roca, and Broyles 2012; Mallia 2008; Pueyo Ayhan 2010). Thus, rather than career success resulting from talent and hard work alone, the practices of the agency creative system often work to ensure masculine heterosexual hegemony and the continued ascendance of men (Bird 1996; Gregory 2009; Nixon 2003; Windels 2011).

In the United Kingdom, the "placement" system all but guarantees the continuation of white, upper-class privilege in advertising by automatically weeding out anyone unable to sustain herself for at least two years at less than minimum wage (Klein 2000; McLeod, O'Donohoe, and Townley 2011). In agencies where teams routinely compete against one another—rather than having account assignments that particular teams "own"—the system automatically puts women at a disadvantage; abundant research shows that women's career success is disadvantaged by competitive environments (Schwartz 2014). In creative departments where intramural competition for assignments is not the norm—for example in agencies such as Huge, Possible, and Wongdoody—we find more women, and more women CDs (Mallia, unpublished data).

Male Models of Work and Unspoken Codes

More than thirty years ago, research identified the power of both psychological and contextual sociological variables, and the interaction between them, in shaping significant differences in the career paths of women and men (Astin 1984). As Steiner (2012, 201) noted in a review of gender across mass media professions, "women have been regarded as the intruder, the exception, the problem." In advertising, the "ideal" advertising creative is still a mid-century male model who myopically pursues his next great achievement, and whose only life is his work. Creatives are still measured against this prevailing (albeit outmoded) cultural standard, and social pressure is strong. Working late is a badge of superior dedication. Creatives who leave the office at 5:30 or 6 p.m., sometimes later, are the recipients of snide remarks such as, "Oh, taking a half day?" (Mallia 2009b). One art director heard that comment from a colleague who knew she had worked all day the day before, entertained a client until 1 a.m., and had started at 8:15 a.m. (Mallia, unpublished research).

If competition makes men manly, then what does it make women? When nice girls finish last, it's because they can't compete with men without being labeled with impolite words, although they can compete against women for recognition from men. Nice white girls are reared to avoid conflict and competition as unladylike; black women, reared to stand up for themselves when no one else will, risk the Sapphire label (Golombisky and Bell 2004). A competitive work environment is recognized as undermining women, who tend to be less self-aggrandizing, and find greater success in more collaborative work environments (Baer and Kaufman 2008; Gneezy and Rustichini 2004; Schwartz 2014; Windels and Mallia 2015). The oft-repeated industry adage "you're only as good as your last ad" is a constant reminder that someone, who might be younger and cheaper, is always nipping at your heels and ready to take your job. Rather, "competition" can mean viewing other women as the opposition. The 1970s version of the "queen bee syndrome" refers to women who manage to succeed to the management level and then thwart the women coming behind them by holding them to higher standards or viewing them as competition for the role of the sole queen bee (Staines, Jayaratne, and Tarvis, 1973). Jane Maas reported, "The more successful a woman is, the less likely she is to mentor other younger women" (Mallia et al. 2012). That may be as much a function of scarcity as lack of interest; the dearth of women leaders means there are too few to meet the mentoring needs of all younger women.

When working long hours and weekends is not merely about putting in the time needed to get the work done, but "proving" oneself, it reinforces the codes of the creative system. Having peers and superiors *witness* one's dedication is necessary, so that means work must happen in the office where it is seen. The phrase "face time," and mention of its importance to creative success, was repeated in countless interviews with creatives (Mallia 2009b; Mallia and Windels 2011). This might explain why so many agencies discourage working from home or steadfastly refuse to formalize flexi-place policies, even when allowing them on a case-by-case basis. Ad hoc individual arrangements communicate, "*You're* special; we're doing you a favor," whereas a corporate policy would convey a stance that having a life outside the office is normative and acceptable.

The availability of flexible work arrangements helps women and men succeed in the workplace ("The Benefits" 2015). Yet such policies are rare in advertising agencies (Mallia 2009b; Mallia and Windels 2011; Mallia and Windels 2015). Because collaboration is considered important in creativity and innovation, some organizations have used that rationale to mandate regular office reporting. Such decisions are more likely about bureaucratic control than fostering innovation, as the creativity literature offers little to support a need for full-time proximity, and many resources exist to facilitate remote collaboration. Creative research supports some positive benefits of synergy and collaborative thinking, but individual ideation is also important to the process (Lubart 2001; Osborn 1957). Much of a creative's work comes after the conceptual process, in solo execution of the idea while crafting copy or dialogue and ad layout and design. A CD mother of two described the clash between rigid entrenched agency policy, perceptions, and reality:

> I worked freelance for an agency for the last year with the promise that I never had to be onsite more than three days a week—the other two from home. Interestingly enough when they wanted me to go full-time and offered me a job, they were no longer comfortable with that setup, despite every team member raving about how I made it work for the last year. (Mallia, unpublished data)

Indeed, freelancers, a significant portion of the labor force working in advertising's creative and allied fields, have successful careers without showing up at the office.

The "model" career path remains a hidebound, gendered, cultural stereotype, a direct trajectory unforgiving of "detours" such as childrearing and eldercare (Hewlett 2007). A recent study found that more than 90 percent of women and men believe taking extended family leave will hurt their position at work ("2015 Women in the Workplace Study" 2016). Leave can be particularly disruptive to a creative career because of fierce jockeying and territoriality surrounding "ownership" of plum accounts and assignments. The career consequences of a hiatus are beginning to be acknowledged in advertising; for example, Sapient-Nitro instituted a formal "REturnship" program akin to an internship to facilitate reentry (Nudd 2015). Numbers of creative women "choose" freelance after motherhood, indicating that full-time agency work and parenting is untenable (Mallia 2009a). One could argue whether that is indeed a "choice" if the system makes it the only option.

Creatives have consuming, demanding jobs that make "having a life" challenging even without children. Without exception, women CDs report that a supportive partner and a full-time or live-in nanny are essential. Women still bear the brunt of childcare and housework, even in households where both partners work full time, according to a 2015 study published by Catalyst ("2015 Women in the Workplace Study" 2016). Among women working full time, 60 percent find it difficult—and 20 percent find it very difficult—to manage family and work responsibilities. Even in egalitarian partnerships, Mom remains the "designated worrier" (Schulevitz 2015). Even well paid women creatives who outsource housework and childcare still report experiencing the stress of "share of mind" issues and role conflict (Mallia 2009b, unpublished data).

There's No Such Thing as Work–Life Balance

The all-consuming nature of the creative process and unpredictable demands of client-service bring time and energy strains for working parents. The buck stops on the "factory" floor. Jane Maas (1986) first said it decades ago: Being a CD requires putting your "career first, husband second, and children third" and she reiterated that contention more recently (Maas 2012). The belief is common among her advertising industry peers (Chatman et al. 1998; Mallia 2009b). This accepted wisdom has the material consequence of forming barriers for parents without nannies. Almost without exception, every woman executive CD in my research has been childless, had a full-time nanny, or had a spouse with a less-demanding job (or no job) who assumes primary responsibility for life outside work (Mallia 2009b). My work shows that being career-primary appears to be a mandate for creatives constrained by prevailing agency codes and practices.

Some have suggested that more generous parental leave policies could help in the retention of creative women because many women leave agencies as children arrive. However, recent data suggest that family-friendly policies alone may not make a difference in creative departments: Even in the nations with the most generous social policies for parental leave (Sweden, for example), the proportion of women in creative departments is actually *lower* than in the United States (see Chapter 9).

PEOPLE ACTUALLY DO CARE, AND OTHER GOOD NEWS

Women's under-representation is on the industry's radar. The surge of research and discussion published in the popular press, in trade publications, and across social media has traveled around the world (Mallia and Jang 2015). Increased press coverage has coincided with the rise of a number of advocacy groups promoting and enabling the cause of women in advertising worldwide (Mallia and Jang 2015). I believe we can say with a fair degree of certainty that more people than ever are concerned. Consider the signs:

The Growth of Advocacy Groups

A burgeoning grassroots "women's movement" in advertising is afoot, with several organizations blossoming simultaneously in varied corners. The 3% Conference (now a full-fledged movement) began as a gathering of like-minded and interested people presented by Kat Gordon, a CD inflamed at the industry's historic denial of gender issues, and buttressed by seeing some of my research on the dearth of creative women (Mallia 2008, 2009a, 2009b) and a doctoral student (Windels 2008) who is now an associate professor also writing in this volume (see Chapter 7). In the few short years since The 3% Conference could not get a single trade press reporter to cover its inaugural event, it has become a global phenomenon, attracting major media attention, sponsors, agencies, and devotees to advancing the cause of women in advertising. The event expanded from one sold-out day in 2012 to two days in 2013, and moved from San Francisco to New York City in 2015, attracting eight hundred attendees. A personal passion project turned into a full-fledged movement demonstrating that the lack of creative women in advertising leadership cannot be attributed to lack of interest or ambition on the part of creative women, the 3% Conference has helped raised awareness on an international scale that diversity is good business (Mallia and Jang 2015).

Other advocacy groups have also experienced interest and rapid growth. To advance the cause of women in the digital media space, SheSays was founded in London in 2007 by Laura Jordan Bambach, creative partner at Mr. President, and Alessandra Lariu, former McCann Digital Executive Creative Director (weareshesays.com). It has since evolved into a global education, networking, and mentoring program with chapters in twenty-five cities in eleven countries, most recently opening in Kuala Lumpur, Malaysia (Mallia and Jang 2015).

MPLS Mad Women started in 2013 as a personal support group for a young mother at Fallon, but membership exploded in a matter of months. Its "hacking the issues" events are so popular that tickets routinely sell out in less than an hour, and eager-to-participate fans outside of the advertising business have contacted the group (Mallia and Jang 2015).

Some strong women leaders have taken the findings of a handful of dedicated academics and marshaled a world of like-minded, ardent women to make the case for gender diversity via advertising and social media and force the advertising industry to finally pay attention and get with the program. They've leveraged the research and told the world loudly and repeatedly that diversity is essential for creativity and that greater creativity means greater profitability. Kat Gordon, founder of The 3% Conference, repositioned the case for creative women from a moral argument to a more compelling business argument, an effective rhetorical strategy that nonetheless has suspect ethical implications.

Broad Industry Activation

In the early 2010s, advertising trade groups launched new diversity initiatives and put the cause of creative women on their agendas, and a number of agencies followed suit. In 2013, The One Club sponsored a three-part lecture series for women ("Creative Women's Leadership Series" 2014; "Where Are All the Black People?" 2014). The Art Director's Club launched a "Let's Make the Industry 50/50" initiative in 2013 ("Art Director's Club" 2013), promising gender-equal juries for its annual awards (Mallia and Windels 2015). Cannes hosted panels on gender diversity in 2014 (Rare Birds of Cannes 2014) and in 2015 launched a Glass Lion to celebrate creative work that challenges gender bias ("Girl Power" 2015). In 2016, six Glass Lions were awarded, including a Glass Grand Prix for a tea brand from India that created the first transgender pop band (Markowitz 2016). The 4A's presented a series of webinars with activist Cindy Gallop ("Glass Ladder Series" 2015). BBDO partnered with The One Club in 2015 to launch a new diversity residency program ("BBDO Partners" 2015). DDB introduced its D3 diversity program in 2015 ("D3" 2015). In the United Kingdom, Ogilvy initiated a program in 2015 specifically to address unconscious bias (Institute of Practitioners in Advertising 2015).

Men are involved, too. Without them, cultural change is impossible. At The 3% MiniCon in Salt Lake City, 25 percent of the attendees were men ("History and Highlights" 2015). Tom Jordan, one of the first "manbassadors" to take up the cause of ad women, highlighted the disconnect between male creators and women consumers (Jordan 2009). Tracy Wong, an agency owner dedicated to egalitarianism in principle and action, announced his $5,000 "Women in Advertising" scholarship in 2015, for women students interested in creative careers. At Wongdoody, women compose 43 percent of the executive team; the creative department is 25 percent women and 17 percent minority ("Introducing Wongdoody's" 2015).

Concerned that their advertising content mirrors the demographics of their consumers, some clients speak up for creative diversity in their agencies. Team diversity was on the agenda at the 2015 conference of the Association of National Advertisers, where a PepsiCo executive reiterated research concerning the effect of team diversity on creativity (Spiegel 2016). Coca-Cola and Unilever have joined the agency diversity discussion as well (Maheshwari 2013).

A study examining the representation of women in creative departments via *Communication Arts* data from 1984 to 2014 revealed that the overall number of women in creative departments had not increased since 1994 (Mallia and Windels 2015). However, the data revealed that the number of women CDs had increased from 2 percent to 9 percent (Mallia and Windels

2015). In 2008, a study found 35 women listed among 249 creative executives in the *Standard Directory of Advertising Agencies* (Redbook), or 14 percent (Beard, pers. comm.), whereas data from a different source indicated just 11 percent of CDs were women at that time (Windels 2008). As mentioned earlier, 2013 Redbook data showed that women represented 25.2 percent of US CDs (Grow and Deng 2014).

Public and client pressure to increase diversity in hiring and promotion may be having some effect. In April 2016, BBDO announced its intent to double female creative leadership in twelve months (Coffee 2014). In 2015 and 2016, several women were named chief creative officers at major agencies: Kate Stanners, Global CCO at Saatchi and Saatchi (Wentz 2016), Chaka Sobhani, Leo Burnett London ("Leo Burnett London" 2016), Susan Credle, Global CCO at FCB (Morrison 2015), and Liz Taylor, CCO at FCB Chicago (Morrison 2016).

With leadership comes power, and if they choose to, women and men can exert influence on discriminatory policies and practices and cultural codes. Research demonstrates that having women at the top has a positive effect on increased gender equity in the organization (Burke and McKeen 1996). In addition, the trend toward increased collaboration throughout industry practice favors diversity because people, especially millennials, are more likely to view heterogeneous work groups as an integral part of the culture when an organization emphasizes collective efforts rather than individual goals (Chatman et al. 1998). In fact, one leading male industry executive penned an *Adweek* article titled, "Why the Perfect Modern Creative Is Fierce, Fearless and Female" (Leonard 2014).

WHERE DO WE GO FROM HERE?

When 91 percent of women claim that advertisers don't understand them (Coffee 2014), and major brands challenge their agencies about their lack of diversity in creative leadership, the issue is more than a moral imperative for advertising. It's a business mandate. Agency and client success depend on the caliber of creative work produced and its resonance with its audience.

Competition for creative talent is increasing, with the likes of Google attracting clever minds that might otherwise go into creative advertising (Diaz 2015; Elliott 2013; Magee 2015; "The Talent-Crunch Crisis" 2014). It is foolish for agencies to ignore more than half of the available creative talent pool.

Scholars need to continue to dig deeper to find new insight in the anomalies in the gender story. Why do women dominate creative positions in China? Why do women have better representation in Poland and South Africa than elsewhere in the world? What is the explanation for Sweden and Canada having fewer CDs than the United States, despite those nations' generous family leave policies? As advertising scholars and educators, we need to make a concerted effort to share our findings more broadly, beyond academic journals, especially knowledge about the role of unconscious bias in the creative process, because bias shapes the work as well as those who create it.

The under-representation of women across race, ethnicity, ability, religion, and sexuality in advertising is not a women's issue; it's everyone's issue. In advertising, this problem of women's exclusion from creative process is symptomatic of broader social issues: Twenty-first-century life is hampered by twentieth-century gender stereotypes that are bound to white, Anglo, heteronormative, able-bodied, First-World ideals and privileges work life above all other human endeavors. We must find a way to make it possible for all talented, passionate, creative people to find success.

REFERENCES

"2015 Women in the Workplace Study." 2016. Lean In, McKinsey and Company. Accessed September 30. http://wit.berkeley.edu/docs/Women-in-the-Workplace-2015.pdf.

"About Us," 2016. Multicultural Advertising Internship Program. http://maip.aaaa.org/ - home.

Acker, Joan. 1990. "Hierarchies, Jobs, Bodies: A Theory of Gendered Organizations." *Gender and Society* 4 (2): 138–59.

Alvesson, Mats. 1998. "Gender Relations and Identity at Work: A Case Study of Masculinities and Femininities in an Advertising Agency." *Human Relations* 51 (8): 969–1005.

Amabile, Teresa M., R. Conti, H. Coon, J. Lazenby, and M. Herron. 1996. "Assessing the Work Environment for Creativity." *Academy of Management Journal* 39 (5): 1154–84.

"Art Directors Club Launches Initiative to Encourage Equal Involvement of Women and Men in the Creative Industry." 2013. *Yahoo! Finance*. Accessed June 20. http://finance.yahoo.com/news/art-directors-club-launches-initiative-195025423.html.

Aryee, Samuel, Vivienne Luk, Alicia Leung, and Susanna Lo. 1999. "Role Stressors, Interrole Conflict, and Well-Being: The Moderating Influence of Spousal Support and Coping Behaviors among Employed Parents in Hong Kong." *Journal of Vocational Behavior* 54 (2): 259–78. doi:10.1006/jvbe.1998.1667.

Astin, Helen S. 1984. "The Meaning of Work in Women's Lives: A Sociopsychological Model of Career Choice and Work Behavior." *The Counseling Psychologist* 12 (3–4): 117–26.

Baer, John, and James C. Kaufman. 2008. "Gender Differences in Creativity." *Journal of Creative Behavior* 42 (2): 75–105.

Barlow, Gail. 2012. “Confessions of a Recovering Workaholic: How This Creative Director Got Her Groove Back.” *The 3% Conference.* http://www.3percentconf.com/blog/confessions-recovering-workaholic-how-creative-director-got-her-groove-back - .WFLscX0sY0w.

“BBDO Partners with One Club on One-Year Diversity Residency.” 2015. Accessed May 30. http://adage.com/article/adtile/bbdo-partners-club-year-diversity-residency/298802/.

Bendick, Marc, and Mary Lou Egan. 2009. *Research Perspectives on Race and Employment in the Advertising Industry.* Washington, DC: Bendick and Egan Economic Consultants. http://www.newyorkemploymentattorneyblog.com/files/2013/06/Research_Perspectives_on_Race_and_Employment_in_the_Advertising_Industry.pdf.

The Benefits of Flexible Working Arrangements. 2012. New York: Future of Work Institute. https://www.bc.edu/content/dam/files/centers/cwf/individuals/pdf/benefitsCEOFlex.pdf.

Bird, Sharon R. 1996. “Welcome to the Men’s Club: Homosociality and the Maintenance of Hegemonic Masculinity.” *Gender and Society* 10 (2): 120–32.

Bosman, Julie. 2005. “WPP Executive Resigns over Remarks on Women.” *New York Times,* October 21. http://www.nytimes.com/2005/10/21/business/21adco.html.

Boulton, Christopher. 2013. “The Ghosts of Mad Men: Race and Gender Inequality Inside American Advertising Agencies.” In *The Routledge Companion to Advertising and Promotional Culture,* edited by Matthew P. McAllister and Emily West. New York: Routledge, 252–66. http://works.bepress.com/chris_boulton/19/.

Bruell, Alexandra. 2015. “Publicis Settles Class-Action Gender-Bias Suit for Nearly $3 Million.” *Advertising Age.* http://adage.com/article/agency-news/publicis-settling-gender-discrimination-suit-2-875-000/300900/.

Burke, Ronald J., and Carol A. McKeen. 1996. “Employment Gaps and Work and Career Satisfactions of Managerial and Professional Women.” *International Journal of Manpower* 17 (1): 47–55. doi:10.1108/01437729610110611.

Cadwalladr, Carole. 2005. “Focus: Sexism Row: This Advertising Boss Thinks Women Make ‘Crap’ Executives.” *The Guardian.* https://www.theguardian.com/media/2005/oct/23/advertising.genderissues.

Chatman, Jennifer A., Jeffrey T. Polzer, Sigal G. Barsade, and Margaret A. Neale. 1998. “Being Different Yet Feeling Similar: The Influence of Demographic and Organizational Culture on Work Processes and Outcomes.” *Administrative Science Quarterly* 43: 749–80.

Coffee, Patrick. 2014. “Study: Advertisers Don’t Understand Women.” *Adweek Agency Spy.* June 26. http://www.adweek.com/agencyspy/study-advertisers-dont-understand-women/68869.

———. 2016. “BBDO Plans to Double Its Female Creative Leadership over the Next 12 Months.” *Adweek AgencySpy,* April 19. Accessed September 30, 2016. http://adweek.it/1SY97tu.

“Companies with More Women Board Directors Experience Higher Financial Performance, According to Latest Catalyst Bottom Line Report.” 2012. *Catalyst.* August 7. http://www.catalyst.org/media/companies-more-women-board-directors-experience-higher-financial-performance-according-latest.

"Confessions of a Female Ad Exec." 2012. Digiday. http://digiday.com/agencies/confessions-of-a-woman-in-advertising/.

Conor, Bridget, Rosalind Gill, and Stephanie Taylor. 2015. "Gender and Creative Labour." *The Sociological Review* 63 (May): 1–22. doi:10.1111/1467-954X.12237.

"Creative Women's Leadership Series." 2014. *The One Club.* Accessed November 18. http://www.oneclub.org/events/?eid=264.

Csikszentmihályi, Mihaly. 1988. "The Flow Experience and Its Significance for Human Psychology." In *Optimal Experience: Psychological Studies of Flow in Consciousness,* edited by Mihaly Csikszentmihályi and Isabella Selega Csikszentmihályi, 15–35. Cambridge, UK: Cambridge University Press.

———. 1996. "The Creative Personality." *Psychology Today* July/August: 36–40

———. 1999. "16 Implications of a Systems Perspective for the Study of Creativity." In *Handbook of Creativity,* edited by Robert J. Sternberg, 313–35. Cambridge, UK: Cambridge University Press.

Cuneo, Alice Z., and Petrecca Laura. 1997. "Women Target Boys Club of Ad Creative." *Advertising Age* 68 (45): 24–24.

"D3: Intern Program." 2015. *DDB.* Accessed November 13. http://www.ddb.com/diversity-creativity/about/d3intern-program/.

Dahlerup, Drude. 2006. "The Story of the Theory of Critical Mass." *Politics and Gender* 2 (04): 511–22. doi:10.1017/s1743923x0624114x.

Della Femina, Jerry, and Charles Sopkin. 1970. *From Those Wonderful Folks Who Gave You Pearl Harbor.* New York: Simon & Schuster.

Diaz, Ann-Christine. 2015. "Former AKQA Execs Rei Inamoto and Rem Reynolds Open Business Invention Studio." *Advertising Age.* Accessed September 29. http://adage.com/article/agency-news/akqa-execs-rei-inamoto-rem-reynolds-open-business-invention-studio/300619/.

"Education Services." 2016. *American Advertising Federation.* http://www.aaf.org/IMIS/AAFMemberR/OUR_EFFORTS/Education_Services/AAFMemberR/Efforts/EdServices.aspx?hkey=51ce707d-d2ba-40cb-b61e-1ec1cf3d955c.

Edwards, Chris. 2015. "Balls: It Takes Some to Get Some." *3% Conference.* Accessed November 13. http://www.3percentconf.com/blog/balls-it-takes-some-get-some.

Edwards, Jim. 2012. "Here's the Brutal Paragraph Cut from This CEO's 'Confessions of a Female Ad Exec.'" *Business Insider.* July 24. http://www.businessinsider.com/heres-the-brutal-paragraph-cut-from-this-ceos-confessions-of-a-female-ad-exec-2012-7.

Eichler, Leah. 2012. "Debunking the Myth of Meritocracy in Business." *Women 2.0.* June 2. http://women2.com/stories/2012/06/03/debunking-the-myth-of-meritocracy-in-business.

Elliott, Stuart. 2013. "A Silicon Valley for Ad Agencies, Only in the Mountains." *New York Times,* August 22. http://www.nytimes.com/2013/08/23/business/media/a-silicon-valley-for-ad-agencies-only-in-the-mountains.html.

Ely, Robin J. 1994. "The Effects of Organizational Demographics and Social Identity on Relationships among Professional Women." *Administrative Science Quarterly* 39: 203–38.

Ewing, Michael T., Julie Napoli, and Douglas C. West. 2001. "Creative Personalities, Processes, and Agency Philosophies: Implications for Global Advertisers." *Creativity Research Journal* 13 (2): 161–70.

Fiddner, Kelly. 2015. "A Healthcare Marketing Checkup: It's Her Economy." *The HC Insighter.* Accessed November 13. http://healthcare.acrobatant.com/blog/tag/greenfield-online-for-arnolds-womens-insight-team/.

Friedman, Ronald S., and Jens Forster. 2001. "The Effects of Promotion and Prevention Cues on Creativity." *Journal of Personality and Social Psychology* 81 (6): 1001–13.

———. 2005. "Effects of Motivational Cues on Perceptual Asymmetry: Implications for Creativity and Analytical Problem Solving." *Journal of Personality and Social Psychology* 88 (2): 263–75.

Fuegen, Kathleen, Monica Biernat, Elizabeth Haines, and Kay Deaux. 2004. "Mothers And Fathers in the Workplace: How Gender and Parental Status Influence Judgments of Job-Related Competence." *Journal of Social Issues* 60 (4): 737–54.

García-González, Aurora, and Teresa Piñeiro-Otero. 2011. "Women in Advertising Production. Study of the Galician Advertising Sector from a Gender Perspective." *Revista Latina de Comunicación Social.* http://www.revistalatinacs.org/11/art/943_Galicia/22_AuroraEN.html.

Gill, Rosalind. 2002. "Cool, Creative and Egalitarian? Exploring Gender in Project-Based New Media Work in Europe." *Information, Communication and Society* 5 (1): 70–89.

"Girl Power Wins Big at Cannes Ad Festival." 2015. *USA Today.* Accessed October 26. http://www.usatoday.com/story/money/2015/06/23/cannes-ad-festival-glass-lion-awards/29173189/.

"Glass Ladder Series: How to Join the C-Suite When Nobody Thinks You Can: With Cindy Gallop." 2015. *4A's.* Accessed May 11, 2017.3. https://vimeo.com/channels/990528/145786745

Gneezy, Uri, and Aldo Rustichini. 2004. "Gender and Competition at a Young Age." *American Economic Review,* 94 (2): 377–81.

Goldin, Claudia, and Cecilia Rouse. 1997. "Orchestrating Impartiality: The Impact of 'Blind' Auditions on Female Musicians." *National Bureau of Economic Research Working Paper Series,* NBER Working Paper No. 5903.

Golombisky, Kim, and Elizabeth Bell. 2004. "Voices and Silences in Our Classrooms: Strategies for Mapping Trails among Sex/Gender, Race, and Class." *Women's Studies in Communication* 27: 294–329.

Gregory, Michele Rene. 2009. "Inside the Locker Room: Male Homosociability in the Advertising Industry." *Gender, Work and Organization* 16 (3): 323–47. doi:10.1111/j.1468-0432.2009.00447.x.

Grow, Jean M., and Sheri J. Broyles. 2011. "Unspoken Rules of the Creative Game: Insights to Shape the Next Generation from Top Advertising Creative Women." *Advertising and Society Review* 12 (1). doi:10.1353/asr.2011.0009.

Grow, Jean M., and Tao Deng. 2014. "Sex Segregation in Advertising Creative Departments Across the Globe." *Advertising and Society Review* 14 (4). doi:10.1353/asr.2014.0003.

Grow, Jean M., David Roca, and Sheri J. Broyles. 2012. "Vanishing Acts: Creative Women in Spain and the United States." *International Journal of Advertising* 31 (3): 657–79.

Guilford, J. P. 1970. "Creativity: Retrospect and Prospect." *The Journal of Creative Behavior* 4 (3): 149–68.

Hackley, Chris. 2003. "From Consumer Insight to Advertising Strategy: The Account Planner's Integrative Role in Creative Advertising Development." *Marketing Intelligence and Planning* 21 (7): 446–52. doi:10.1108/02634500310504296.

Hackley, Chris, and Arthur J. Kover. 2007. "The Trouble with Creatives: Negotiating Creative Identity in Advertising Agencies." *International Journal of Advertising* 26 (1): 63–78.

Heilman, Madeline E., and Michelle C. Haynes. 2005. "No Credit Where Credit Is Due: Attributional Rationalization of Women's Success in Male-Female Teams." *Journal of Applied Psychology* 90 (5): 905–16.

Heilman, Madeline E., and Tyler G. Okimoto. 2008: "Motherhood: A Potential Source of Bias in Employment Decisions." *Journal of Applied Psychology* 93 (1): 189–98.

Heilman, Madeline E., Aaron S. Wallen, Daniella Fuchs, and Melinda M. Tamkins. 2004. "Penalties for Success: Reactions to Women Who Succeed at Male Gender-Typed Tasks." *Journal of Applied Psychology* 89 (3): 416–27.

Helgesen, Sally. 1990. *The Female Advantage: Women's Way of Leadership.* New York: Currency Doubleday.

Helgesen, Sally. 2015. "At Most Tech Firms, the C-Suite Is Still a Boy's Club." *Strategy + Business Blog,* March 4. http://www.strategy-business.com/blog/At-Most-Tech-Firms-the-C-Suite-Is-Still-a-Boys-Club?gko=19b32.

Hendryx, Nancy. 2012. "The Double-Bind Dilemma for Women in Leadership: Damned if You Do, Doomed if You Don't." *Catalyst.* October 24. http://www.catalyst.org/knowledge/double-bind-dilemma-women-leadership-damned-if-you-do-doomed-if-you-dont-0.

Henry, Colette. 2009. "Women and the Creative Industries: Exploring the Popular Appeal." *Creative Industries Journal* 2 (2): 143–60. doi:10.1386/cij.2.2.143/1.

Hewlett, Sylvia A. 2007. "Off-Ramps and On-Ramps." *Women and Leadership: The State of Play and Strategies for Change,* 407–30.

Hirschman, Elizabeth C. 1989. "Role-Based Models of Advertising Creation and Production." *Journal of Advertising* 18 (4): 42–53.

"History and Highlights." 2015. 3% Conference. Accessed November 13, 2015. http://www.3percentconf.com/about.

Ibarra, Herminia. 1992. "Homophily and Differential Returns: Sex Differences in Network Structure and Access in an Advertising Firm." *Administrative Science Quarterly* 37 (3): 422–47.

Institute of Practitioners in Advertising. 2015. *IPA: Briefing and Consultation on New Diversity Strategy.* https://www.youtube.com/watch?v=JbfrHhvWwGE.

"Introducing Wongdoody's Women in Advertising Scholarship." 2015. Accessed November 13. http://www.wongdoody.com/feed/wongdoodys-new-5000-women-in-advertising-scholarship/.

Jordan, Tom. 2009. In *Re-Render the Gender: Why the Vast Majority of Advertising Is Not Connecting with Women—And What We Can Do about It.* New York, NY: Booksurge.

Jung, Kiju, Sharon Shavitt, Madhu Viswanathan, and Joseph M. Hilbe. 2014. "Female Hurricanes Are Deadlier than Male Hurricanes." *Proceedings of the National Academy of Sciences* 111 (24): 8782–87. doi:10.1073/pnas.1402786111.

Kanter, Rosabeth Moss. 1977. "Some Effects of Proportions on Group Life: Skewed Sex Ratios and Responses to Token Women." *American Journal of Sociology* 82 (5): 965–90.

Kestin, Janet. 1998. "Where the Girls Aren't: A Y-Chromosome Is Not the Measure of a Creative Person. So What's with the Dearth, Still, of Women Creatives?" *Marketing Magazine* 103 (45): 56.

Klein, Deborah. 2000. "Women in Advertising, 10 Years On: Findings and Recommendations." *Study Commissioned by the Institute of Practitioners in Advertising (IPA).* London: Institute of Practitioners in Advertising.

Kover, Arthur J. 1995. "Copywriters' Implicit Theories of Communication: An Exploration." *Journal of Consumer Research* 21 (4): 596–611.

"Leo Burnett London Appoints Chaka Sobhani as New Chief Creative Officer." 2016. *Leo Burnett.* Accessed October 2. http://leoburnett.com/articles/news/leo-burnett-london-appoints-chaka-sobhani-as-new-chief-creative-officer.

Leonard, Nils. 2014. "Why the Perfect Modern Creative Is Fierce, Fearless and Female." *Adweek.* Accessed October 2. http://www.adweek.com/news/advertising-branding/why-perfect-modern-creative-fierce-fearless-and-female-160473.

Lubart, Todd I. 1994. "Product-Centered Self-Evaluation and the Creative Process." PhD diss., Yale University.

Lubart, Todd I. 2001. "Models of the Creative Process: Past, Present and Future." *Creativity Research Journal* 13 (3–4): 295–308.

Maas, Jane. 1986. *Adventures of an Advertising Woman.* Queen Creek, AZ: Turn Page Media.

———. 2012. *Mad Women: The Other Side of Life on Madison Avenue in the '60s and Beyond.* New York: St. Martin's.

Magee, Kate. 2015. "Apple Poaches Grey Global Creative Chief Tor Myhren." Accessed December 19. http://www.campaignlive.com/article/apple-poaches-grey-global-creative-chief-tor-myhren/1377416.

Maheshwari, Sapna. 2013. "Facebook's Sandberg Details Lack of Progress for Women at Top." *Bloomberg.* Accessed February 13. Accessed May 11, 2017. http://www.newsmax.com/Finance/InvestingAnalysis/Facebook-Progress-Women-Top/2012/03/09/id/432031/

Mallia, Karen L. 2008. "New Century, Same Story: Women Scarce When Adweek Ranks 'Best Spots.'" *Journal of Advertising Education* 12 (1): 5–14.

———. 2009a. "Creativity Knows No Gender, But Agency Creative Departments Sure Do." *Advertising Age.* August 31. http://adage.com/article/talentworks/advertising-motherhood-mix-creative-directing/138709/.

———. 2009b. "Rare Birds: Why So Few Women Become Ad Agency Creative Directors." *Advertising and Society Review* 10 (3). doi:10.1353/asr.0.0032.

———. 2014. "Women Now 11% of Ad Agency Creative Directors. Hooray?" *Media Report to Women* 42 (4): 22–24.

Mallia, Karen L., and Kasey Windels. 2011. "Will Changing Media Change the World? An Exploratory Investigation of the Impact of Digital Advertising on Opportunities for Creative Women." *Journal of Interactive Advertising* 11 (2): 30–44

———. 2015. "Female Representation in the Communication Arts Advertising Annual." Presented at the Association for Education in Journalism and Mass Communication, San Francisco, CA, August 6.

Mallia, Karen L., and S. Mo Jang. 2015. "Examining Media Coverage and the Global Awakening of the Creative 'Women's Movement' in Advertising." *Proceedings of the 2015 Global Conference of the American Academy of Advertising*. http://www.aaasite.org/page-1503249. (Members-only access).

Mallia, Karen L., Jane Maas, Becky Swanson, Liz Taylor, Mary Barber, Sheri J. Broyles, and Kim Golombisky. 2012. "Mad Women Attack Topic." Panel at the annual conference of the Association for Education in Journalism and Mass Communication, Chicago, IL, August 9.

Mallia, Karen L., Kasey Windels, and Sheri J. Broyles. 2013. "An Examination of Successful Leadership Traits for the Advertising-Agency Creative Director." *Journal of Advertising Research* 53 (3): 339–53.

Manago, Bianca, and Catherine J. Taylor. 2015. "Occupational Sex-Segregation, Workplace Interactions, and Chronic Physiological Stress Exposure." Paper presented at the Annual Meeting of the American Sociological Association, August, Chicago, IL.

Markowitz, Chloe. 2016. "Cannes Lions/The Glass Lion Winners." *Contagious Communications*. Accessed September 30. http://www.contagious.com/blogs/news-and-views/cannes-lions-the-glass-lion.

Martín Llaguno, Marta. 2007. "La Mujer en la Industria Publicitaria. La Segregación Vertical en la Comunicación Comercial: Techo de Cristal Y Suelo Pegajoso." ("Women in the Advertising Industry: Vertical Segregation in Commercial Communication: Glass Ceiling and Tacky Floor.") http://rua.ua.es/dspace/handle/10045/25692.

McLeod, Charlotte, Stephanie O'Donohoe, and Barbara Townley. 2011. "Pot Noodles, Placements and Peer Regard: Creative Career Trajectories and Communities of Practice in the British Advertising Industry." *British Journal of Management* 22 (1): 114–31. doi:10.1111/j.1467-8551.2010.00705.x.

Morrison, Maureen. 2015. "Susan Credle Named Global Chief Creative of FCB." *Advertising Age,* June 9. Accessed August 23, 2016. http://adage.com/article/agency-news/susan-credle-named-global-chief-creative-fcb/298935/

———. 2016. "FCB Chicago Names Ogilvy's Liz Taylor Chief Creative Officer." *Advertising Age,* August 23. Accessed August 23, 2016. http://adage.com/article/agency-news/fcb-chicago-names-ogilvy-s-liz-taylor-cco/305576/.

National Center for Education Statistics. 2012. "Bachelor's, Master's and Doctor's Degree Conferred by Postsecondary Institutions, by Sex of Student and Discipline Division." National Center for Education Statistics.

Nixon, Sean. 2003. *Advertising Cultures: Gender, Commerce, Creativity*. London: Sage.
Nixon, Sean, and Ben Crewe. 2004. "Pleasure at Work? Gender, Consumption and Work-Based Identities in the Creative Industries." *Consumption Markets and Culture* 7 (2): 129–47. doi:10.1080/1025386042000246197.
Nudd, Tim. 2015. "Did You Leave Advertising for a Few Years? Here's the Painful Truth about Getting Back In." *Adweek*. Accessed November 8. http://www.adweek.com/adfreak/did-you-leave-advertising-few-years-heres-painful-truth-about-getting-back-167785.
Olson, Millie. 2007. "Where Are All the Women in This Biz?" *Advertising Age*, July 10. Accessed July 20, 2015. http://adage.com/article/small-agency-diary/women-biz/119118/.
Osborn, Alex F. 1957. *Applied Imagination: Principles and Procedures of Creative Thinking*. New York: Charles Scribner's Sons.
Prakash, Ved, and R. Caeli Flores. 1985. "A Study of Psychological Gender Differences: Applications for Advertising Format." *Advances in Consumer Research* 12 (1): 231–37.
Pueyo Ayhan, Natalia. 2010. "Sex Structure of Occupations in the Advertising Industry: Where Are the Female Ad Practitioners?" *Observatorio (OBS*)* 4 (3). http://obs.obercom.pt/index.php/obs/article/view/416.
Rare Birds of Cannes. 2014. "The #SeeItBeIt Diary." http://rarebirdsofcannes.tumblr.com/.
Rhode, Deborah L. 2003. *The Difference "Difference" Makes: Women And Leadership*. Stanford, CA: Stanford University Press.
Roca, David, Daniel Tena, Patrícia Lázaro, and Alfons González. 2016. "Is There Gender Bias When Creative Directors Judge Advertising? Name Cue Effect in Ad Evaluation." *International Journal of Advertising* 35 (1): 1–16.
Rohrback, Jeneal. 2003. "Dumbing Sideways." *Adweek* 18 (1): 11.
Rossini v. Ogilvy and Mather, Inc., 80 F.R.D. 131; 1978 U.S. Dist. Lexis 14888.
Rudman, Laurie A., and Stephen E. Kilianski. 2000. "Implicit and Explicit Attitudes toward Female Authority." *Personality and Social Psychology Bulletin* 26 (11): 1315–28.
Rudman, Laurie A., Corinne A. Moss-Racusin, Julie E. Phelan, and Sane Nauts. 2012. "Status Incongruity and Backlash Effects: Defending the Gender Hierarchy Motivates Prejudice against Female Leaders." *Journal of Experimental Social Psychology* 48 (1): 165–79.
Runco, Mark A. 2007. "A Hierarchical Framework for the Study of Creativity." *New Horizons in Education* 55 (3): 1–9.
Sandberg, Sheryl. 2013. *Lean In: Women, Work, and the Will to Lead*. New York: Alfred A. Knopf.
Saner, Emine. 2016, June 26. "Cindy Gallop: 'Advertising Is Dominated by White Guys Talking to White Guys.'" *The Guardian*. Accessed September 30. https://www.theguardian.com/media/2016/jun/26/cindy-gallup-advertising-white-men-sex-tapes.
Shulevitz, Judith. 2015. "Mom: The Designated Worrier." *New York Times*. Accessed May 9. http://www.nytimes.com/2015/05/10/opinion/sunday/judith-shulevitz-mom-the-designated-worrier.html?nytmobile=0.

Schwartz, Ariel. 2014. "If You Want Female Employees to be Creative, Don't Make Them Compete at Work." *Co.Exist.* Accessed September 9. http://www.fastcoexist.com/3034820/if-you-want-female-employees-to-be-creative-dont-make-them-compete-at-work.

Schwartz, Tony. 2014. "What Women Need at Work to Give Their All." *DealBook.* October 31. http://dealbook.nytimes.com/2014/10/31/what-women-need-at-work-to-give-their-all/.

Slaughter, Anne-Marie. 2013. "Why Women Still Can't Have It All." *The Atlantic.* Accessed February 5. http://www.theatlantic.com/magazine/archive/2012/07/why-women-still-can-8217-t-have-it-all/9020/.

Spiegel, Benjamin. 2016. "Brands Need to Make Agency Diversity a Requirement." *Advertising Age.* Accessed April 28. http://adage.com/article/agency-viewpoint/brands-make-agency-diversity-a-requirement/301087/.

Staines, Graham, Toby Jayaratne, and Carol Tavris. 1973. "The Queen Bee Syndrome." In *The Female Experience,* edited by C. Tarvis. Del Mar, CA: CRM Books.

Steiner, Linda. 2012. "Failed Theories: Explaining Gender Difference in Journalism." *Review of Communication* 12 (3): 201–23. doi:10.1080/15358593.2012.666559.

Sternberg, Robert J. 2006. "The Nature of Creativity." *Creativity Research Journal* 18 (1): 87–98.

Stuhlfaut, Mark W. 2011. "Language at a Different Level: The Creative Code of Ethnically Oriented IMC Agencies." *International Journal of Integrated Marketing Communications* 3 (2): 77–89.

Stuhlfaut, Mark W., and Chan Yun Yoo. 2011. "A Tool for Evaluating Advertising Concepts: Desirable Characteristics as Viewed by Creative Practitioners." *Journal of Marketing Communications* 19 (2): 81–97. doi:10.1080/13527266.2010.550009.

Target Market News. 2012. "Survey Contrasts Perceptions between Multicultural and White Ad Professionals," April. http://targetmarketnews.com/storyid04131201.htm.

"The Talent-Crunch Crisis: We've Got to Step Up Outreach to Young People." 2014. *Advertising Age.* Accessed October 11. http://adage.com/article/guest-columnists/ad-industry-talent-crunch-means-reach-young-people/236468/.

Tsui, Anne S., and Barbara A. Gutek. 1984. "A Role Set Analysis of Gender Differences in Performance, Affective Relationships, and Career Success of Industrial Middle Managers." *Academy of Management Journal* 27 (3): 619–35.

Vagnoni, Anthony. 2005. "Ads Are from Mars, Women Are from Venus." *America's Graphic Design Magazine* 59 (2): 52–55.

Van der Pool, Lisa. 2002. "What Women Think." *Adweek Eastern Edition* 43 (22): 28.

Volpi, Jack. 1998. "What Makes Men Perfect for Creative? Respondents Baffled: Agency Execs Put Subjective Gender Spin on Some Posts." *Advertising Age* 69 (49): 8.

Vonk, Nancy, and Janice Kestin. 2005. *Pick Me.* Hoboken, NJ: John Wiley and Sons.

Wallas, Graham. 1926. *The Art of Thought.* New York: Harcourt, Brace and Company.

Watson, Carol. 2011. "Impact Study 2011: From Where I Stand . . . Advertising Diversity and Inclusion Perspectives." Tangerine-Watson. http://www.ana.net/miccontent/show/id/kp-tangerine-impact-study.

Weisberg, Larry, and Brett Robbs. 1997a. "Creative Department Still Boys' Playground." *Advertising Age,* November 24: 28.

———. 1997b. "A Study of the Underrepresentation of Women in Advertising Agency Creative Departments." Paper presented at the Association for Education in Journalism and Mass Communication (AEJMC), Chicago, IL. http://list.msu.edu/cgi-bin/wa?A3=ind9710b&L=AEJMC&E=7BIT&P=1117976&B=–&T=TEXT%2FPLAIN;%20charset=US-ASCII.

Wentz, Laurel. 2016. "Kate Stanners Is Saatchi's New Global CCO." *Advertising Age,* April 6. Accessed April 7, 2016. http://adage.com/article/agencies/kate-stanners-saatchi-s-global-cco/303448/.

West, Douglas C. 1993. "Cross-National Creative Personalities, Processes, and Agency Philosophies." *Journal of Advertising Research* 37: 53–62.

"Where Are All the Black People: Part 3 [press release]." 2014. *The One Club.* Accessed November 17. http://www.oneclub.org/oc/press/-where-are-all-the-black-peoplea-part-3.

"Why Getting More Women onto Award Show Juries Could Be the Ultimate Ad Industry Hack." 2015. *Little Black Book Online.* Accessed January 24. http://lbbonline.com/news/why-getting-more-women-onto-award-show-juries-could-be-the-ultimate-ad-industry-hack/.

Williams, Christine L., Chandra Muller, and Kristine Kilanski. 2012. "Gendered Organizations in the New Economy." *Gender and Society* 26 (4): 549–73. doi:10.1177/0891243212445466.

Windels, Kasey Farris. 2008. "Proportional Representation and Regulatory Focus: The Case for Cohorts among Female Creatives." PhD diss., University of Texas.

Windels, Kasey. 2011. "What's in a Number? Minority Status and Implications for Creative Professionals." *Creativity Research Journal* 23 (4): 321–29. doi:10.1080/10400419.2011.621820.

Windels, Kasey and Karen L. Mallia. 2015. "How Being Female Impacts Learning and Career Growth in Advertising Creative Departments." *Employee Relations* 37 (1): 122–40. doi:10.1108/ER-02-2014-0011.

Windels, Kasey, Karen L. Mallia, and Sheri J. Broyles. 2013. "Soft Skills: The Difference between Leading and Leaving the Advertising Industry?" *Journal of Advertising Education* 17 (2): 17.

Windels, Kasey and Wei-Na Lee. 2012. "The Construction of Gender and Creativity in Advertising Creative Department." *Gender in Management: An International Journal* 27 (8): 502–19.

Windels, Kasey, Wei-Na Lee, and Yi-Hsin Yeh, 2010. "Does the Creative Boys' Club Begin in the Classroom?" *Journal of Advertising Education* 14 (2): 15–24.

Chapter 9

Exporting Gender Bias

Anglo-American Echoes in Swedish Advertising Creative Departments

Jean M. Grow

"At the top of the industry is a closed loop of White guys talking to other White guys" (Ember 2016a, B1). So says Cindy Gallop, founder and former chair of BBH London and an outspoken supporter of women in advertising. She underscores the power and pervasiveness of heteronormative gender cultural norms in advertising, whether in Sweden or any other country where the global advertising powerhouses Omnicom, Interpublic, WPP, or Publicis have influence.

Previous work has explored the under-representation of women in advertising creative departments (Broyles and Grow 2008; Grow and Broyles 2011; Grow, Roca, and Broyles 2012; Klein 2000; Mallia 2009; Mallia and Windels 2011; Nixon 2003; Nixon and Crew 2006; Weisberg and Robbs 1997; Windels 2011; Windels and Lee 2012; Windels, Mallia, and Broyles 2013). Such studies have investigated women's experiences in the United States and in Britain, homes to three of the world's major advertising holding companies: Omnicom and Interpublic in the United States and WPP in Britain. A fourth, Publicis, is French. This work also demonstrates that the advertising industry functions within a heteronormative gender system, which presumes women and men to be different (Broyles and Grow 2008; Grow 2009; Grow and Broyles 2011; Mallia 2009; Nixon 2003; Windels and Lee 2012). Further, they confirm that the cultural norms, those unconscious understandings governing individual behaviors within this cultural group, tend to be stereotypically masculine. The resulting "boys' club" (Grow and Broyles 2011) environment within advertising creative departments privileges men, while negatively affecting the hiring, retention, and promotion of women (Broyles and Grow 2008; Grow and Broyles 2011; Klein 2000; Mallia 2009; Mallia and Windels 2011; Nixon and Crew 2006; Weisberg and Robbs 1997; Windels 2011; Windels and Lee 2012; Windels, Mallia, and Broyles 2013).

In this chapter, I explore the experiences and perceptions of women working in advertising creative departments in Sweden, the most egalitarian country in the world (Rothstein 2012). In doing so, I offer further evidence of the global pervasiveness of the Western heteropatriarchal gender culture in advertising creative departments. My work is framed by feminist theory, which helps articulate how Anglo-American heteronormative sexism is also experienced by Swedish women creatives and suggests that locally specific or indigenous cultural norms and values have limited influence within advertising creative departments. Ultimately, I argue that gender bias is exported around the world as part of an industry-wide white, Anglo-American, heteropatriarchal cultural norm.

To provide context, I begin with an overview of women in advertising, followed by a review of Swedish cultural norms and values and of the Swedish advertising industry. Next, I outline relevant feminist thought before turning to the theoretical underpinnings that frame the gendered system that defines advertising. I then address the method I used to gather information, in-depth interviews with management-level Swedish women creatives. The analysis, based on the experiences and perceptions of these Swedish creatives, echoes the experiences and perceptions of women creatives in Britain and the United States. I contend that an Anglo-American version of advertising creative culture has been exported around the world. In the process, gendered practices have become the norm, creating and reinforcing a systemic heteronormative masculine culture that pervades advertising creative departments, despite their geographic location or the local norms. I write as a white, heterosexual, feminist woman who made a career in advertising before joining the academy.

CULTURAL CONTEXT

To help readers understand the cultural context in which advertising women creatives work, I first provide a brief overview of women working in the advertising industry before focusing on women working in creative departments. I then turn to a discussion of Swedish cultural norms and values, and the Swedish advertising industry.

Women in Advertising

Creative departments are the location where ads are concepted (conceptualized) and created. People working here are referred to as *creatives* and include art directors, copywriters, and creative directors, who are the creative managers. In the United States, women make up 56 percent of the advertising workforce (Equal Employment Opportunity Commission 2014);

a study by the British Institute of Practitioners in Advertising (IPA) found that women represent 49 percent of the British advertising workforce (Klein 2000). According to the Swedish Association of Communication Agencies (KOMM), an organization that parallels IPA, women make up 49 percent of Sweden's advertising workforce (KOMM 2014). Although these data suggest that women in advertising are employed in roughly equal numbers, in creative departments things look different. In a study using advertising industry data across fifty countries, Tao Deng and I found that worldwide women make up only 20.3 percent of all creatives and only 14.6 percent of all creative directors (Grow and Deng 2014). We also found that in the United States women make up 27.7 percent of the creative department and 25.2 percent of creative directors; in Britain women make up just 13.9 percent of the creative department and 8.1 percent of creative directors. Data from KOMM (2014) show that in Sweden, women make up 38 percent of the creative department and 16 percent of creative directors.

In addition to limited numbers of women being employed in advertising creative departments, creative women earn less than creative men (Grow and Broyles 2011; Mallia 2009; Windels, Mallia, and Broyles 2013). One of the key factors that can increase a creative's salary and provide the ability to rise into management is winning creative awards, such as the Cannes Festival of Creativity, the One Show, the Effies in marketing, the American Advertising Federation's Addys, *Communication Arts*' CA Awards, and the Clio Awards. However, when it comes to these coveted awards, women win far fewer than men (Mallia 2009; Windels and Lee 2012). A 2014 study found that 11.5 percent of the *Communication Arts* award winners were women creative directors, representing a 319 percent increase from six years earlier, when women were only 3.6 percent of the award winners (3% Conference 2014). Awards competitions are further complicated by the fact that very few women judge these awards (Mallia 2009; Windels and Lee 2012). This is a significant problem, according to Jean Batthany, executive creative director at DDB: "If all the advertising is being created through that dominant male lens and you look at what the result is, there's a bias in that and there's only one perspective" (Ember 2016a, B1).

The scarcity of women creatives and the gender bias that drives it are not new topics. We should be shocked by stories such as the recent ouster of J. Walter Thompson's CEO, Gustavo Martinez, for allegations of gender and racial bias and sexual harassment exemplified by speaking of raping women who did not comply with his wishes, and calling African-American employees "monkeys" (Birkner 2016; Coffee 2016; Ember 2016b; Vranica and Tadena 2016). But the truth is, gender bias garners headlines infrequently, and the trade press largely ignores racial bias. Publicis' CEO Maurice Lévy referred to Martinez's comments as a "one-time mistake" and not something "endemic of what's happening in our industry" (Birkner 2016, 34). In a swift and powerful response, WPP's CEO, Maurice Sorrell, said he "violently" disagreed with Lévy and noted that "when we get to senior levels of management, the number of women drops, unacceptably, to a third [of all executives]" (Brikner 2016, 34). It should not surprise us that fear silences many women. "It is difficult for them [women] to address gender bias in the [advertising] industry . . . because they want to protect relationships in the industry" (Ember 2016a, B1).

It is important to note that, despite Martinez's Argentinean heritage, advertising is largely a white, Anglo industry. Further, the topics of racial bias or minority hiring in advertising draw little attention from the trade press. African Americans accounted for just 5.3 percent of the employees within marketing communications (including advertising and public relations), yet they represent 11.7 percent of the US workforce (Vranica and Tadena 2016). Hispanics make up 11.7 percent of marketing communications employees, yet they represent 16.4 percent of the US workforce (Vranica and Tadena 2016). Further complicating matters is a siloed industry structure with non-whites and non-Anglos largely employed within multicultural advertising agencies. These agencies are segregated from the elite general market agencies (Altstiel and Grow 2017). As I turn my thoughts to Sweden, I am struck by the need for scholars to expand our work to address minority representation in American advertising.

Swedish Cultural Norms and Values

For the purpose of this study, I chose Sweden because it highlights a counterpoint to the Anglo-American cultural norms that frame American and British advertising agencies. Sweden is the most egalitarian country in the world (Rothstein 2012). According to the Gender Equity Index (2015), an index produced by the European Institute for Gender Equality to measure gender equity in Europe, Sweden demonstrates the most gender-neutral cultural norms and equitable social practices of any European country. Cultural norms are the unconscious understandings that govern an individual's behaviors; cultural values are ways in which society or social groups express cultural norms (De Mooij 2014). Stereotypical masculine cultural norms may be expressed in ways including, but not limited to, competitiveness, risk-taking, toughness, and so on (Broyles and Grow 2008; Grow and Broyles 2011; Mallia 2009). Stereotypical feminine cultural norms may be expressed in ways including, but not limited to, collaboration, empathy, and good listening skills (Broyles and Grow 2008; Grow and Broyles 2011; Mallia 2009). Equitable cultural norms are norms that both women and men may embrace (De Mooij 2014). Considering that the mean gender equity score, on a scale of 0 to 100, for all twenty-seven EU countries is 54, whereas Sweden's score is 74.3 (The Local 2013), it is fair to say that Sweden may be one country where legal and social structures encourage social institutions and commercial enterprises to robustly support gender equity.

Sweden's embrace of equality began in the 1970s; it emerged out of the women's movement and is based on redistributive social justice. Swedish policy changes ultimately enshrined values of equity and social justice within Swedish legal structures (Swedish Institute 2013). For instance, Swedes have long had universal healthcare and institutionalized childcare subsidies (Järvklo 2013). In 2002, parental leave was increased to 480 days, and in 2009 a strict Discrimination Act solidified Sweden's egalitarian values into the social fabric of Swedish life (Swedish Institute 2013). Yet, according to a United Nations report from the Commission on the Status of Women, Swedish women still take more parental leave than men and work part time in greater numbers (United Nations 2013). In addition, Swedish women working full time are paid lower salaries than men (Statistics Sweden 2012). Despite Sweden's commitment to equality, disparities remain. Nonetheless, gender equity is higher in Sweden than virtually any other country in the world (Järvklo 2013; Swedish Institute 2013).

Like agencies in the United States and Britain, Swedish advertising agencies are located in major urban centers with the majority located in Stockholm, along with a few in Gothenburg. Although women and men are employed in generally equal numbers in Swedish advertising, women constitute just 38 percent of the creative workforce and account for only 16 percent of all creative directors (KOMM 2014). Further, according to the KOMM, creative women are paid less than men. Women copywriters younger than thirty earn 10 percent less than men, whereas women copywriters older than fifty earn 11 percent less than men, and women creatives at mid-career, ages thirty to fifty, earn 32 percent less than men creatives (KOMM 2012). The *Gender Equity Index* places Sweden as the leader in gender equity overall (The Local 2013). Yet in terms of both hiring and compensation for women creatives, it seems creative gender equity is not found in Swedish advertising.

Alvesson's (1998) early work on the institutional culture of Swedish advertising finds it, as a whole, more feminine. That is, he suggests its structure is collaborative with pairs or couples at the nexus of creative production. He also highlights structural forms of support including childcare, flexible work hours, and a generally more malleable work environment, all of which appear to reflect Swedish cultural values. However, Alvesson (1998, 984) also observes that Swedish advertising agency practices are "extraordinarily patriarchal," which he defines as having an institutional culture where "masculine values are predominant and gender oppression [is] pronounced." Taken in totality, it appears that Swedish advertising agencies are also dominated by masculine, heterosexist norms, not dissimilar to the culture within Anglo-American advertising agencies in the United States and Britain.

GENDERING THE SYSTEM

Cultural and organizational feminism, along with feminist perspectives on language, support my analysis of in-depth interviews I conducted with Swedish women creatives to shed light on the gendered creative culture in which they work.

Feminist Perspectives

As citizens of the Western world, we live in a predominately masculine culture, which constrains women by privileging men. Women and men are socialized into gender roles, which "operate in relatively autonomous yet interrelated spheres" (Calasanti and Bailey 1991, 38). *Gender* refers to a culturally determined set of characteristics ascribed to women and men (Tannen 1999). In that sense, gender functions as a "mechanism that enjoin(s) people to live as women and men" (Golombisky 2015, 391). Gender is also "politically constructed" (Dow and Condit 2005, 449). In fact, "gender and sex have been repeatedly attended to throughout history as a means of controlling and subordinating women" (Dow and Condit 2005, 453). The subjugation of women is the foundation for gender-based social and economic inequities (Calasanti and Bailey 1991; Jamieson 1995; Tong 2013). Further, women within Western cultures are often sanctioned if they claim to be different from men or the same as men. In this way, women are held to a different set of standards. In other words, women are systematically trapped in a nearly intractable double bind (Jamieson 1995).

In advertising agencies, there are norms and codes that frame its fraternity culture (Broyles and Grow 2008; Grow 2009; Grow and Broyles 2011; Klein 2000; Mallia 2009; Mallia and Windels 2011; Nixon 2003; Nixon and Crew 2006; Weisberg and Robbs 1997; Windels 2011; Windels and Lee 2012; Windels et al. 2013). This fraternity culture can also be explained, in part, by cultural feminism, which suggests that women and men are reared in and experience life in separate gendered cultures. Cultural feminism posits that women and men "perform [gender] in different ways in different cultures" (Dow and Condit 2005, 455). Living in separate cultures and performing gender differently reinforces culturally constructed gender differences.

Fletcher's (1998, 164) feminist relational theory delves into how gender influences relationships and draws "attention to what has been hidden, obscured, or invisible." Drawing attention to women's frequent invisibility makes clear the culturally constructed differences that separate women and men. Through the lens of cultural feminism, this research draws our attention to this culturally constructed gender divide, which is powerfully articulated by the "laddish" behaviors within advertising creative departments that create "fundamental barriers to women" (Nixon 2003, 98). Fletcher (1998) might argue that in doing so, everyone's interests are preserved. However, preserving everyone's interest is not the goal within the advertising industry. For advertising "is shot through with gendered understandings of the creative person" (Nixon 2003, 115). Those who run advertising creative departments, predominately white men, are "complicit in reinforcing links between masculinity and creativity" (Nixon 2003, 104). In the end, "women's knowledge has been absent from what we believe we know to be true about the world" (Golombisky 2010, 169). In the same way, women creatives' expression of what it means to be creative is missing from advertising culture.

Feminist perspectives on organizational management suggest that organizations, including advertising agencies, are never gender neutral. "Organizations have been created by and for men and are based on male experiences" (Meyerson and Fletcher 2000, 129). Organizational systems are framed by gendered "interactions and interrelatedness of various components that make up the environment in which an organization functions" (Creedon 1993, 158). Organizational feminism further argues that the inequities that hamper women's success in business have been "rendered invisible" (Lewis 2014, 1846). This is, in part, because the "identified connection between masculinity and management is always interpreted as detrimental to women because of their difference from the norm [men]" (Lewis 2014, 1847). There is no point, from the perspective of the powerbrokers (men), to explore these gendered differences. Thus these differences, particularly the differences that hold women back, remain invisible.

Higgins, (1997) regulatory fit model proposes that there are two distinct organizational environments: promotion-oriented and prevention-oriented. Promotional environments welcome self-promotion, especially for men who have gender privilege. Prevention-oriented environments discourage self-promotion, especially for women who lack gender privilege. Thus, regardless of whether women work in prevention or promotional organizations, they are likely to experience the constraints of a sexist system, just as Jamieson's (1995) double bind predicts. Complicating matters, Carlson and Crawford (2011, 361) argue that "masculine principles and practices pervade organizational life under the guise of gender neutrality . . . making conforming to them a prerequisite for managerial success." Yet these biases "erect powerful but subtle and often invisible barriers for women that arise from cultural assumptions and organizational structures, practices, and patterns of interaction that inadvertently benefit men while putting women at a disadvantage" (Ibarra, Ely, and Kolb 2013, 64).

This is particularly true in advertising's "culture of commerce" where there is a masculine "cult of creativity" (Nixon 2003, 166). This cult of creativity is exemplified by "masculine juvenility and the childlike qualities of creative people . . . [creating] intense bonds between young male creatives and the older men who manage creative departments that helped to fix the culture" (Nixon 2003, 163). Ultimately, organizations reinforce gendered arrangements in formal and informal ways (Acker 1990; Carlson and Crawford 2011; Creedon 1993; Ibarra, Ely, and Kolb 2013; Lewis 2014; Meyerson and Fletcher 2000). In advertising, these arrangements are "complicit in reinforcing the link between masculinity and creative jobs" (Nixon 2003, 104).

The Power of Language

I also find it useful in gender analysis to consider language in the context of interactions, as we know gendered language patterns are pervasive in organizational culture. Language has significant influence on social formation and cultural evolution. We often bring with us the language we have been socialized to use (Tannen 1990, 1999). Tannen (1990) suggests women are socialized to be listeners and not speakers, just as men are socialized to be speakers and not listeners. Men tend to use talk as a "means to preserve independence and negotiate and maintain status in a hierarchal social order" (Tannen 1990, 77). Women use language as a way of building rapport, "a way of establishing connections and negotiating relationships" (Tannen 1990, 77). Although Tannen's (1990, 1999) work largely reflects a white world, so, too, does advertising. Within this social context, women can feel invisible in conversations with men. However, according to Kendall and Tannen (1997, 97), "researchers must ask not only about power, but also about how power and solidarity (or status and connection) interact." In a heteropatriarchal advertising culture, the socialized and stereotypically gendered use of masculine language creates powerful interactions, which negatively affect women creatives more than men creatives. For example, in advertising, men are viewed as youthful and creative (Gregory 2009; Nixon 2003), whereas in broader culture, "women are seen as severe and lacking in humor" (Tannen 1999, 237). For women working in creative departments, this can be especially detrimental as youth and humor are significant drivers of postmodern advertising. Further, humor is judged through a masculine prism, which further limits women creatives' access to creative departments. Finally, there is the use of the word *girl,* which is common in American culture. The problem is that the word *girl* sexualizes and infantilizes women (Duschinsky 2013). Not surprisingly, the word *girl* is a common linguistic reference for women within the advertising industry. This proves problematic for women. Women creative workers are sexualized and infantilized, but so too are the women within the images that the advertising industry creates.

Sexism remains; "it has just gone underground" (Meyerson and Fletcher 2000, 128). The problem with the underground nature of gender inequity is that it creates "a subtle pattern of systemic disadvantage, which blocks all but a few women from career advancement" (Meyerson and Fletcher 2000, 128). Within the heteropatriarchal advertising industry, men benefit from this unfair advantage. This advantage also truncates creative outcomes by trapping creative departments within a masculine paradigm, which disadvantages women and limits everyone's ability to think about advertising and creativity in other perhaps more creative ways. Further, even if women creatives choose to conform to masculine cultural norms, women creatives still remain women. As such, they remain outsiders judged to be inadequate by sole virtue of their gender. In the end, women working in advertising creative departments are not less creative. They are simply stymied by a system defined and replicated by and for men.

THE STUDY

In an effort to investigate to what extent local norms might affect the culture within Swedish advertising creative departments, I interviewed Swedish women creatives, gathering interpretations of their experiences.

Women creative directors were chosen as the participants for two reasons. First, individuals with more extensive work histories offer the greatest potential for teasing out patterns (Dodd 2012). Second, Swedish advertising is a small community; women in creative management with more job security may feel more comfortable speaking about their experiences than entry- or mid-level creatives, thus offering the greatest potential for candor.

I contacted the KOMM, which provided a list of twenty women creative directors, reflecting just how small the Swedish advertising community is. All potential participants were contacted via e-mail and told I was interested in their experiences working as advertising creatives in Sweden. I guaranteed them anonymity and let them know the interview would be done via Skype. Ten women agreed to participate. I knew only one of the participants prior to the interviews. Each interview lasted, on average, one hour, and all were conducted near the end of the workday or after hours. I conducted all the interviews in English, recorded them, and then immediately transcribed them. Follow-up e-mails were used to obtain clarifications. I asked open- and closed-ended questions, and I collected demographic information. I began each interview with broad, open-ended questions, allowing for a "more complete understanding of the phenomenon through the eyes of the informants" (Windels and Lee 2012, 507). I also allowed the women to take the discussion where they wanted it to go.

Using grounded theory (Glaser and Strauss 1967), I conducted inductive analyses of the transcripts as a whole, allowing themes to emerge. The categories that emerged were observed differences, hiring and promotion, practitioner descriptors, and suggestions for change. Verbatim quotes, which verified themes, were clustered under each of the four thematic categories. To honor anonymity, no references to particular participants are used in the present analysis. Third, I conducted inductive analysis within each of the four thematic categories. This analysis allowed me to focus on interpreting the thematic discourse, which in turn allowed me to contextualize the world in which Swedish women creatives work. Fourth, where appropriate, I employed a simple nonstatistical quantitative analysis to quantify responses. Finally, I applied feminist theories to interpret and articulate the nuances within and across the four thematic threads.

Additionally, I asked questions to capture and quantify demographic details. The ten Swedish women creative directors ranged in age from thirty-six to fifty-four and had been in advertising an average of 22.3 years. Five women held the title of creative director; two, founder–creative director; two, partner–creative director; and one, chief executive officer–creative director. Each woman had worked in management, as a creative director or higher, for an average of 8.5 years. Two women worked at large multinational agencies with thirty or more people in the creative department. Six worked at mid-sized agencies with five to fifteen people in the creative department. Two worked in small boutique shops with fewer than five creative employees. Each woman worked across a range of product categories, although every woman, at some point, had been assigned to women-oriented products such as feminine hygiene, hair care, or cleaning products. Only three of the women had worked on premier brands traditionally targeting men, such as beer, automotive, or finance. All participants were married and referred to their partners as men, and each had an average of 2.5 children. All the women were white and of Swedish or mixed Swedish–European ancestry.

ANGLO-AMERICAN ECHOES: AN ANALYSIS OF WOMEN CREATIVES' EXPERIENCES IN SWEDEN

The experiences and perceptions shared by these Swedish women creatives point to a heterogendered culture within Swedish advertising creative departments, despite egalitarian cultural norms within Sweden. The insights these women shared articulate four themes: career trajectory through the lens of gender; perceptions of gendered differences and the experience of discrimination; practitioner descriptions and the silos they illustrate; and suggestions for change to break down barriers, which I include in my closing remarks. My initial analysis is guided by cultural and organizational feminism, which build on each other, as they both share the common thread of making the invisible visible. My analysis articulates the systemic nature of heteronormative gender bias, which echoes across the advertising industry, particularly in creative departments. I argue that the fundamental barriers that limit women creatives in Sweden reflect the same barriers that limit women creatives working in Western-style advertising environments worldwide, that is, a sexist culture that supports a masculine "cult of creativity" (Nixon 2003, 166).

Career Trajectories through the Lens of Gender

There was strong agreement among the participants that women are underrepresented in Swedish advertising creative departments. Three aspects emerged related to women creatives' career trajectories: hiring, promotion, and salary.

Nine of the women perceived a lack of hiring equity based on either gender bias or the need to fit in, which feminists would argue is gender bias. For instance, one woman said, "There are more men in recruiting positions, and men tend to recruit other men." Another observed, "The pressure of companies today is to have women creatives. But I think . . . the men are always going to recognize themselves in the man's portfolio and not the girl's." This response, referring to women as "girls," articulates how women creatives are routinely infantilized (Duschinsky 2013). Organizational feminism, including regulatory fit (Higgins 1997), provides context to these comments. It suggests that men will hire other men within promotionally driven environments, like advertising creative departments, which privilege men, whereas cultural feminism suggests that a heteronormative gender culture creates barriers to women. The single woman I interviewed who viewed hiring as equitable thought it was because "it is much easier in Sweden." This may imply that local Swedish values have some positive effect in terms of hiring. It may also indicate external pressure, as suggested by the woman who spoke of the "pressure of companies today is to have women creatives," despite what appears to be a tendency to ignore this external pressure.

Perspectives on promotion followed a similar pattern. Six women perceived that women creatives experience promotional inequity, and two indicated there was equity but qualified their responses, essentially demonstrating inequity. Two women were unsure. Those speaking of promotional inequity linked it to gender, noting pay disparities or unconscious bias on the part of the men making the decisions. This speaks to both cultural and organizational feminist arguments that many of the inequities that hamper women are rooted in invisible bias, in large part because heteronormative gender rules require conforming to masculine principles and practices to fit into the organizational culture (Carlson and Crawford 2011; Creedon 1993; Dow and Condit 2005; Ibarra, Ely, and Kolb 2013; Lewis 2014). One woman put it this way: "Men get more opportunities all the time because it's other men who rule the opportunities. And I'm not certain that they are aware of it." Another woman mentioned family as a factor, yet ultimately brought her comments back to men promoting men: "Women suffer from the fact they are still often more burdened with the responsibilities for family and children, which limits how much they can give and thereby limits their promotions. . . . Men tend to promote other men." Another woman who qualified her responses said this: "Clients ask for women. . . . If you are super good in Stockholm today, it's easier for me to get a job because I'm a woman." Notice, however, her perception that women need to be "super good." Yet she provided no acknowledgement of the gender bias that her perception illustrates. Finally, the two women who were also unsure suggested family was a factor. "When you [are] having children, perhaps you will fall back." In this way, a masculine code is articulated, suggesting that family is feminine and implying that women (and not men) with families lack commitment.

When discussing salary, all of the women perceived compensation to be inequitable. Most women simply said "no" when asked if there was pay equity. However, some expanded their comments. Said one woman, "I know for a fact that men have higher salaries than women." Another woman perceived that women lacked negotiation acumen and confidence: "I think women are not good when you discuss salary. I think men are much better. They [men] know what they are worth." The idea that some women perceive themselves as less confident fits into Higgins's (1997) model of regulatory fit, in that these women appear to meet the gender expectations of androcentric organizational culture. Yet organizational feminism argues that gender bias prevents women from successfully promoting themselves and then blames the women for lack of career advancement. This is a systemic organizational problem and not an individual issue. The promotional struggles these women expressed also illustrate the classic double bind (Jamieson 1995). The ubiquitous privileging of masculine gender truncates Swedish women creatives' advancement, but it also distorts perceptions of work-style differences within Swedish advertising creative departments.

Perceptions of Differences and the Experience of Discrimination

In discussions about work-style behavioral differences between women and men, three patterns of responses emerged: perceived differences, perceived discrimination, and why women leave advertising creative departments.

Eight of ten women perceived gender-based work-style differences between creative women and men. These women framed the differences around the masculine cultural norms that dominate Swedish advertising creative departments. One woman said, "Boys stick together very tight with the same outfits, the same interests, the same attitudes. And being a minority, being a girl, in the group makes it more difficult." Another woman commented, "They (men) share the same humor and jokes. They build a culture that is very encouraging and nourishing for them. Because women are in the minority, we often just become the audience to this culture." Four of the eight women who perceived differences pointedly discussed men's way of expressing themselves. One woman said, "Men act more confident whether they are or not. They claim more space. They speak louder. They are heard. They confirm each other." Another woman suggested, "It's always better if you mix genders when you build a team." Both of the previous comments illustrate gender performance and its negative effect on women. The two women who noted no gender-based work-style differences were ambivalent or perhaps unconsciousness of any bias that they, or others, might face. As one stated, "Of course, there are preferences (for working with one gender over another) between different persons. But I can't say that when I work with women it's a different thing than when I work with men."

Seven women identified what they perceived as discriminatory attitudes or behaviors. The women's responses suggest that discrimination is more prominent early in women creatives' careers. As one woman said: "It was quite hard when I was younger. . . . I don't think that's so much a problem now [at my age]." Other women observed discrimination in purported attempts to hire other women creatives. One woman recalled being told, "We would really like to hire a woman, but they [women] don't have any good ideas." This suggests a cultural feminist explanation that in a masculine creative culture, men's creativity would be highly valued while women's creative ideas would be less valued. However, the most common experience women related was being ignored in favor of men. This is at the heart of both cultural and organizational feminist arguments. One woman stated, "They [men] went to the presentations [with my ideas], and I wasn't allowed to come." Another participant said: "I stand up for an hour and talk about the presentation and tell them [the clients] all about what we think. Then he [the client] asks his question to the man in the room instead of me. It happens a lot." All seven of the women who perceived discrimination related their experiences as "a subtle thing." Of the three women who said they had experienced "nothing major," one woman said she thought it was a "plus to be a woman."

I next turn to why women leave Swedish advertising creative departments. In fact, seven of the women indicated they believe that women leave advertising for different reasons than men. Among these women, some thought women creatives leave because of family and the work–life challenges that children can bring. As one woman said, "It's often because they [women] don't get their family life and work to match." Another woman said, "I don't think it's biology." This woman thinks that women are socialized to take responsibility for the family; at the same time women are not recognized for having time-consuming family responsibilities or good time-management skills in the professional world. These comments suggest that women have difficulty finding a fit, as they lack gender privilege, which is an articulation of the power of regulatory fit (Higgins 1997). One woman spoke of her perceptions that the creative department is "so male." A different woman said, "It's so much about rules that men put up." Yet another woman simply said, "Women are not recognized," which speaks to feminist perspectives on women's invisibility. Finally, another woman said: "Women feel alienated. They don't really feel like they belong." These comments support organizational feminist thought, which suggests that "organizations have been created by and for men and are based on male experiences" (Meyerson and Fletcher 2000, 129). Three women felt gender did not influence why women leave advertising creative. One woman stated, "I think it's an age problem for both [women and men]," adding, "My female friends often do it [leave] because they think it's [advertising] too shallow." Another woman simply said, "It's [advertising] not easy." Yet another said, "After a while you get tired of it [the work]." These comments also might be interpreted as a problem of regulatory fit because it is more difficult to work in an environment in which one does not fit into the culture.

Practitioner Descriptors

To explore the perceptions these women creatives had of their fellow Swedish creatives, both women and men, I asked participants two parallel questions designed to elicit top-of-mind reactions. Specifically, I asked the women to state the first three words that come to mind when they think of Swedish women creatives and then the first three words that come to mind for Swedish men creatives. Eight thematic categories emerged (see Table 9.1). Five were attributed to both women and men creatives, two were exclusively attributed to men creatives, and one was exclusively attributed to women creatives. The five categories attributed to both women and men were "bold" (twelve cites for women and nine for men), "thoughtful" (five cites for women and three for men), "smart" (four cites for women and three for men), "alive" (four cites for women and two for men), and "creative" (two cites for women and three for men). The two categories exclusively attributed to men were "ego"

Table 9.1 Thematic Categories

Attributions	*Women and Men*	*Women and Men*	*Women and Men*	*Women and Men*	*Women and Men*	*Men Only*	*Men Only*	*Women Only*
Thematic Categories	Bold	Thoughtful	Smart	Alive	Creative	Ego	Humor	Responsible
Attribution Distribution	12 Women 9 Men	5 Women 3 Men	4 Women 3 Men	4 Women 2 Men	2 Women 3 Men	5 Men	5 Men	3 Women

Note: Attributions were derived from interviews with the 10 participants who were asked to state the first three words that come to mind when they thought of Swedish women creatives and Swedish men creatives.

(five cites) and "humor" (five cites). The single thematic category attributed only to women was "responsible" (three cites). In the category "creative," the word was repeated multiple times. Likewise for the category and word "responsible." Other categories represent a clustering of the same and similar words. For example, the "bold" category includes words such as "strong." Other paired matches included "thoughtful" and "conscientious," "smart" and "intelligent," "alive" and "energetic," "ego" and "egotistic," as well as "humor" and "funny."

I begin with an analysis of the two categories shared by both genders. Nine out of ten women perceived men creatives as being bold. All ten women perceived women creatives to be bold, with one of the women repeating the word "bold" three times in her description of women creatives. These Swedish women creatives clearly perceived the need to be "bold" as a significant quality, no matter the gender. Tannen's (1990, 1999) work suggests "bold" and "strong" in the present case have stereotypical masculine connotations. The women's perception of boldness as the most common behavior trait powerfully points to Swedish advertising as a masculine world (Alvesson 1998). The women also said that creative women are bolder than creative men. Organizational feminism suggests that boldness and strength present "masculine principles and practices [that] pervade organizational life under the guise of gender neutrality . . . making conforming to them a prerequisite for managerial success" (Carlson and Crawford 2011, 361). This suggests that Swedish women creatives see either a compelling need to conform to the environmental cultural norms in which they work or a need for boldness to survive within the highly masculine culture. "Creative" is also a quality shared by both women and men working in Swedish creative departments. "Creative" had less than half as many references as "bold," despite the fact that "creative" described the work these women do. Regardless of gender, the quality of being "bold," a powerful masculine behavior quality, appears to trump the art of creativity. Indeed, I might argue women require a degree of boldness to attempt to compete in a patently masculine environment in the first place.

Two categories of behavioral qualities, "ego" and "humor," were perceived by the Swedish women creatives as exclusive to men. Swedish women creatives perceived "ego" as an exclusively male trait. One could argue that there is a US taboo against nice women exhibiting "ego" because women are meant to be invisible and selfless, which are traits incompatible with egotism. As Alvesson (1998, 984) observes, Swedish advertising agencies are "extraordinarily patriarchal." The second category that was perceived as exclusive to men was "humor." Tannen (1999) argues that women are perceived as lacking in humor. Without the cultural capital of "humor," women are less likely to find success in the advertising creative department. The power of male humor was also demonstrated earlier when some of the women creatives spoke of jokes as a way of "nourishing" men, while diminishing women by scripting them as "audience to this [men's] culture." By citing "humor" as related only to men, these Swedish women creatives reinforced their role as silent audience members rather than active participants in creative culture.

Finally, the single behavioral category perceived as exclusive to Swedish women creatives was a stereotypically female trait, "responsible" (Broyles and Grow 2008; Grow and Broyles 2011; Mallia 2009). The fact that the women perceived themselves to be "responsible" while perceiving the men as having "ego" and "humor" correlates with socialized gendered norms. These norms are part of formal and informal arrangements that organizations use to reinforce gender conformity (Acker 1990; Carlson and Crawford 2011; Creedon 1993; Ibarra, Ely, and Kolb 2013; Lewis 2014; Meyerson and Fletcher 2000). These arrangements, evident in Swedish creative departments described here, are "complicit in reinforcing the link between masculine and creative jobs" (Nixon 2003, 104). If advertising creative departments nurture and protect a youthful lad culture of bad boys goading one another to push the boundaries and see how much they can get away with to achieve individual acclaim, then women *as women* creative directors might be positioned as babysitters and mothers "responsible" for making sure no one gets hurt. This frames creatives as naughty boys just trying to have a bit of fun while humorless mothers look on at the risk of being labeled spoilsports. A review of the words these Swedish women creatives chose to be descriptors for those practicing creative in Sweden supports what the limited number of women have already told us: The contributions women creatives make are largely invisible and block "all but a few women from career advancement" (Meyerson and Fletcher 2000, 128).

Moreover, these Swedish women creatives, with an average of 22.3 years of experience, have articulated an organizational culture within Swedish creative departments that reflects the organizational culture within American and British creative departments. This, despite the fact that Sweden is viewed to be the most egalitarian country in the world (Rothstein 2012), with cultural and social values rooted in social justice. As one of the women said, Swedish advertising creative "women feel alienated; they don't really feel like they belong." Although the women interviewed here perceived the discrimination and marginalization they experience to be "a subtle thing," it is also a real thing. It's time to consider that these experiences, like the experiences of their counterparts in the United States and Britain, are likely to be part of systemic organizational gender bias deeply rooted in advertising creative culture and exported around the world.

CLOSING THE BORDERS TO GENDER BIAS EXPORTATION

This study points to a system of gender bias in advertising creative departments in Sweden that parallels findings from studies in the United States. Despite being the first study to explore the experiences and perceptions of Swedish women creatives, this work has limitations. First, interviewing creative directors provided only the perspectives of women in creative management. Second, Skype interviews may have limited the intimacy and possibly truncated the depth of the women's responses. Third, it is always a disadvantage to conduct interviews in a nonnative language. Finally, ten participants are a small dataset, albeit an insightful one. The words of these Swedish women creatives open fresh understandings, including suggestions for change in terms of what Swedish women creatives can do for themselves and what advertising powerbrokers can do for Swedish women creatives.

In terms of what women can do for themselves, the women in this study saw senior Swedish women creatives as being a "source of power" for junior creative women. In other words, woman-to-woman mentoring is viewed as paramount to enabling women's success in advertising creative departments. Senior women can help junior women, guiding them through the complexities of Jamieson's (1995) gender double bind. The women also spoke of simple things the more junior Swedish women creatives can do for themselves. One women said, "Show off more." "Claim more space," another urged. Yet another advised, "Speak slowly and men will listen more." These strategies speak to a fundamental tenant of both cultural and organizational feminism: making oneself more visible and pushing back against regulatory fit (Higgins 1997). Another woman urged, "never think that you are a girl; you are someone within a team." This directly confronts gender-biased language that sexualizes and infantilizes women (Duschinsky 2013). It encourages junior women creatives to break down the hierarchal social order that men use to maintain their status and privilege (Tannen 1990). Finally, one woman counseled: "Do it your way. Don't be afraid."

Still, changing gendered behaviors does not change the system or its culture. Every woman in this study spoke of the importance of powerbrokers at the top facilitating change, suggesting CEOs could make the biggest difference for Swedish women working in creative. CEOs must offer women equal opportunities, create environments with more open attitudes, create pay equity, and simply hire more women because, as one woman said, "When you start to have more equal [numbers of women] . . . something happens." Lewis (2014) speaks of organizational inequities that render women invisible, whereas Ibarra, Ely, and Kolb (2013) suggest that when women see other women in positions of power, the often-invisible barriers women face begin to come down. The Swedish women creatives also spoke of making agency

CEOs accountable for change, including making men accountable for their unconscious biases. It is time for men and women creatives to account for the ways that advertising's masculine "cult of creativity" is reinforced and perpetuated as normal and ideal.

If, as I believe, we are exporting the US culture of misogyny in the advertising industry's idealized myth of the creative department around the world, then we are also exporting our racism, homophobia, ageism, and ableism. More cross-cultural studies can enhance our understanding of how advertising culture is shared globally.

REFERENCES

3% Conference. 2014. "Female CDs on the Rise." *3% Conference,* October 22, 2015. http://www.3percentconf.com/downloads/female-cds-rise.

Acker, Joan. 1990. "Hierarchies, Jobs, Bodies: A Theory of Gendered Organizations." *Gender and Society* 4 (2): 139–58.

Altstiel, Tom, and Jean Grow. 2017. *Advertising Creative: Strategy, Copy, and Design.* Los Angeles: Sage.

Alvesson, Mats. 1998. "Gender Relations and Identity at Work: A Case Study of Masculinities and Femininities in an Advertising Agency." *Human Relations* 51 (8): 969–1005.

Birkner, Christine. 2016. "Martin Sorrell Addresses JWT Lawsuit, Acknowledging Sexism Is an Industrywide Problem." *Adweek,* March 23. http://www.adweek.com/news/advertising-branding/martin-sorrell-talks-jwt-lawsuit-sexism-industry-and-media-rebates-170386.

Broyles, Sheri J., and Jean M. Grow. 2008. "Creative Women in Advertising Agencies: Why So Few 'Babes in Boyland'?" *Journal of Consumer Marketing* 25 (1): 4–6.

Calasanti, Toni, and Carol Bailey. 1991. "Gender Inequality and the Division of Household Labor in the United States and Sweden: A Socialist-Feminist Approach." *Social Problems* 38 (1): 34–53.

Carlson, Jessica, and Mary Crawford. 2011. "Perceptions of Relational Practices in the Workplace." *Gender, Work and Organization* 18 (4): 359–76.

Coffee, Patrick. 2016. "Agency CEO's Downfall Leaves Ad Industry Questioning if It's Truly Left the Mad Men Era." *Adweek,* March 18. http://www.adweek.com/news/advertising-branding/agency-ceos-downfall-leaves-ad-industry-questioning-if-its-truly-left-mad-men-era-170295.

Creedon, Pamela. 1993. "Acknowledging the Infrasystem: A Critical Feminist Analysis of Systems Theory." *Public Relations Review* 19 (2): 157–66.

De Mooij, Marieke. 2014. *Global Marketing and Advertising: Understanding Cultural Paradoxes,* 4th ed. Thousand Oaks: Sage.

Dodd, Fiona. 2012. "Women Leaders in the Creative Industries: A Baseline Study." *International Journal of Gender and Entrepreneurship* 4 (2): 153–78.

Duschinsky, Robbie. 2013. "The Emergence of Sexualization as a Social Problem: 1981–2010." *Social Politics* 20 (1): 137–56.

EEOC. 2014. "2014 Job Patterns for Minorities and Women in Private Industry." *Equal Employment Opportunity Commission,* March 22, 2016. Washington, DC. Accessed May 12, 2017. https://www1.eeoc.gov/eeoc/statistics/employment/jobpat-eeo1/2014/index.cfm?redirected=1

Ember, Sydney. 2016a. "It's a 'Mad Men' World." *New York Times, Late Edition (East Coast),* May 2, B1.

———. 2016b. "Lawsuit's Accusations Shake Up Ad Industry." *New York Times, Late Edition (East Coast),* March 16, B1.

Fletcher, Joyce. 1998. "Relational Practice: A Feminist Reconstruction of Work." *Journal of Management Inquiry* 7 (2): 163–86.

Gender Equity Index. 2015. "Measuring Gender Equality in the European Union, 2005–2012 Report." *European Institute for Gender Equality,* October 30, 2015. http://eige.europa.eu/sites/default/files/documents/mh0215616enn.pdf

Glaser, Barney, and Anselm Strauss. 1967. *The Discovery of Grounded Theory: Strategies for Qualitative Research.* Chicago: Aldine.

Golombisky, Kim. 2010. "Feminist Methodology." In *Communication Research Methods in Postmodern Culture: A Revisionist Approach,* edited by Larry Z. Leslie, 167–236. Boston: Allyn and Bacon.

———. 2015. "Renewing the Commitments of Feminist Public Relations Theory from Velvet Ghetto to Social Justice." *Journal of Public Relations Research* 27: 389–415.

Gregory, Michele. 2009. "Inside the Locker Room: Male Homosociability in the Advertising Industry." *Gender, Work and Organizations* 16 (3): 323–47.

Grow, Jean M. 2009. "The Gender of Branding: Early Nike Women's Advertising a Feminist Antenarrative." *Women's Studies in Communication* 31 (3): 310–343.

Grow, Jean M., and Sheri J. Broyles. 2011. "Unspoken Rules of the Creative Game: Insights to Shape the Next Generation from Top Advertising Creative Women." *Advertising and Society Review* 12 (1). DOI: 10.1353/asr.2011.0009.

Grow, Jean M., and Tao Deng. 2014. "Sex Segregation in Advertising Creative Departments across the Globe." *Advertising and Society Review* 14 (4). DOI: 10.1353/asr.2014.0003, https://muse.jhu.edu/article/534556.

Grow, Jean M., David Roca, and Sheri J. Broyles. 2012. "Vanishing Acts: Creative Women in Spain and the United States." *International Journal of Advertising* 31 (3): 657–79.

Higgins, E. T. 1997. "Beyond Pleasure and Pain." *American Psychologist* 52 (12): 1280–300.

Ibarra, Herminia, Robin Ely, and Deborah Kolb. 2013. "Women Rising: The Unseen Barriers." *Harvard Business Review* 91 (9): 60–66.

Jamieson, Kathleen. 1995. *Beyond the Double Bind: Women and Leadership.* New York: Oxford University Press.

Järvklo, Nicolas. 2013. "Parental Leave Policy in Sweden: Evolution, Lessons Learned." Paper presented at fifty-seventh session of United Nations Commission on the Status of Women, New York.

Kendall, Shari, and Deborah Tannen. 1997. "Gender and Language in the Workplace." In *Gender and Discourse,* edited by Ruth Wodak, 81–105. London: Sage.
Klein, Debbie. 2000. *Women in Advertising—10 Years On: Findings and Recommendations.* London: Institute of Practitioners in Advertising.
KOMM. 2012. Internal Report, August 23.
KOMM. 2014. Internal Report, January 11.
Lewis, Patricia. 2014. "Postfeminism, Femininities and Organization Studies: Exploring a New Agenda." *Organization Studies* 35 (12): 1845–66.
Mallia, Karen. 2009. "Rare Birds: Why So Few Women Become Ad Agency Creative Directors." *Advertising and Society Review* 10 (3). DOI: 10.1353/asr.0.0032.
Mallia, Karen, and Kasey Windels. 2011. "Will Changing Media Change the World? An Exploratory Investigation of the Impact of Digital Advertising on Opportunities for Creative Women." *Journal of Interactive Advertising* 11 (2): 30–40.
Meyerson, Debra, and Joyce Fletcher. 2000. "A Modest Manifesto for Shattering the Glass Ceiling." *Harvard Business Review* 78 (1): 126–36.
Nixon, Sean. 2003. *Advertising Cultures: Gender, Commerce, Creativity.* London: Sage.
Nixon, Sean, and Ben Crew. 2006. "Pleasure at Work? Gender, Consumption and Workplace Identities in the Creative Industry." *Consumption, Markets and Culture* 7 (2): 129–47.
Rothstein, Bo. 2012. "The Reproduction of Gender Inequality in Sweden: A Causal Mechanism Approach." *Gender, Work and Organization* 19 (3): 324–44.
Statistics Sweden. 2012. "Women and Men in Sweden Facts and 2012 Figures 2012." *Statistiska centralbyrån.* Stockholm: July 2, 2015. http://www.scb.se/statistik/_publikationer/le0201_2012A01_Br_X10Br1201eNg.pdf.
Swedish Institute. 2013. "Gender Equality: The Swedish Approach to Fairness." July 2, 2015. www.sweden.se/wp-content/uploads/2013/11/Gender-equality-high-res.pdf.
The Local. 2013. "Sweden Most Gender Equal Country in the EU." October 22, 2015. http://www.thelocal.se/20130614/48494.
Tannen, Deborah. 1990. *You Just Don't Understand: Women and Men in Conversation.* New York: Ballantine.
———. 1999. "The Display of (Gendered) Identities in Talk at Work." In *Reinventing Identities: The Gendered Self in Discourse,* edited by Mary Bucholtz, A. C. Liang, and Laurel Sutton, 221–40. New York: Oxford University Press.
Tong, Rosemarie. 2013. *Feminist Thought: A More Comprehensive Introduction.* Boulder: Westview.
United Nations. 2013. *Commission on the Status of Women, Official Records, Economic and Social Council,* October 22, 2015. http://www.un.org/ga/search/view_doc.asp?symbol=E/2013/27.
Vranica, Suzanne, and Nathalie Tadena. 2016. "Lawsuit Sparks Soul-Searching on Madison Avenue over Diversity." *Wall Street Journal* (March 13). http://www.wsj.com/articles/madison-avenue-grapples-with-a-lack-of-diversity-1457914997.
Weisberg, Larry, and Brett Robbs. 1997. "Creative Departments Still Boys' Playground." *Advertising Age* 68 (November 24): 28.

Windels, Kasey. 2011. "What's in a Number? Minority Status and Implication for Creative Professionals." *Creativity Research Journal* 23 (4): 321–29.
Windels, Kasey, and Wei-Na Lee. 2012. "The Construction of Gender and Creativity in Advertising Creative Departments." *Gender in Management* 27 (8): 502–19.
Windels, Kasey, Karen Mallia, and Sheri J. Broyles. 2013. "Soft Skills: The Difference between Leading and Leaving the Advertising Industry?" *Journal of Advertising Education* 18 (2): 17–27.

Part III

DECODING: FEMINIST ANALYSES OF INTERSECTIONAL ADVERTISING AUDIENCES

Chapter 10

Engaging in Consumer Citizenship

Latina Audiences and Advertising in Women's Ethnic Magazines

Jillian M. Báez

Despite the growth of advertising directed toward Latinx audiences, there is little research on Latinas and advertising, especially from a feminist perspective.[1] In particular, we know little about how Latina audiences make sense of advertising targeted to them. This essay offers a glimpse into how Latina audiences interpret print advertisements in a women's magazine catered to a Latina readership. Interviews with Latinas about ads in *Latina* magazine suggest that readers engage with these images through consumerist logic that positions them as gendered consumer-citizens. More specifically, although Latinas in the present study are generally reflexive about the commercial purpose of advertising and the medium's attendant objectification of women's bodies, the women interviewed here nonetheless view advertising's attention to Latinas as potential consumers with buying power as a form of visibility and belonging to the market, and by extension, the nation.

In this essay, I focus on Latina readers' general impressions of magazine advertising in a publication directed at Latinas. Elsewhere I explored Latina audiences' interpretations of specific print advertisements in magazines, magalogues, and billboards (Báez 2008). In this essay, I foreground women's general impressions because they illuminate audiences' commonsense understandings of and relationships to advertising, especially as they pertain to issues of gender, ethnicity, and race. Although there is a robust feminist literature on the content of women's magazines (e.g., Cortese 2015; Currie 1999; Goffman 1976; Hermes 1995; Jhally, Kilbourne, and Rabinovitz 2010; McRobbie 1991), the research is primarily concerned with general-market publications. There is little scholarship available on magazine advertising in ethnic women's magazines, let alone content that is specifically targeted to Latina readers. Research specifically on ethnic women's magazines is necessary because studies indicate that advertisers address women differently according to race and ethnicity (see Fernandez et al. 2005; Hirshman 2011). There is some research available on Latina/os and advertising (e.g., Alaniz and Wilkes 1995; Astroff 1997; Báez 2008; Dávila 2012; Fernandez et al. 2005; Hirshman 2011; Kreshel 2017; Peñaloza 1994; Subervi-Vélez et al. 1997; Taylor and Bang 1997; Taylor, Lee, and Stern 1995), but only some of that scholarship examines magazine advertising. Women's magazine advertising is an apt place to explore issues of feminism and niche marketing given that magazines historically were one of the first forms of media to focus on segmented audiences. Additionally, magazines' revenue stream increasingly relies more on advertising than subscriptions. Advertisements commonly occupy half or more of a hardcopy magazine issue's content (Moses 2009).

Although feminist media scholars have analyzed the content of women's magazines rigorously, reception studies are less common, partly because of the time and cost of human subject research. In particular, we know little about Latina audiences. This essay contributes to the scholarship on women's magazine advertising by foregrounding how niche marketing that targets Latinas is interpreted by Latina audiences. I provide some grounding for studying Latinas and advertising, particularly from an audience studies perspective. In so doing, I argue that Latinas are ambivalent yet critical consumers who desire to be interpellated as professionals by advertising.

This study is based on thirty-five in-depth interviews with Latinas about the print edition of *Latina* magazine.[2] I conducted interviews with both individuals and small groups consisting of Latinas of various ages, classes, nationalities, and sexual orientations. The diversity of the sample echoes the heterogeneity of the Latinx population in the United States. The Latina/o population includes people of twenty-seven nationalities, different citizenship statuses (undocumented, residents, citizens), languages (English, Spanish, and indigenous languages such as Nahuatl and Quechua), racial identifications (e.g., white, black, indigenous, mixed), and socioeconomic statuses (poor, working class, middle class, and upper class). Participants were recruited in Chicago, Illinois, a location chosen for its diverse Latina/o nationalities and history of Latina/o immigration dating to the nineteenth century. The interviews consisted of questions about *Latina* magazine and participants' broader understandings of how Latinas and their bodies are depicted in mainstream and Latina/o media. I recruited participants through snowball sampling, advertisements posted on the Internet, and community organizations in Chicago serving Latina/os. I conducted interviews at locations that were convenient to each participant. These locations included the women's homes, workplaces, and coffee shops.

I chose to interview audiences about advertising in *Latina* because of the periodical's wide distribution across the United States. Targeting eighteen- to forty-five-year-old, middle-class, and professional Latinas, *Latina* magazine's content is mostly in English. *Latina* was launched in 1996 by Christy Haubegger, a recent law school graduate who felt that Latinas were an underserved market. As a Mexican-American woman, Haubegger noted that Latinas, particularly "successful" (read: highly educated or professional) Latinas, were not represented in magazines. She modeled *Latina* after the long-standing African-American women's magazine *Essence* (http://www.makers.com/christy-haubegger). During the early years of the publication, Haubegger struggled to recruit advertisers because of stereotypes about Latina/os. For example, in an interview, Haubegger explains, "I've had great information on [Latino] buying power for years, but when people close their eyes and picture Hispanic women, they picture someone who cleans up their office at night. We don't get to do a sales job in this market, we do an education job" (Weissman 1999, 37). *Latina*'s advertising revenue reached $20.9 million in the first three quarters of 2011 (Vega 2011). *Latina* magazine currently has a readership of two million women and a visible online presence (*Latina* 2016).

In addition to its popularity and long-standing publishing record, compared with other magazines geared toward Latinas that have folded, *Latina* is an appropriate object of analysis for this study. To contextualize how audiences are reading the ads in relation to the editorial content of the magazine, I draw on research that examines the content of *Latina* (e.g., Calafell 2001; Martinez 2004, 2008). I also build on a Fernandez et al. (2005) study that examines cigarette advertising in women's magazines. Analyzing *Glamour en Español* and *Cosmopolitan en Español,* Fernandez et al. (2005) find that Latinas are addressed more frequently in cigarette ads by less expensive brands, perhaps partly because of advertisers' assumptions that Latinas earn lower incomes than other women. The 2005 cigarette advertising study offers some insight into magazine advertising directed to Latinas and how advertisers might perceive this niche market, but the publications studied primarily include articles translated into Spanish and do not cater to English-dominant and second-plus-generation Latinas living in the United States.

The principal theoretical frameworks that guide the analysis are feminist audience studies and Chicana/Latina feminist theories. Feminist audience studies provide a lens to understand media texts as polysemic and often contradictory because they have the potential to reinforce patriarchy *and* enable women's agency (Ang 1996; Parameswaran 2003; van Zoonen 1994). Feminist audience studies are also a useful entry point because they take feminized popular culture forms, such as women's magazines, seriously as sites where women audiences reflect on and imagine their subjectivities (Ang 1985; Currie 1999; Hermes 1995; Levine 2015; McRobbie 1991; Radway 1984). The analysis also builds on Chicana and Latina feminist epistemologies that position Latinas as hybrid transnational subjects whose experiences are shaped by colonization, migration, and racialization in the United States (Anzaldúa 1987; Valdivia 2003). Central to this approach is an intersectional optic that considers various axes of difference (e.g., gender, nationality, sexual orientation, ethnicity, and class) (Hill Collins 2000; Shohat and Stam 1994). In particular, Chicana and Latina feminisms insist on an intersectional analysis to understand the tensions underlying agency and structure (Anzaldúa 1987; Valdivia 2000). This understanding of Latinas' lived experience as one that encompasses overlapping identities provides a particularly useful approach to exploring how Latinas use advertising to make claims to citizenship.

My positionality is noteworthy in terms of how I accessed and interacted with participants; it also shapes my analysis. As a second- and third-generation Puerto Rican, cis-gendered woman with a working-class background and current middle-class status who is bilingual and has legal citizenship, my relationship to the participants oscillated between insider and outsider. I never discussed my sexual orientation with the participants, but I was often presumed to be heterosexual. I am a light-skinned brunette with dark eyes and curly hair and was often perceived by participants as fitting what media industries call the "Latin look" (Dávila 2012). My physicality differed from many of the participants who embodied more indigenous features (i.e., straight black hair, deep brown skin) or women who identified as Afro-Latina. I provide more detail on my positionality as a researcher in my forthcoming book (Báez, forthcoming 2018).

CHICANA/LATINA FEMINIST PERSPECTIVES ON ADVERTISING

Chicana/Latina feminism emerged out of the civil rights movements in the late 1960s, but Chicana/Latina feminists largely ignored or dismissed advertising and most commercial media. Instead, Chicana/Latina feminists in the 1960s and 1970s were interested in creating radical and alternative forms of media, such as independent film, which included feminist perspectives and revisionist histories. Certainly, this sentiment was shaped by the exclusionary history of advertising whereby Latinas (and also Latinos) were rarely visible; when they were represented, the images offered reductionist constructions. Until very recently, Latina representation in mainstream advertising followed this pattern. For example, in the mid-1990s, Taylor and Bang (1997) and Taylor, Lee, and Stern (1995) found Latinos highly underrepresented in magazine advertising.

The advertising industry dubbed the 1980s the "Decade of the Hispanic" because of the growing Latinx population in the United States (Dávila 2012). According to the US Census Bureau (1983) in 1980 there were 14.6 million

Latina/os in the United States, composing 6.4 percent of the population. By the 1990s, 22.4 million Latina/os were in the United States, making up 9 percent of the population. Dovetailing with the launch of Spanish-language broadcast television network Univision in 1987, advertisers began to pay more attention to Latinx consumers by placing ads in Spanish-language media and in emerging bilingual ethnic media outlets.[3] It is important to note that this attention to the Latina/o market was not only a response to a growing Latinx population. Advertisers deliberately constructed a Latina/o market by grouping together Latina/os of various nationalities on the basis of language. In other words, advertisers created a homogenous Spanish-language market, a niche that necessitated its own media outlets (e.g., Univision). In doing so, Spanish-language media have often flattened differences and nuances within the Latinx community (Dávila 2012; Levine 2001). Despite Latina/o visibility in advertising in Spanish-language media, Latina/os were still largely underrepresented in mainstream English-language advertising campaigns. Part of this erasure is due to advertising firms' employment of pan-continental advertising campaigns (e.g., Coca-Cola) to reach consumers in Spanish in both Latin America and the United States. In so doing, advertisers were not tasked with creating content specifically for Latina/os in the United States that might reflect their bilingual language competencies or bicultural experiences.

Following the success of pop star Gloria Estefan in the 1980s, the death of Tejano singer Selena in 1995 ushered a Latin music boom in the United States. The outpouring of fans for Selena was so large that *People* magazine released a tribute issue to the slain star. After the issue sold one million copies on the day of its release, *People* decided to launch *People En Español* to capitalize on the Latina/o market. Selena's postmortem mainstream popularity also paved the way for "crossover" Latina/o pop artists moving from the Spanish-language to the English-language market.[4] Some of these "crossover" successes included Ricky Martin, Shakira, and Marc Anthony. Although this was certainly not the first time Latin music garnered the attention of mainstream popular culture (consider the mambo craze in the 1950s), this particular boom intensified media industries' interest in the Latina/o audience with an emphasis on the so-called buying power of the Latina/o market, estimated at $489 billion in 2000 (Selig Center for Economic Growth 2009) and $1.5 trillion in 2015 (Rodriguez 2015). The twenty-first century has witnessed more images of Latina/os in advertising, partly stemming from recent interest in the Latina/o market and also from the advertising industry's growing preference for racially and ethnically ambiguous-looking models (often Latinas) to appeal to as many potential audiences as possible (Molina Guzmán 2013).

The number of publications targeted to Latinas in both English and Spanish has grown, especially among mainstream publishers (Vega 2011).

With an increase in Latina representation, more feminist scholars are analyzing Latina/o-oriented advertising and other forms of commercial media in the United States. Most of the work in this growing body of scholarship (see Cepeda 2015), unfortunately, does not focus on advertising, instead emphasizing film, television, and music. The limited literature on advertising and Latinas suggests that they are depicted within the virgin–whore dichotomy (Báez 2008; Hirshman 2011). In her study of black and Latina women in advertisements, Hirshman (2011) finds that advertising targets Latinas as mothers. In doing so, the advertising industry's emphasis on the Latina role as caretaker of the family and the home consequently negates Latina contributions outside the home. Hirshman contends that this trope is similar to 1950s mainstream advertising messages to women that positioned women consumers as domestic goddesses. She also notices a preference for more fair-skinned Latina actresses and models in advertisements directed to Latinas.[5] Other studies find that Latinas are hypersexualized, that is, extremely sexualized, in a heteronormative fashion (Alaniz and Wilkes 1995; Báez 2008; Dávila 2012). In US contemporary popular culture, women are often sexualized to an imagined (heterosexual) male gaze. Hypersexualization involves an extreme heterosexualization whereby the actress or model is positioned as a passive object to be consumed by a heterosexual male viewer. Hypersexualization of Latinas in advertising is achieved through form-fitting clothing, large areas of exposed bare skin, curvaceous silhouettes, use of the color red (especially in clothing and lipstick), and animal prints. In terms of demeanor, Latinas are regularly depicted as "sexually available and proficient" (Valdivia 2000). Similar to Latina representation in film and television, research documents that Latinas are often objectified, or presented as mere body parts, in advertising (Báez 2008). The objectification of Latinas in advertising is especially accentuated in ads that hone in on women's hips and derrieres.

LATINAS AS MARKETS AND AUDIENCES

In the last twenty years, Latina/os shifted from being invisible within advertising to being viewed as a lucrative market. This growing visibility signals a departure from the under-representation in earlier advertising and other media content, what Tuchman (1978) termed "symbolic annihilation." Latinas are currently perceived to be the most desirable segment of the Latinx audience (Meraji 2013; Sebastian 2013; Vega 2011). Nielsen's (2013) report titled "The Latina Power Shift" positions Latinas as an audience segment attractive to advertisers because they are socially and economically upward bound and are making significant contributions as citizens and consumers:

> US Hispanic women, also known as Latinas, have recently and rapidly surfaced as prominent contributors to the educational, economic, and cultural wellbeing of not only their own ethnicity, but of American society and the consumer marketplace. This rise of Latinas is driven both by strong demographics and a healthy inclination to embrace and retain their Hispanic culture even as they make significant strides toward success in mainstream America. (2)

In the report, Nielsen also locates Latinas as lucrative consumers because of their role as the primary decision-makers about spending in their families, rising educational attainment, and connectivity to large networks via social media. In particular, Nielsen emphasizes the buying power of "ambicultural" Latinas who navigate both US and Latin American culture and often are bilingual. Perceiving Latinas as a lucrative market, publishing industries are targeting Latinas through specialized media products. For example, in 2012, the long-standing women's magazine *Cosmopolitan* launched *Cosmo for Latinas,* a special issue released four times a year in English and directed to Latina readers. *Women's Day* released *Women's Day for Latinas* in 2013, and *Parents* launched *Parents Latina*; both publish quarterly issues that are mailed directly to Latina subscribers. These publications, along with more established magazines outside the mainstream such as *Latina,* present an alternative to how Latinas have historically been addressed in Spanish by the media (Beer 2002; Johnson 2000, 2005).[6]

Although more attention is being focused on Latinas as consumers in the contemporary media landscape, virtually nothing is known about Latina audiences. A limited number of studies explore Latina media audiences through a feminist lens; however, those studies largely focus on television and music (Báez 2008; Cepeda 2008; Rojas 2004; Vargas 2009). As such, it behooves scholars to learn more about Latina audiences of advertising as an increasingly important niche market within US advertising.

In the next section, I provide insight into how Latina audiences in this study make sense of current magazine advertising directed toward them as a market. To do so, I present findings from interviews in Chicago with thirty-five Latinas about advertising in *Latina* magazine. I interpret the data through the frameworks of feminist audience studies and Chicana/Latina feminist theories to make sense of the reception process among audiences through an intersectional optic.

ENGAGING IN CONSUMER CITIZENSHIP

In this section I offer a snapshot of how Latina audiences interpret magazine advertising targeted directly to them. The thirty-five interviews indicate that the Chicago-based women in the study engage with these images through consumerist logic and seek to be addressed as middle-class professionals. Hermes's (1995) research on how audiences read women's magazines suggests that readers use magazines as aspirational tools to imagine their ideal selves. Because of the commercial nature of women's magazines, which heavily rely on advertising for revenue, the aspirations promoted are presented as attainable mostly through consumption. Research concludes that women's magazine advertising also tends to be contradictory, oscillating between traditional femininity and progressive feminist values (Cortese 2015; Douglas 2010). Likewise, magazines directed toward Latinas reinforce these notions and advise women to be traditional caretakers in the home while simultaneously seeking educational and professional advancement (Beer 2002). However, magazines like *Latina* also attempt to express pride in one's ethnicity (Calafell 2001; Martinez 2004, 2008).

All of the interviewees in this study reported some familiarity with *Latina* magazine. This familiarity is partly because *Latina,* owned by the long-standing African-American women's magazine *Essence,* is available in many urban newsstands nationwide. *Latina* also currently has a strong digital presence with two million monthly unique visitors (*Latina* 2016). Most of the interviewees perceived *Latina* as an important publication because it foregrounds Latinas and their experiences. In particular, some of the women appreciated that the magazine is available in English and focuses on second- and third-generation Latina experiences in contrast to the Spanish-language magazines that center on Latin American or immigrant perspectives. Some women were impressed that the magazine has been available since the mid-1990s and was created by a Latina. Historically, *Latina* filled a gap in the media landscape by addressing one segment of the Latina/o audience: educated, upwardly mobile, English-dominant, US Latinas. This group previously had not been represented in US media efforts to target Latina/os. *Latina* markets its magazine to potential advertisers as "acculturated":

> Our role is to act as a mirror that reflects her life, experiences and interests. For 20 years, Latinas have turned to our brand to serve as a guide for her goals and aspirations, whether they are looking and feeling her best, forging a successful career, continuing traditions, juggling family life or starting a business—all while staying connected to her culture. Everything we do as a company is about serving our acculturated Latinas, who are the most pivotal consumers in the Hispanic market. (*Latina* 2016)

However, while many of the interviewees remarked that *Latina* is notable for its emphasis on Latinas, more than half of the women mentioned disappointment with current issues of the magazine. For example, a handful of participants said that they used to subscribe to the magazine, but they no longer do because the magazine's content has shifted from a focus on political and cultural issues affecting Latinas to more articles on beauty and fashion. Moreover, among these Chicago women, those in their forties and fifties who previously subscribed to *Latina* in the late 1990s and early 2000s also observed that the amount of advertising has significantly increased over the years. In 2015, *Latina* hired a "politics and culture editor," Raquel Reichard, to address readers' desire for more content in that area. In an e-mail to the author on May 17, 2016, Reichard reported that she regularly receives e-mails and messages on social media from readers "telling me how much they appreciate my work, asking for more and thanking me for bringing a 'change' to the magazine." She said, "I also get a lot of, 'if it wasn't for Raquel, I wouldn't read *Latina* at all' or 'I only read *Latina* articles when they're by Raquel.' A lot of my readers are blunt about hating the magazine [outside of her articles]."

Overall, most of the readers in this study said that *Latina* lacked substantive content, and they desired less advertising. Previously I found that Latina audiences generally recognize, and sometimes bemoan, the ubiquity of advertising in everyday life (Báez 2007, 2014). Like other audiences, Latina audiences are fairly reflexive about commercial media and recognize how media reinforce laborious, and often unattainable, aspirations toward a perfect self (Sender 2012). My research suggests that Latina audiences demonstrate some media literacy in deciphering and sometimes challenging dominant ideologies in various forms of media (Báez 2014). For example, Latina audiences tend to realize that most media images are digitally edited. However, these same audiences still desire to be represented in media *and* also to have input into the production of content. For example, several participants mentioned wanting to be selected for market research surveys and focus groups. These women wanted to have a say in what sorts of media are produced and circulated *about* and *for* Latinas. Participants especially felt that Latinas were excluded from most market research. Elena, a twenty-nine-year-old Puerto Rican occupational therapist, described her disappointment:

> I've only done one [focus group], but one of my friends she does this all the time. There's a woman who recruits people to do [a] survey, and it's for make-up and everything under the sun. So I'm on her list when she sends out these surveys, but almost every time I'm having a discussion—almost every time it's [recruitment calls] not for Latinas. It's rarely African American or Latino. It's always—"I'm looking for Caucasian females." But it's for television shows—like all things that we consume. I was telling my friend it's pretty frustrating because obviously we're not an important market.

Elena's comment differs from the current industry interest in Latinas described in the previous section of this chapter. Whereas media industries might tout Latinas as a lucrative market, Elena laments that they are not interested in gathering Latina audiences' input, particularly in relation to general-market media.

In one interview with a college student, the interviewee related an experience participating in market research specifically for *Latina* magazine. Although Audrey, a Mexican woman in her early twenties, was appreciative of having been paid to participate in a focus group, she made a distinction between consulting a reader for input and targeting an advertising audience. Audrey communicated disappointment with *Latina*'s market research. She observed that the research was primarily concerned with advertising and the most effective ways to sell products to the readers. Audrey was much more interested in commenting on the content within the magazine, something she later revealed in the interview as lacking in substantive material on Latinx culture:

> I don't usually read it [*Latina*] a lot and speaking of it now, I remember one time me and a friend did a research thing on it where there were like ten girls, and we all had to say what we thought about the magazine. . . . But that was more geared towards advertising, not what we thought about the media in it. I think that it was just about making money. It wasn't about how we related to it [the magazine] or what we felt for it.

Interviewees such as Elena and Audrey long for more inclusion of Latinas' perspectives within market research on advertising as well as within the media content in which advertisements are placed.

Scholarship on representations of Latinas in commercial media indicates that Latinas are often hetero-hypersexualized in media, more so than other women (Molina Guzmán 2010; Molina Guzmán and Valdivia 2004; Peña Ovalle 2011). *Latina* magazine features ads that foreground the heterosexualized female body alongside some ads that emphasize women as more traditional and modest caretakers of the family and the home. Like general-market women's and men's magazines, heterosexualized images in *Latina* are similar to mainstream ads of passive, objectified women (Jhally 2010; Reichert and Carpenter 2004). Although the content of *Latina* magazine tends to emphasize education, professionalization, and financial independence for Latina women (Beer 2002), many of the advertisements tend to align more with mainstream and Spanish-language television and radio ads that objectify and exoticize Latina bodies. Similar to general-market women's magazines, *Latina* is aspirational in tone and suggests that its readers can attain upward socioeconomic mobility through consuming the products displayed in the magazine's advertising of clothing, cosmetics, and hair-care products. These types of aspirational messages are ubiquitous in US media. *Latina* spins this aspirational message by underscoring Latinas' history of marginalization in society, noting in its content how Latinas are underrepresented in higher education and white-collar work.

Despite the presence of some nonsexualized images of women in *Latina*'s ads, the women in the study primarily recalled the heterosexualized advertisements. For example, in reference to an outdoor billboard in Chicago for the Mexican beer Tecate, one participant, Elizabeth, observed, "This looks like one of the ones that would be in *Latina* magazine." Mexican beer companies are notorious for depicting highly heterosexualized Latinas in their advertisements (Alaniz and Wilkes 1995). Elizabeth, a Puerto Rican poet in her fifties, is familiar with *Latina*, having read it on and off for nearly fifteen years. She is convinced that the ads in *Latina* are primarily about sex appeal. For Elizabeth and many other participants, *Latina* tends to reproduce the prevalent image of the hetero-hypersexual Latina.

Reception studies with Latinas find that Latina audiences tend to be frustrated with pervasive media representations of Latinas as hetero-hypersexual (Báez 2008; Rojas 2004). In the present study, this frustration emerges when two lesbian participants expressed concern over sexualized images of Latinas that seem to be created for Anglo heterosexual men. Most of the participants associated representations of overt sexuality with poor, working-class, and uneducated women. This is unsurprising given that poor and working-class women tend to be heterosexualized in more excessive ways than middle-class and wealthy women in media (Valdivia 2000). In her study of Latina audiences of Spanish-language television, Rojas (2004) found that the participants critiqued hypersexualized images of Latinas and distanced themselves from these images to maintain respectability. In other words, in seeking upward mobility, these Latina audiences disavow heterosexualized images because of their class markers. For many of my Chicago participants, the frustration with the prevalence of the hypersexual Latina trope in both mainstream and Spanish-language media fuels a desire to see images of professional (read: nonsexualized) Latinas. Participants seek middle-class images of Latinas similar to those they assumed would be present among images of Anglo women in general-market women's magazines. Although images of women in advertisements in general-market women's magazines might also be overly heterosexualized, Latina audiences perceive that they are less so because of the overarching media stereotype of the hypersexual, heterosexual Latina. These assumptions can be attributed to the differences in how Latinas are represented in mainstream and Latinx media. In mainstream media, Latinas are overwhelmingly portrayed as working class when compared with Anglo women (Valdivia 2000). Representations of Latinas outside of the working class only appear in mainstream media in the form of Latina celebrities (e.g., Jennifer Lopez, Salma Hayek, and Eva Longoria). In Spanish-language media, class representations include both the poor and the wealthy.[7] However, magazines directed to Latinas privilege middle-class femininity because the upper middle class to middle class are the target audience (Dávila 2008; Martinez 2004, 2008). Magazines' primary function is to sell issues, and, in the magazine industry's reliance on advertising, to sell consumer products. The catalog-like nature of magazines necessitates locating Latinas as middle class to sell Latina readers as viable consumers to advertisers. It may be that Latina audiences internalize the magazine's need to sell lucrative (read: middle class with disposable income) audiences to advertisers. Nonetheless, readers' preference for representations of professional, middle-class women eclipses depictions of working-class Latinas, especially domestic workers, who are not constructed as lucrative segments of the Latinx market. As such, only women who are hailed as middle class will be able to partake in consumer citizenship, meaning seeking belonging and recognition through the market.

However, not all of the interviewees were critical of advertising in *Latina*. Although some of the participants complained about the excessive amount of advertising in the magazine, most of the women reported being accustomed to the use of women's bodies to sell products and services. For example, Sofia, a Puerto Rican government worker in her fifties, observed that women are often used to advertise products. She noted that advertisers show "models with boats and cars and so on and so forth so I guess it's [sexualized advertising] more than acceptable, especially for the young people I think." Sofia accepts and expects that heterosexual sex appeal, in the form of women's bodies, will be deployed to promote products. She thinks sexualized images will be appealing to younger audiences because they are, in her words, "less conservative and religious" than older generations. For her, the objectification of women's bodies is an advertising industry norm, and she does not question or challenge it. Sofia was one of the few participants who seemed to internalize Douglas's (2010) "enlightened sexism" by not questioning the excessive use of hypersexuality or consumption in the magazine. The majority of the participants, most of whom were younger than Sofia, were also more apt to critique sexualized imagery, although most did not question consumption.

The interviews discussed in this section suggest that the participating *Latina* readers are critical of the amount and the content of the advertising in the magazine. Even audience members who are less critical, such as Sofia, demonstrate a basic understanding of how advertising functions, in particular the commonplace objectification of women. Others long for more input into the magazine and its advertisements as demonstrated in the interviewees who desired to participate in market research. Most crucially, in countering stereotypical representations of Latinas as heteronormatively hypersexual, the Chicago-based Latinas who contributed to this study yearned for more images of Latinas as professionals within both the articles and advertisements in the magazine. In demanding this type of recognition in advertising, Latina audiences perform consumer citizenship, a neoliberal form of asserting their belonging to the market and by extension to the nation. Scholars argue that modernity characterizes individuals as consumer-citizens whereby very little distinction is made between one's belonging to the market and the nation (Flores 2000; García Canclini 2001; Spring 2003; Stevenson 2003; Yúdice 1995). Advertising, thus, is a significant arena where historically marginalized groups such as Latinas might pursue recognition. This type of citizenship should be neither celebrated nor dismissed. For Dávila (2008), the problem with Latina/os seeking power through visibility in the market is that doing so establishes a false link between cultural visibility and political power. From a feminist perspective, Douglas (2010) reminds us that we are in a moment of "enlightened sexism" when women are encouraged to seek agency in two ways: by heteronormatively objectifying the body and by consuming beauty and fashion products. Latina audiences might internalize their subjectivities as consumers. Yet it should come as no surprise that Latinas embody this sensibility of consumer citizenship because it is by participation in the market that they receive the most affirmative attention in the public sphere. In other areas, namely immigration, Latinas are often cast as unworthy of citizenship (Molina Guzmán 2010). If we are to follow the attention Latina/os receive in the news and media trade presses, it seems that the only path toward visibility and recognition is located in Latinx "buying power." Latina audiences similarly perceive advertising representations of upward class mobility—although not as present in the media as they wish—as another means to gaining visibility and power. Nevertheless, as Phelan (1993, 10) puts it, "If representational visibility equals power, then almost-naked young white women should be running Western culture."

CONCLUSION

Latina audiences have a relationship to advertising that is shaped by the assumption that being wooed as a consumer is a form of power. For the Chicago-area Latinas in the present study, visibility is simultaneously desired and critiqued. Magazine ads offer narrow conceptions of Latina womanhood, and Latina participants recognize this and, for the most part, contest limited notions of femininity. For example, the *Latina* magazine readers in this study are critical of the sexualization, especially objectification, of women's bodies in advertising. Although not all the participants were critical of the heteronormativity embedded in magazine advertising, some did recognize that heteronormativity is produced through a heterosexual male gaze. Equally important, a majority of the participants perceived that in everyday life (outside of media), Latinas are also hetero-hypersexualized. The case study presented in this essay illuminates some of the important issues surrounding gender and ethnicity in advertising and its reception. The issues include how niche audiences interpret being wooed by advertisers, the continued heterosexualization of women, and the internalization of a neoliberal consumer-citizen subjectivity. Most importantly, the interviewees' engagement with advertising indicates that Latina audiences have fraught relationships with commercial media where participants simultaneously are frustrated with narrow representations of Latina womanhood and yet fiercely seek to be recognized as an important market.

Although consumer citizenship is one of the main ways that Latina audiences in this study engage with magazine advertising, I want to emphasize that consumer citizenship has its limitations. I concur with Beer (2002, 165) in her analysis of Latina-oriented magazines, including *Latina*. She argues that "because the magazines define Latinas primarily as consumers, they are a limited forum for women to explore nonconsumerist identities, challenge hegemony, or express oppositional points of view." Therefore, magazines like *Latina* will only contain content that is for readers constructed as consumers. There, only certain kinds of Latina/os are deemed worthy to target—those who are middle class. Poor and working-class Latina experiences will not be represented because they are not the segments of the Latina/o market deemed most profitable. Certainly, advertisers are not interested in targeting unprofitable segments of a Latina/o market; media are not interested in reaching those audiences because the industry's goal is to secure revenue. However, because advertising is one of the few spaces in public culture where Latina/os are readily visible and sometimes cast in a favorable light, the industry must be held accountable as prominent storytellers about Latinx communities.

Indeed, advertising's insistence on addressing niche markets, such as Latina/os, through specialized media (e.g., Spanish-language outlets, women's magazines, etc.) raises the larger question of how the industry recognizes diverse groups without reifying difference as exceptional rather than ordinary (Acosta-Alzuru and Kreshel 2002; Dávila 2012; Kreshel 2017). How can advertising represent difference without exploiting it? Advertising cannot address these challenges of inclusivity without deeper knowledge about Latinx reception. Moreover, having quantitatively more diverse images within a commercial media system must not be confused with equity.

NOTES

1. *Latinx* refers to communities of Latin American descent living in the United States. *Latinx* is preferred over the more widely used term *Latina/o* because it is gender neutral and inclusive of nonconforming gender and transgender individuals. At

times, however, I use the term *Latina/o* to avoid redundancy. Because of the study's focus on gender, I use *Latina* to refer to women and *Latino* to refer to men. The terms *Latinx* and *Latina/os* are not used to flatten difference within this pan-ethnicity, but instead used to discuss these groups in relation to one another. Also, I prefer to use *Latinx* and *Latina/o* over *Hispanic* given that the latter term was imposed by the US government and privileges cultural and linguistic ties to Spain over indigenous and African elements within Latina/o culture. My use of *Latina/o* departs from advertising and governmental general usage of the term *Hispanic*. The US government devised the term *Hispanic* for census purposes under the Nixon administration. In the 1980s and 1990s, advertisers also began deploying "Hispanic" as a market to target. See Oboler (1995) for a deeper discussion of the origins and usage of *Hispanic* and *Latina/o*.

2. Similar to Sender (2015), who draws from data collected for a larger book project to make some larger theoretical claims, this essay is based on interview data from a forthcoming book-length audience research project (Báez, forthcoming 2018). Whereas the book explores how Latina audiences interpret a variety of types of Latina/o-oriented media and draws from additional methodologies such as participant observation and textual analysis, this essay hones in on interviews specifically on magazine advertising not deeply explored in the book.

3. Prior to 1987, what is now known as Univision operated as the *Spanish International Network,* which first broadcast Spanish-language television in the United States in 1955. See Wilkinson (2015) for more details on the history of Univision.

4. See Paredez (2009) for a more elaborate discussion on the significance of Selena in mainstream media industries' perceptions of Latina/o audiences.

5. Johnson, Prabu, and Huey-Ohlsson (2003) also find this pattern in the nonadvertising content of Latina-oriented magazines.

6. It is also notable that magazines like *Latina* and the now defunct *Moderna* were forerunners to English and bilingual media content created specifically for US Latina/o audiences. Television networks such as Univision and Telemundo are foraying into this type of content now, but magazines were instrumental to this shift.

7. Within Spanish-language media, particularly *telenovelas,* representations of class differences are often more extreme. Storylines tend to hinge on the very poor versus the very rich. These depictions are partly a reflection of the lack of a large middle class in most Latin American countries.

REFERENCES

Acosta-Alzuru, Carolina, and Peggy J. Kreshel. 2002. "'I'm an American Girl . . . Whatever That Means: Girls Consuming Pleasant Company's American Girl Identity." *Journal of Communication* 52 (1): 139–61.

Alaniz, Maria, and Chris Wilkes. 1995. "Reinterpreting Latino Culture in the Commodity Form: The Case of Alcohol Advertising in the Mexican American Community." *Hispanic Journal of Behavioral Sciences* 17 (4): 430–51.

Ang, Ien. 1985. *Watching Dallas: Soap Opera and the Melodramatic Imagination.* New York: Methuen.

———. 1996. *Livingroom Wars: Rethinking Media Audiences for a Postmodern World.* London: Routledge.
Anzaldúa, Gloria. 1987. *Borderlands/La Frontera: The New Mestiza.* San Francisco: Aunt Lute Books.
Astroff, Roberta. 1997. "Capital's Cultural Study: Marketing Popular Ethnography of US Latino Culture." In *Buy This Book: Studies in Advertising and Consumption,* edited by A. B. Mica Nava, Lain MacRury, and Barry Richards, 120–36. London: Routledge.
Báez, Jillian M. 2007. "(Re)membering the Latina Body: A Discourse Ethnography of Gender, Latinidad, and Consumer Culture." In *Globalizing Cultural Studies: Ethnographic Interventions in Theory, Method and Policy,* edited by Cameron McCarthy, Aisha S. Durham, Laura C. Engel, Alice Filmer, Michael Giardina, and Miguel A. Malagreca, 189–203. New York: Peter Lang.
———. 2008. "Mexican/Mexican American Women Talk Back: Audience Responses to Representations of Latinidad in US Advertising." In *Latina/o Communication Studies Today,* edited by Angharad Valdivia, 257–81. New York: Peter Lang.
———. 2014. "Latina/o Audiences as Citizens: Bridging Culture, Media, and Politics." In *Contemporary Latina/o Media: Production, Circulation, Politics,* edited by Arlene Dávila and Yeidy Rivero, 267–84. New York: New York University Press.
———. Forthcoming 2018. *In Search of Belonging: Latinas, Media, and Citizenship.* Urbana, IL: University of Illinois Press.
Beer, Amy. 2002. "Periodical Pleasures: Magazines for US Latinas." In *Sex and Money: Feminism and Political Economy in the Media,* edited by Eileen R. Meehan and Ellen Riordan, 164–80. Minneapolis: University of Minnesota Press.
Calafell, Bernadette. M. 2001. "In Our Own Image?!: A Rhetorical Criticism of *Latina* Magazine," *Voces: A Journal of Chicana/Latina Studies* 3 (1–2): 12–46.
Cepeda, Maria Elena. 2008. "Survival Aesthetics: US Latinas and the Negotiation of Popular Media." In *Latina/o Communication Studies Today,* edited by Angharad N. Valdivia, 237–56. New York: Peter Lang.
———. 2015. "Beyond 'Filling in the Gap': The State and Status of Latina/o Media Studies. *Feminist Media Studies* 16 (2): 1–17.
Cortese, Anthony J. 2015. *Provocateur: Images of Women and Minorities in Advertising,* 2nd ed. Lanham, MD: Rowman & Littlefield.
Currie, Dawn. 1999. *Girl Talk: Adolescent Magazines and Their Readers.* Toronto: University of Toronto Press.
Dávila, Arlene. 2008. *Latino Spin: Public Image and the Whitewashing of Face.* New York: New York University Press.
———. 2012. *Latinos, Inc.: The Marketing and Making of a People,* 2nd ed. Berkeley: University of California Press.
Douglas, Susan J. 2010. *The Rise of Enlightened Sexism: How Pop Culture Took Us from Girl Power to Girls Gone Wild.* New York: Times Books.
Fernandez, Senaida, Norval Hickman, Elizabeth A. Klonoff, Hope Landrine, Kennon Kashima, Bina Parekh, Catherine R. Brouillard, Michelle Zolezzi, Jennifer A. Jensen, and Zorahna Weslowski. 2005. "Cigarette Advertising in Magazines

for Latinas, White Women, and Men, 1998–2002: A Preliminary Investigation." *Journal of Community Health* 30 (2): 141–51.

Flores, Juan. 2000. *From Bomba to Hip Hop: Puerto Rican Culture and Latino Identity*. New York: Columbia University Press.

Garcia Canclini, Nestor. 2001. *Consumers and Citizens: Globalization and Multicultural Conflicts*. Minneapolis: University of Minnesota Press.

Goffman, Erving. 1976. *Gender Advertisements*. New York: Harper & Row.

Hermes, Joke. 1995. *Reading Women's Magazines: An Analysis of Everyday Media Use*. Cambridge: Polity Press.

Hill Collins, Patricia. 2000. *Black Feminist Thought: Knowledge, Consciousness, and the Politics of Empowerment,* 2nd ed. New York: Routledge.

Hirshman, Elizabeth C. 2011. "Motherhood in Black and Brown: Advertising to US Minority Women." *Advertising and Society Review* 12 (2). Accessed December 15, 2015. http://muse.jhu.edu/journals/advertising_and_society_review/v012/12.2.hirshman.html.

Jhally, Sut. 2010. *The Codes of Gender: Identity and Performance in Popular Culture,* DVD. Written and directed by Sut Jhally. Amherst, MA: Media Education Foundation.

Jhally, Sut, Jean Kilbourne, and David Rabinovitz. 2010. *Killing Us Softly 4: Advertising's Image of Women*. Northampton, MA: Media Education Foundation.

Johnson, Melissa A. 2000. "How Ethnic Are US Ethnic Media: The Case of Latina Magazines." *Mass Communication and Society* 3 (2–3): 229–48.

———. 2005. "Constructing a New Model of Ethnic Media: Image-Saturated Latina Magazines as Touchstones." In *A Companion to Media Studies,* edited by Angharad N. Valdivia, 272–92. Malden, MA: Blackwell.

Johnson, Melissa A., David Prabu, and Dawn Huey-Ohlsson. 2003. "Beauty in Brown: Skin Color in Latina Magazines." In *Brown and Black Communication: Latino and African American Conflict and Convergence in Mass Media,* edited by Diana I. Ríos and A. N. Mohamed, 159–73. Westport, CT: Praeger.

Kreshel, Peggy J. 2017. "Niche Markets, Niche Media." In *Media Ethics: Cases and Moral Reasoning,* 10th ed., edited by Clifford G. Christians, Mark Fackler, Kathy Mckee Richardson, Peggy J. Kreshel, and Robert H. Woods, Jr. New York: Routledge.

Latina Magazine. "Media kit." 2016. Accessed January 2, 2016. http://www.latina.com/files/pdf/lmv_media_kit_2016.pdf.

Levine, Elana. 2001. "Constructing a Market, Constructing an Ethnicity: US Spanish Language Media and the Formation of a Latina/o Identity." *Studies in Latin American Popular Culture* 20: 33–50.

———. 2015. "Introduction: Feminized Popular Culture in the Twenty-First Century." In *Cupcakes, Pinterest and LadyPorn: Feminized Popular Culture in the Twenty-First Century,* edited by Elana Levine, 1–14. Urbana, IL: University of Illinois Press.

Martinez, Katynka Z. 2004. "*Latina* Magazine and the Invocation of a Panethnic Family: Latino Identity as It Is Informed by Celebrities and *Papis Chulos*." *The Communication Review* 7: 155–74.

———. 2008. "Real Women and Their Curves: Letters to the Editor and a Magazine's Celebration of the 'Latina body.'" In *Latina/o Communication Studies Today,* edited by Angharad N. Valdivia, 137–59. New York: Peter Lang.

McRobbie, Anglela. 1991. *Feminism and Youth Culture: From "Jackie" to "Just 17."* Boston: Unwin Hyman.

Meraji, Shereen Marisol. 2013. "Latinas Drive Hispanic Purchasing Power in the US." NPR's *Code Switch.* August 13. http://www.npr.org/sections/codeswitch/2013/08/12/211411085/latinas-drive-hispanic-purchasing-power-in-the-u-s.

Molina Guzmán, Isabel. 2010. *Dangerous Curves: Latina Bodies in the Media.* New York: New York University Press.

———. 2013. "Commodifying Black Latinidad in US Film and Television." *Popular Communication: The International Journal of Media and Culture* 11 (3): 211–26.

Molina Guzmán, Isabel, and Angharad N. Valdivia. 2004. "Brain, Brow, and Bootie: Iconic Latinas in Contemporary Popular Culture." *The Communication Review* 7 (2): 205–21.

Moses, Lucia. 2009. "The Ad/Edit Balancing Act." *AdWeek.* January 18. http://www.adweek.com/news/press/adedit-balancing-act-111116.

Nielsen. 2013. "Latina Power Shift." *Latina Power Shift* (Diverse Intelligence Series): 1–24.

Oboler, Suzanne. 1995. *Ethnic Labels, Latino Lives: Identity and the Politics of (Re)presentation in the United States.* Minneapolis: University of Minnesota Press.

Parameswaran, Radhika E. 2003. "Resuscitating Feminist Audience Studies: Revisiting the Politics of Representation and Resistance." In *A Companion to Media Studies,* edited by Angharad N. Valdivia, 311–36. Oxford: Blackwell.

Paredez, Deborah. 2009. *Selenidad: Selena, Latinos, and the Performance of Memory.* Durham, NC: Duke University Press.

Peña Ovalle, Priscilla P. 2011. *Dance and the Hollywood Latina: Race, Sex, and Stardom.* New Brunswick, NJ: Rutgers University.

Peñaloza, Liza. 1994. "¡Ya Viene Atzlan! Images of Latinos in US Advertising." *Media Studies Journal* 8 (3): 133–42.

Phelan, Peggy. 1993. *Unmarked: The Politics of Performance.* London: Routledge.

Radway, Janice. 1984. *Reading the Romance: Women, Patriarchy, and Popular Literature.* Chapel Hill: University of North Carolina Press.

Reichert, T., and Courtney Carpenter. 2004. An Update on Sex in Magazine Advertising: 1983 to 2003. *Journalism and Mass Communication Quarterly* 81 (4): 823–35.

Rodriguez, Ashley. 2015. "Retailers Duke It Out for Hispanic Shoppers' Dollars." *Advertising Age,* April 6. http://adage.com/article/cmo-strategy/retailers-duke-hispanic-shoppers-dollars/297902/.

Rojas, Viviana. 2004. "The Gender of Latinadad: Latinas Speak about Hispanic Television." *The Communication Review* 7 (2): 125–53.

Sebastian, Michael. 2013. "Magazines' Next Big Goal: Reaching Latinas in English." *Advertising Age,* November 8. http://adage.com/article/media/publishers-reaching-latina-audiences-english/245036/.

Selig Center for Economic Growth. 2009. "The Multicultural Economy 2009." *Georgia Business and Economic Conditions* 69 (3). http://www.terry.uga.edu/media/documents/selig/GBEC0903q.pdf.
Sender, Katherine. 2012. *The Makeover: Reality Television and Reflexive Audiences*. New York: New York University Press.
———. 2015. "Reconsidering Reflexivity: Audience Research and Reality Television." *The Communication Review* 18: 37–52.
Shohat, Ella, and Robert Stam. 1994. *Unthinking Eurocentrism: Multiculturalism and the Media*. New York: Routledge.
Spring, Joel. 2003. *Educating the Consumer-Citizen: A History of the Marriage of Schools, Advertising, and Media*. Mahwah, NJ: Lawrence Erlbaum Associates.
Stevenson, Nick. 2003. *Cultural Citizenship: Cosmopolitan Questions*. Maidenhead, Berkshire, UK: Open University Press.
Subervi-Velez, Federico, with Charles Ramirez Berg, Patricia Constantakis-Valdés, Chon Noriega, Diana I. Ríos, and Kenton T. Wilkinson. 1997. "Hispanic-Oriented Media." In *Latin Looks: Images of Latinas and Latinos in the US Media*, edited by Clara E. Rodríguez, 225–38. Boulder, CO: Praeger.
Taylor, Charles R., and Hae-Kyong Bang. 1997. "Portrayals of Latinos in Magazine Advertising." *Journalism and Mass Communication Quarterly* 74 (2): 285–303.
Taylor, Charles R., Ju Yung Lee, and Barbara B. Stern. 1995. "Portrayals of African American, Hispanic, and Asian Americans in Magazine Advertising." *American Behavior Scientist* 38 (4): 608–21.
Tuchman, Gaye. 1978. "Introduction: The Symbolic Annihilation of Women." In *Hearth and Home: Images of Women in Mass Media*, edited by Gaye Tuchman, Arlene Kaplan Daniels, and James Benet, 3–38. New York: Oxford University Press.
U.S. Bureau of the Census. 1983. *Census of Population and Housing, 1980*. Bureau of the Census, Washington, DC, https://www2.census.gov/prod2/decennial/documents/1980/1980censusofpopu8011u_bw.pdf
Valdivia, Angharad N. 2000. *A Latina in the Land of Hollywood: And Other Essays on Media Culture*. Tucson: The University of Arizona Press.
———. 2003. "Racial Hybridity: Latina/s as the Paradigmatic Transnational Post-Subculture." In *The Post-Subcultures Reader*, edited by David Muggleton and Rupert Weinzeil, 151–65. New York: Berg.
van Zoonen, Liesbet. 1994. *Feminist Media Studies*. Thousand Oaks: Sage.
Vargas, Lucila. 2009. *Latina Teens, Migration, and Popular Culture*. New York: Peter Lang.
Vega, Tanzina. 2011. "Marketers, and Media Companies, Set Their Sights on Latin Women." *New York Times Magazine*, December 9, 3.
Weissman, Rachel X. 1999. "Los Niños Go Shopping." *Advertising Age*, May 1, 37.
Wilkinson, Kenton T. 2015. *Spanish-Language Television in the United States: Fifty Years of Development*. New York: Routledge.
Yúdice, George. 1995. "Civil Society, Consumption and Governmentality in an Age of Global Restructuring. *Social Text* 45 (4): 1–25.

Chapter 11

"You Get a Very Conflicting View"

Postfeminism, Contradiction, and Women of Color's Responses to Representations of Women in Advertisements

Leandra H. Hernández

Advertising plays a prominent role in constructing definitions and perceptions of health, beauty, and success for women. Advertisements send messages to women about what is *healthy*—how a woman should look in terms of beauty and weight, what kinds of food she should eat to contribute to better health, what kinds of physical alterations she should make to be healthier, and what she should do to feel better about herself overall. Furthermore, advertisements are important social agents, as consumers are bombarded by advertisements throughout a variety of traditional, new, social, digital, and out-of-home media. It is estimated that consumers are exposed to more than five thousand advertisements and brands daily (Johnson 2014). This exposure has the potential to affect consumers in powerful ways. Kilbourne (1999, 34) argues that advertising is "both a creator and perpetuator of the dominant attitudes, values, and ideology of the culture, the social norms and myths by which most people govern their own behavior." Kang (1997, 980) elaborates upon this by noting that "advertising as signifying practices gives meaning to words and images; through this process, advertising diffuses its meanings into the belief systems of the society." The meanings advertising circulates in society have the potential to affect women's self-image and body perception.

Women featured in advertisements are often tall, thin, tanned, and flawless with perfect hair and makeup, thereby creating unrealistic and often unattainable representations of women (Hawkins et al. 2004). The typical thin woman depicted in advertisements—Caucasian with European features and standards of beauty—is biologically and practically impossible to attain for the majority of women who view them (Attie and Brooks-Gunn 1989). This practice, compounded by the fact that women of color are underrepresented in advertisements and then characterized by ethnic and racial stereotypes when they are depicted (Cortese 2015), raises questions regarding the ways women of color decode, interpret, and evaluate representations of women in advertising. Although research has explored how demographic groups such as Caucasian women (e.g., Stevens, Maclaran, and Brown 2003) and Caucasian and African-American teens (e.g., Duke 2000) make sense of depictions of women in advertising, little research has explored how women of color decode and respond to depictions of women in advertising. In this study, I analyze the ways in which twenty-five women of color make sense of how women are portrayed in magazine advertisements.

First, I situate this analysis within key areas: postfeminism, representations of women in advertising, and feminist approaches to audience studies. Second, I describe the participant selection and interview process that I employed, and revisit postfeminism and feminist approaches to audience studies to set up the framework through which I analyze the transcripts. Third, I analyze participants' interpretations of representations of women in advertisements as mediated by their intersectional positionalities of race, ethnicity, class, gender, and body image, and I share the three themes that surfaced. My argument is twofold: (1) postfeminist paradoxes that emerged from participants' multilayered interpretations of representations of women in advertising simultaneously empowered participants to feel confident about their body shapes and beauty, yet insidiously reinforced their anxieties about their weight, body shapes, and health success through constant corporeal surveillance; (2) the whiteness of postfeminist representations of women in advertising obfuscates women of color's ability to identify with advertisements, thus rendering certain advertisements ineffective and problematic.

POSTFEMINISM, CONTRADICTION, AND WOMEN IN ADVERTISEMENTS

Cultural Standards of Health, Beauty, and Thinness

The term *health* is defined and conceptualized depending on the interplay between and among factors such as cultural context, media constructions, and interpersonal relationships, to name a few. The term *health* has traditionally been conceptualized within two models: the biomedical and the biopsychosocial. The biomedical approach to health, which dominates Western medicine, conceptualizes health in purely biological and scientific ways as the absence of disease and illness (Engel 1980). The biopsychosocial model, created by George Engel (1980) in the 1970s, serves as the focus of this study. The biopsychosocial model conceptualizes health in a more holistic sense by taking into consideration factors such as culture (mass media, race, ethnicity), social relationships (with friends, family members, and spouses), and psychology (intrapersonal communication and self-perceptions). Although the biopsychosocial model was initially conceptualized for and implemented within clinical interpersonal contexts, in this study I bridge the two contexts to investigate how the biopsychosocial approach to conceptualizing health can shed light on the relationships between women of color's perceptions of women in advertisements and their self-image and health.

Cultural ideals contribute to how women view themselves and construct definitions of *health, beauty, thinness,* and *attractiveness* (Couch et al. 2016). The pressures that women experience to be thin and beautiful are often confused with pressures to be healthy (Couch et al. 2016). Today's Western society values thinness and a particular narrow definition of beauty. Indeed, slenderness is generally associated with traits such as happiness, youthfulness, social acceptability, and success (Grogan 1999). From a social comparison perspective, individuals view their weight and their peers' weight as outcomes of either personal efforts to achieve the thin ideal or a failure to succeed in this arena (Pidgeon and Harker 2013). Furthermore, individuals who are overweight are stigmatized because of their weight and appearance, which is partially attributed to the perception that overweight and obese people are accountable for their health and weight (Mulder, Rupp, and Dijkstra 2015). Thinness can also be a physical, embodied representation of and expression of achievement, meaning it is the ability to master a physical and cultural ideal that not all can accomplish (Ferreira, Gouveia, and Duarte 2013). It is an ideal that women seek to attain "as a competitive weapon to assure a secure place in the social world" (Ferreira, Gouveia, and Duarte 2013, 15).

Representations of Women in Advertising

Feminist scholars have long been interested in representations of women in advertising. Gill (2007, 1) notes, "Starting from the proposition that representations matter, feminist analyses of the media have been animated by the desire to understand how images and cultural constructions are connected to patterns of inequality, domination, and oppression." Representations of women in advertising in particular have been criticized because of their role in objectifying and symbolically annihilating women, which is why research suggests that advertising is one of the most visible and constant indicators of patriarchal ideology in our culture (Nowak, Abel, and de Bruin 2010). First, as to objectification, advertisements that both feature and target women often portray women in sexist and sexually objectifying ways via sexually provocative and subordinate positions with minimal clothing and as props to sell products (Cortese 2015; Goffman 1976; Krawczyk and Thompson 2015; Mager and Helgeson 2011; Zotos and Tsichla 2014).

Second, regarding symbolic annihilation, representations of women in advertisements are problematic because they simultaneously depict women in sexist ways and then fail to represent women of all genders, races, ethnicities, sexualities, class statuses, and physical abilities. Symbolic annihilation describes the ways in which the mass media are implicated in patterns of discrimination through the "condemnation, trivialization, or 'absence'" of women in media content (Tuchman 1978, 8). Gallagher (2014, 23) elaborates by noting that "when women are 'visible' in media content, the manner of their representation reflects the biases and assumptions of those who define the public—and therefore the media—agenda."

More specifically, women of diverse races, genders, ethnicities, class statuses, and abilities are symbolically annihilated, as well (Behm-Morawitz and Ortiz 2013). Gender and ethnic representations in advertising are linked to power and social cultural arrangements. From a symbolic annihilation perspective, lack of representation—the absences of women of color in advertising—reflects the status of groups that do not possess significant power (Cortese 2015). Moreover, when women of color are depicted in advertisements, they are portrayed stereotypically. Black women are portrayed as servants or animalistic sexual predators, whereas Latinas are portrayed as luscious, hypersexual, erotic, and irrational (Cortese 2015; Hirshman 2011).

Advertising and Women's Health Messages

Negative representations of women coincide with another problematic aspect of advertising, that of health messages that target women as consumers. Advertising health messages, while under the guise of creating and promoting "healthy" products and behaviors, not only focus more on appearance than health but also employ contradictory messages. First, content analyses of advertisements suggest that the lean female body shape and thin models have become the standard in advertisements, with more than 50 percent of models being lean and thinner than recommended body and health standards (Wasylkiw et al. 2009; Willis and Knobloch-Westerwick 2014). Moreover, magazines that specifically focus on women's health overwhelmingly feature white women in their body-shaping and weight-loss messages, which compose 80 percent of magazine content overall (Conlin and Bissell 2014). Appearance-related behaviors and messages are more prominent than health-related behaviors and messages (Aubrey and Hahn 2016; Willis and Knobloch-Westerwick 2014). Thus "health" messages in magazines focus less on healthy behaviors (healthy eating, moderate exercise, and positive mental health behaviors) and more on thinness and body appearance (extreme dieting and extreme weight loss), which potentially influence women to adopt unhealthy habits to achieve unrealistic, even unattainable, cultural ideals of attractiveness and thinness (Aubrey and Hahn 2016).

Postfeminism, Contradiction, and Advertising to Women

Postfeminism provides a useful lens to examine representations of women and health in advertising. *Postfeminism* is a recently created ideological constellation of arguments that undermines the successes of feminism and presents "true happiness" and "empowerment" through hyper–self-awareness, luxury consumerism, and matrimonial and maternalist models of female subjectivity (Negra 2009). By casting and caricaturing feminism as a dead and irrelevant movement, postfeminism "offers the pleasure and comfort of (re)claiming an identity uncomplicated by gender politics, postmodernism, or institutional critique" (Negra 2009, 2). Postfeminism operates through tropes such as freedom and choice (McRobbie 2004). Postfeminist discourse, including advertising, encourages women to engage in luxury consumerism, to purchase products to enhance their beauty, and to work on their bodies under the guise of personal freedom and empowerment through beauty practices and bodily hypermodification (Lazar 2011).

Postfeminist logic in advertising is dangerous and problematic because it "ensures that real problems for women are concealed under a guise of individual self-empowerment, superficial solutions, and artificial transformations that in fact undermine true agency and real feminist change" (Crymble 2012, 63). Advertisers deploy postfeminist discourses of choice and freedom to link normative practices of beautification with the notion of an emancipated identity, which operates through the overarching message that women have a right to be beautiful (Lazar 2011). The problem, however, lies in the fact that women's right to be beautiful is often confused with women's right to be healthy and the practices women undergo to achieve these beauty and health standards (Duncan and Klos 2014). Women's magazines that advertise health, beauty, and fitness messages are characterized by contradiction because they produce feminine bodies that are rigged for failure. This phenomenon, what Duncan and Klos (2014) refer to as *paradoxes of the flesh,* is characterized by the multiple contradictions embedded in health, fitness, and beauty advertising discourses. Examples of such contradictions include, among others, the notions that diets are freeing, pounds will disappear if women love their bodies as they are, women can lose weight if they stop trying to lose weight, and dieting is a behavior that indicates one cares about one's self (Duncan and Klos 2014). Overall, these contradictory frames emphasize that achieving health and beauty through controversial means is essential—required—to ensure that embodied neoliberalism and postfeminism successfully operate within magazine advertising discourses (Cairns and Johnston 2015; Duncan and Klos 2014). From an embodied, material consumer point of view, however, women consumers find themselves in a no-win situation as they struggle to achieve these health and beauty ideals (Duncan and Klos 2014).

Although research has analyzed representations of women in advertising using textual and content analyses, little research has used audience reception to analyze how consumers respond to representations of women and health in advertising. Most advertising audience research seeks to understand and manipulate purchasing patterns. Audience reception analyses, however, understand audiences as active or resistant agents who make meaning. The few studies from both social science and critical-cultural studies traditions that have analyzed Caucasian women's and Latina women's responses to representations of women in advertising suggest that women's beliefs and attitudes about these images are "complex, shaded, and sometimes contradictory" (Goodman 2002, 722). Both groups of women compare themselves to women in advertisements, even though these images provoke dissatisfaction, and women continue to incorporate ideologies of thinness and self-awareness evident in advertisements into their everyday lives. However, Latinas use their ethnic identity and perceptions of their cultural values and cultural preferences to mediate, and perhaps even buffer, the ways in which they are influenced by representations of women in advertising (Goodman 2002; Schooler and Daniels 2014). Goodman (2002) found that Caucasian women and Latinas defined *health* in terms of losing weight and toning their bodies to mirror women in advertisements; they pursued the mediated ideal, as this was viewed as a sense of self-power. Latinas, however, were more critical of the mediated ideal, which they attributed to their cultural values that preferred curvier women and more voluptuous feminine forms (Goodman 2002). Moreover, Báez (2008) found in her study of Mexican-American women's responses to Latinidad in advertising that Latina consumers were vocal in criticizing the oversimplified, limiting, hypersexualized, and incorrect representations of Latina femininity and sexuality. Thus, at least for Latina consumers, ethnic identity can serve as one factor that buffers negative representations of women in advertising. Given this literature, my study asked how women-of-color participants respond to representations of women in advertising, especially in relation to participants' perceptions of health, agency, and self.

THE STUDY

This study used qualitative methods because interpersonal conversations with participants can help researchers understand the ways in which individuals create social and personal identities, as well as the ways in which cultural institutions shape body image. Given that women of color are a traditionally underrepresented and understudied group in audience studies, qualitative research allows women-of-color participants to "speak back, against, and to mainstream institutions such as media" (Báez 2008, 261). Furthermore, participants and researchers in discussion during interviews have the opportunity to co-construct meanings of health attributed to representations of women in advertisements. As a middle-class pansexual Mexican-American woman who is both a media consumer and feminist media researcher, I engaged in detailed co-constructed conversations with participants about how women are represented in advertisements and accompanying health messages.

The participant group consisted of twenty-five women from Houston, Texas. Participants' ages ranged from twenty-two to twenty-eight, and participants self-identified as Caucasian, Hispanic, Italian, or mixed race and mixed ethnicity. Sixteen participants identified as Hispanic, two participants identified as Italian, two participants identified as black, and five participants identified as mixed race or mixed ethnicity. Each participant had at least a bachelor's degree, and two-thirds of the participants were master's degree students at the time the study was conducted in 2011. Participant recruitment began with a convenience sample of women of color I knew from graduate school and other graduate programs, and then I used the snowball method to gather more women of color as participants. Women from some of the participants' social networks agreed to participate, and I stopped scheduling interviews once I reached data saturation.

After attaining Institutional Review Board approval, I conducted in-depth, semistructured individual interviews with each participant. I asked the participants to explore (1) how images of women in advertisements make them feel, (2) their perceptions of how representations of women in advertisements shape their self-image, and (3) how they define *health.* I asked questions about these broad themes to explore the relationships among self-image, body image, representations of women in advertising, and participants' overall health. Instead of preselecting advertisements for discussion during the interviews, participants were asked about perceptions of women in advertising generally to elicit advertisements and campaigns salient to the women-of-color participants. The interviews progressed as natural give-and-take conversations with me prompting for more information when needed. Interviews lasted approximately thirty minutes to one hour and were audiorecorded and transcribed with participant consent. In sum, the interviews resulted in two hundred pages of single-spaced transcripts. Participants were assigned pseudonyms to maintain confidentiality. For the present purpose, readers can assume participants referred to here are Hispanic or mixed unless otherwise noted.

To answer the research questions, I conducted a thematic analysis in which I created categories and a coding scheme based on patterns, similarities, and notable exceptions in the data. Thematic analysis is a way of seeing (Boyatzis 1998). Specifically, it is a method for identifying, analyzing, and reporting patterns (themes) within data (Braun and Clarke 2006). The three main themes that characterized participants' responses to representations of women in advertising include (1) positive and negative advertisements, (2) healthy and unhealthy advertising images, and (3) positive and negative self-images in reaction to representations of women in advertising, all of which I explain in more detail in this chapter.

WOMEN OF COLOR SPEAK OUT: POSITIVITY, CONTRADICTION, AND WOMEN IN ADVERTISING

Overall, a majority of the participants saw a relationship between representations of women in advertising and their own health and body image. Twenty-one of the twenty-five participants defined *health* in biopsychosocial ways and described health as being most optimal when their physical, emotional, mental, and spiritual health were aligned. As opposed to being defined as the absence of disease, many participants defined *health* holistically as an "all-encompassing state." Marie defined *health* as "maintenance on yourself on all different facets." Similarly, Sarah incorporated happiness in her definition when she said, "Someone is healthy when they are happy with themselves—they are mentally and physically well, they have good self-esteem, and they have high aspirations for themselves." Most of the participants disagreed with the notion that health should be related to physical appearance and success, yet many contradicted this statement as interviews progressed, a phenomenon I discuss later. Marilyn said, "I don't think health should have anything to do with a woman's appearance. We're built differently, and you can have the heart of a horse and be overweight or underweight, and you can look ideal and have an unhealthy mind, body, spirit, and soul." Lana also pointed to a perceived disconnect between health and body size and then said, "Being beautiful doesn't mean you're healthy in any shape or form."

When asked about depictions of women in advertisements and the coinciding health messages, participants discussed what they interpreted to be both positive and negative representations of women in advertisements, along with what they perceived to be negative and positive ways in which the advertisements affected them. Participants define positive interpretations as a perceived improvement in the representations in advertisements, including "real, average women." Negative interpretations were defined as the tendency for advertisements to emphasize thinness and beauty.

Positive and Negative Advertisements: "It's Better than Nothing"

During interviews, participants consistently described both the positive and negative aspects of depictions of women in advertising, and the first theme focuses on the various ways in which participants perceived these depictions to be both "positive and normal," yet simultaneously "negative and stereotypical."

Roughly two-thirds of the participants were pleased with and appreciated what they perceived to be a new trend in advertising of showcasing "real, average women," as opposed to the typical thin cultural ideal documented in a majority of magazine advertising (Wasylkiw et al. 2009; Willis and Knobloch-Westerwick 2014). Rosie said that she appreciates that advertising images have become better: "Before, it was really skinny, glorified women, and it was unrealistic. You can't live up to that just as a normal, everyday person." She also said, "I've always been conscious of my weight, but it definitely affected me more negatively before when it was only skinny people in the media." Olivia expressed similar sentiments when she said that seeing more average and realistic women in advertising opened her eyes to the unrealistic nature of seeing "typical thin models" in advertisements. Overall, participants said that they enjoyed seeing more "realistic women" in advertisements, such as the Dove Campaign for Real Beauty advertisements, because they offer new perspectives on the relationship between beauty and health and helped them realize that being thin or beautiful does not necessarily equate to being healthy. From a representation standpoint, seeing more "realistic women" in advertising empowered participants to feel more positive about their body image, which was encapsulated by Rosie's statement: "Seeing women like me in advertisements makes me feel like I matter, like I'm normal, too."

Two participants explicitly mentioned that they enjoyed Dove commercials and advertisements because of Dove's perceived "progressive representations of women of all shapes and colors." Yet this appreciation was mediated by a critical consciousness and reading of the advertisements. Elizabeth said, "God bless Dove." She said she enjoyed the Dove Beauty Campaign advertisements: "They have the best commercials, and they put *us* on TV—us, average USA—they put us on TV and in magazines and make you realize, you know what? She didn't have a six-pack, but she still looked beautiful in that commercial or that advertisement."

The explicit naming of the Dove Campaign for Real Beauty advertisements is noteworthy, as participants used this campaign as an exemplar of positive advertising and positive depictions of women in advertising. Featuring "real women" of various races, ethnicities, and body shapes, the Dove Campaign for Real Beauty showcased women who "radiated happiness and friendship" and who sought to represent all women (Johnston and Taylor 2008, 951). Although some women consumers have viewed the Dove campaign positively (Millard 2009) or as a "better than nothing" alternative (Taylor, Johnston, and Whitehead 2016)—as participants did in in my study—feminist scholars critique the campaign for its inherent contradiction (promoting real beauty, yet selling beauty products) and its continued reliance on beauty expectations and myths that its campaign and advertisements purport to reverse (Dye 2009; Murray 2013). Additionally, Dove's campaigns continue to align women's worth with beauty, however generously defined. Still, as participants noted, it is a step in the right direction. Therefore, even though the "positive" presentation of "real" women in advertisements coincides with most participants' definitions of health and body image perceptions, participants agreed that there is room for improvement in advertising.

Although many participants said they were pleased with what they perceived as a new advertising trend of including more realistic women in advertisements, many said that the majority of representations are still negative ("stupid" or "stereotypical"), unrealistic ("completely warped and twisted"), and unhealthy because of the continual depiction of thin, white women in advertisements. Elizabeth, for example, said, "The media don't put big disclaimers on there that say this person doesn't eat and was airbrushed. You look at these people and say, 'That's successful and beautiful. That's what I should strive for.'" Ava believes that many beauty and health advertisements tell women how to look, both explicitly and implicitly, because the women depicted are "too coiffed, too perfect, and too ideal; there is a certain boob size that's perfect, a certain waist that's perfect, and a certain hair color and a certain general look that is a little too over-emphasized." In terms of stereotypical representations, Chloe said, "All advertisements keep showing white women who are super tall and super skinny. That's not common of normal people, and that's negative. Where is the Latina of average body size?" Sarah shared similar sentiments: "Models in advertisements are idealized. They're impossible and fake. I think they're probably all underweight and not eating enough."

In addition to interpreting images of women in advertisements as unhealthy and unrealistic, when asked how images of women in advertising make them feel, participants said that they experience difficulties identifying with women portrayed in advertisements for two reasons: (1) because of the models' body shapes and perceived lifestyles and (2) because of the models' races and ethnicities. When asked how depictions of women in advertisements make her feel, Marilyn replied, "Utterly inadequate." She went on to say, "All of those maternity ads and mothers in commercials are always so thin with perfect shiny hair and decent makeup, and their outfits match, and they work ninety-hour weeks and they're completely sexually fulfilled, and I have just absolutely no identification with that." Elizabeth said, "Even when the advertisements are about healthy living, the models are still too thin. How can real women relate to that?" Finally, Chloe said, "Being from Venezuelan descent, there's a lot of tall, skinny, big-breasted white women, which I'm actually kind of short, not super skinny, and I kind of have boobs. No way do I fit what I see in ads."

Thus participants described first what they perceive to be positive and negative aspects of depictions of women in advertising. Although they felt that depictions of women in some advertising are becoming positive because of a newer focus on portraying "realistic" and "average, real-life" women, thus indicating a potentially positive trend, participants still described what they perceived as negative aspects of advertisements, including continuing stereotypical depictions and limited representations of models who are women of color. This indicates two important findings: First, participants responded negatively to what they judged to be stereotypical depictions of women in advertisements. They perceived too little variation in body shapes and too much focus on the thin ideal. Second, through a lens of symbolic annihilation, the omission of both representations of more average women and women-of-color models communicated to participants that they "did not matter" because they could not see themselves represented in these advertisements. Granted, advertisements, and the companies and brands behind their creation, have a primary goal of selling products. However, in spite of this, these findings suggest that advertisers continue to use Crymble's (2012) contradiction and identity dissonance in product marketing. As Crymble (2012, 80) notes in her study of feminine complexity and gender identity dissonance in magazine advertisements, dissonant advertisements explicitly illustrate the "unreasonable social constructions that frame female gender identity," even as this dissonance might offer an "important liberatory space for resistant readings and social critiques." This same trend of contradiction and dissonance characterized participants' interpretations of health messages that they saw in advertising, as well.

Healthy and Unhealthy Advertising Images: "It's Great in Theory, But. . . ."

When considering advertisements that include both representations of women and perceived health messages, participants noted that health messages have improved, yet are still problematic because of the conflicting and persistent focus on body modification and quick fixes. "Health messages" that emerged during the interviews ranged from public health awareness about healthy eating to product advertisements for exercising and weight-loss supplements. In terms of positive health messages, participants noted that this "positive trend" is a step in the right direction, yet there is still room for improvement. Rosie, for example, enjoyed positive health messages from American Heart Association advertisements in women's magazines, such as *Shape* and *In Touch,* because they send a "positive 'We as Americans know we have a problem, so let's do something about it' message." For Rosie, framing weight loss as related to heart disease was more credible and believable because the weight loss message focused on a "real public health problem with an average-looking woman" and less on quick-weight-loss scams or extreme exercise. Olivia shared similar sentiments when she said that she felt advertisements targeting women for healthy eating and food products have improved over time. When probed, Olivia said, "[These advertisements] have gotten better because they're focusing more on real health and less on products that are unhealthy scams that really don't work." Sarah also felt that health messages in advertisements are improving because they're "becoming more realistic," yet she continues to read these advertisements critically. When asked about why she thinks advertising is contradictory, Sarah said: "They have commercials and advertisements about different health things, but they have models that are uber-skinny, which sends the wrong message. Although some advertisements, like the Dove campaign, are promoting healthy lifestyles, I still wouldn't consider some of these models to be healthy."

Other participants stressed, however, that they perceived "health" messages in advertisements to be unhealthy and negative because they focus on quick fixes and promote negative health practices and ideals. This portion of Elizabeth's interview focused heavily on quick fixes. For her, advertisements that focused on healthy living via weight loss promoted too many quick fixes, such as two-day detoxes, pills, and supplements, instead of focusing on moderate exercise and a well-balanced diet. She referred to this advertising strategy as a "Band-Aid" fix. She said, "Advertising says, 'Yes, you've got this issue, but look at all these quick fixes and products we have to help you fix it temporarily!' It's a very instant gratification and fix-it-now type thing, which you can see as accompanied by stick-thin models who don't even need this product in the first place." Another participant, Marilyn, also referred to this phenomenon when she said, "That's it in a nutshell. If there is something wrong with you, we've got a product for that." Marie, referring to quick-weight-loss products, said, "These messages make me want to scream because they really are communicating that there is a quick fix, that you can do this, and it won't be a big challenge and that is the ideal you want to lose. Everyone wants to lose twenty pounds." This phenomenon that participants are referring to, the "Band-Aid fix" phenomenon, is problematic because it promotes unhealthy behaviors under the guise of "fast, healthy alternatives." These often contradictory and confusing messages, referred to as a *dietary cacophony* (Rousseau 2015), are even more problematic when promoted as "healthy" by celebrities because this adds an unsupported credibility to the products. Overall, these products rest on questionable science and research findings, threaten scientific and public health literacy, and also pose a threat to those who are trying to lose weight (Rousseau 2015). Many of the participants referred to their graduate school education as giving them strategies for resisting these products and advertisements. However, the participants are operating with an education privilege that most consumers do not enjoy.

In addition to the perception of quick fixes as a negative component of health advertising, participants noted that health messages both directly and indirectly promote negative health practices and ideals. Viviana said that "quick-fix" advertisements tell women that they are unhealthy, and this frame is used to promote products: "It's very in your face, like the latest diet pill, the latest diet, the latest detox, the latest exercise that's going to flatten your stomach in seven minutes—there's never a stopping point, like too fit, and that's unhealthy." Addie thought that advertisements equate health with thinness, which "is bad because that's the popular thing." Addie said, "From the images they show, skinny is the predominant one. Women should know that you can be healthy and not be that bony, that you can be healthy and full-sized." Olivia said that health messages have shifted over the last few years because she perceives that advertisers are using health-framed messages to get to audiences who "are over the old messages." Olivia said, "They used to be, 'You need to be thin to be attractive,' and now they're using health messages to push another message which is, 'Buy this product because you're not good enough as you are now."

A few participants also believed that advertising indirectly promotes negative health practices by not addressing health or by using "general messages" that don't specify what sorts of behaviors could be used to make women healthier. In other words, advertising messages that do not provide clear-cut health behaviors or actions did not help participants improve their health behaviors. By focusing more on beauty and less on healthy eating and realistic workout routines, participants felt that advertisers are missing an important consumer information preference. Chloe and Michelle said that advertisements do not talk about health very much. "I don't think [advertisements] ever say anything about being healthy or exercising," said Chloe. "They never promote exercising. They always focus on different things, rather than actually being healthy and taking care of your body." When Chloe was prompted about the role of advertising to sell products to consumers, she replied, "That's true, but advertisers should have an ethical obligation to promote healthy things, too, not just products to make you beautiful." Michelle said, "I don't really know if there's a lot of stuff out there saying, 'Oh, be healthy.' I don't really think [advertisements] communicate about good health all that much, really." Last, Ava said of advertisements, "You get a very conflicting view." Ava elaborated that the contradiction lies in the products that are marketed to make women beautiful and the weight-loss products to make women thinner. Ava's view encapsulated other participants' views on this subject when she said, "It's like I just can't win."

To summarize, participants perceived advertising to be both positive and negative, which stemmed from both representations of women in advertising and also the health messages embedded within these advertisements. Although some participants felt empowered by certain depictions and were happy to see what they perceived to be more realistic depictions, other participants felt that advertising images of women continue to be unhealthy, unrealistic, and ineffective at communicating "real health."

Positive and Negative Self-Perceptions: "It's a Confidence Thing"

When asked about their self-perceptions regarding health and beauty, participants perceived themselves to be both healthy and unhealthy at the same time when compared with images of women and the health messages embedded in advertisements. Some participants used their education and their media consciousness as modes to protect themselves from depictions of thin women in advertising. Yet other participants, in spite of their graduate training and media consciousness, struggled with eating disorders and body dysmorphia, which compounded their penchant to compare themselves to models in advertisements.

Lana, Addie, Rosie, and Viviana, for example, said they did not compare themselves to thin models in advertisements because they think the models are unhealthy and not a good basis for comparison. Viviana said that she did not compare herself because she knew she would be unhappy and unsatisfied with herself if she did. She said, "It's a confidence thing. I have to be confident in myself before anyone can have confidence in me. If I'm constantly comparing myself to a goal I can't reach, like a body type I'm not born to have, then it would really be unhealthy and unintelligent of me to do that." Similarly, Rosie said she did not compare herself to thin models in advertisements because she is not a superstar and does not have personal trainers, a beauty staff, and nutritionists on call, all resources that she believes models have access to. Moreover, Rosie said that her family is an important factor that helps her "be a better person":

> I know my life is different from a model. I'm big on "Beauty is not just how you look. Are you a good person? That's what makes you beautiful." There are a lot of heavy people in my family, but we're pretty, and we're good. I would rather be huge and ugly and fat and be good than be skinny, pretty, and crappy. I just don't compare myself to models. We're on different life tracks.

Rosie created a dichotomy between advertising models and "normal women" in her interview, as she discursively constructed "normal women" to have wrinkles, extra weight, and intellect and models to have thinness and beauty, but perhaps not much else. Not all of the participants shared these sentiments, but this line of thinking was one of Rosie's mechanisms that helped ameliorate unrealistic depictions of women in advertising.

On the other hand, some participants felt unhealthy when they reflected on images of women in advertising and compared themselves to these depictions frequently. Marilyn said that her preference to read magazines such as *Vogue* and *In Style* shaped her perceptions of women in advertising: "We look at these advertisements, and it's like we're looking at Barbies. It's like I don't even identify with them. Like they're completely separate beings from everyone who exists. I know I shouldn't compare myself to them, but it's hard not to." Similarly, Megan said that she doesn't identify with women in advertisements, which frustrates her and reduces her self-esteem: "First off, they're almost all white, which is not me. I don't feel like they represent me or even the average woman." Megan later said of models in advertising: "I know I can't relate to these women. I don't identify with them. It's hard not to want to look like them, though."

Thus participants described their self-images as affected both positively and negatively by representations of women in advertising. Some participants did not compare themselves to depictions of women in advertisements because of their confidence and media literacy. Other participants struggled with social comparison because they did not identify with models in advertisements and also because the thin ideal continued to influence them negatively. By feeling that they were not represented accurately in advertisements and by continually comparing themselves to women in advertisements, certain participants engaged in paradoxical comparison: They knew that they were very different from the models featured in advertisements, yet they could not refrain from societal and media pressures to compare themselves to the models.

CONTRADICTION, WOMEN OF COLOR, AND WOMEN IN ADVERTISING

As feminist scholars have long argued, advertising is an important cultural socialization tool because of its ubiquity and the power it has to transmit messages about thinness, beauty, and health (Gil 2007; McRobbie 2004; Negra 2009). The diverse women interviewed in this study interpreted representations of women in advertisements in both positive and negative ways—in the actual depiction of women in advertisements and also in the ways in which participants perceived advertisements as shaping and affecting their self-images. First, participants noted that they were pleased with the "new media trend" of portraying women in more realistic ways, which indicates that there could be a positive advertising trend emerging, especially in the wake of social and digital activism advocating for less airbrushing and digital manipulation. This trend made participants feel valued because, from a body shape perspective, participants felt that more realistic women models were being included in some advertising. However, from a cultural, racial, and ethnic perspective, participants did not identify with the overreliance on white, thin models with predominantly Eurocentric beauty features, which decreased the efficacy of the advertisements and contributed to participants' dissatisfaction with the advertisements and the products being advertised. Additionally, participants expressed frustration and exasperation as they described stereotypical depictions of women in advertising. Similar to Báez's (2008) findings, the women in this study were dissatisfied with one-dimensional images of white models as beautiful and hyperthin. These hegemonic depictions of women in advertisements led participants to three conclusions: (1) advertising models are pictured as unhealthy, (2) it is unhealthy for consumers to see these kinds of models, and (3) the participants perceive themselves as inadequate in their inability to "measure up" to the thin ideal. Finally, the participants recalled advertisements that focused on weight loss, body fat reduction, and quick fixes to solve health ailments. Their interpretations resulted in a contradiction between health literacy and media literacy as they worked to discern accurate, helpful health messages and advertisements from negative and inaccurate advertisements.

This study has three important implications pertaining to contradiction and postfeminism, the role of race and ethnicity, and media literacy education helping consumers make sense of advertisements. First, in terms of contradiction and postfeminism, participants experienced cognitive dissonance as they tried to make sense of depictions of women in advertising and resulting messages about health, beauty, thinness, and success. Part of this could be attributed to the postfeminist nature of advertising to women, namely the ways in which women are told that they are beautiful and perfect as they are, yet are encouraged to become *more* beautiful, healthy, and thin by engaging in consumerism and purchasing products in a never-ending and unattainable quest for perfection. This phenomenon, which I am referring to as a *postfeminist advertising paradox,* was experienced by participants as they attempted to make sense of advertisements and their own responses to depictions of women in advertising, especially when self-image and self-perceptions were concerned. As Crymble (2012, 79) argues, these dissonant advertising representations present women with a "disconcerting array of ideal(ized) identities," which are problematic because of their unclear health messages. However, the contradiction also lies in the goal to "promote anxiety-fueled consumption and to reach the widest variety of consumers" (Crymble 2012, 79).

Second, previous research has found that culture and ethnicity, particularly for Latinas, can help mediate the ways in which Latinas respond to the unrealistically thin white model ubiquitous in contemporary advertising (Báez 2008; Goodman 2002; Schooler and Daniels 2014). However, in this study, even with a majority Latina participant group, culture and ethnicity did not surface as a factor that helped participants respond more critically to depictions of women in advertising. What did surface, however, was the participants' use of their graduate education and perceived critical media consciousness as a means of resisting the temptation to compare themselves to advertising models. Although a few participants were distraught that, in spite of their education, they continued to compare themselves to thin models in advertising, many participants noted that the media concepts they learned in classes, coupled with their increasing self-confidence, helped them interpret depictions of women in advertising more critically.

In conclusion, although depictions of women in advertisements might be described as an improvement with the inclusion of more realistic women and models, a postfeminist contradiction continues between depictions of women in advertising and the health and beauty messages presented in advertisements. This postfeminist advertising paradox continues to argue that women are healthy, successful, and beautiful, yet that women still need to improve themselves via consumerism and extreme bodily attention, sometimes in unhealthy ways (Gill 2011). What is more, advertisements of this nature emphasize bodily scrutiny as a gendered practice, which further positions women as neoliberal consumers who constantly need to engage in self-surveillance to strive for perfection (Cairns and Johnston 2015). By using feminist audience reception studies as an approach and a method, we can (1) understand the complexities associated with the multifaceted ways that women of different races, ethnicities, sexualities, classes, and abilities interpret representations of women in advertising and the factors that assist them in reading such representations more critically; (2) understand the loci of resistance and agency that women employ to reject contradictory messages and body types in advertisements; and (3) use these findings to partner with women consumers to create media literacy campaigns to assist and empower women in this context. By the same token, such optimism once again positions women to fix themselves—to become better at resisting—rather than laying the onus on advertising professionals, researchers, educators, and students to work to improve advertising practices that use unidimensional images of young, anorexic, white women to obfuscate beauty and health messages.

REFERENCES

Attie, Ilana, and Jeanne Brooks-Gunn. 1989. "Development of Eating Problems in Adolescent Girls: A Longitudinal Study." *Developmental Psychology* 25 (1): 70.

Aubrey, Jennifer Stevens, and Rachel Hahn. 2016. "Health versus Appearance versus Body Competence: A Content Analysis Investigating Frames of Health Advice in Women's Health Magazines." *Journal of Health Communication* 21 (5): 1–8.

Báez, Jillian M. 2008. "Mexican (American) Women Talk Back: Audience Responses to Latinidad in US Advertising." In *Latina/o Communication Studies Today,* edited by Angharad N. Valdivia, 257–81. New York: Peter Lang.

Behm-Morawitz, Elizabeth, and Michelle Ortiz. 2013. "Race, Ethnicity, and the Media." In *The Oxford Handbook of Media Psychology,* edited by Karen E. Dill, 252–67. New York: Oxford University Press.

Boyatzis, Richard E. 1998. *Transforming Qualitative Information: Thematic Analysis and Code Development.* Thousand Oaks, CA: Sage.

Braun, Virginia, and Victoria Clarke. 2006 "Using Thematic Analysis in Psychology." *Qualitative Research in Psychology* 3 (2): 77–101.

Cairns, Kate, and Josee Johnston. 2015. "Choosing Health: Embodied Neoliberalism, Postfeminism, and the 'Do-Diet.'" *Theory and Society* 44 (2): 153–75.

Conlin, Lindsey, and Kim Bissell. 2014. "Beauty Ideals in the Checkout Aisle: Health-Related Messages in Women's Fashion and Fitness Magazines." *Journal of Magazine and New Media Research* 15 (2): 1–19.

Cortese, Anthony J. 2015. *Provocateur: Images of Women and Minorities in Advertising,* 2nd ed. Lanham, MD: Rowman and Littlefield.

Couch, Danielle, Samantha L. Thomas, Sophie Lewis, R. Warwick Blood, Kate Holland, and Paul Komesaroff. 2016. "Obese People's Perceptions of the Thin Ideal." *Social Science and Medicine* 148: 60–70.

Crymble, Sarah B. 2012. "Contradiction Sells: Feminine Complexity and Gender Identity Dissonance in Magazine Advertising." *Journal of Communication Inquiry* 36 (1): 62–84.

Duke, Lisa. 2000. "Black in a Blonde World: Race and Girls' Interpretations of the Feminine Ideal in Teen Magazines." *Journalism and Mass Communication Quarterly* 77 (2): 367–92.

Duncan, Margaret Carlisle, and Lori A. Klos. 2014. "Paradoxes of the Flesh: Emotion and Contradiction in Fitness/Beauty Magazine Discourse." *Journal of Sport and Social Issues* 38 (3): 245–62.

Dye, Lauren. 2009. "Consuming Constructions: A Critique of Dove's Campaign for Real Beauty." *Canadian Journal of Media Studies* 5 (1): 114–28.

Engel, G. 1980. "The Clinical Application of the Biopsychosocial Model." *American Journal of Psychiatry* 13 (5): 535–44.

Ferreira, Claudia, Jose Pinto Gouveia, and Cristiana Duarte. 2013. "Drive for Thinness as a Woman's Strategy to Avoid Inferiority." *International Journal of Psychology and Psychological Therapy* 13 (1): 15–29.

Gallagher, Margaret. 2014. "Media and the Representation of Gender." In *The Routledge Companion to Media and Gender,* edited by Cynthia Carter, Linda Steiner, and Lisa McLaughlin, 23–31. New York: Routledge.

Gill, Rosalind. 2007. *Gender and the Media*. Malden: Polity Press.
———. 2011. "Sexism Reloaded, or, It's Time to Get Angry Again." *Feminist Media Studies* 11 (1): 61–71.
Goffman, Erving. 1976. *Gender Advertisements*. New York: Harper Colophon.
Goodman, J. Robyn. 2002. "Flabless Is Fabulous: How Latina and Anglo Women Read and Incorporate the Excessively Thin Body Ideal into Everyday Experience." *Journalism and Mass Communication Quarterly* 79 (3): 712–27.
Grogan, Sarah. 1999. *Body Image: Understanding Body Dissatisfaction in Men, Women, and Children*. London: Routledge.
Hawkins, Nicole, P. Scott Richards, H. Mac Granley, and David M. Stein. 2004. "The Impact of Exposure to the Thin-Ideal Media Image on Women." *Eating Disorders* 12 (1): 35–50.
Hirshman, Elizabeth C. 2011. "Motherhood in Black and Brown: Advertising to US Minority Women." *Advertising and Society Review* 12 (2). DOI: 10.1353/asr.2011.0015,
Johnson, Sheree. 2014. "New Research Sheds Light on Daily Ad Exposures." *SJ Insights*, September 29. https://sjinsights.net/2014/09/29/new-research-sheds-light-on-daily-ad-exposures/.
Johnston, Josee, and Judith Taylor. 2008. "Feminist Consumerism and Fat Activists: A Comparative Study of Grassroots Activism and the Dove Real Beauty Campaign." *Signs: Journal of Women in Culture and Society* 33 (4): 941–66.
Kang, Mee-Eun. 1997. "The Portrayal of Women's Images in Magazine Advertisements: Goffman's Gender Analysis Revisited." *Sex Roles* 37 (11–12): 979–96.
Kilbourne, Jean. 1999. *Can't Buy My Love: How Advertising Changes the Way We Think and Feel*. New York: Simon & Schuster.
Krawczyk, Ross, and J. Kevin Thompson. 2015. "The Effects of Advertisements That Sexually Objectify Women on State Body Dissatisfaction and Judgments of Women: The Moderating Roles of Gender and Internalization." *Body Image* 15: 109–19.
Lazar, Michelle M. 2011. "The Right to be Beautiful: Postfeminist Identity and Consumer Beauty Advertising." In *New Femininities: Postfeminism, Neoliberalism, and Subjectivity*, edited by Rosalind Gill and Christina Scharff, 37–51. New York: Palgrave Macmillan.
Mager, John, and James G. Helgeson. 2011. "Fifty Years of Advertising Images: Some Changing Perspectives on Role Portrayals along with Enduring Consistencies." *Sex Roles* 64 (3): 238–52.
McRobbie, Angela. 2004. "Post-Feminism and Popular Culture." *Feminist Media Studies* 4 (3): 255–64.
Millard, Jennifer. 2009 "Performing Beauty: Dove's 'Real Beauty' Campaign." *Symbolic Interaction* 32 (2): 146–68.
Mulder, Laetitia B., Deborah E. Rupp, and Arie Dijkstra. 2015. "Making Snacking Less Sinful: (Counter-)moralizing Obesity in the Public Discourse Differentially Affects Food Choices of Individuals with High and Low Perceived Body Mass." *Psychology and Health* 20(2).
Murray, Dara Persis. 2013."Branding 'Real' Social Change in Dove's Campaign for Real Beauty." *Feminist Media Studies* 13 (1): 83–101.

Negra, Diane. 2009. *What a Girl Wants: Fantasizing the Reclamation of Self in Post-feminism*. New York: Routledge.

Nowak, Anita, Sue Abel, and Marjan de Bruin. 2010. "Contextualizing Women/Advertising/Representation." In *Women, Advertising, and Representation: Beyond Familiar Paradigms,* edited by Sue Abel, Marjan de Bruin, and Anita Nowak, 11–28. Cresskill: Hampton.

Pidgeon, Aileen, and Rachel A. Harker. 2013. "Body-Focused Anxiety in Women: Associations with Internalization of the Thin-Ideal, Dieting Frequency, Body Mass Index and Media Effects." *Open Journal of Medical Psychology* 2: 17–24.

Rousseau, Signe. 2015 "The Celebrity Quick-Fix: When Good Food Meets Bad Science." *Food, Culture and Society: An International Journal of Multidisciplinary Research* 18 (2): 265–87.

Schooler, Deborah, and Elizabeth A. Daniels. 2014. "I Am Not a Skinny Toothpick and Proud of It: Latina Adolescents' Ethnic Identity and Responses to Mainstream Media Images." *Body Image* 11 (1): 11–18.

Stevens, Lorna, Pauline Maclaran, and Stephen Brown. 2003. "'*Red* Time Is Me Time:' Advertising, Ambivalence, and Women's Magazines." *Journal of Advertising* 32 (1): 35–45.

Taylor, Judith, Josee Johnston, and Krista Whitehead. 2016. "A Corporation in Feminist Clothing? Young Women Discuss the Dove 'Real Beauty' Campaign." *Critical Sociology* 42 (1): 123–44.

Tuchman, Gaye. 1978. "Introduction: The Symbolic Annihilation of Women by the Mass Media." In *Hearth and Home: Images of Women in the Mass Media,* edited by Gaye Tuchman, Arlene Kaplan Daniels, and James Benet, 3–38. New York: Oxford University Press.

Wasylkiw, L., A. A. Emms, R. Meuse, and K. F. Poirier. 2009. "Are All Models Created Equal? A Content Analysis of Women in Advertisements of Fitness versus Fashion Magazines." *Body Image* 6: 137–40.

Willis, Laura E., and Silvia Knobloch-Westerwick. 2014. "Weighing Women Down: Messages on Weight Loss and Body Shaping in Editorial Content in Popular Women's Health and Fitness Magazines." *Health Communication* 29: 323–31.

Zotos, Yorgos C., and Eirini Tsichla. 2014. "Female Stereotypes in Print Advertising: A Retrospective Analysis." *Procedia: Social and Behavioral Sciences* 148: 446–54.

Chapter 12

Social Exclusion and Gay Consumers' Boycott and Buycott Decisions

Wanhsiu Sunny Tsai and Xiaoqi Han

In America's current multicultural market, a plethora of consumer niches exist, including various minority groups. This chapter highlights the socio-political tension surrounding gay and lesbian consumers' socially conscious, politically informed consumption decisions in relation to their disadvantaged social status and direct experience of discrimination. We use the acronym *LGBT* generically, following the National Lesbian and Gay Journalists Association's stylebook, for "lesbian, gay, bisexual, and transgender" when referring to this heterogeneous community, which includes lesbian women and gay men, among others. Although a proliferation of identity labels address gender diversity and sexual orientation, and the term employed often differs by discipline and street politics, here we adopt *LGBT* because it is the most commonly used term by marketing and advertising agencies that specialize in this consumer market as well as by the Human Rights Campaign in its online buyer's guide based on its LGBT workplace equality index. Nonetheless, in the present chapter, we focus on lesbian women and gay men, the *L* and the *G* in LGBT, respectively. We write from the perspective that gay and lesbian consumers face heterosexist and heteronormative oppression that enforces and normalizes traditional gender roles and performances (Jackson 2006; Warner 1991). Eliminating oppression and discrimination on the basis of gender, gender identity, gender expression, and sexual orientation, as well as other identities and identifications, remains the central concern of feminists. The history of feminism and the development of women's studies echo a commitment to the interrogation of identity, power, and privilege that goes far beyond the category "woman" (National Women's Studies Association 2016), with the ultimate goal of improving the lives of not only diverse women but also self-defined gender and sexual minorities (Golombisky 2015).

POLITICAL CONSUMPTION

Hamilton (2013) argued that as citizens have become frustrated with the stiff resistance to national legislation on various sociopolitical and environmental issues, citizens have turned to the increasingly politicized marketplace to exercise their consumer power to demand social changes. At the same time, the transition of social movement targets from regulatory to corporate fields reflects both growing corporate power and citizens' limited avenues for influencing corporate behavior (Gardberg and Newburry 2010). Indeed, consumer activism for ethical or socially responsible consumption to effect changes in the marketplace and society at large has gained momentum in the past decade. Consumers increasingly take into account not only their personal needs but also the interests of society and the world as a whole when making their purchase decisions (Miller 2001). Their consumption decisions thus reflect an understanding of commercial goods and businesses as symbolizing complex and interconnected sociocultural and political systems (Stolle, Hooghe, and Micheletti 2005). To these critical consumers, politically motivated purchases, or withdrawal from purchases, are another important form of political engagement. Based on survey data, scholars report that consumers who engage in politically motivated consumption (i.e., political consumption) are also more likely to be involved in traditional forms of civic and political acts, such as voting, donating, volunteering, organizing community events, and discussing politics (Atkins 2012; Nelson, Rademacher, and Paek 2007).

In particular, instead of relying solely on governmental institutions and traditional political actions, many consumers have pursued boycotting—defined as "social action where individuals withhold resources to punish a firm for actions or policies perceived as illegitimate or socially irresponsible" (Gardberg and Newburry 2010, 322). Consumers might engage in boycotting to protest and demand changes in corporate or industry strategies, policies, or practices (Newman and Bartels 2011). Consumers have joined boycotts to express their concerns for international politics (e.g., American consumers' boycotting of French products because of France's opposition to the war in Iraq), environmental concerns (e.g., boycotting Shell for its plan for offshore drilling in Alaska's arctic waters), and human rights (e.g., boycotting Nike for its sweatshops in developing countries). Participation in boycotts has steadily increased in recent decades and has in fact demonstrated faster growth than other forms of political engagement (Stolle, Hooghe, and Micheletti 2005). The number of boycotts organized worldwide is also increasing (Friedman 1999). An international poll of 15,500 consumers from seventeen countries revealed that 36 percent of consumers have boycotted at least one brand (GMI Poll 2005).

Prior research has identified the psychological traits and motivations of boycotters, including susceptibility to normative influence (Sen, Gürhan-Canli, and Morwitz 2001), dominant personality (Webster 1975), and self-enhancement (Klein, Smith, and John 2004). Perceptual factors such as issue egregiousness, boycott efficacy (Klein, Smith, and John 2004), and boycott–personal goal consistency (Sen, Gürhan-Canli, and Morwitz 2001) also encourage boycotting. In contrast, factors like personal cost (Garrett 1987) and product dependence (Klein, Smith, and John 2004) diminish boycott tendency. Research generally suggests that boycotting is unlikely if no alternatives are available, and the likelihood of boycotting decreases when personal cost or sacrifice is high in terms of product price, quality, and convenience (Klein, Smith, and John 2004).

Consumers around the globe have also voted with their dollars in the market ballot through "buycotts"—the purchase of specific products to reward a business for ethical or political reasons (Atkins 2012; Friedman 1999). Buycotts now commonly include fair trade, community-supported, or environmentally friendly products (for a comprehensive review, see Harrison, Newhom, and Shaw 2005). In contrast to boycotting, buycotting directs rather than prohibits purchases. Research has reported key differences between boycotters and buycotters. Specifically, buycotters are more likely to be women and tend to be more trusting, involved in more associations, and more altruistic than boycotters; furthermore, both boycotters and buycotters are generally more altruistic and less competitive than nonpolitical consumers (Neilson 2010). Notably, studies suggest that consumers are more likely to sanction unethical behaviors than to reward ethical ones (Folkes and Kamins 1999) because it is easier not to buy than actively seek out alternative products. In other words, consumers may more readily engage in boycotting than in buycotting, which may require more thought and effort (Neilson 2010).

Regardless of boycotting or buycotting, the literature suggests that consumers who are women, highly educated, and young tend to be political consumers because they are more likely than others to look beyond utilitarian concerns such as price, quality, and convenience to consider the broader consequences of their consumption (Bennett 1998; Stolle, Hooghe, and Micheletti 2005). However, recent boycotts by minority consumers suggest that for marginalized consumers, who are often limited in their access to and resources in the conventional political arena, political consumption such as boycotts may constitute an important means to express their voice and concerns.

In the consumer literature, political consumption can be classified as being either a beneficiary or conscience action (Friedman 1999). *Beneficiary behaviors* refer to scenarios in which the sponsor and beneficiary belong to the same constituency, such as gay consumers boycotting antigay corporations or buycotting gay-friendly companies. Conscience behaviors address situations in which the sponsor and beneficiary are of different constituencies, such as American consumers' boycotting companies that use sweatshop labor in foreign countries. To understand the far-reaching consequences of minority consumers' collective experience of discrimination and powerlessness, we focus on the conscience aspects of political consumption that is beyond minority consumers' identity-centric concerns.

MINORITY CONSUMERS' POLITICAL CONSUMPTION

Minority consumers who belong to groups that are few in number and have little social power are often acutely aware of the political relations and meanings that permeate the consumer market because they constantly struggle for acceptance and equal treatment within it (Campbell 2005; Tsai 2011). The literature has documented discrimination in the marketplace, particularly as it relates to race and ethnicity (Walsh 2009). Existing evidence points to a myriad of venues from hotels and restaurants to department stores where racial minorities receive inferior service or pay more compared with their white counterparts. For instance, in Feagin and Sikes's (1994) study, middle-class African-American respondents described experiences of discrimination ranging from poor service in restaurants and focused surveillance in department stores to outright harassment in public accommodations (Pager and Shepherd 2008). In 2004, the Justice Department announced the filing and settlement of a racial discrimination lawsuit against the chain restaurant Cracker Barrel in light of evidence of discriminatory treatment against African-American customers, such as segregating customer seating by race and seating white customers before African-American customers who arrived earlier. In addition, a 2005 report by New Jersey Citizen Action revealed that African Americans and Hispanics were disproportionately subject to finance markup charges at car dealerships (Pager and Shepherd 2008). As part of the ongoing fight for respect and acceptance in the late 1990s marketplace, a well-known example of minority-led protests included Latino Americans' boycott against Taco Bell because of the company's offensive television commercials that used a Spanish-speaking Chihuahua. In 2012, gay consumers led a boycott against Chick-fil-A for its CEO's opposition to same-sex marriage and donations to antigay organizations.

Research further suggests that minority consumers' awareness of marginalization and their collective experience of discrimination play a critical role in dictating their consumption behaviors (Barnhart and Peñaloza 2013; Tsai 2011). For instance, being conscious of the underclass stigma often attached to them, immigrant consumers and African-American consumers tend to use conspicuous consumption and prestigious brand purchases to counter the stigma and to signal self-worth (Kwak and Sojka 2010; Lamont and Molnár 2001). Similarly, Wyatt, Gelb, and Geiger-Oneto (2008, 61) found a high percentage of racial minorities expressed concerns of being viewed as "second class," which may have led them to favor well-known national brands over private-label counterparts (Dhar and Hoch 1997).

In the management literature, marginalization has been shown to be a powerful source of social identity (Creed and Scully 2000), which is a critical means of mobilizing social movements (Rowley and Modoveanu 2003). Racial minorities were found to have a high propensity for joining social movements (Friedman 1999). At the same time, Freidberg (2004) proposed that citizens may become more powerful by leveraging their identities as consumers. Along this line of reasoning, minority groups with limited social and political resources may strategically wield their consumer power by participating in political consumption campaigns with the ultimate goal of effecting changes in objectionable corporate practices and policies.

Empirical data, albeit limited, suggest that marginalized groups are more likely to participate in boycotts than the general population. Research suggests that racial minorities not only are more likely to engage in protest activism (Sherkat and Blocker 1994), but also place a higher priority on corporate social performance and responsibility and are more likely to find corporate actions objectionable, as compared with privileged groups (Smith et al. 2001). Gardberg and Newburry (2010) also found African Americans, Hispanics, and Native Americans are more likely to be more critical of corporate actions and to engage in boycotts than their Caucasian counterparts. The researchers argue that marginalization is a critical factor dictating boycotting behavior. Focusing on young consumers, Harp et al. (2010) found that African-American adolescents were more likely than their Caucasian counterparts to participate in political consumerism, to engage in civic activities, to be politically involved in online and offline settings, to talk about news, and to demonstrate. Because minorities possess fewer political resources than elite group members, they might be more inclined to embrace boycotting as an accessible and viable response to objectionable corporate policies and practices. To advance the knowledge on minority consumers and their politically informed consumption decisions, in this chapter, we focus on another historically marginalized group that remains under-researched in the literature—the gay and lesbian community.

POLITICIZED GAY CONSUMER CULTURE

The sociohistoric construction of personal identity based on sexual orientation is intricately intertwined with American economic and market structures

(Tsai 2011). D'Emilio (1983, 470) points out that the financial autonomy bestowed by the capitalistic labor system allowed same-sex desires to materialize into a personal identity "based on the ability to remain outside the heterosexual family and to construct a personal life based on attraction to one's own sex." By the same token, the contemporary gay consumer market is neither an accident nor a natural progression resulting from a supposed increased acceptance of lesbians and gays. It has been cultivated by the gay press' and gay marketing firms' active enticement, marketers' niche marketing strategies, and the post-Stonewall gay rights movements (Chasin 2000; Sender 2012). Although contemporary advertising and marketing discourse has embraced the umbrella term *LGBT* to describe marketing efforts targeting the heterogeneous lesbian, gay, bisexual, and transgender community, gay and lesbian consumers receive the lion's share of marketing dollars, with a few exceptions of truly inclusive campaigns, such as Marriott's 2014 #LoveTravels campaign that featured ordinary same-sex couples as well as famous celebrities such as openly gay NBA player Jason Collins and transgender activist Geena Rocero. Moreover, the LGBT community is composed of disparate subgroups embracing different identities and beliefs in relation to sexuality, gender, race, ethnicity, and class, resulting in dissimilar experiences of marginalization among members of this diverse community.

Peñaloza (1996, 22) pointed out that an important component of the gay niche market is the minority consciousness that has developed as a result of gays' and lesbians' "history of common interests and experiences, particularly their exclusion, mobilization, and struggle in response to how they have been treated by others." The marginalized status of the gay community in the marketplace can be illustrated by the research objective of numerous studies that evaluated the potential risks and tradeoffs of targeting the highly controversial gay market (e.g., Oakenfull, McCarthy, and Greenlee 2008; Tuten 2005) and focused on the negative nontargeting effects of evoking straight consumers' hostile responses (e.g., Um 2014). In addition, previous studies on minority consumers were primarily concerned with advertising effectiveness and investigated the moderating roles of advertising models, subcultural cues, and strength of group identification on minority consumers' advertising responses (e.g., Appiah and Liu 2009; Green 1999). This approach largely ignored how consumers experiencing prolonged discrimination negotiate political tension as they forge market relations (Tsai 2011).

Sen (1996) argued that controversies surrounding the gay and lesbian community have taken the center stage in contemporary civil rights debates. Some commentators postulated that with the historic gay rights victory arising from the case of *Obergefell v. Hodges* (2015) in which the US Supreme Court struck down state bans on same-sex marriage, gays and lesbians might no longer be disenfranchised minorities. However, the battle for equal rights is far from over. Without doubt, gays and lesbians continue to face widespread legally and socially sanctioned discrimination throughout the United States. No national laws exist to prohibit discrimination in the workplace, housing, or public accommodations based on sexual orientation (Jones 2015). The Protecting Freedom of Conscience from Government Discrimination Act, which passed in Mississippi in April 2016, allows businesses, individuals, and religiously affiliated organizations to deny service to same-sex couples. Based on surveys conducted by the Gay, Lesbian and Straight Education Network, 64 percent of gay youth felt unsafe at school because of their sexual orientation (NoBullying.com 2016), and lesbian, gay, and bisexual youth are four times more likely than heterosexual youth to attempt suicide (Kann 2016). The 2016 Orlando Pulse nightclub shooting further reminds us of the profound ongoing prejudice against the gay community.

As a marginalized community, gay and lesbian consumers may make their consumption decisions based on political concerns. Schuppe (2016) argued that consumer boycotts have become an essential lever of the gay rights movement. Tsai's (2011) ethnographic study also reports that, highly cognizant of their desirable target consumer status and encouraged by the marketing myth of gay affluence, many gay consumers often strategically advocate consumer power to alleviate their own marginality and to forge a positive sense of self-identity. The gay participants in that study widely regarded the free market of the United States as a legitimate battlefield in which minority groups could demand market reform and social changes by exercising their consumer power.

Within the broader LGBT communities, there have always been notable efforts to raise awareness of the political implications of their economic activities. For instance, the Human Rights Campaign, the largest gay equal rights organization in the United States, publishes the annual *Buying for Workplace Equality Guide* and has created smartphone apps to educate the community about supporting LGBT-friendly businesses that offer antidiscrimination protection, diversity training, and transgender-inclusive benefits, along with avoiding organizations that continue to exclude LGBT rights from their corporate policies. These efforts highlight the tie between the LGBT rights movement and corporate America. Recently, this moral stand has also been embraced by LGBT-friendly corporations such as Apple, IBM, and the NFL, which have opposed attempts by certain states to limit antidiscrimination protections for LGBT people by threatening to move their investments, resources, and jobs elsewhere. To appreciate gay and lesbian consumers' political consumption, we now turn to the field of social psychology and applied social exclusion theory to understand the effects of systematic, institutional-level discrimination on minority consumers' boycott and buycott decisions.

SOCIAL EXCLUSION

Social exclusion refers to the broad phenomenon of individuals involuntarily being put into a condition of solitude or denied social contact (Blackhart et al. 2009). Social exclusion has been shown to generate a wide variety of behavioral responses. Some studies have reported that it can encourage prosocial, appeasing, and affiliative actions (Williams 2007). For instance, socially excluded people tend to express greater interest in making new friends, collaborating with others, and assigning rewards to new interaction partners (Maner et al. 2007). They also tend to engage in unconscious mimicry of other individuals (Lakin, Chartrand, and Arkin 2008) and generally become more sensitive to social cues (Pickett, Gardner, and Knowles 2004). In contrast, other studies have reported that social exclusion can encourage aggressive, antisocial, retaliatory behaviors, such as providing a more negative job evaluation for someone who has offered insults (Twenge et al. 2001); blasting a target with a higher level of aversive, stressful noise (Twenge et al. 2001); and allocating more hot sauce to a stranger known to dislike spicy food (Warburton, Williams, and Cairns 2006). DeWall et al. (2009) further pointed out that excluded individuals are inclined to perceive neutral information or ambiguous scenarios as hostile, which contributes to aggressive responses, even to persons who are not involved in the situation.

Scholars have only recently begun to explore the effects of social exclusion in a consumption context, finding that social exclusion has critical implications for consumer behavior. In four experiments, Mead et al. (2011) demonstrated that consumption constitutes an important tool for ostracized people to form new social relationships. The researchers found that excluded individuals might strategically purchase products that signal loyalty and group membership, tailor their consumption preferences to mirror those from whom they may gain acceptance, purchase unappealing products that their peers explicitly favor, and even go so far as to try illegal drugs when doing so may help them forge alliances. Loveland, Smeesters, and Mandel (2010) demonstrated that social exclusion increases consumers' interest in nostalgic products, such as previously popular movies, television programs, foods, or automobiles that provide opportunities to reconnect with the past and their associated communities. Focusing on financial decision making, Duclos, Wan, and Jiang (2013) reported that feeling isolated may cause consumers to pursue riskier but potentially more lucrative financial opportunities. Their experimental results showed that interpersonal rejection exacerbates financial risk taking by heightening the instrumentality of money as a means to obtain control and power when individuals lack social connections and the associated resources. The limited literature thus suggests that being socially excluded tends to induce prosocial responses via affiliative consumption for the purpose of redeveloping social connections, or to prompt aggressive risk taking to regain a sense of control, sometimes at the expense of individuals' real desires or financial well-being.

Yet prior studies have predominantly explored the effects of *interpersonal* exclusion (Blackhart et al. 2009). For instance, in experiments by Mead et al. (2011), participants were told that their assigned interaction partner refused to meet with them after watching a self-introductory video about them. The rejection feedback was designed to make the participants feel that "there is something wrong with them" (Mead et al. 2011, 905). However, the cause of the rejection was never explained, permitting it to be disregarded as a whim of the interacting partner. Another common manipulation of exclusion involves having a research participant play a computer-simulated ball-tossing game, during which the simulated partners suddenly and without explanation cease to throw the ball to the participant, thus inducing feelings of being ignored (Blackhart et al. 2009). In some experiments, social exclusion is not directly experienced but is instead projected for the future, for example, by informing participants that they are likely to end up being alone based on their scores on a personality test (e.g., Mead et al. 2011; Twenge et al. 2001). Other studies have asked research participants to recall and write down an incident in which they felt excluded, but again, the reason for the exclusion experience is never specified (e.g., Lee and Shrum 2012; Molden et al. 2009). The effects of systematic, institutionalized ostracism, such as in the case of minority groups, are left unexamined. Mead et al. (2011) called for more empirical research examining the effects of chronic exclusion on consumer behavior. We thus focused on the ongoing, prolonged, and, more importantly, identity-based exclusion that many minority consumers have commonly and continuously experienced in their everyday life.

Molden et al. (2009) theorized about two different forms of social exclusion—being ignored versus being rejected. Being ignored entails implicit and indirect exclusion, whereas being rejected is direct and overt. Lee and Shrum (2012) suggested that the two forms of social exclusion threaten different types of personal needs and in turn produce dissimilar outcomes of prosocial versus self-focused consumption behaviors. Being ignored tends to make people feel socially invisible and nonexistent, threatening their feelings of power, control, and meaningful existence (Williams 2009). When these efficacy needs are thwarted, individuals strive to regain power and control. In contrast, being rejected typically involves explicit criticism that an individual is undesirable and unacceptable, posing a direct threat to relational needs, including self-esteem (Leary et al. 1995). Individuals whose relational needs are threatened are then motivated to restore relational appreciation (Lee and Shrum 2012). In four experiments, Lee and Shrum (2012) reported that participants who had experienced being ignored were more likely to engage in self-focused, attention-grabbing conspicuous consumption, whereas those who experienced being rejected were more likely to engage in prosocial behaviors of helping others and donating money. Along this line of reasoning, ignored individuals, whose sense of control is jeopardized, may be more likely to adopt the coercive, punitive measure of boycotting to restore their sense of control. Moreover, studies show that social exclusion heightens people's desire for money as an embodiment of power and control, hence leading them to cling to it (Zhou, Vohs, and Baumeister 2009).

However, prior studies have not considered social exclusion in terms of minority consumers' discrimination experiences, particularly when the cause of exclusion is directly linked to their minority identity (e.g., sexual orientation or ethnicity). Therefore, to illuminate the political tension surrounding disenfranchised minorities who are chronically rendered invisible or ostracized, we paid special attention to the effects of prolonged, ongoing, and identity-based exclusion at the sociopolitical and institutional level (i.e., exclusion in the form of workplace antidiscrimination policies). Exclusion is operationalized herein as systematic and institutionalized discrimination that is directly linked to minority consumers' self-identity factor, which is distinct from previous research that predominantly focused on social exclusion at the interpersonal level.

Although Lee and Shrum (2012) distinguish between feelings of being ignored and feelings of being rejected, both are commonly experienced by marginalized consumers. Adopting Lee and Shrum's approach of distinguishing dissimilar types of social exclusion, we tested how feelings of being ignored versus being rejected might influence the inclination to engage in boycotting action. Prior studies have suggested that practical concerns such as the availability, quality, price, and convenience of a substitute product as well as consumers' intrinsic preference for the boycotted product determines the likelihood of boycott (Carrigan and Attalla 2001; Klein, Smith, and John 2004). To accurately capture boycott decisions, we not only incorporated the availability of a socially responsible substitute, but also considered consumers' option of deferring to make a choice when the only available option was a socially irresponsible product. Therefore, we evaluated consumers' boycott decision in two specific ways. First, when the only consumption choice was a socially irresponsible product, we assessed consumers' boycott decision by capturing their decision of deferring the choice (i.e., taking time to look for other alternatives). Second, when a socially responsible alternative was available, consumers' boycott decision was captured by the likelihood of choosing the alternative or deferring the choice.

Prior research revealed that the lower the personal cost (e.g., price, convenience, and quality) associated with a boycott, the more likely consumers will participate in it (Sen, Gürhan-Canli, and Morwitz 2001). Because the availability of suitable substitutes lowers the cost of a boycott (Sen, Gürhan-Canli, and Morwitz 2001), when a suitable alternative is available, consumers are likely to engage in a boycott by purchasing the substitute, rather than deferring choice to look for other alternatives. Therefore, we predicted that minority consumers are more likely to boycott a socially irresponsible company by buying substitutes when a suitable substitute is available. However, when there is no substitute, the consumers are more likely to boycott the socially irresponsible company by deferring choice and looking for more alternatives.

> H1: When no substitute is available, minority consumers are likely to boycott a socially irresponsible product by deferring choices and looking for more alternatives.

> H2: When a socially responsible substitute exists, minority consumers are likely to boycott a socially irresponsible product by purchasing the substitute (vs deferring the choice).

However, a boundary condition may exist when the perceived risk of choosing an alternative is high. Prior research showed that when the risk of the available choice set increases, consumers are more likely to defer making a choice (Gunasti and Ross 2009). Hence, a higher risk associated with an alternative may keep consumers from selecting it even though it is offered by a socially responsible company. Therefore, we predicted that ignored individuals are likely to engage in boycotting irresponsible companies by choosing socially responsible substitutes but only when the risk associated with buying them is low. By the same token, when no substitutes are available or the risk from buying substitutes is high, ignored individuals who are more cautious about how they spend their money and more prudent in their purchase decisions are more likely to defer the buying decision to search for ideal substitutes:

> H3: When no substitute is available, ignored consumers (vs rejected consumers vs control) are more likely to boycott the socially irresponsible product by deferring the choice and looking for more alternatives.

> H4: When a substitute exists and the risk associated with buying it is low (vs high), ignored consumers (vs rejected consumers vs control) are more likely to boycott the irresponsible product by buying the substitute.

OUR STUDY

The participants for this study were recruited from a national online consumer panel managed by a major marketing research company. A total of 308 participants (162 men, 146 women) who self-identified as gay or lesbian participated in the online study and were compensated through the marketing research company. To avoid participants knowing the purpose of the study, they were told that they would participate in several short separate studies. For the first study, they were told to think about the consequences of a company's policies and practices based on a recent news article about the company. For the second study, they were told that they would be presented with a purchasing choice scenario as a consumer.

The experiment was a 3 (rejected vs ignored vs control) × 3 (no substitute vs high-risk substitute vs low-risk substitute) between-subjects design. Participants were randomly assigned to the ignored, rejected, or control condition. To manipulate these conditions, participants were told to think about the consequences of Company X's policies based on an excerpt of a news article about the company. In the rejected condition, participants read that the company explicitly refused to include sexual orientation in its existing employment policy and had denied benefits such as domestic partnership to its gay and lesbian employees. In the ignored condition, participants read that the company intended to hire and retain an executive management and employee staff based on equal participation and opportunity for all, regardless of race, gender, age, national origin, religion, or any other legally protected characteristic. However, sexual orientation was not included in the company's definition of diversity. In the control conditions, the history of Company X and its recent marketing practices was described, without mentioning the company's workplace policy. After reading the excerpts, participants were asked to rate how implicitly ignored and explicitly rejected they felt on two 7-point scales (1 = not at all, 7 = very much), respectively.

Next, in an ostensibly different task, all participants were told that they were planning a vacation in a scenic town fifteen minutes from surrounding cities. They were instructed to decide on a hotel where they would stay for three days. One-third of the participants were assigned to the no-substitute condition in which only two options were available: they could stay in the socially irresponsible Hotel A or defer the choice and look for alternatives, which would incur a fifteen-minute drive to a nearby town. The rest of the participants were assigned to the substitute-available conditions in which the socially responsible alternative, Hotel B, was available. Participants were instructed to read short descriptions of a labor dispute against Hotel A's denial of medical benefits to its workers, as well as the charity donations and community outreach activities of Hotel B. Additionally, in the low-risk substitute condition, Hotel B had positive online reviews emphasizing its good service, pleasant amenities, and competitive price. By contrast, in the high-risk substitute condition, Hotel B did not have any online customer reviews because it had only recently opened. Participants could choose Hotel A or B, or they could forgo both choices and look for other alternatives in the nearby town. Participants then answered two questions regarding their intention to boycott Hotel A and buycott Hotel B.

STUDY RESULTS

Results revealed that when the only buying option was a socially irresponsible product without other substitutes readily available, participants were more likely to defer the choice. The proportion of choice deferral was significantly greater in the no-substitute condition than in the substitute-available conditions. By contrast, when a socially responsible substitute existed, participants were more likely to choose the alternative product, regardless of the risk level associated with it, thus supporting H2.

To test H3 on ignored participants' likelihood to boycott the only option, the socially irresponsible Hotel A, via choice deferral, a series of chi-squared tests were conducted. As expected, compared with individuals in the control condition, participants in the ignored condition were more likely to defer making a choice ($\chi^2(1) = 5.33$, $p < .05$). The difference was not found when the rejected condition was compared with the control condition ($\chi^2(1) = 1.9$, $p > .1$), thus supporting H3.

When Hotel B was available as a socially responsible substitute and when the consumption risk associated with Hotel B was low relative to those in the control condition, ignored participants were more likely to select Hotel B than Hotel A ($\chi^2(2) = 7.39$, $p < .05$). The same pattern was not observed in the control condition or in the rejection condition ($\chi^2(2) = 4.5$, $p > .1$). Similarly, this pattern was not observed when the risk associated with choosing Hotel B was high ($p > .4$).

We then went a step further to assess participants' boycotting inclination by analyzing the continuous measure of boycott (vs buycott) intention. Results revealed that consumers were more motivated to boycott in the no-substitute condition ($M_{\text{no-substitute}} = 5.03$) and in the high-risk substitute-available condition ($M_{\text{low-risk-substitute}} = 3.31$, $t(204) = 5.78$, $p < .0001$) compared with the low-risk substitute-available condition ($M_{\text{high-risk-substitute}} = 5.48$, $t(204) = 7.33$, $p < .0001$). This pattern was observed across all social exclusion conditions. Moreover, in a comparison of the willingness to boycott versus buycott in the substitute-available conditions, the willingness to boycott was stronger than that to buycott ($M_{\text{boycott}} = 5.48$, $M_{\text{buycott}} = 3.37$, $t(103) = 8.05$,

$p < .0001$) when the alternative was associated with a higher consumption risk ($M_{boycott} = 3.31$, $M_{buycott} = 3.47$, $t(101) < 1$). No difference was found when the risk of buying the responsible alternative was low, and no difference emerged across the ignored and rejected conditions. This pattern of results thus suggests that when no substitution is available, participants' decision to defer the choice is indeed motivated by punishment of the socially irresponsible company. Moreover, when the substitute is deemed acceptable (i.e., low risk), the intention to boycott and buycott is similarly accessible. However, when the substitute is less acceptable (i.e., high risk), the intention to boycott outweighs buycotting.

DISCUSSION AND CONCLUSION

Gardberg and Newburry (2010, 319) cautioned that "the stakeholders who may be most negatively affected by corporate behavior are those with the least power—marginalized groups." By connecting social exclusion theory to the growing trend of political consumption and by focusing on the underrepresentation of gay and lesbian consumers in the advertising literature, this chapter highlights the complex processes and motivations underlying how marginalized consumers turn to the free market as a lever for civic expression and political participation. Highlighting the far-reaching effects of minority consumers' marginalization awareness and experience, we explored social exclusion in one context and its consequences on boycott decisions in a different, irrelevant consumption context. We examined the two forms of social exclusion in the context of prolonged, systematic, institutionalized, and more importantly, identity-based discrimination that many minority consumers routinely experience to shed light on the political tension underlying minority consumers' boycott and buycott decisions.

Findings lend direct support to Gardberg and Newburry's (2010) proposition that marginalization drives boycotting behaviors. When contending with an irresponsible company, gay and lesbian consumers are inclined to boycott either by choice deferral or by buycotting responsible substitutes. The consumers' willingness to boycott is particularly prominent when a lack of socially responsible alternatives exists, regardless of their exclusion experience. Additionally, when the buying risk associated with choosing the responsible product is high, gay and lesbian consumers' purchase choices were more concerned with punishing the unethical company than with rewarding the responsible one.

More importantly, because boycott decisions reflect consumers' willingness to exercise their consumer power to punish socially irresponsible companies, the experiment results provide evidence that ignored individuals whose need for power and control is threatened (Lee and Shrum 2012) are more motivated to penalize the unethical company to compensate for the feeling of power deprivation. That is, in comparison with consumers who experience rejection, ignored consumers are more likely to boycott the irresponsible product and to pursue other alternatives (i.e., choice deferral) when no other options are readily available. Additionally, when they are presented with a low-risk suitable substitute, the ignored consumers would opt for the substitute, but not when the perceived risk of choosing the socially responsible option is high. In this way, the findings also suggest that minority consumers' boycotting and buycotting decisions are contingent on the practical concern of buying risk, in this case, purchase uncertainty.

Companies tend to discount organized boycotts as having little or no effect on sales (Davidson, Worrell, and El-Jelly 1995), likely to avoid legitimating the tactic. However, not only have consumer boycotts become a growing phenomenon around the globe, but the prevalence and efficiency of social media has also further fueled publicity surrounding boycotts, hence increasing the corporate costs of legal fees and public relations expenses, disrupting business operations, and tarnishing corporate reputation (Eesley and Lenox 2006). Moreover, consumer boycotts may be harbingers of shifting social norms, as in the case of environmentalism (Gardberg and Newburry 2010). Corporate leaders should pay close attention to the requests of consumer boycotts and monitor public sentiment surrounding the issues. In particular, the experimental findings suggest that social minorities are a potentially powerful force in initiating, advocating, and publicizing boycotting campaigns and thus lead social trends. Given that minority consumers, particularly ignored individuals, are more likely to boycott via choice deferral or buycotting responsible alternatives, advertisers should examine their corporate policy on equality and diversity to design inclusive messages that preempt minority consumers' punitive intentions. If companies are constantly criticized and boycotted for various issues in today's politics-laden consumer market, then advertising and public relations campaigns that highlight a company's bona fide inclusive and nondiscriminatory policies as well as its sincere efforts to support minority causes might validate and empower minority stakeholders, as well as strengthen corporate trust, enhance reputation, and prevent boycotts.

Beyond the key finding of minority consumers' strong inclination to boycott socially irresponsible companies, our findings also suggest that minority consumers' buycotting decisions are contingent on the practical concern of buying risk. An increasing number of companies have turned to corporate social responsibility as a primary positioning and brand differentiation strategy (Du, Bhattacharya, and Sen 2007). However, managing the perceived buying risk of cost, price, uncertainty, quality, and convenience is key to effectively winning over socially conscious consumers. Prior research suggests that consumers are likely to be willing to pay more for ethically produced products, such as "green" or "fair trade" products (Clarke et al. 2007; O'Rourke 2005). But studies with minority consumers suggest that they may not always be willing to support socially responsible businesses when the perceived buying risk is high. Gardberg and Newburry (2010) also reported that economically upwardly mobile members of minority groups show the highest rate of boycott participation possibly because they might be more financially comfortable in pursuing socially responsible alternatives. Minority consumers with relatively limited resources, power, and financial security might be more cautious with their purchases and thus more readily inclined to engage in boycotts rather than buycotts.

Finally, with regard to gay and lesbian consumers and the broader LGBT community, the consumer segment wielded buying power of nearly $1 trillion in 2015 (Green 2016). During the past decade, many marketers have taken steps ahead of public policy to offer equal rights and benefits to LGBT employees, and many LGBT consumers have looked to companies to fill the void in public policy. Specifically, many gay and lesbian consumers have used purchases, loyalty, and advocacy to support gay-friendly companies that provide domestic partner benefits and corporate financial support of gay causes, feature gay models in their marketing communications, and place advertisements in gay media (American Marketing Association 2016). Although the study findings should not be generalized to the broader, diverse LGBT community, we observed that gays and lesbians tend to be critical consumers whose purchase decisions involve ethical and social considerations of a company's practices and policies, beyond their identity-oriented concerns of supporting gay-friendly companies and boycotting homophobic businesses. In fact, a 2011 national poll reported that gay consumers are more environmentally conscious than their heterosexual counterparts (Koch 2011). Therefore, companies and organizations emphasizing their corporate social responsibility brand positioning and core business strategies could integrate the gay community as a key target consumer group in their segmentation strategy.

An individual's self-identity is constructed, embodied, prioritized, performed, and experienced differently depending on multifaceted identifications of gender, sexuality, race, ethnicity, religion, ability, and age, among others, not the least of which is socioeconomic status. Similarly, gays' and lesbians' experiences with sexism and heterosexism vary depending on their position in interlocking systems of oppressions (Golombisky 2015). More empirical investigations to explore the marginalization effects of gay and lesbian consumers' intersecting distinctive identities (e.g., being a working-class lesbian of color) (Aaker, Brumbaugh and Grier 2000) on their consumption decisions will achieve a more holistic understanding of how marginalization drives political consumerism.

REFERENCES

Aaker, Jennifer L., Anne M. Brumbaugh, and Sonya A. Grier. 2000. "Nontarget Markets and Viewer Distinctiveness: The Impact of Target Marketing on Advertising Attitudes." *Journal of Consumer Psychology* 9 (3): 127–40.

American Marketing Association. 2016. "LGBT Consumers Look to Companies to Fill Void of Public Policy." Accessed October 11. https://www.ama.org/publications/JournalOfPublicPolicyAndMarketing/Pages/pr-jppm.12.050.aspx

Appiah, Osei, and Yung-I Liu. 2009. "Reaching the Model Minority: Ethnic Differences in Responding to Culturally Embedded Targeted- and Non-Targeted Advertisements." *Journal of Current Issues and Research in Advertising* 31 (1): 27–41.

Atkins, Lucy. 2012. "Buying into Social Change: How Private Consumption Choices Engender Concern for the Collective." *The Annals of the American Academy of Political and Social Science* 644 (1): 191–206.

Barnhart, Michelle, and Lisa Peñaloza. 2013. "Who Are You Calling Old? Negotiating Old Age Identity in the Elderly Consumption Ensemble." *Journal of Consumer Research* 39 (6): 1133–53.

Bennett, W. Lance. 1998. "The Uncivic Culture: Communication, Identity, and the Rise of Lifestyle Politics." *PS: Political Science and Politics* 31 (4): 741–61.

Blackhart, Ginette C., Brian C. Nelson, Megan L. Knowles, and Roy F. Baumeister. 2009. "Rejection Elicits Emotional Reactions but Neither Causes Immediate Distress nor Lowers Self-Esteem: A Meta-Analytic, Review of 192 Studies on Social Exclusion." *Personality and Social Psychology Review* 13 (4): 269–309.

Campbell, Howard. 2005. "Chicano Lite: Mexican-American Consumer Culture on the Border." *Journal of Consumer Culture* 5 (2): 207–33.

Carrigan, Marylyn, and Ahmad Attalla. 2001. "The Myth of the Ethical Consumer: Do Ethics Matter in Purchase Behaviour?" *Journal of Consumer Marketing* 18 (7): 560–78.

Chasin, Alexandra. 2000. *Selling Out: The Lesbian and Gay Movement Goes to Market.* New York: St. Martin's.

Clarke, Nick, Clive Barnett, Paul Cloke, and Alice Malpass. 2007. "The Political Rationalities of Fair-Trade Consumption in the United Kingdom." *Politics and Society* 35 (4): 583–607.

Creed, W. E. Douglas, and Maureen A. Scully. 2000. "Songs of Ourselves: Employees' Deployment of Social Identity in Workplace Encounters." *Journal of Management Inquiry* 9 (4): 391–412.

Davidson, Wallace N., Dan L. Worrell, and Abuzar El-Jelly. 1995. "Influencing Managers to Change Unpopular Corporate Behavior through Boycotts and Divestitures: A Stock Market Test." *Business and Society* 34 (2): 171–96.

D'Emilio, John. 1983. *Sexual Politics, Sexual Communities: The Making of a Homosexual Minority in the United States, 1940–1970.* Chicago: University of Chicago Press.

DeWall, C. Nathan, Jean M. Twenge, Seth A. Gitter, and Roy F. Baumeister. 2009. "It's the Thought that Counts: The Role of Hostile Cognition in Shaping Aggressive Responses to Social Exclusion." *Journal of Personality and Social Psychology* 96 (1): 45–59.

Dhar, Sanjay, and Steven Hoch. 1997. "Why Store Brand Penetration Varies by Retailer." *Marketing Science* 16 (3): 208–27.

Duclos, Rod, Echo Wen Wan, and Yuwei Jiang. 2013. "Show Me the Honey! Effects of Social Exclusion on Financial Risk-Taking." *Journal of Consumer Research* 40 (1): 122–35.

Du, Shuili, Chitrabhan B. Bhattacharya, and Sankar Sen. 2007. "Reaping Relational Rewards from Corporate Social Responsibility: The Role of Competitive Positioning." *International Journal of Research in Marketing* 24 (3): 224–41.

Eesley, Charles, and Michael J. Lenox. 2006. "Firm Responses to Secondary Stakeholder Action." *Strategic Management Journal* 27 (8): 765–81.

Feagin, Joe R., and Melvin P. Sikes. 1994. *Living with Racism: The Black Middle-Class Experience*. Boston: Beacon Press.

Folkes, Valerie S., and Michael A. Kamins. 1999. "Effects of Information about Firms' Ethical and Unethical Actions on Consumers' Attitudes." *Journal of Consumer Psychology* 8 (3): 243–59.

Freidberg, Susanne. 2004. "The Ethical Complex of Corporate Food Power." *Environment and Planning D: Society and Space* 22: 513–31.

Friedman, Monroe. 1999. *Consumer Boycotts: Effecting Change through the Marketplace and the Media.* New York: Routledge.

Gardberg, Naomi A., and William Newburry. 2010. "Who Boycotts Whom? Marginalization, Company Knowledge, and Strategic Issues." *Business and Society* 52: 318–57.

Garrett, Dennis E. 1987. "The Effectiveness of Marketing Policy Boycotts: Environmental Opposition to Marketing." *Journal of Marketing* 51: 46–57.

GMI Poll. 2005. "More Than a Third of All Consumers Boycott at Least One Brand," last modified January 1. Accessed October 11, 2016. http://www.holmesreport.com/latest/article/more-than-a-third-of-world's-consumers-boycott-brands.

Golombisky, Kim. 2015. "Renewing the Commitments of Feminist Public Relations Theory from Velvet Ghetto to Social Justice." *Journal of Public Relations Research* 27 (5): 389–415.

Green, Corliss. 1999. "Ethnic Evaluations of Advertising: Interaction Effects of Strength of Ethnic Identification, Media Placement, and Degree of Racial Composition." *Journal of Advertising* 28 (1): 49–64.

Green, Jeff. 2016. "LGBT Purchasing Power near $1 Trillion Rivals Other Minorities," last modified July 20. Accessed October 11, 2016. http://www.bloomberg.com/news/articles/2016-07-20/lgbt-purchasing-power-near-1-trillion-rivals-other-minorities

Gunasti, Kunter, and William T. Ross Jr. 2009. "How Inferences about Missing Attributes Decrease the Tendency to Defer Choice and Increase Purchase Probability." *Journal of Consumer Research* 35 (5): 823–37.

Hamilton, Trina. 2013. "Beyond Market Signals: Negotiating Marketplace Politics and Corporate Responsibilities." *Economic Geography* 89 (3): 285–307.

Harp, Dustin, Ingrid Bachmann, Tania C. Rosas-Moreno, and Jaime Loke. 2010. "Wave of Hope: African American Youth Use Media and Engage More Civically, Politically Than Whites." *Howard Journal of Communications* 21 (3): 224–46.

Harrison, R., Terry Newholm, and Deirdre Shaw. 2005. "Introduction: Defining the Ethical Consumer." In *The Ethical Consumer,* edited by Rob Harrison, T. Newholm, and D. Shaw, 1–8. London: Sage.

Human Rights Campaign. *Buying for Workplace Equality*. Accessible at: http://www.hrc.org/apps/buyersguide/ranking.php?category=1219#.WFV0ntRZha4.

Jackson, Stevi. 2006. "Gender, Sexuality and Heterosexuality: The Complexity (and Limits) of Heteronormativity." *Feminist Theory* 7 (1): 105–21.

Jones, Robert. 2015. "After Same-Sex Marriage, Then What?" last modified June 20. Accessed October 11, 2016. http://www.theatlantic.com/politics/archive/2015/06/after-same-sex-marriage-then-what/396659/.

Kann, Laura. 2016. "Sexual Identity, Sex of Sexual Contacts, and Health-Related Behaviors among Students in Grades 9–12—United States and Selected Sites, 2015." *Morbidity and Mortality Weekly Report, Surveillance Summaries,* August 12. Accessed October 11, 2016. http://www.cdc.gov/mmwr/volumes/65/ss/ss6509a1.htm.

Klein, Jill Gabrielle, N. Craig Smith, and Andrew John. 2004. "Why We Boycott: Consumer Motivations for Boycott Participation." *Journal of Marketing* 68 (3): 92–109.

Koch, Wendy. 2011. "Harris Poll: Gays Are Greener Than Heterosexuals." Last modified January 19, 2011. Accessed October 11, 2016. http://content.usatoday.com/communities/greenhouse/post/2011/01/gays-greener-harris-poll/1#.V3QXofkrLrc.

Kwak, Lynn Eunjung, and Jane Z. Sojka. 2010. "If They Could See Me Now: Immigrants' Use of Prestige Brands to Convey Status." *Journal of Consumer Marketing* 27 (4): 371–80.

Lakin, Jessica L., Tanya L. Chartrand, and Robert M. Arkin. 2008. "I Am Too Just Like You: Nonconscious Mimicry as an Automatic Behavioral Response to Social Exclusion." *Psychological Science* 19 (8): 816–22.

Lamont, Michèle, and Virág Molnár. 2001. "How Blacks Use Consumption to Shape Their Collective Identity: Evidence from Marketing Specialists." *Journal of Consumer Culture* 1 (1): 31–45.

Leary, Mark R., Ellen S. Tambor, Sonja K. Terdal, and Deborah L. Downs. 1995. "Self-Esteem as an Interpersonal Monitor: The Sociometer Hypothesis." *Journal of Personality and Social Psychology* 68: 518–30.

Lee, Jaehoon, and L. J. Shrum. 2012. "Conspicuous Consumption versus Charitable Behavior in Response to Social Exclusion: A Differential Needs Explanation." *Journal of Consumer Research* 39 (3): 530–44.

Loveland, Katherine E., Dirk Smeesters, and Naomi Mandel. 2010. "Still Preoccupied with 1995: The Need to Belong and Preference for Nostalgic Products." *Journal of Consumer Research* 37 (3): 393–408.

Maner, Jon K., C. Nathan DeWall, Roy F. Baumeister, and Mark Schaller. 2007. "Does Social Exclusion Motivate Interpersonal Reconnection? Resolving the 'Porcupine Problem.'" *Journal of Personality and Social Psychology* 92: 42–55.

Mead, Nicole L., Roy F. Baumeister, Tyler F. Stillman, Catherine D. Rawn, and Kathleen D. Vohs. 2011 "Social Exclusion Causes People to Spend and Consume Strategically in the Service of Affiliation." *Journal of Consumer Research* 37 (5): 902–19.

Miller, Daniel. 2001. *The Dialectics of Shopping*. Chicago: The University of Chicago Press.

Molden, Daniel C., Gale M. Lucas, Wendi L. Gardner, Kristy Dean, and Megan L. Knowles. 2009. "Motivations for Prevention or Promotion following Social

Exclusion: Being Rejected versus Being Ignored." *Journal of Personality and Social Psychology* 96: 415–31.
National Women's Studies Association. 2016. "What Is Women's Studies?" Accessed October 11. http://www.nwsa.org/womensstudies.
Neilson, Lisa A. 2010. "Boycott or Buycott? Understanding Political Consumerism." *Journal of Consumer Behavior* 9 (3): 214–27.
Nelson, Michelle R., Mark A. Rademacher, and Hye-Jin Paek. 2007. "Downshifting Consumer = Upshifting Citizen? An Examination of a Local Freecycle Community." *The Annals of the American Academy of Political and Social Science* 611: 141–56.
Newman, Benjamin J., and Brandon L. Bartels. 2011. "Politics at the Checkout Line: Explaining Political Consumerism in the United States." *Political Research Quarterly* 64 (4): 803–17.
NoBullying.com. 2016. "LGBT Bullying Statistics." Last modified November 7. Accessed April 15, 2017. https://nobullying.com/lgbt-bullying-statistics/.
Oakenfull, Gillian K., Michael S. McCarthy, and Timothy B. Greenlee. 2008. "Targeting a Minority without Alienating the Majority: Advertising to Gays and Lesbians in Mainstream Media." *Journal of Advertising Research* 48 (2): 191–198.
Obergefell v. Hodges. 2015. 135 S. Ct. 2071.
O'Rourke, Dara. 2005. "Market Movements: Nongovernmental Organization Strategies to Influence Global Production and Consumption." *Journal of Industrial Ecology* 9 (1–2): 115–28.
Pager, Devah, and Hana Shepherd. 2008. "The Sociology of Discrimination: Racial Discrimination in Employment, Housing, Credit, and Consumer Markets." *Annual Review of Sociology* 34: 181–209.
Peñaloza, Lisa. 1996. "We're Queer and We're Going Shopping: A Critical Perspective on the Accommodations of Gays and Lesbians in the US Marketplace." *Journal of Homosexuality* 31 (1/2): 9–41.
Pickett, Cynthia L., Wendi L. Gardner, and Megan Knowles. 2004. "Getting a Cue: The Need to Belong and Enhanced Sensitivity to Social Cues." *Personality and Social Psychology Bulletin* 30: 1095–107.
Rowley, Timothy I., and Mihnea Moldoveanu. 2003. "When Will Stakeholder Groups Act? An Interest- and Identity-Based Model of Stakeholder Group Mobilization." *Academy of Management Review* 28 (2): 204–19.
Schuppe, Jon. "Corporate Boycotts become Key Weapon in Gay Rights Fight." Last modified March 26, 2016. Accessed October 11, 2016. http://www.nbcnews.com/news/us-news/corporate-boycotts-become-key-weapon-gay-rights-fight-n545721.
Sen, Sankar. 1996. "Marketing and Minority Civil Rights: The Case of Amendment 2 and the Colorado Boycott." *Journal of Public Policy and Marketing* 15 (2): 311–18.
Sen, Sankar, Zeynep Gürhan-Canli, and Vicki Morwitz. 2001. "Withholding Consumption: A Social Dilemma Perspective on Consumer Boycotts." *Journal of Consumer Research* 28 (3): 399–417.
Sender, Katherine. 2012. *Business, Not Politics: The Making of the Gay Market*. New York: Columbia University Press.

Sherkat, Darren E., and T. Jean Blocker. 1994. "The Political Development of Sixties' Activists: Identifying the Influence of Class, Gender and Socialization on Protest Participation." *Social Forces* 72: 821–42.
Smith, Wanda J., Richard E. Wokutch, K. Vernard Harrington, and Bryan S. Dennis. 2001. "An Examination of Diversity and Stakeholder Role on Corporate Social Orientation." *Business and Society* 40 (3): 266–94.
Stolle, Dietland, Marc Hooghe, and Michele Micheletti. 2005. "Politics in the Supermarket: Political Consumerism as a Form of Political Participation." *International Political Science Review* 26 (3): 245–69.
Tsai, Wanhsiu Sunny. 2011. "How Minority Consumers Use Targeted Advertising as Pathways to Self-Empowerment: Gay Men's and Lesbians' Reading of Out-of-Closet Advertising." *Journal of Advertising* 40 (3): 85–97.
Tuten, Tracy L. 2005. "The Effect of Gay-Friendly and Non-Gay-Friendly Cues on Brand Attitudes: A Comparison of Heterosexual and Gay/Lesbian Reactions." *Journal of Marketing Management* 21 (3/4): 441–61.
Twenge, Jean M., Roy F. Baumeister, Dianne M. Tice, and Tanja S. Stucke. 2001. "If You Can't Join Them, Beat Them: Effects of Social Exclusion on Aggressive Behavior." *Journal of Personality and Social Psychology* 81: 1058–69.
Um, Nam-Hyun. 2014. "Does Gay-Themed Advertising Haunt Your Brand?" *International Journal of Advertising* 33: 811–32.
Walsh, Gianfranco. 2009. "Disadvantaged Consumers' Experiences of Marketplace Discrimination in Customer Services." *Journal of Marketing Management* 25 (1): 143–69.
Warburton, Wayne A., Kipling D. Williams, and David R. Cairns. 2006. "When Ostracism Leads to Aggression: The Moderating Effects of Control Deprivation." *Journal of Experimental Social Psychology* 42: 213–20.
Warner, Michael. 1991. "Introduction: Fear of a Queer Planet." *Social Text* 29: 3–17.
Webster Jr., Frederick E. 1975. "Determining the Characteristics of the Socially Conscious Consumer." *Journal of Consumer Research* 2 (3): 188–96.
Williams, Kipling D. 2007. "Ostracism." *Annual Review of Psychology* 58: 425–52.
———. 2009. "Ostracism: A Temporal Need-Threat Model." In *Advances in Experimental Social Psychology,* edited by Mark P. Zanna, 275–314. New York: Academic.
Wyatt, Rosalind J., Betsy D. Gelb, and Stephanie Geiger-Oneto. 2008. "How Social Insecurity and the Social Meaning of Advertising Reinforce Minority Consumers' Preference for National Brands." *Journal of Current Issues and Research in Advertising* 30 (1): 61–70.
Zhou, Xinyue, Kathleen D. Vohs, and Roy F. Baumeister. 2009. "The Symbolic Power of Money: Reminders of Money Alter Social Distress and Physical Pain." *Psychological Science* 20: 700–706.

Part IV

PROFESSIONAL DEVELOPMENT: HISTORIOGRAPHY AND BIOGRAPHY

Chapter 13

The Curious Story of Home Economics' Contribution to Women's Careers in Advertising

Kimberly Wilmot Voss

The five women students gathered around a microphone as guests on home economist, teacher, and radio host Aline Hazard's Homemakers Program in the home economics department at the University of Wisconsin. The students—four white women and one woman of color—were smartly dressed and surrounded the host. These were serious women training for professional careers in home economics. They were not taking classes to become better homemakers—they were training for paid employment, often in advertising. Hazard's home economics radio program, which ran from 1933 through 1965, included descriptions of new products and offered cooking advice. It enjoyed a significant following (Apple 2003). For example, in 1962, Hazard received more than ten thousand letters from listeners.

Fast forward to the image of home economics in the late 1960s and the early 1970s. Many home economics students of that era recall making tasteless casseroles and memorizing table settings (Shapiro 1986). Home economics as a career seemed behind the times as women were entering the workplace in roles historically reserved for men. When Robin Morgan, author of *Sisterhood Is Powerful* (1970), spoke to the national home economics convention in 1972, she addressed the home economists in the audience as the "enemy" (Morgan 1973, 13). The field that had welcomed women for generations and kept them gainfully employed was discovering that it had become an unappealing leftover.

Yet women majoring and working in the home economics field in the 1950s and 1960s were living the issues that would become part of the mission of the second-wave women's movement. In truth, the women who chose home economics as a career were closer to their activist sisters as acquaintances than as enemies. One popular introductory textbook in 1965, *Introduction to Home Economics,* was written by Kansas State University home economist professor Ruth Hoeflin. The book began with quotes from a report, "American Women," which highlighted women's employment and documented the difficulties facing women in the workplace (Hoeflin 1965). The quotes were based on a 1962 report from President Kennedy's Commission on the Status of Women, which predicted a new role for women in society and identified problems of potential workplace gender discrimination. The textbook addressed a range of jobs that the home economics field offered, including advertising (Hoeflin 1965). Hoeflin cited an article in *Cosmopolitan* magazine that described home economists as "Today's Glamour Girls" (Younger 1965, 12). These were not jobs but rather careers with potential.

For nearly one hundred years, mass communication combined with home economics provided paid employment for US women, especially in jobs creating messages that targeted women in the home. For example, at newspapers, women journalists worked in the women's pages from the 1880s through the retirement of those sections as anachronisms in the 1970s. The content of these sections has been described as the nonthreatening topics of the four F's: family, fashion, food, and furnishings. The women's pages provided jobs for a growing number of women who wanted not only to write newspaper articles but also to create and sell ads (Fahs 2012). According to Sivulka (2009, 290), women working in advertising today are linked to advertising women of the past: "Their market is women; their business is advertising; and their new agencies would specialize in food, fashion and home furnishing—the modern expression of the enduring feminine role." Ad women worked in a number of roles, among them agency copywriters, department store merchandisers, test kitchen managers, and mail-order advertising designers.

Many of the women working both in newspaper women's pages and as advertising copywriters found their careers through home economics. Stories of educated women's paid employment are often defined by careers as nurses, teachers, or librarians. Yet home economics, a field initially called *domestic science,* was a popular college major for women who found careers upon graduation (Shapiro 1986). As part of the major, women learned about writing copy, understanding new technologies, and educating consumers. They went on to work in the advertising industry, creating ads, selling ads, and serving as consultants. They also worked at advertising consumer food products, developing new recipes, overseeing cooking contests, running test kitchens, and answering letters about promoted products. They largely addressed a white, middle-class audience who did their own cooking and cleaning. The increased number of consumer goods for the home created a need to educate and persuade the women who ran households not only of the benefits of purchasing these products but also of the most efficient, artful, and scientific ways of consuming them on behalf of their families. To that end, women trained as home economists represented readymade experts for the advertising industry.

Feminist historian Joan Wallach Scott (1993, 235) writes that a fuller accounting of history "requires not a simple linear narrative, but a more complex one, that takes into account the changing position not only of women's history, but of the feminist movement and the discipline of history." In making a case for the importance of home economics' history to the history of women's movement, much of the work of home economists was between the first and second waves. Until recently, home economists were largely written off as old-fashioned and irrelevant. Their accomplishments were marginalized, as more vocal crusaders for women's rights garnered the media's attention. In this chapter, I tell the story of the mostly forgotten synergy between home economics and advertising in providing women with a professionalized career path through much of the twentieth century.

AMERICAN WOMEN SPEAKING TO AMERICAN WOMEN IN ADVERTISING HISTORY

Even before 1900, US advertising agencies enlisted women's voices to create advertising copy to speak to women as consumers. Sivulka (2009, 13) writes, "To retell the history of advertising and the making of American consumer culture, I emphasize that women took their place alongside men and played an important role in the development of the American economy as both consumers and ad women." Some advertising agencies had segregated women-only departments, similar to newspapers' women's pages. Moreover, food and appliance companies regularly employed home economists to help advertise their products. Sivulka (2009, 13) writes, "If you are selling to women, nothing succeeds like a woman's viewpoint." At the same time, academic home economics programs focused on developing women's expertise and their ability to communicate with other women. Graduates were trained to write advertising copy and encouraged to find paid employment. As scholars have noted, a significant part of a home economist's education was convincing consumers what they needed to buy (Goldstein 2012).

As early as the 1870s, German immigrant and widow Mathilde C. Weil sought advertising for a German society newspaper. She was soon selling advertising space in newspapers. Later, she joined with Meta Volkman to create the general advertising agency M. C. Weil, and others like Weil and Volkman found opportunities in the advertising business after the Civil War as the United States rebuilt and capitalized on industrial advancements (Sivulka 2009). Changing laws that allowed women to earn their own income and sign contracts helped encourage more women to go into advertising and allied jobs. By 1901, the advertising industry trade publication *Printers' Ink* included an ad for women to write advertisements. Records document women in the early 1900s writing advertising copy for clients such as White Sewing Machines, Libby Glass Company, and Cream of Wheat, among dozens of others (Sivulka 2009). The US tradition of women employed in the advertising public sphere to persuasively speak to women as consumers toiling in the private sphere parallels the rise of consumer goods manufacturing and the need to market goods to women running households.

Meanwhile, early pioneers of the domestic sciences focused on household efficiency and health, which also required messages to be crafted rhetorically for the so-called lady of the house. Before long, these home economists were recommending products. For example, Christine McCaffey Frederick published the 1929 *Selling Mrs. Consumer,* one of the first publications telling advertisers how to address women as consumers. Described as a "home efficiency expert, an advertising consultant and a consumer advocate" (Rutherford 2003, 2), Frederick exemplified the irony of professional women instructing, indeed constructing, women's modern role inside the home. As Frederick once said, "Our greatest enemy is a woman with a career" (Sivulka 2009, 148).

Advertisers learned early on that advertising appealing to women was big business. This opened opportunity for women to excel as advertisers, as long as they sold products to women using women-focused media. Much of advertising copy targeting women ran in women's magazines. These magazines with large circulations exerted significant influence not only on the advertising and consumer products industries but also on popular understandings of the ideal American household (Walker 1998). An article in a 1954 issue of *Printers' Ink* argued, "Credibility demands a woman on household products and other merchandise sold to and largely used by women" (Sivulka 2009, 247).

Popular radio announcer Mary Margaret McBride edited the 1948 book *How to Be a Successful Advertising Woman,* published by the Advertising Women of New York. The book suggested that women could play almost any role in advertising and public relations. One contributing author, a freelance writer, illustrator, and lecturer, wrote, "One of the nicest things about careers in advertising art is that you can free-lance and combine career with marriage" (Hardy 1948, 23).

Helen Woodward's 1960 book *The Lady Persuaders* noted the importance of advertising in women's magazines, which were especially important before the widespread adoption of television and the advent of daytime programming targeting white, middle-class women. "To the uninitiated, a woman's magazine may seem merely a powdery bit of fluff," Woodward (1960, 5) wrote "No notion could be more unreal or deceptive." Although content reinforced women's role in the private sphere, stories of career women and community development by women volunteers appeared in the pages as well. Arguing that women were required to effectively communicate with women was a convenient economic logic for women who wished to work outside the home in advertising, an industry wholly dependent on its ability to persuade.

INTRODUCING APPLIANCES AND TECHNOLOGY TO THE US HOME

A major part of many women's jobs in home economics and advertising was to interpret new products and develop a demand for new technology among consumers (Goldstein 2012, 286). This largely was accomplished in two ways: writing recipe booklets for food companies and demonstrating appliances to audiences at department stores and other public events. Some of the earliest examples of using home economists to advertise and sell products can be found in the history of kitchen appliances. An "all-electric kitchen" of the future existed as early as 1893, where it appeared at the Chicago World's Fair. Of course, Americans first would need to be convinced that they needed electricity. It was not until the 1920s, then, that most houses were wired so that kitchens could have electric lighting and a few small appliances. Cooking on wood or coal stoves was decreasing over the same period as gas cooking became popular. Meanwhile, iceboxes were being replaced by refrigerators. Homemakers in the United States of the 1920s were urged on many fronts to update their kitchens. Home economics presentations to women's clubs and pamphlets targeted women with advice such as, "When a baby's health hangs in the balance, the intelligent mother will see to it that the ice supply never runs too low" (Robinson 1997, 259). In 1926, the Bureau of Home Economists promoted "Convenience Kitchens," with the idea that efficiency and convenience were not mutually exclusive. At the same time, although mechanical refrigerators were available to purchase for home use, the Bureau of Home Economics decided that they remained too expensive. The refrigerator industry was not to be deterred. Between 1927 and 1931, the popular *Ladies' Home Journal* featured two to three refrigerator ads per issue. The ads were part of a mission by home economists "to solve a common problem: to determine and communicate the health effects of refrigeration" (Goldstein 2012, 125). The relationship between consumers and companies producing household technologies grew. According to one 1930 study, "Home economists were recommending six cubic feet of refrigerator storage as the standard for an 'average family'" (Nickles 2002,

706). The growing feminized household consumer culture in the United States was largely guided by home economists who advised advertising copywriters or wrote the copy themselves.

New products and inventions for the kitchen were being introduced throughout the twentieth century, and home economists were ready to explain their value. A review of scholarship produced by home economics students shows an emphasis on the scientific understanding of the new appliances. For example, a 1923 home economics master's thesis examined the efficiency of stoves (Davison 1923). A 1948 article in the *Journal of Home Economics* explained the results of a study of dry versus steam irons (Breckenridge and Peet 1948). In conducting and publishing the results of home economics research, a form of advertising endorsement was forming. A trustee at Iowa State University, which helped establish home economics as an academic field of study, explained the equipment studies part of home economics this way: "We must teach the girls to acquire by practice a thorough knowledge of the art of conducting a well regulated [*sic*] household" (Bix 2002, 731). Home economics graduates were expected to have a scientifically grounded understanding of technologies in the home. Yet this equipment was not affordable or available for everyone. For this reason, home economists were trained broadly. The 1949 edition of the textbook *Household Equipment* addressed iceboxes along with electric, gas, and kerosene refrigerators. The book continued to have sections covering wood, coal, and kerosene ranges until the 1961 edition—mostly because these products were still on the market.

Technology advances were not limited to appliances; food companies began to market prepared and packaged products. For example, after World War II, advances in food technology led food companies to easier ways to make a cake. There was a problem: The dessert was created with too much ease. Did this lack of effort mean a homemaker loved her family less? A 1950 home economics study looked at the quality and efficiency of cake mixes versus those made from scratch. The study's researchers found a variety of opinions on taste and texture between the two styles (Gross and Mackley 1950), but by 1958 the cake mixes were considered a success story. The home economists of Betty Crocker reassured home cooks that no love was lost when a dessert was made using a mix rather than by scratch (Nelson 2006). In 1955, the General Foods Consumer Center employed sixty home economists (Goldstein 2012). These women knew how to sell products and develop new ideas. They incorporated this knowledge into their recipe writing—a form of advertising and a mainstay of home economics work. In 1958, an ad written by a home economist featured a recipe for cheesecake that nearly doubled sales of Jell-O lemon instant pudding (Goldstein 2012).

HOME ECONOMICS EDUCATION WITH A SIDE OF ADVERTISING

Many of the women who joined advertising agencies or the advertising departments of food companies took the home economics journalism path in college. Land-grant colleges originally developed home economics programs for women to complement agriculture programs for men. In 1871, the first college class in domestic economy was offered at Iowa State University, and in 1873 Kansas State began a domestic economy curriculum. One scholar noted that the emphasis on an applied science curriculum for Midwestern men created a place for women students: "In many ways, household equipment studies developed as a feminine parallel to agricultural engineering" (Bix 2002, 731). At several conferences in Lake Placid between 1899 and 1907, women defined their domestic applied science field, debating what it should be called. It became *domestic science* before transitioning into *home economics.*

The conversation about transitioning to home economics had been started by pioneering scientist Ellen Swallow Richards, the first woman to earn a bachelor of science from the Massachusetts Institute of Technology. Richards had looked at public health issues such as sanitation and nutrition since the 1870s. Although she focused on social reforms, her message was largely directed to women, whether it was creating a community of educators or helping a homemaker become more efficient. Indeed, home economics was not contrary to feminist principles under Richards's vision. It was an academic program that would "liberate" women from housework and provide opportunities for women to spend their time elsewhere, including in the public sphere (Dyas 2014).

By 1909, the American Home Economics Association was officially established with a mission to improve "living conditions in the home, the institutional household and the community" ("Was Home" 2001). Creating domestic science or home economics invited women into the public sphere without threatening traditional gender roles. As historian Shapiro (1986, 9) explains:

> The women who chose domestic science had no quarrel with women's rights, but neither did they have any desire to call themselves feminists. They wanted to have a career and they needed a cause, but they weren't interested in breaking very many rules, reordering society, or challenging men on their own turf.

In 1914, Congress passed the Smith-Lever Act; it created the Agriculture Extension Service to provide farm women with an education in domestic science. During World War I, home economists taught the nation's homemakers about rationing and food substitution. By 1914, there were home economics courses in 250 universities. Many of these academic programs developed partnerships with large food manufacturing companies, which would later employ graduates in the business of marketing communication and advertising (Biltekoff 2002). The US Department of Agriculture (USDA) created the Bureau of Home Economics in 1923 to research consumer behavior and to modernize rural homes. The process of modernizing resulted in increased advertising for kitchen products, thus forming an unlikely partnership between the government and industry. The Purnell Act of 1925 offered federal money for the scientific investigation of vitamins and rural home management research. Granted only to women, Cornell's first graduate degree in home economics was awarded in 1922 and its first home economics doctoral degree in 1930.

According to a history of Iowa State University, the 1920s through the 1950s were good years for home economics journalism graduates. According to the school, "Manufacturers of food products and household equipment discovered that home economics–trained women could write reports and directions" (Eppright and Ferguson 1971, 202). That concept was spreading to schools across the country. A 1963 article in *Journalism Quarterly* addressed "Opportunities and Preparation in Home Economics Journalism." The author described the home economics curriculum as including classes in business, advertising, journalism, and home economics and textiles (Baird 1963). The classes were professional and intended for careers rather than homemaking.

The 1918–1919 catalog at Iowa State University invited women to major in home economics with an emphasis in technical journalism that included an advertising class. The following year's catalog explained that there were two sequences: editorial and advertising (Eppright and Ferguson 1971). Katherine Goeppinger, a well-known home economics journalism professor at Iowa State from 1936 until 1960, wrote the foreword and a chapter in the textbook *How to Write for Homemakers* (Richardson and Callahan 1951). The premise was that women writers were more likely to understand the woman consumer and sell her products. Students in the home economics journalism program at Iowa State took a wide range of communication classes. During the sophomore year, students took three classes in technical writing. The following year, students took principles of broadcasting, technical advertising, copyediting, and magazine editing. During the senior year, there were two technical writing classes along with one radio-writing class. The curriculum clearly operated on the assumption of women gaining skills to enter the workforce upon graduation.

Kansas State University had a home economics program beginning in 1873. Helen Pansy Hostetter joined the faculty to teach journalism to home economics students in 1926. She worked on and off for the university for the next twenty years, sometimes taking leave to work for the USDA and as editor of the academic *Journal of Home Economics*. In 1949, she became the first woman named a full professor of journalism. At the same time, there was a new curriculum for home economics journalism that trained its graduates to be more employable. According to Hostetter, "Ten years hence girls who have these journalism courses will be earning at least $1,000 more a year than will equally bright colleagues who haven't had them. They will know how to write and will have subject matter about which to write" (Hoeflin 1965, 149).

ADVERTISING CAREERS FOR HOME EC GRADS CHAMPIONING WOMEN

During the heyday of home economics education, graduates were in demand. Mass media and food companies employed home economists with writing experience to create and test recipes. During the 1950s, the advertising firm J. Walter Thompson Company published newsletters that explained the importance of home economics knowledge to clients. For example, a January 1951 memo highlighted new recipes developed for the Good Luck line of pie fillings and crusts. "Recipes would be the backbone of the campaign," according to the memo. The ad campaign appeared in the food sections of newspapers in twenty-one eastern cities ("Best Wishes" 1951). Later that year, a Thompson memo addressed a successful advertising campaign for Kraft salad dressings: The "Salad Carnival" campaign included grocery store point-of-sale displays and in-store demonstrations by home economists ("Account Changes" 1951).

According to a 1963 academic study in *Journalism Quarterly,* "The sales promotion department offers women some of their best career opportunities in the field of advertising" (Baird 1963, 374). There were clearly appeals to female college graduates. In 1963, J. Walter Thompson recruited women in college with a brochure that explained that women worked at all levels at the agency, including the management and executive levels. According to the introduction, "Advertising is a particularly promising field for women because so much advertising is directed to women and so many products are purchased by women" (*Advertising: A Career* 1963, 6). Suggested majors for future advertising careers were English, journalism, or home economics. Women were featured in each of the photos in the twenty-five-page document.

Home economists took various paths to their professional careers. Some companies had established home economics departments, especially in the food and home technology fields. In other cases, home economists took the initiative to create positions for themselves in trade associations or industry groups. One home economics teacher told a student she could be just as successful in an advertising job as she could be as a diplomat, artist, copywriter, or nurse (Goldstein 2012). Home economists' training was broad enough for many possible careers.

On a practical level, remaining in a women-dominated field allowed for career advancement and a level of expertise that likely would have eluded women in fields and professions that remained aspirational for men. Home economists worked within the system to become a voice for women. Some home economics journalism graduates hosted radio programs for homemakers. These sponsor-driven programs, sometimes known as "corporate home economics shows," breached the firewall separating advertising and journalism as the host promoted the product within the program. For example, Spry Shortening sponsored the "Aunt Jenny's Real Life Stories" radio program, featuring "Aunt Jenny" in her kitchen preparing dishes which of course required Spry Shortening. Segments and stories also ran between Aunt Jenny's recipe preparation demonstrations in a format that mixed advertising and conversation (Elias 2008).

One of the strongest examples of these "sisterhood of pen-and-ink home economists" can be found in the advertising campaigns based on "live trademarks" (Shapiro 2005, 30). Women characters, such as Patricia Collier at Dole and Mary Blake at Carnation, became branding synecdoche. Home economist Ellen Pennell became the first Ann Pillsbury. These kinds of pseudonyms were used by several home economists to create trusted personas who could sell products to help the busy homemaker. At Pillsbury, Pennell designed the company's first test kitchen, planned radio and television programs, and oversaw food photography. She went on to be a home economics faculty member at Kansas State (Eppright and Ferguson 1971).

The best known and the longest lasting of these live trademarks, however, is Betty Crocker, used by General Mills to "help" women with their baking using General Mills products. Significant scholarship has been published about the creation of Betty Crocker (Castagna 2011; Marks 2010; Shapiro 2005). Researchers agree that Betty Crocker's origins lie in a 1921 advertising campaign for Gold Flour that resulted in thousands of consumer responses asking questions such as how to make pancakes fluffier and requesting recipes. The all-male advertising department decided that it might seem strange for a man to respond to cooking questions. So they came up with Betty Crocker. The name "Betty" was chosen because it sounded friendly, and "Crocker" referred to a longtime company executive. Women employees submitted sample Betty Crocker signatures to be used on letters. The winning signature, submitted by secretary Florence Lindeberg, is still used today ("The Story of Betty Crocker" 2). The character Betty Crocker got her own radio program in 1924 as "The Betty Crocker Cooking School of the Air," which ran for almost three decades.

Betty Crocker also wrote cookbooks and recipe booklets that connected the company with customers.

Betty Crocker truly came to life through Marjorie Child Husted, who was hired as a home economist by the Washburn Crosby firm in 1924. Husted would go on to manage a staff of forty in the Betty Crocker Homemaking Service, and she became the voice of Betty Crocker on the radio for many years. She edited the "Big Red" cookbook, which grew to be so popular that in 1951, only one year after publication, sales of the cookbook were close to that of the Bible (Marks 2010). Husted's work in promoting Betty Crocker was so successful that in 1945 Crocker was the second most popular woman in the country, second only to First Lady Eleanor Roosevelt, according to *Fortune* magazine (Marks 2010). During the 1940s, surveys showed that Betty Crocker was known to nine out of ten American homemakers ("The Story of Betty Crocker" 3). In recognition of her contributions, Husted received a Woman of the Year Award from the Women's National Press Club in 1948, and the following year, she won the Advertising Woman of the Year Award from the Advertising Federation of America.

Husted viewed her role as a champion for women, both in the workplace and in the home. She regularly contributed columns that addressed gender issues to the *Journal of Home Economics*. One 1948 article, "Would You Like More Recognition?" called for empowering women. Husted also created a "bias quiz" for men to take to determine their innate prejudice toward women. A member of the American Association of University Women (AAUW), Husted was appointed to the group's Committee on the Status of Women in 1949. She helped to develop the 1953 AAUW Money Management Portfolio for Women. Looking back at the Betty Crocker years, Husted said:

> It is very interesting to me to look back now and realize how concerned I was about the welfare of women as homemakers and their feelings of self respect. Women needed a champion. Here were millions of them staying at home alone, doing a job with children, cooking, cleaning on minimal budgets—the whole depressing mess of it. They needed someone to remind them that they had value. (American Association of University Women 2014)

In 1945, Patricia Roth (later Anfinson) was a new home economics graduate of the University of Minnesota. She recalled thinking that she would love to work for Betty Crocker but understood the prospect was unlikely: "Marjorie Husted, the woman who runs the kitchens is tough. She's probably got a line of girls dying to work there." Regardless, her brother-in-law convinced her to go to the company's headquarters. "You have two minutes to tell me why I should hire you," Husted demanded once Roth had gained access. Whatever

Roth's response, she landed the job and was soon answering the phone as Betty Crocker and fielding home economics questions from callers. She also answered letters from customers, signing each letter as Betty Crocker (McAndrews, nd).

Roth, who stayed at home for a few years while rearing her six children before returning to the paid workforce, was like many home economists of that era. They may not have used the term *feminism,* but in practice they did much to help other women while finding their own place in a workforce that often was not welcoming. Indeed, despite her status as a piece of advertising fiction, Betty Crocker herself might be described as practicing a kind of feminism (Geraci and Demers 2011). Dozens of home economists over the years found employment as "Betty Crocker," and I would argue those Betty Crockers, answering phones and letters and serving as the face of the company, were effectively mentoring women everywhere.

Yet Betty Crocker's role as a teacher for home cooks made her a target, as changing views about women's place in society shifted in the late 1960s. In 1972, the Minneapolis-St. Paul chapter of the National Organization for Women accused Betty Crocker of being a racist, sexist image. The chapter filed a class-action complaint against General Mills, which was later dropped. General Mills subsequently updated Betty Crocker's image that year to one with a more ambiguously ethnic, multicultural appearance (Castagna 2011).

ENTER THE SECOND WAVE AND QUESTIONS ABOUT FEMINISM

By the 1960s, change was on the horizon as society began questioning the gendered division of labor, family gender roles, and the function that home economics served. As home economics historian Carolyn M. Goldstein (2012, 1) writes:

> For feminist historians seeking to understand the forces and factors that conspired to limit women's opportunities in the public sphere, home economics was an easy target. In blaming home economists for confining women to the domestic sphere, this type of analysis reinforced assumptions that home economics was concerned only with private matters of the home.

Soon the second-wave women's movement would reject the ideological premise of a field that had propelled women into economically independent lives for close to a century. As Stage and Vincent (1997, 1) note, "The feminists of the 1970s cast off their aprons long before they burned their bras."

For decades, despite the appearance that home economics was all about homemaker training, the field served as a significant path to employment for women before it was redesigned and renamed in the 1970s. By then, a general perception of its old-fashioned views ended home economics, as earlier generations of alumnae would have recognized it. Goldstein (2012, 290) writes, "Reacting to both feminist cries against domesticity and attacks from male administrators, many college home economics programs took steps to eliminate the word 'home' from their names." This transition began in 1960, and, within twenty years, there were thirty different names for the field (Goldstein 2012). Today, the most common name for the field is *human ecology* ("Was Home Economics a Profession" 2001), which reframes the field away from the original idea of applied domestic science to realign it with contemporary public health and geo sciences—human geography and environmental science, for example—among others, such as textiles and family studies.

Although some dismissed traditional "home economics" as irrelevant and "little more than a conspiracy to keep women in the kitchen" (Stage and Vincent 1997, 1), recent interest in studying its history has encouraged reinterpretation of what the field has meant for women. New research casts home economics as a more complex and diverse field than previously thought. How home economists working in advertising viewed feminism is complex, as well. These women clearly advocated for better lives for homemakers from efficiency in the kitchen to wider appreciation for the work homemakers did. Home economists, however self-serving, also worked to legitimize the realities of working mothers. Home economists not only professionalized their own field to provide career opportunities for themselves, they also conducted research that showed that mothers working outside the home did not have a detrimental effect on their children. In 1952, the president-elect of the American Home Economics Association, Elizabeth Sweeney Herbert, gave a speech titled "Occupation Housewife" sponsored by the American Medical Association to an audience of healthcare practitioners. Her talk, a roundup of the research on mothers working outside of the home, was meant to advocate on behalf of working women. Sweeney Herbert said that family relationships are more important than a clean house, and she argued that mothers spending their time with children is more important than how much time they spend with children. She also said mothers need time for themselves, away from the children (Sweeney Herbert 1952).

Nevertheless, Golombisky and Holtzhausen (2005, 12) caution against "projecting feminism onto the past," ascribing conscious feminist intent to historical figures without evidence: "Historically significant women do not necessarily identify with feminism or even so-called feminist issues." Golombisky and Holtzhausen (2005, 12), however, do argue that all historical research about women has "latent feminist potential," and they write that women's historians need not refrain from noting a woman's historical importance to feminism or women's movement, regardless of her professed politics or lack thereof. There were undoubtedly home economists, famous and obscure, who acted in ways compatible with definitions of feminism, even if they did not call themselves feminists or subscribe to "women's lib," per se. They worked within a field that was accepting of women. At the same time, in the advertising industry, these women typically were limited to selling women's products, even as they made the most of their limitations. Creedon (1993, 71), illustrating a liberal feminist philosophy, observed that to remain in any field "women must conform in some ways to the norms." That was clearly the place that home economists found themselves.

In an irony bordering on tragedy, the white, well-educated, middle-class, liberal feminist second-wave women's movement, in campaigning for women's right to equal access to mostly white-collar careers outside the home, participated in ending one of the few careers simpatico with such a politics. When Robin Morgan addressed home economists at their national convention in 1972, she said she was there to help end the oppression of women, and she urged her audience to quit their jobs as home economists. "You run the risk of becoming obsolete," she warned the women. "Those institutions that home economics has been hooked into are dying, and they are dying even without the feminist revolution" (Morgan 1973, 13).

Home economists, like Christine Frederick, were "caught in the crossfire between persisting old and emerging new visions for women" (Rutherford 2003, 3). They walked a fine line between stereotypes about women's place in the home and women's ability to succeed in a man's world of work. The safest path was balancing the status quo with an eye toward a more enlightened future. For example, in 1954, the Betty Crocker Search for the All-American Homemaker of Tomorrow was initiated. High school senior girls competed in a cooking competition for college scholarships. While these competitions were grounded in the idea of a young woman eventually becoming a housewife, the prizes often led to careers outside the home. In 1970, the winner in Nevada was Joyce Kay Nelson. In her application she wrote about an exciting trip she had taken to Mexico where she learned about the culture and the people. She described what she thought was important in a homemaker: "By keeping the home as clean and comfortable as possible, the homemaker can provide an escape from the growing pressures of the outside world" (Nelson 1970). But upon winning the prize, she used the scholarship to attend veterinary school.

Historians were late to uncover the curious story of home economics education and the advertising careers home economists pursued in the twentieth century. As they say, "Well-behaved women seldom make history" (Ulrich 2008). Women with backgrounds in home economics, and home economics itself, have not been considered historically significant because they were successful in a feminized field composed of women working in the public sphere serving women working in the private domestic sphere. Unless women are mothers or wives of famous men, or women achieve a level of fame considered prestigious for men, women's history too often remains unexplored or merely a footnote. In the present case, it was US home economists who used advertising to shape the food and kitchen equipment that changed America's dinner tables and found a career for themselves along the way.

REFERENCES

"Account Changes." 1951. *J. Walter Thompson Company News,* January 1. New York: J. Walter Thompson Company Papers, Duke University Libraries. http://library.duke.edu/digitalcollections/jwtnewsletters_jwtnl10001/.

Advertising: A Career for Women. 1963. New York: J. Walter Thompson Company Papers, Duke University Libraries.

American Association of University Women. 2014. "Have This with Your Cupcake: Betty Crocker Was a Feminist!" June 2. http://www.aauw.org/2014/06/12/the-real-betty-crocker/.

Apple, Rima. 2003. *The Challenge of Constantly Changing Times.* Madison, WI: Parallel.

Baird, Gladys A. 1963. "Opportunities and Preparation in Home Economics Journalism." *Journalism Quarterly* 40 (3): 371–74.

"Best Wishes for 1951." 1951. *J. Walter Thompson Company News,* January 1. New York: J. Walter Thompson.

Biltekoff, Charlotte. 2002. "Strong Men and Women Are Not Products of Improper Food: Domestic Science and the History of Eating and Identity." *Journal for the Study of Food and Society* 6 (1): 60–69.

Bix, Amy Sue. 2002. "Equipped for Life: Gendered Technical Training and Consumerism in Home Economics, 1920–1980." *Technology and Culture* 43 (4): 728–54.

Breckenridge, Harriet B., and Louise J. Peet. 1948. "Combination Dry and Steam Flatirons Tested." *Journal of Home Economics* 40 (1): 137–139.

Castagna, JoAnn E. 2011. "Betty Crocker." In *Icons of American Cooking,* edited by Victor W. Geraci and Elizabeth S. Demers, 79–90. Santa Barbara, CA: Greenwood.

Creedon, Pamela. 1993. "Framing Feminism: A Feminist Primer for the Mass Media." *Media Studies Journal* 7(1–2): 69–80.

Davison, Eloise. 1923. *Stove Efficiency Tests.* Master's thesis, Iowa State College.

Dyas, Brie. 2014. "Who Killed Home Ec? Here's the Real Story behind Its Demise." *HuffPost Home,* September 30. http://www.huffingtonpost.com/2014/09/29/home-ec-classes_n_5882830.html.

Elias, Megan J. 2008. *Stir It Up: Home Economics in American Culture.* Philadelphia: University of Pennsylvania Press.

Eppright, Ercel Sherman, and Elizabeth Storm Ferguson. 1971. *A Century of Home Economics at Iowa State University.* Ames: Iowa State University.

Fahs, Alice. 2012. *Out on Assignment: Newspaper Women and the Making of the Public Sphere*. Chapel Hill: University of North Carolina Press.

Frederick, Christine McCaffey. 1929. *Selling Mrs. Consumer*. New York: Business Bourse.

Geraci, Victor W., and Elizabeth S. Demers, editors. 2011. *Icons of American Cooking*. Santa Barbara, CA: Greenwood.

Goldstein, Carolyn M. 2012. *Creating Consumers: Home Economists in Twentieth-Century America*. Chapel Hill: University of North Carolina Press.

Golombisky, Kim, and Derina Holtzhausen. 2005. "'Pioneering Women' and 'Founding Mothers': Women's History and Projecting Feminism onto the Past." *Women and Language* 28: 12–22.

Gross, Bernice, and Kay Young Mackley. 1950. "Should the Homemaker Use Ready-Made Mixes?" *Journal of Home Economics* 42 (6): 451.

Hardy, Kay. 1948. "Advertising Art Careers." In *How to Be a Successful Advertising Woman,* edited by Mary Margaret McBride, 23–46. New York: McGraw-Hill.

Herbert, Elizabeth. 1952. "Occupation Housewife." Speech to the American Media Association.

Hoeflin, Ruth. 1965. *Introduction to Home Economics*. Manhattan, KS: Kansas State University.

"Home Economics?" 2001. Division of Rare and Manuscript Collections, Carl A. Kroch Library, Cornell University. http://rmc.library.cornell.edu/homeEc/masterlabel.html.

Husted, Marjorie Child. 1948. "Would You Like More Recognition?" *Journal of Home Economics* 40 (8): 459–460.

Marks, Susan. 2010. *Finding Betty Crocker: The secret Life of America's First Lady of Food*. New York: Simon & Schuster.

McAndrews, Meghan. n.d. "The Snickerdoodle Lady." https://www.bettycrocker.com/menus-holidays-parties/mhplibrary/parties-and-get-togethers/vintage-betty/the-snickerdoodle-lady

McBride, Mary Margaret, editor. 1948. *How to Be a Successful Advertising Woman.* New York: McGraw Hill.

Morgan, Robin. 1970. *Sisterhood Is Powerful*. New York: Vintage.

Morgan, Robin. 1973. "What Robin Morgan Said in Denver." *Journal of Home Economics* 65 (January): 13. Transcript of invited speech at American Home Economics Association Conference, 1973.

Nelson, Joyce Kay. 1970. "Questionnaire for Betty Crocker Search for the American Homemaker of Tomorrow, April 3, 1970." Ann Valder Collection, Special Collections, University of Nevada, Las Vegas.

Nelson, Rick. 2006. "The Original Happy Homemaker." *Minneapolis-St. Paul Star Tribune,* January 24, 2006.

Nickles, Shelley. 2002. "Preserving Woman: Refrigerator Design as Social Process in the 1930s." *Technology and Culture* 43 (4): 693–727.

Richardson, Lou, and Genevieve Callahan, editors. 1951. *How to Write for Homemakers*. Ames: Iowa State College.

Robinson, Lisa Mae. 1997. "Safeguarded by Your Refrigerator." In *Rethinking Home Economics: Women and the History of a Profession,* edited by Sarah Stage and Virginia B. Vincent, 253–270. Ithaca, NY: Cornell University Press.

Rutherford, Janice Williams. 2003. *Selling Mrs. Consumer: Christine Fredericks and the Rise of Household Efficiency.* Athens: University of Georgia Press.

Scott, Joan Wallach. 1993. "Women's History." In *American Feminist Thought at Century's End,* edited by Linda S. Kauffman, 246–237. Cambridge, MA: Blackwell.

Shapiro, Laura. 1986. *Perfection Salad: Women and Cooking at the Turn of the Century.* New York: Farrar, Straus and Giroux.

Shapiro, Laura. 2005. "'I Guarantee': Betty Crocker and the Woman in the Kitchen." In *From Betty Crocker to Feminist Food Studies,* edited by Arlene Voski Avakian and Barbara Haber, 29–40. Boston: University of Massachusetts Press.

Sivulka, Juliann. 2009. *Ad Women: How They Impact What We Need, Want, and Buy.* New York: Prometheus Books.

Stage, Sarah, and Virginia B. Vincent. 1997. "Introduction: Home Economics, What's in a Name?" In *Rethinking Home Economics: Women and the History of a Profession,* edited by Sarah Stage and Virginia B. Vincent, 1–13. Ithaca, NY: Cornell University Press.

"The Story of Betty Crocker." http://www.bettycrocker.com/menus-holidays-parties/mhplibrary/parties-and-get-togethers/vintage-betty/the-story-of-betty-crocker.

Ulrich, Laurel Thatcher. 2008. *Well-Behaved Women Seldom Make History.* New York: Knopf.

Walker, Nancy A., editor. 1998. *Women's Magazines, 1940–1960: Gender Roles and the Popular Press.* New York: Bedford/St. Martins.

"Was Home Economics a Profession?" 2001. Online supplement to exhibition: From Domesticity to Modernity: What Was Home Economics?" Cornell University. http://rmc.library.cornell.edu/homeEc/cases/namechange.html.

Woodward, Helen. 1960. *The Lady Persuaders.* New York: Oboloensky.

Younger, Joan. 1965. "Home economists—Today's Glamour Girls." *Cosmopolitan,* April: 12.

Chapter 14

A Woman's Place

Career Success and Early Twentieth-Century Women's Advertising Clubs[1]

Jeanie E. Wills

In the early years of the twentieth century, the United States was settling into what has been called a "culture of professionalism" (Bledstein 1978; Kwolek-Folland 1998, 87). This culture, a product of transformations brought about in part by industrialization and urbanization, structured a new relationship between individuals, work, and society. As the nation developed an exaggerated respect for the specialist, members of occupations as varied as baseball player, mortician, private detective, and advertiser sought to have their fields recognized as professions (Bledstein 1978).

During that period, advertising practitioners undertook a number of activities to establish the industry's "professional" image. These efforts included among other things, the formation of academic advertising programs, the development of trade publications, and the formation of local advertising clubs and national associations. These clubs provided institutional support that was instrumental in developing a professional consciousness among advertising practitioners. Schultze (1978, 43) points out that "without the shared values and techniques that associations and journals fostered, ad men would not have been able to hold a common conception of the role of advertising in the new urban nation."

What of the women working in advertising? Advertising men began organizing clubs in the 1890s, the first in Denver in 1891 (Roche 1989). These clubs met regularly; however, ad women rarely were allowed to become members or to attend meetings. The exceptions were "some of the western clubs—out in sections where women's suffrage [was] in vogue"; in those clubs, women were admitted to membership on equal terms with men ("Ad Women at Convention" 1916). The first women-only advertising club, the League of Advertising Women of New York, later the Advertising Women of New York (AWNY), and most recently She Runs It, was founded in 1912, and other women's advertising clubs soon followed. These clubs challenged a dominant social understanding that anchored women in the domestic sphere and helped a subset of primarily white, middle-class women experience success in the professional sphere, increasing women's influence in the growing advertising industry. Women benefitted from support the clubs offered to individual members, including exclusive opportunities for networking and professional development. At the same time, the visibility and credibility of individual members helped develop a professional ethos and enhanced the clubs' legitimacy. Here, I argue that this mutually beneficial relationship reinforced affirmations of the importance of women's participation in advertising, supported women working in the field, and ultimately shaped professional dimensions of the industry. I begin by locating the contribution of my work to the limited historical work on advertising women.

THE HISTORIES OF WOMEN IN ADVERTISING

Scanlon (1995, 171) argues, "Women who worked in the advertising business have been overlooked by historians of women, historians of advertising, and historians of consumer culture." Traditional histories of advertising (e.g., Ewen 1976; Presbrey 1929) largely ignored women's experiences, although more recently a number of advertising historians (Fox 1984; Lears 1994; Marchand 1985) have acknowledged women's contributions. Others (Scanlon 1995, 2013; Sivulka 2009; Sutton 2009) have reclaimed the careers of early modern advertising women, focusing exclusively on women working in advertising agencies. A number of "semiautobiographical" and "insider" works by women have appeared on occasion (e.g., Hamburger 1939; Lyon 1943; Maas 1986, 2012; Polykoff 1975; Wells Lawrence 2002; Woodward 1926); however, those are primarily anecdotal. In short, our historical view of advertising culture has come largely through the eyes of men (e.g., Della Femina 1970; Hopkins 1927; Ogilvy 1963, 1978) or through accounts of advertising men's lives (e.g., Cummings 1984). This limited acknowledgment of women's experiences is not without consequence. Feminist historians have noted that once women's experiences are integrated into history, events take on a "wholly different character of meaning from the normally accepted one" (Kelly-Gadol 1987, 16). Histories of advertising women "deserve to be rescued from their obscurity" (Dickenson 2016, 2).

In this chapter, I add to the limited literature on women working in advertising not merely as a matter of equity, but to contribute to our historical understanding of the advertising industry by adopting a feminist standpoint. I trace the connections between a single ad woman's career and the opportunities afforded to her by membership in three women's advertising clubs in the early years of the twentieth century. Drawing on archival documents of the clubs—AWNY, the Philadelphia Club of Advertising Women (PCAW), and the Women's Advertising Club of Chicago (WACC)—and the papers of career ad woman Dorothy Dignam, a member of all three clubs, I construct a case study of Dignam's advertising club experiences. This narrative provides a glimpse into the history of mutually beneficial interrelationships that developed between women's advertising clubs and ad women's careers.

I begin by describing the historical and social milieu in which women's advertising clubs emerged as context for my discussion of the clubs' work. Next, I identify standpoint theory and intersectionality as the feminist lenses through which I view the archival materials I draw on in this account. From there, I briefly introduce the subjects in this study: the three clubs and Ms. Dignam. Finally, I examine Dignam's experiences in these club communities, focusing on the professional-development opportunities made possible through her membership and highlighting her achievements in the clubs and in the broader advertising industry.

WOMEN'S CLUB WORK: SOCIAL AND HISTORICAL BACKGROUND

In the United States, women's clubs thrived during the latter half of the nineteenth and the first half of the twentieth centuries. As early as the 1800s, women formed clubs ranging from religious groups; to literary, culture, and self-improvement clubs; to reform movements.

These clubs "rendered obsolete the notion that 'woman's place is in the home,' and thereby made a significant contribution to women's struggle for autonomy" (Blair 1980, 119). Cramer (1998) suggests that although women's clubs were generally segregated by race and class, they functioned to construct gendered forms of citizenship. Clubs "propelled women out their front doors" and pushed them "to confront public problems" (Schneider and Schneider 1993, 95), helping women work collaboratively to achieve a variety of ends, providing opportunities for women to exert influence in public life and on public policy, establish public service institutions, contribute to cultural change, and work toward intellectual self-improvement (Gere 1997).

THE EMERGENCE OF WOMEN'S ADVERTISING CLUBS

Amid the developing culture of professionalism, a favorable attitude toward business, and an increase in the number of white middle-class women participating in public life, "[w]omen solidified their position in the working world"

(Schneider and Schneider 1993, 104). The number of women's professional organizations multiplied. Kwolek-Folland (1998, 98) notes that "[a] striking feature of turn-of-the century America was the sense that business offered special, perhaps even unique opportunities to [white, middle-class] women. Many saw business almost as a panacea for women."

Women had "gained importance in the economy as America's primary consumers, but most middle-class married women continued to center their lives on the private home" (Rutherford 2003, 3). A "domestic science" movement promoting "the betterment of the home" developed late in the nineteenth century, and universities began to offer home economics curricula. Like advertising women, home economists "staked a set of professional claims as technical experts about consumer goods and consumer behavior," developing "a woman's professional and feminized culture of expertise" (Goldstein 2012, 2–3, 74). Women educated in home economics often sought employment in advertising (see Chapter 13).

Businesses, that is advertisers—primarily white, middle- to upper-middle-class men—viewed white, middle-class women as their primary customers. A 1918 headline in a J. Walter Thompson agency ad in *Advertising Club News* declared that "Eighty-five percent of all retail purchases are made by women." The copy continued: "In selling goods to women, you hear much of the women's point of view. It is spoken of as if there were some mystery about women, which perhaps some woman, properly gifted could divulge" (quoted in Sutton 2009, 1). Toward that end, advertisers saw the value of women's guidance in their efforts to sell products to women. In response, advertising women, like home economists and many of the abolitionists and suffragists before them, "developed careful arguments to bolster their ethos, often relying on popular beliefs about women's domestic natures" (Sharer 2004, 17). White, middle-class women hoping to work in advertising adopted an essentialist claim of feminine intuition and touted their homemaking experience as a professional skill set that enabled them to make the connection with consumers. The possession of the "women's viewpoint" provided women an entrée into the profession (Marchand 1985). Thus, in the early years of the twentieth century, advertising was widely recognized as a profession open to women.

Marchand (1985, 34) has noted, "Rare was the advertising woman who escaped being typecast as an expert on the 'woman's viewpoint.'" Despite finding a niche for themselves, advertising women recognized that they often were "welcomed" into the industry only grudgingly, based on their "viewpoint" more so than for their strategic skills and creativity. Advertising women were well aware that advertising men viewed them as being less than equal. They were primarily limited to working on "women's products," often segregated into "women's departments," and rarely allowed to meet with clients. Most relevant to the discussion here, ad women rarely were allowed to become members of advertising men's clubs or even to attend club meetings. They were unable to take advantage of educational and networking opportunities, involvement in industry "gossip," and participation in advertising industry development that the men's clubs provided. In short, existing clubs excluded women from numerous professional aspects of the industry in which they worked.

As noted earlier, in response to this exclusion, advertising women in New York City established the first women-only advertising club in New York in 1912. More clubs soon followed, among them clubs in Los Angeles (1915), Philadelphia (1916), St. Louis (1917), and Chicago (1918).[2] In 1916, eight hundred advertising women from all over the country attended the Associated Advertising Clubs of the World convention in Philadelphia, held a meeting of their own, and formed the Women's Advertising Association of the World ("Ad Women at Convention" 1916). One goal of that meeting was to secure a "women's advertising club in every important city, or a provision by which advertising women may be admitted to existing clubs on equal terms with advertising men" ("Make Plans" 1916).

Women's ad clubs provided support and opportunities to many women, yet the clubs could hardly be termed "inclusive." They did not practice overt racial exclusion, but reflected the systematic employment discrimination endemic in office work at the time.[3] Chambers (2008, 10) has noted that because advertisers did not recognize blacks as an important consumer group, "for most of the twentieth century both advertisements and the advertising industry remained 'lily-white.'"

Seeking to distinguish themselves as professional organizations rather than social clubs, many women's advertising clubs had a strategy of only allowing women who were already established in the advertising industry to become members. In this way, the clubs constructed and nurtured an "ideal" advertising woman: a white, middle-class professional, eager to share experiences and challenges with colleagues like herself, and educate other American women—white and middle class—in consumption habits. Although advertising club members were not overtly feminist in their undertakings or philosophies, Blair (1980, 1) argues that many clubwomen were "feminists under the skin." Women's advertising clubs did not explicitly advocate that all women have careers, nor were their members all active reformers. Instead, these women undertook the conscious creation of a community of professional advertising women to advance their agenda of supporting the careers of women working in the advertising industry. In the following section, I introduce the feminist lenses through which I developed my understanding of the clubs.

FEMINIST STANDPOINT AND INTERSECTIONAL ANALYSIS

Feminist standpoint theory argues that knowledge, politics, and science are socially situated. The theory's analytical power derives from taking note of the "gap between the understanding of the world available if one starts from the lives of people in the exploited, oppressed, and dominated groups and the understanding provided by dominant conceptual schemes" (Harding 1991, 147). Standpoint theory advocates that marginalized identities offer an advantage in both the production and analysis of social knowledge: "women's oppression can be turned to an epistemic advantage" (Code 1995, 180). According to feminist standpoint theory, the establishment of a standpoint is a political achievement. That is, "a standpoint is not merely a perspective that is occupied simply by dint of being a woman; . . . a standpoint is earned through the experience of collective political struggle" (Bowell n.d.).

Women's advertising clubs were founded by white, middle-class women who challenged gendered social norms that confined women to the domestic sphere and entered the public sphere of business and advertising. These women, conscious of their marginalized position within a profession dominated by middle-class, white men, found voice through the establishment of women's advertising clubs and national associations. The clubs struggled against gendered stereotypes; they were viewed by the industry to be more social than professional (Burt 1998), and often were tagged with disparaging monikers (e.g., "Jane Martin's Sewing Circle," an allusion to the first president of the AWNY). Feminist standpoint theory thus informs an understanding of the women's clubs as the collective voice of women marginalized by gendered social norms of the profession in which they worked and the society in which they lived at that historical moment. Club mandates, membership requirements, programs, and activities were linked to goals of professionalism, mutual support, education of both consumers and ad women, and community service.

Intersectionality "highlights the ways in which existing institutional structures are set up in such a way as to be inhospitable to the unique needs of women of color" (Tong and Botts 2014, 215). Club members were almost exclusively white, middle-class women. Although nothing in the club records indicates that women of color were prohibited from membership, at the time, advertisers saw little economic reason to pursue the black market. Chambers (2008, 10) argues, "Executives had little interest in upsetting the existing social fabric by hiring an African American for the intimate role of communicating with the white, middle-class women who were the targets of most advertising (or to work with the white women who crafted that advertising)." The absence of women of color on the clubs' membership rolls likely reflected broader social inequalities of the period, and controlling white advertiser perceptions of the limited economic influence of the black consumer market.

Because white ad women sought professional recognition from the industry and in the larger society, membership qualifications often were stringent. This worked to constrain the advertising work that counted as "professional" for women working in the industry. Although it was not uncommon for women to enter the advertising business "on a stenographic basis" (Dignam 1939, 18), those working in secretarial pools often were explicitly excluded from membership. Although these women often sought to advance beyond secretarial work, and no doubt would have benefitted from association with the women's clubs, they were denied access to the clubs' professional networks. In this way, clubs benefitted from the public recognition and experience of women who had "made it" in the advertising industry. The following section offers a brief introduction to the three women's clubs examined in this research—the AWNY,[4] the PCAW, and the WACC—in the chronological order by which they were established.

BRIEF HISTORY OF THREE WOMEN'S ADVERTISING CLUBS

This establishment and growth of clubs for advertising women near the turn of the century suggest that many women found advertising to be an "agreeable" career. Similarities in the clubs' mandates, membership policies, structure, activities, and publicity suggest that these advertising women shared concerns, encountered similar barriers to professional advancement, felt a sense of urgency to overcome those barriers, and adopted a vision of how to go about doing so.

At the time the AWNY was founded, none of the organizations of advertising men that had been established admitted women to membership or allowed women to attend meetings. J. George Frederick, publisher and advertising man, and his wife Christine Frederick, home economist and contributing household editor of the *Ladies Home Journal,* were instrumental in getting the League started. Although existing accounts of the club's founding vary slightly in detail, Christine Frederick (1939) recounted the story in "Historical Introduction" in *Advertising Careers for Women.* According to Frederick, Marie Bronson from Macy's department store asked J. George Frederick if she could attend a Men's Advertising League of New York meeting. She could not. He suggested instead that advertising women start a club of their own. The vestiges of long-held gender stereotypes are reflected in Bronson's response that because "women don't club together very well" she couldn't organize a club (Frederick 1939, xvi). However, she submitted the Fredericks could.

In March 1912, at the invitation of the Fredericks, forty women met at a fashionable New York restaurant to form the first professional organization of advertising women, the AWNY. The club's "statement of purpose" was to:

> improve the level of taste, ethics and knowledge throughout the communications industry by example, education and dissemination of information. [The club] strives to encourage cooperation among those engaged in various aspects of communications and, through education and dissemination of useful information, to inspire a keener interest in communication. Thus those engaged in various fields of communications are enabled to serve the public more effectively, as well as their own careers.[5]

The club undertook a wide variety of activities. Regular meetings featured prominent speakers not only from advertising and business, but also from law, entertainment, and politics. Other speakers represented "causes" in which the League was involved such as suffrage, child- and infant-labor laws, and repealing the 1916 Adamson Act's eight-hour workday. A publicity committee promoted League activities and member achievements in a monthly newsletter for members and in local newspapers. The League hosted social events—bridge parties, luncheons, and an annual formal ball—sometimes merely to bring members together, but in other instances as fundraisers for League activities. The "mutual fund" provided temporary financial assistance to members when needed and was maintained in part by loan repayment and also through the proceeds of social events (Kreshel 1991).

Theodore E. Ash started the PCAW four years later, in 1916. Ash was a member of the Poor Richard Club, a private club of advertising men. As general secretary of the Poor Richard Convention Committee, he established the PCAW in anticipation of the Advertising Association of the World convention to be held in Philadelphia that year. The club would "join with the New York League of Advertising Women in entertaining the women delegates to the convention who are active workers in the advertising business."[6] Advertising women had more than entertainment in mind. The club adopted a mandate to "secure for members the benefits of discussion and cooperation in matters of interest for the purpose of mutual advancement; and to emphasize the work that woman is doing and is specially qualified to do, in the field of sales promotion and in the many-sided business of advertising."[7]

The PCAW did not explicitly exclude clerical workers from membership, but the process of becoming a member suggests the club actively policed its boundaries to establish professional stature. Only a woman nominated by a member in good standing, seconded by another, and able to provide references that were "satisfactory" to the club was considered for membership.[8] In 1934, the PCAW had a membership of about 150 women whose work ranged from account executives to advertising artists, copywriters to space buyers, and direct mail to engraving and printing services across a variety of venues including manufacturing firms, department stores, public utilities, banks, insurance companies, retail stores, newspapers, and radio stations.

The PCAW published a members' newsletter and promoted club activities in other publications. They also hosted dinners and balls to raise money for the club in support of its involvement in various community outreach activities, such as sending underprivileged girls to camp and helping education efforts of veterans convalescing after returning from war.

The PCAW focused on providing educational opportunities for members as well as other young women considering advertising as a career. The club began providing advertising education to girls and women in 1926, offering scholarships for girls to attend the Charles Morris Price School of Advertising and Journalism, a professional "graduate" school for advertising and marketing majors who sought business careers as well as writers and journalists (Nickels 2012). In 1928, members of the PCAW started teaching their own classes, which ran from January to May, one evening a week for twenty weeks. Over the following six years, more than five hundred women enrolled in PCAW courses.

This successful foray into advertising education prompted the club to create a textbook that discussed the many careers available to women in advertising and ways to move into those careers. Written by club women for women, *Advertising Careers for Women* was published in 1939. It consisted of twenty-two lectures by experts in various fields, and "set forth the fields of opportunity to which advertising beckons women" (Clair and Dignam 1939, title page). Those opportunities included advertising agencies; retail advertising; promotional advertising; and advertising for cosmetics, food, home equipment, industrial companies, and insurance, among others.

In another educational effort, the PCAW celebrated the achievements of historically significant women by producing a radio series. *Famous Women of Yesteryear* was broadcast on Philadelphia WFIL, with the aim of "reminding men, as well as women, that Women—as Women—today and yesterday, are and were important in the scheme of things."[9] In the process of developing the series, and raising the public visibility of the club, members sharpened skills fundamental in advertising work: conducting research on women in Philadelphia, Pennsylvania, the United States, and the world,[10] writing scripts, and performing on air.

Farther west in Chicago, the WACC was established in 1918. WACC's constitution clearly outlined the duties of its members and the vision of the club: "to discuss and study advertising in all its phases, to encourage and promote the work of women in the advertising field, and to assist in the civic and national work where knowledge of publicity is of value."[11] Like the other two clubs examined here, the WACC produced a monthly newsletter for its members and promoted recognition of members' achievements.

Like the PCAW, the WACC had an explicit, exclusive membership policy, which stated that members had to be active advertising professionals. The minutes of the July 1, 1920, meeting provided the qualifications for club membership: "Any woman actively engaged in an executive capacity or in buying, selling or purchasing advertising, is eligible to active membership. This shall not be construed as admitting those engaged in purely clerical work."[12]

The WACC had an educational fund, a financial assistance fund much like AWNY's "mutual fund," and also undertook a range of activities supporting professional ad women as well as a variety of community outreach efforts to help expand business interests and generate publicity for the club. For example, in 1933, WACC members helped establish a business library for the Fort Sheridan Business Men's club, a study club founded to assist "splendid men who have come out of the war crippled or otherwise handicapped."[13] According to an article in *Associated Advertising* ("Give Library" 1920, 66): "With the seal of the Women's Advertising Club of Chicago in every volume more than 200 well-chosen books have been forwarded to the men in the collection of which every girl of the Chicago club has taken part."

In summary, these three advertising clubs provided opportunities for members to create communities in which they could voice their collective concerns and share their experiences in the male-dominated industry, develop greater proficiency in advertising, create awareness of emerging opportunities, enjoy a supportive environment, and gain professional stature in the industry. Membership was limited to women who already had attained some degree of success in advertising; participation of those women in turn suggested the professional legitimacy of the clubs within the industry, and enhanced public recognition. These women's advertising clubs reinforced a particular understanding of middle-class, white women as the standard of good taste and appropriate consumption practices. They promoted a consistent image of professional advertising women, articulated ideals guiding their role in the broader advertising community, and identified what constituted proper training and education in advertising.

One of the many professional advertising women who participated in the club community was Dorothy Dignam. In the next section, I introduce Dignam and then detail her engagement with each of the three women's advertising clubs discussed here.

DOROTHY DIGNAM: AD WOMAN AND CLUB MEMBER

Dorothy Dignam was born in 1896 in Cleveland, Ohio. Retrospectively, it seems she had been interested in writing since childhood, having written a children's column, "Cousin Dorothy," for her father's magazine, *Dignam's Magazine,* at age twelve. At eighteen, following her high school graduation, Dignam was on her way to becoming a successful writer, initially becoming a journalist. During a career that spanned more than four decades (1918–1962), Dignam wrote public relations articles for various community clubs and society columns for newspapers, worked as a copywriter in several advertising agencies, conducted marketing research abroad, and published numerous articles in *Printers' Ink* and other trade publications. She was an outspoken advocate for women, particularly for women in advertising, and authored numerous articles aimed at women readers explaining how to succeed in the business. She also wrote several articles targeting men in which she explained that ad women were crucial to creating successful advertising campaigns, and were therefore crucial to the advertising industry. She edited the PCAW text *Advertising Careers for Women* with Blanche Clair, and was recognized as one of the leading advertising copywriters in the late 1920s (Marchand 1985, 34). Her involvement with women's advertising clubs, which continued well into the 1950s, began in Chicago in 1920 and continued in Philadelphia in 1929 and then in New York in 1939.

In the following sections, I develop a chronological case study, highlighting Dignam's involvement in each of the clubs. This narrative illustrates Dignam's professional growth as a member of the clubs, and recognition the club achieved, in part as a result of the collective contributions of Dignam and others like her. It also suggests that women's participation began to alter the dimensions of an advertising industry, a "masculine stronghold" (Dignam 1939, 19).

WACC and Dignam's Chicago Career

Dignam began her career in newspapers, first at *The Women's Press* and then at the *Chicago Herald,* writing headlines for society-page pictures. She later wrote stories without being credited with a byline; then wrote for the city desk as Henrietta Hale, a stock pseudonym provided by the paper; and finally wrote the society-page columns "Have You Heard by Priscilla" and "Chicago Girl."[14]

Like many privileged, middle-class, white women of the era, Dignam was ambitious, had high aspirations, and was not satisfied doing the kind of work that was deemed *suitable* for a woman. The sudden sale of the *Herald* to Hearst in 1918 was something Dignam retrospectively identified as "a good fork" because it led her to a job in the advertising department of Contented Cow Milk. Her first advertising agency job was as a copywriter with that company's former advertising agency, Chicago's Vanderhoof and Sons, where she worked from 1919 to 1921.[15] She then joined another Chicago agency, the McJunkin Agency.[16] While at these Chicago agencies, Dignam worked on accounts for women's cosmetics, clothing, fabric, and sanitary products, as well as a range of home appliances. In addition to agency writing, she wrote pamphlets for the Commonwealth Edison Electric Shop about laborsaving devices, including electric washers and irons, ice cream makers, and other small electrical appliances such as blow dryers, curling irons, and facial vibrators.[17]

Dignam attended the organizational meeting of the WACC in 1918 as a guest of a friend, but was not eligible to become a member at the time because she was a journalist. Writing of that experience, she noted, "The initial meeting of the club was my first experience with a group of business women, all smarter than I was and on the make professionally."[18] She joined the WACC in 1920, when she had begun her work in advertising. Dignam's press and public relations experience, combined with her personal ambition and a flair for self-promotion, made her an ideal club member. She served on the club's board as historian and sometimes as acting secretary. An outgoing WACC president once described Dignam as "a master mind in a youthful body."[19]

Perhaps reflecting the growing interest in the home economics movement, Dignam took a one-year leave from her agency job in Chicago in 1928 and spent ten months "investigating the electrical appliance situation in Europe."[20] Traveling to London, Paris, Switzerland, and Germany, she was a "European correspondent" for several trade journals, sending international marketing news to American producers and advertisers. On her return to the states in 1929, she published several articles in *Printers' Ink* based on the trip offering insight into differences between Europe and the United States: "The British Like Cold Toast for Breakfast" (March 1930), and "We Stand Accused of Too Much Color Scheming" (December 1930). She frequently gave presentations to varied consumer, industry, trade, and professional groups. Dignam became a copywriter at N. W. Ayer and Son, on July 1, 1929, and moved to Philadelphia.

PCAW and Dignam's Philadelphia Career

Dignam joined the PCAW in 1929. There her interest in promoting advertising careers for women was nurtured and subsequently thrived. She immersed herself in club activities that educated women about the varied opportunities available to women in advertising. She routinely shared stories of successful advertising women as encouragement to those seeking to enter the field. By then a "successful advertising woman" herself, Dignam frequently lectured at the PCAW's advertising classes on topics ranging from "The Appeal" and "Style"[21] to "Women in Advertising Agencies."[22]

Dignam worked with Blanche Clair, another PCAW member, to develop the club's advertising education classes, which began in 1928. She later suggested the club produce a book about women's careers in advertising prepared by well-known women in the industry. Viewing the book as a possible "money-maker and prestige builder" for the club, the PCAW decided to move forward with the idea.

Dignam used the upcoming book as a promotional tool to market the club's education classes; pamphlets promised students that they would find the course "doubly interesting because [they] will be *living the making of a book*." And, there would be no need to take notes because the lectures would be published in book form and sent to every enrolled student.[23]

Dignam took the lead as an editor of the book. She recruited a number of nationally known advertising women, primarily from Philadelphia, to lecture in the PCAW advertising classes, and subsequently edited their lectures into chapters for a book that became *Advertising Careers for Women: Twenty-Two Lectures on Advertising Vocations Presented by the Philadelphia Club of Advertising Women, Setting Forth the Fields of Opportunity to Which Advertising Beckons Women* (Clair and Dignam). It was published in 1939 by Harper and Brothers.

As the title suggests, the PCAW book included twenty-two lectures presented by experts in various fields. Dignam's (1939) chapter, "Ideas and Copy," described the "agency copywriter at work" and included advice about conducting research and creating sales appeals. In part an introduction to work in advertising agencies, Dignam also used the chapter as a platform to spread what was to become her signature theme: Women can bring crucial knowledge and skills to the advertising industry and can find work in advertising and success in their careers. The advertising agency, she wrote, "is and probably always will be, a masculine stronghold" (1939, 19), but she suggested one of the requirements for a copywriter: "You must be a woman—if an agency wanted only a copywriter they'd hire a man! As a woman you must know other women and be interested in them" (1939, 24). Here then, was a clear articulation of the power of a woman's viewpoint, its value to the advertising industry, and its value to women seeking to become involved in the industry.

Dignam went on to emphasize the importance of knowing something about the "five main interests of American women," which she identified as food, fashion, children, home equipment, and special interests (among those interests: "her club, her garden, reading, sewing, gossiping, shopping, movies") (Dignam 1939, 24). It is clear that Dignam, like many of the women working in the field of advertising during that moment, viewed the consumer to be like her, white and middle class, "not in the position of the newly landed immigrant or the working-class shop girl, factory worker, or seamstress" (Sutton 2009, 3). Writing about the J. Walter Thompson company at the time, Sutton notes, "The women whose lives [were] reflected in the JWT ads [were] the very women who created the ads. . . . [The ads] reflect the experience of a minority while making appeals to an imagined majority" (Sutton 2009, 3).

Advertising Careers for Women was widely reviewed and well received. A September 1940 issue of *Printers' Ink* named it to a list of the recommended books for advertising novices. That list also included Claude Hopkins's *My Life in Advertising* (1927), which remains a classic in the field today.[24] Club archival material noted that the book was "highly recommended by the United States Department of Education, by the Journal of Marketing [*sic*] . . . and by other authorities. *Printers' Ink* includes it among the first ten of 50 books on advertising."[25]

The PCAW collected the royalties from the book, which was marketed to alumnae from Temple University advertising courses and the Wharton School of Business among others. Club records indicate that, by 1940, the book, which they claimed was the first textbook written exclusively for women, had earned the club "three figures" in revenue.

In addition to preparing, delivering, and publishing educational material for the PCAW, Dignam participated in many club activities promoting women's lives, accomplishments, and careers, one of which was the *Famous Women of Yesteryear* radio series emphasizing women's "importance in the scheme of things," mentioned earlier.[26] Dignam and PCAW members performed another radio play, *Let's Scrap It,* ten times during the first three months of 1936.[27] *Let's Scrap It* was written by Anna Steese Richardson, a member of AWNY as a response to the rise of the consumer movement.

Dignam also was instrumental in developing a Consumers' Clinic for the "examination and diagnosis of 'consumer troubles.'"[28] The clinics were likely a response to activist criticism of advertising (Westkaemper 2017). In announcing the clinics in 1937, Dignam indicated that the "study-course" was a response to members' requests for "up-to-date information on the co-operative movement . . . on consumer education . . . and on . . . organizations such as the important, nation-wide Consumers' Relations Council." Equally important, the clinic would then "restate, simply and clearly, the place of Advertising in our changing economic pattern."[29] Dignam transferred from Philadelphia to the New York Ayer and Son offices in 1939, but remained a member of PCAW even after joining the AWNY. She remained a member of the PCAW and continued to participate in PCAW's advertising courses.[30]

AWNY and Dignam's New York Career

During her time at AWNY, Dignam, having been in the advertising business for more than fifteen years, came into her own as a spokesperson for women and the value of their skills, and as a fierce promoter of women's careers. Dignam used speaking engagements and publishing efforts to support and encourage women like her to succeed in advertising. She advocated for women's pursuit of careers, especially in advertising, routinely focusing on two themes: the celebration of women's accomplishments and the importance of breaking into male strongholds.

For example, in "She's a Stylist in Paris," an article published in *The Chicago Girl* in 1930, Dignam celebrated Constance Miller's career with a brief biography.[31] Miller had become a freelance writer in Britain in the 1920s, then worked for a trade journal, *Advertising World,* in London, and finally wrote a book about how to write advertising. She then became a "style adviser to the Curtis Publishing Company" stationed in France. Dignam wrote that Miller's "steady ascent . . . points [to] a comforting moral," concluding, "Our first job or even our present one needn't foreclose on our future." Dignam's own biography was instructive for women with career ambitions.

In a 1933 lecture, "Up the Ladder We Must Go"[32] at the Women's Advertising Club of Providence,[33] Dignam argued that although the nation was in the depths of the Great Depression, "most folks don't realize that women are not usurping men's jobs. . . . [T]hey're largely creating new ones for themselves." She went on to talk about women entrepreneurs starting their own businesses, taking executive positions in companies, and working in sales and marketing. Then too, she suggested, as she would continue to do throughout her career, that men controlled advertising agencies. Yet because a woman was useful as "an interpreter of women and her buying ways," women aspiring to be successful advertising professionals should "keep a stiff upper lip, with some lipstick on it."[34]

Writing in a similar vein, in a 1939 *Printers' Ink* article, "Some Women Have Made Good in Advertising But as for Others . . .," Dignam emphasized that, although the number of women in the advertising industry had increased, they were not yet professionally recognized.[35] She noted the absence of women's stories in advertising publications such as *Printers' Ink: Fifty Years 1888–1938* (1938) and went on to recount women's careers in advertising and the start of the AWNY. She concluded by asking that young women be given apprenticeships. In a 1943 *Printers' Ink* article,[36] Dignam summarized the results of a survey of employment of women in advertising, and concluded by saying that women's motto for "the changing times" should be "never be afraid of any job."

In a 1948 career guide, *How to Be a Successful Advertising Woman* (McBride 1948), Dignam's (1948, 203) chapter, "Women's Place in

Advertising," begins by noting, "Women have been making their impression on this [advertising] business for some eighty years." Still, she notes that "The first truth about the advertising business is this: it is still highly masculine" (Dignam 1948, 203). Women are "outnumbered by men at least five to one. Not a single big, nationally known advertising agency has a woman president and only a handful have women vice-presidents" (204). She points out that "every girl takes her ultimate orders or receives her final pay from a man" (204). Still, she encourages women to make incursions into the world of advertising, because there are more places for women to look for advertising work, writing, "Women are coming into the advertising of home building supplies, heating systems, flooring, roofing and insulating materials, glass brick, tile, and other construction products, and all the new mechanical marvels for house and garage, even including the new automobile" (213). Dignam (1948, 204) continues, "So what chance do women really have for an advertising career, especially now with all the men back and rightfully getting first choice at the jobs?" Dignam's overarching message was positive and encouraging as well as rhetorically nuanced. She offered assurance that jobs were available for women, and they are not jobs being taken from men returning from World War II. "There are more places to *look* for jobs," she noted. Women had "penetrated production work and were staying with it; that they were undaunted in art departments, that they were giving the red and green lights in advertising agency traffic departments, and that they had even moved into press-agentry for the movies, into labor relations for industry, and into billposting for an outdoor advertising company" (204).

Dignam's belief that women had a place in advertising, indeed, that women were critical to the industry's well-being, was unequivocal. She recounted success stories to encourage more success stories. Her work as a club historian, first for the PCAW and later, beginning in the early 1940s, for AWNY, reflected her belief that that women's efforts should be well documented and preserved. In 1951, as AWNY prepared for its fortieth anniversary, Dignam consented to prepare a biography of the "League of Advertising Women" (as the AWNY club was called in its early days). Identifying herself as a "'predestined' historical researcher," she prepared a digest of all written material that had accumulated in files since the organization began. In a letter to Mabel Stringer, Board Advisor, in 1951, Dignam outlined her approach to creating the "running history" of all the club's significant activities. She wrote, "I am including color, amusing incidents, trends, and all things that make good reading—not just dates and places." She noted there were discrepancies and contradictions that "must be cleared up to the best of our ability and then the final statement must stand."[37] It is largely through Dignam's work as club historian that I have been able to write this narrative.

A WOMAN'S PLACE

In the early years of the twentieth century, the middle-class woman was recognized as the primary consumer, but who was she? In a chapter in *Masters of Advertising Copy,* Christine Frederick (1924 225, 227), a home economist, defined the "so-called average woman" this way: "She invariably is the result of a fantastic, often distorted picture developed in the mind of the individual who conceives her. The picture is *only* in his mind, and is the result of whatever he can conjure up mentally." As white middle-class women increasingly ventured beyond the confines of home, women seeking work in advertising, some of them convinced advertising men that the advertising industry needed women because only women knew what women wanted and needed. Advertising welcomed women far earlier and in greater numbers than other businesses.

Yet, as feminist historian Joan Wallach Scott (1999, 178) reminds us, acceptance is more than numbers. She suggests more important questions: "[H]ow are those who cross the threshold received? If they belong to a group different from the one already 'inside' what are the terms of their incorporation? How do the new arrivals understand the place they have entered? What are the terms of identity they establish?"

In this historical account, I examined the relationship between advertising women and the advertising clubs they created in the early years of the twentieth century, while attempting to account for standpoint and intersectional positionalities. White middle-class advertising women, keenly aware of their marginalized status within the advertising field, established women's advertising clubs as part of a broader struggle of advertising women to achieve professional recognition, to raise a collective voice, to say, "We are a vital part of the advertising industry." I argue that the relationship was a strategic and mutually beneficial one.

Advertising women organized to educate other women on the opportunities available to them in advertising and to encourage more women to enter the business. Club activities, such as advertising classes, provided a platform from which advertising women could speak with authority about their profession. Women's advertising clubs served as communities that provided the institutional support needed to develop a professional consciousness and a private ethic as white, middle-class advertising women, and to realize their own value. Those efforts were advertising white, middle-class women's initial steps toward negotiating the boundaries of the advertising industry.

Then, too, advertising clubs provided opportunities for women like Dorothy Dignam to develop public careers. Dignam sharpened her knowledge of professional practices and took advantage of opportunities in education, publishing, and public speaking. In short, membership in advertising clubs helped Dignam develop her voice, expertise, recognition in the profession, and visibility in the public realm. She created a successful career for herself and encouraged other women aspiring to join the industry. Her success in achieving both these goals served to elevate the stature of white women within the still-white-male-dominated industry. At the same time, Dignam's reputation as a talented and successful professional helped to build and reinforce the stature of the white women's advertising clubs and solidify white women's place in advertising as well as the professional stature the industry sought to attain.

Although it is easy to celebrate the virtues of these clubs, I also recognize their imperfections. Advertising women occupied a paradoxical situation. Recognizing that their value to the profession was rooted in essentialist notions, advertising women capitalized on their "domestic nature," and in writing ads, perpetuated the very stereotypes they sought to escape. At the same time, they worked to distinguish themselves from the "average woman" whose viewpoint they theoretically shared. For example, when Jane J. Martin, president of AWNY, attended the St. Louis meeting of the Associated Ad Clubs of the World, she refused to register on a woman's registration card. When asked why, she noted, "We come here to attend the convention as the equals of the men. Those cards were intended for the wives of the men and for social purposes and not for women who are doing the real work of advertising."[38] Similarly, Scanlon (1995, 190) notes that the advertising women "often praised the 'woman at home,' but they also grew frustrated with her." Scanlon concludes, "These advertising women wrote effective advertisements for that consumer, but they attempted also to broaden the definition of woman consumer and citizen to include themselves."

Finally, reflecting the advertising industry's lack of interest in the black consumer market, people of color were largely absent from the advertising workplace and hence, from women's advertising clubs. Narrow definitions of "professional advertising work" excluded working-class women, and women working in clerical and secretarial positions in advertising even as they strengthened women's sense of a professional identity as an advertising woman. Club members, primarily white and middle class, reinforced mainstream, white, middle-class notions in advertising representations, and in the industry. The voices and experiences of women of color and working-class women remain largely silent.[39]

NOTES

1. I thank the University of Saskatchewan for awarding me a President's Social Science Humanities Research Council grant, which provided funding for archival

research at Radcliffe Harvard, University of Illinois at Chicago, and Duke University. I also received a travel grant from Schlesinger Library at Radcliffe Harvard for travel funding.

2. Advertising Women of New York additional records, 1912–1983: "Women's Clubs in AFA." 86-M216, Carton 2. Schlesinger Library, Radcliffe Institute, Harvard University.

3. See Sharon Hartman Strom's *Beyond the Typewriter: Gender, Class, and the Origins of Modern American Office Work, 1900–1930* (Urbana: University of Illinois Press, 1992), especially Chapter 6 for a discussion of race in office work culture.

4. Established as the League of Advertising Women of New York, the club became the Advertising Women of New York (AWNY) in 1934. Suggesting that the organization was broadening its scope and representing women who lead at every level in marketing and media, AWNY became She Runs It in 2016.

5. Advertising Women of New York additional records, 1912–1983: "Statement of Purpose." 87-M31, Carton 1. Schlesinger Library, Radcliffe Institute, Harvard University.

6. Article (no publication identified) dated 1916. Dorothy Dignam papers 1907–1962: Dorothy Dignam's scrapbook 2 (May 1916–March 1918). Wisconsin Historical Society.

7. Philadelphia Club of Advertising Women Records, 1916–1984: Special Collections Department, Pamphlet, "Philadelphia Club of Advertising Women: Founded 1916," Box 11, Folder 63. Bryn Mawr College.

8. Ibid.

9. Philadelphia Club of Advertising Women Records, 1916–1984, Box 1, Folder 53. Bryn Mawr College.

10. Philadelphia Club of Advertising Women Records, 1916–1984: "Adland News" Pamphlets, Box 1, Folder 33. Bryn Mawr College.

11. Women's Advertising Club of Chicago papers: "Meetings 1920," Box 7, Folder 63. Richard J. Daly Library, Special Collections, University of Illinois at Chicago.

12. Women's Advertising Club of Chicago papers: "Meetings 1920," Box 7, Folder 63. Richard J. Daly Library, Special Collections, University of Illinois at Chicago.

13. Women's Advertising Club of Chicago papers: "Meetings," 1920, Box 7, Folder 63. Richard J. Daly Library, Special Collections, University of Illinois at Chicago.

14. Dorothy Dignam papers 1907–1962: Dorothy Dignam's scrapbook. Wisconsin Historical Society.

15. Dorothy Dignam papers 1907–1962: Dorothy Dignam's scrapbook. Wisconsin Historical Society.

16. Women's Advertising Club of Chicago papers: "Meetings 1920," Box 7, Folder 63. Richard J. Daly Library, Special Collections, University of Chicago at Illinois.

17. Dorothy Dignam papers 1896–1960: "Commonwealth Edison Electric Shop Pamphlet," A-114, Box 3, Folder 20. Schlesinger Library, Radcliffe Institute, Harvard University.

18. Dorothy Dignam papers 1907–1962: "Think Backs by Dorothy Dignam." Wisconsin Historical Society.

19. Women's Advertising Club of Chicago papers: Box 7, Folder 63. Richard J. Daly Library, Special Collections, University of Illinois at Chicago.

20. Dorothy Dignam papers, 1907–1962: Dorothy Dignam's scrapbook. Wisconsin Historical Society.

21. Philadelphia Club of Advertising Women Records, 1916–1984: Box 1, Folder 33. Bryn Mawr College.

22. Philadelphia Club of Advertising Women Records, 1916–1984: Box 2, Folder 15. Bryn Mawr College.

23. Philadelphia Club of Advertising Women Records, 1916–1984: Box 5, Folder 53. Bryn Mawr College.

24. Philadelphia Club of Advertising Women Records, 1916–1984: Box 1, Folder 33. Bryn Mawr College.

25. Philadelphia Club of Advertising Women Records, 1916–1984: Box 12, Folder 4. Bryn Mawr College.

26. Philadelphia Club of Advertising Women Records, 1916–1984: Box 2, Folder 15. Bryn Mawr College.

27. See Inger Stole's *Advertising on Trial: Consumer Activism and Corporate Public Relations in the 1930s* (Urbana: University of Illinois Press, 2006), especially Chapter 2 for a discussion of the rise of the consumer movement.

28. "Women of Philadelphia Plan Consumer Clinics," n.d., publication unidentified, Dorothy Dignam Papers, 1907–1962: Dorothy Dignam's scrapbook. Wisconsin Historical Society.

29. Philadelphia Club of Advertising Women Records, 1916–1984: Box 2, Folder 15. Bryn Mawr College.

30. Philadelphia Club of Advertising Women Records, 1916–1984, Box 1, Folder 67. Bryn Mawr College.

31. Dorothy Dignam papers, 1896–1988: A-114, Box 3, Folder 23. Schlesinger Library, Radcliffe Institute, Harvard University.

32. Dorothy Dignam papers, 1896–1960: "Up the Ladder We Must Go." A-114, Box 3, Folder 19. Schlesinger Library, Radcliffe Institute, Harvard University.

33. Dorothy Dignam papers, 1907–1962: "The Development of a Copywriter." Box 5. Wisconsin Historical Society.

34. Dorothy Dignam papers, 1896–1988: "Up the Ladder We Must Go" (speech transcript), 1933. Box 3, Folder 19. Schlesinger Library, Radcliffe Institute, Harvard University.

35. Dorothy Dignam papers, 1896–1988: A-114, Box 3, Folder 18. Schlesinger Library, Radcliffe Institute, Harvard University.

36. Dorothy Dignam papers, 1896–1988: A-114, Box 3, Folder 18. Schlesinger Library, Radcliffe Institute, Harvard University.

37. Dorothy Dignam papers, 1907–1962: Box 1, Folder 1, "Correspondence, 1926–1955." Wisconsin Historical Society.

38. Dorothy Dignam papers, 1907–1962: Dorothy Dignam's scrapbook 2. Wisconsin Historical Society.

39. As this chapter was going to press, I became aware of a recent book that gives voice to African-American women's experiences in advertising: Jody Foster Davis,

Pioneering African-American Women in the Advertising Business: Biographies of MAD Black WOMEN (New York: Routledge, 2016).

REFERENCES

"Ad Women at the Convention." 1916. *Printers' Ink.* 17 June. In Dorothy Dignam Papers 1907–1962: Dorothy Dignam's scrapbook 2, May 1916–March 1918. Wisconsin Historical Society.

Advertising Women of New York records, 1912–1970: Newspaper clippings, Box 29, Folder 4. Schlesinger Library, Radcliffe Institute, Harvard University.

Blair, Karen. 1980. *Clubwoman as Feminist: True Womanhood Redefined, 1868–1914.* New York: Holmes and Meier.

Bledstein, Burton. 1978. *The Culture of Professionalism: The Middle Class and the Development of Higher Education in America.* New York: Norton.

Bowell, Tracy. n.d. "Feminist Standpoint Theory," *Internet Encyclopedia of Philosophy.* http://www.iep.utm.edu/fem-stan/

Burt, Elizabeth. 1998. "Challenges in Doing Women's History." *Clio: Among the Media* 31 (1): 17–19.

Code, Lorraine. 1995. *Rhetorical Spaces: Essays on Gendered Locations.* New York: Routledge.

Chambers, Jason. 2008. *Madison Avenue and the Color Line: African Americans in the Advertising Industry.* Philadelphia: University of Pennsylvania Press.

Claire, Blanche, and Dorothy Dignam, eds. 1939. *Advertising Careers for Women.* New York: Harper and Brothers.

Cramer, Janet M. 1998. "Woman as Citizen: Race, Class, and the Discourse of Women's Citizenship, 1894–1909." *Journalism and Mass Communication Monographs* 165: 1–39.

Cummings, Bart. 1984. *The Benevolent Dictators: Interviews with Advertising Greats.* Chicago: Crain Books.

Della Femina, Jerry. 1970. *From Those Wonderful Folks Who Gave You Pearl Harbour: Front Line Dispatches from the Advertising War.* New York: Simon & Schuster.

Dickenson, Jackie. 2016. *Australian Women in Advertising in the Twentieth Century.* Houndmills, Basinstoke, UK: Palgrave Macmillan.

Dignam, Dorothy. 1939, "Ideas and Copy." In *Advertising Careers for Women,* edited by Blanche Clair and Dorothy Dignam, 17–33. New York: Harper and Brothers.

Dignam, Dorothy. 1948. "Women's Place in Advertising." In *How to Be a Successful Advertising Woman,* edited by Mary Margaret McBride, 203–223. New York: McGraw Hill.

Ewen, Stuart. 1976. *Captains of Consciousness: Advertising and the Social Roots of the Consumer Culture.* New York: McGraw Hill.

Frederick, Christine. 1924. "Advertising Copy and the So-Called 'Average Woman.'" In *Masters of Advertising Copy,* edited by George Frederick, 225–246. New York: Garland.

Frederick, Christine. 1939. "Historical Introduction." In *Advertising Careers for Women,* edited by Blanche Clair and Dorothy Dignam, xiii–xi. New York: Harper and Brothers.

Fox, Stephen. 1984. *The Mirror Makers: A History of American Advertising and Its Creators*. Urbana: University of Illinois Press.

Gere, Anne Ruggles. 1997. *Intimate Practices: Literacy and Culture Work in U.S. Women's Clubs, 1880–1920.* Urbana: University of Illinois Press.

"Give Library to Fort Sheridan Men." 1920. *Associated Advertising,* June: 66.

Goldstein, Carolyn M. 2012. *Creating Consumers: Home Economists in Twentieth-Century America.* Chapel Hill: The University of North Carolina Press.

Hamburger, Estelle. 1939. *It's a Woman's Business*. New York: Vanguard.

Harding, Sandra. 1993. "Reinventing Ourselves as Other: More New Agents of History and Knowledge." In *American Feminist Thought at Century's End: A Reader,* edited by Linda S. Kaufman, 140–164. Cambridge: Blackwell.

Hopkins, Claude. 1927. *My Life in Advertising.* New York: Harper.

Kelly-Gadol, Joan. 1987. "The Social Relation of the Sexes: Methodological Implications of Women's History." In *Feminism and Methodology,* edited by Sandra Harding, 15–28. Bloomington: University of Indiana Press.

Kreshel, Peggy J. 1991. "Integrating Women's Experiences into the History of Advertising: The League of Advertising Women of New York." Paper presented at Fifth Conference on Historical Research in Marketing and Marketing Thought, East Lansing, Michigan.

Kwolek-Folland, Angel. 1998. *Incorporating Women: A History of Women and Business in the United States.* New York: Palgrave.

Lears, Jackson. 1994. *Fables of Abundance: A Cultural History of Advertising in America*. New York: Basic.

Lyon, Marguerite. 1943. *And So to Bedlam: A Worm's Eye View of Advertising*. New York: Cornwall.

Maas, Jane. 1986. *Adventures of an Advertising Woman.* New York: St. Martin's.

Maas, Jane. 2012. *Mad Women: The Other Side of Life on Madison Avenue in the '60s and Beyond.* New York: St. Martin's.

"Make Plans to Form Women's Clubs." 1916. Publication unknown. Dorothy Dignam Papers 1907–1962: Dorothy Dignam's scrapbook 2. Wisconsin Historical Society.

Marchand, Roland. 1985. *Advertising the American Dream: Making Way for Modernity 1920–1940.* Berkeley: University of California Press.

McBride, Mary. 1948. *How to Be a Successful Advertising Woman.* New York: McGraw-Hill.

Nickels, Thom. 2012. "The Last Word, Philly's Charles Morris Price School and the Poor Richard Club." *From the Field: Thom Nickels* (blog), February 5. http://thomnickels.blogspot.com/2012/02/last-word-phillys-charles-morris-price.html.

Ogilvy, David. 1963. *Confessions of an Advertising Man.* New York: Athenuem.

Ogilvy, David. 1978. *Blood, Brains and Beer: The Autobiography of David Ogilvy.* New York: Athenuem.

Polykoff, Shirley. 1975. *Does She or Doesn't She? And How She Did it!* Garden City, NY: Doubleday.

Presbrey, Frank. 1929. *The History and Development of Advertising.* Garden City, NY: Doubleday, Doran and Company, Inc.

Printers' Ink: Fifty Years 1888–1938. New York: Garland.

Roche, Bruce. 1989. "The Advertising Club Movement in the United States, 1890–1970." Paper [research in progress] presented at the American Journalism Historians Convention, Atlanta, Georgia.

Rutherford, Janice Williams. 2003. *Selling Mrs. Consumer: Christine Frederick and the Rise of Household Efficiency.* Athens: The University of Georgia Press.

Scanlon, Jennifer. 1995. *Inarticulate Longings: The Ladies' Home Journal, Gender, and the Promises of Consumer Culture.* New York: Routledge.

Scanlon, Jennifer. 2013. "'A Dozen Ideas to the Minute': Advertising Women, Advertising to Women." *Journal of Historical Research in Marketing* 5 (3): 273–290.

Schneider, Dorothy, and Carl J. Schneider. 1993. *American Women in the Progressive Era, 1900–1920.* New York: Facts on File.

Schultze, Quentin. 1978. "Advertising, Science, and Professionalism 1885–1917." Ph.D. diss., University of Illinois.

Scott, Joan Wallach. 1999. "American Women Historians, 1884–1984." In *Gender and the Politics of History,* edited by Joan Wallach Scott, 178–198. New York: Columbia University Press.

Sharer, Wendy. 2004. *Vote and Voice: Women's Organizations and Political Literacy, 1915–1920.* Carbondale: Southern Illinois University Press, 2004.

Sivulka, Juliann. 2009. *Ad Women: How They Impact What We Need, Want, and Buy.* Amherst, NY: Prometheus Books.

Sutton, Denise. 2009. *Globalizing Ideal Beauty: Women, Advertising, and the Power of Marketing.* New York: Palgrave McMillan.

Stole, Inger. 2006. *Advertising on Trial: Consumer Activism and Corporate Public Relations in the 1930s.* Urbana: University of Illinois Press.

Tong, Rosemarie, and Tina Fernandes Botts. 2014. "Women of Color Feminisms." In *Feminist Thought: A More Comprehensive Introduction,* 4th ed., edited by Rosemary Tong, 211–254. Boulder: Westview.

Wells Lawrence, Mary. 2002. *A Big Life (in Advertising).* New York: Simon & Schuster.

Westkaemper, Emily. 2017. *Selling Women's History: Packaging Feminism in Twentieth-Century American Popular Culture.* New Brunswick, NJ: Rutgers University Press.

Woodward, Helen. 1926. *Through Many Windows.* New York: Harper and Brothers.

Chapter 15

Closing Arguments

A Feminist Education for Advertising Students

Kim Golombisky

When I began my advertising career in 1982, I was unprepared for the sexism I encountered. I was asked to "man" the front desk and phones while the receptionist went to lunch because "obviously" none of the men would do it. I was accused of feminine deceit because I had the impudence to become pregnant. I wasn't the one promoted because the other *guy* had a family to support. I was the one chosen for the layoff because I wasn't "ladylike enough." I was advised that I needed "to learn how to bark at clients like a man." I was assigned accounts that "needed a woman's touch," and I had to give up accounts that required "the firm hand of a man." It was all illegal even then, but how was I to know, and even if I did, how was I empowered to act on my own behalf? My advertising education gave me not a hint of probable discrimination, let alone tools to deal with it. I think I was angrier that no one had given me a heads-up than at the gendered double standards I kept running up against.

In putting together the original chapters for this volume, Peggy Kreshel and I, and the contributing scholars, have been interested in exploring relationships between advertising practices and feminist thought. Our focus on the advertising industry, however, leaves the subject of advertising content unexamined. We remedy that lapse in our next volume (Golombisky and Kreshel forthcoming). Nor does the present project touch on advertising education, except for Kimberly Voss's glimpse into the origins of advertising education via home economics and journalism (Chapter 13). To conclude our work here, then, I wax theoretical to offer a feminist advertising educator's thinking about an introductory feminist curriculum for advertising students. This introduction includes reflecting on assumptions about gender, practicing intersectional analysis, unpacking waves of women's movement, and discerning "brands" of feminisms. Such an introduction then provides students with some tools for interpreting advertising issues they face in terms of advertising history and education, advertising professional concerns, advertisers and their brands, advertising technologies and channels, advertising messages and representation, advertising audiences and consumers, and advertising political economy.

DEFINING GENDER

To begin at the beginning, then, is to unpack gender. Women's movement and feminist advocacy by definition are concerned with the status of women. Interest in a group of people defined by gender necessitates some understanding of gender as the mechanism by which women become women, for example, as students in the classroom, target demographics, or advertising employees. My University of South Florida (USF) colleague Sara Crawley argues, with all due respect to the trans+ community, "We are all trans" (Obeid and Crawley 2015). Dr. Crawley means that gender is more fluid than any simple woman–man dichotomy. Given that all human identities are fluid, we are all always transitioning into our next selves. So, as I argue, it is more productive to think about identity, including gender, as an embodied (*we cannot flee our bodies*) accomplishment (*success is not guaranteed despite years of practice*) always in the process of becoming through language (*yes, the self and the self's body are mediated by language*) and social interaction (*think uber peer pressure even when no one is looking*). Dr. Crawley says that because we are always accountable to our social context, we are gender *re*actors, rather than gender actors. To her point, I also argue that we would be better off thinking about our identities as identifications (*both the ones we are assigned and the ones we sign up for*), which is to say that identity is something we *do,* instead of what we *are* or what we *have*.

Most communication scholars understand gender as a social construction in that what it means to embody and practice womanhood or manhood depends on the social milieux, as opposed to what feminists critique as essentialist beliefs in gender as predetermined by some essence from nature or anatomy. Anne Fausto-Sterling (2012) writes a comprehensive contemporary explanation of the complexities of the social-biological matrix of sex/gender, which should dissuade us from any naïve expectation that gender can be pinned to any one variable, either cultural or physiological. In the present volume, however, none of the contributors explicitly defines gender, which seems to suggest they assume an *a priori* category called "woman."

Nonetheless, some contributors do refer to the social construction of gender obliquely. For instance, Leandra Hernández (Chapter 11) as well as Jacque Lambiase, Carolyn Bronstein, and Catherine Coleman (Chapter 2) write that the advertising industry socially constructs gender norms by holding up idealized versions of white womanhood dependent on youth, ableism, and misogynist heterosexism, to suggest what is "normal" for all women. In that way, the industry produces gender "as-ifness" in hailing a group of people as so-called *female* consumers, decision-makers, or target markets, and so on. Gender as-ifness refers to the ways we act *as if* binary heteronormative gender were not just real but important. Thus, the industry quite literally constructs "women" as a social category, as well as who is included in and excluded from that category.

Kasey Windels (Chapter 7) takes a different although not incompatible tack toward gender; her analysis depends on a discursive model: Gender is a symbolic production dependent on human communication systems and language. Her participant ad practitioners revealed their assumptions about racialized heteronormative gender in how they talked about women and men. It is this *languaging* of gender that shapes its material expression—gender as-ifness. What we say about gender—the poststructuralist's speech act, as it were—is how we make it so. Dr. Windels's participant practitioners didn't recognize the potentially dangerous double standard they endorsed that applauds black women who defy restrictive traditional gender norms for women but then encourages white men to reassert their traditional gendered power as men. What happens when rebellious black women and intractable white men collide?

Accommodating both the social constructionist's symbolic social interaction and the poststructuralist's symbolic order, gender understood as performative affords a slightly more elastic view of gender by accounting for individual embodiment and agency, however mightily constrained by social taboo, discourse, and, yes, perhaps, even biology and physiology. Performative understandings of gender both emerged independently in communication and preceded Judith Butler (1990, 1993a, 2004). I give communication feminist Lana Rakow (1986) credit for arguing that gender is a verb before Candace West and Don Zimmerman's (1987) famous essay, "Doing Gender." Performative gender, then, is not about parody, faking it, or theatrical or flamboyant pretense. Rather, performative gender is about ritually *making* it every day, all day long, all our lives as embodied subjects accountable to social context and constrained by symbolic order, which in the United States has required everyone to align with one or the other of two categories, woman or man. I do credit Dr. Butler (1990) with pointing out what feminists and queer theorists now view as obvious, which is that there is no "real" gender to which we aspire or subscribe; instead, gender enactments are citations of nonexistent originals. In that sense, then, we are all in drag, in the sense of Joan Riviere's (1929) masquerade.[1] There is no single independent variable called "sex" or "gender" that produces gendered individuals; instead gender as-ifness and gender enactments produce our understanding of gender. Subscribing to James Carey's (1992) ritual model of communication, I prefer gender performativity because it accommodates peoples' bodies and individuality, ontologically known, however obliged to language, symbolic order, social relations, historical genealogy, and natural sciences.

Because advertising hails people, in Louis Althusser's (1972) sense of interpellation, as *gendered* audiences, markets, consumers, and workers, unpacking our assumptions about gender does matter. As Jean Grow notes in Chapter 9, the boy's club of the creative department presents women with a gender double-bind: Competent women are not creative, and competent creatives are not women, to paraphrase Kathleen Hall Jamieson (1995). Beyond women and men, we also actively gender things and ideas, too, such as the pink aisle for children's toys and the form of creativity to which we in advertising give deference to the exclusion of all other possible ways of defining, measuring, and doing creativity, and, therefore, being creative. For example, Dr. Grow and Dr. Windels both find that, among ad professionals, humor is regarded as both the purview of men and a requirement for working as a creative. Thus, we *do* gender—we practice it—and we wield gender as a verb. We ritually (as in habitually) perform and enforce (as in inhabit and inhibit) gender. Examining gender also reveals the ways we use binary gender to prescribe asymmetrical differences between women and men such that men and things that are said to be manly and masculine accrue more status, power, and privilege than women and things that are said to be womanly and feminine. We blame women for their inferior status but refuse to recognize the ways that sexism and—let us call it what it is—misogyny are institutionalized and systemic in the creative department, to pluck admittedly low-hanging fruit.

Performative gender is also operationally empirical. We in the social sciences needn't get bogged down in unfalsifiables, such as what goes on inside our heads, lower abdomens, genes, or hormones. And once we understand that we are constantly inventing gender then we also might be able to pry apart the binary expectation, too. We have an unfortunate habit of turning relative difference into ranked opposites, like plusses and minuses, or ones and zeros. But gender is not necessarily binary, despite a history of trying to enforce gender performances as strictly one thing or another. We, in the United States, have had a low tolerance for ambiguity and ambidexterity when it comes to gender identity and gender expression, which may or may not align with each other—or our sexuality, for that matter—not to mention either–or dualisms. As my USF colleague David Rubin (2017) demonstrates, the very existence, not to mention range, of anomalous categories that today fall under the umbrella term *intersex* disproves strictly binary sex and gender.

THE PARADOXES OF GENDER AND IDENTITY POLITICS

Three additional points about gender are worth considering: first, the paradox of gender and all identity politics for feminists; second, intersectionality and the impossibility of making claims about all women without always excluding some women; and third, the distinction between difference and equality advocacy. First, as to the paradox of gender for feminists, because of pervasive unacknowledged and unrepentant sexism, feminists address the status of women as a category. The paradox arises when, in order to be women's advocates, feminists can't help but trade in the binary gender system they critique (Golombisky 2006a, 2012b, 2015, 2017). Women circumscribed as a "natural" group, such as women's media, is an invention. The same is true of all segmentation strategies.

In Chapter 5, Joanna Jenkins quotes Nielsen audience research (2014) commodifying African-American women as a business opportunity, like a natural resource just waiting to be developed by advertisers. At the same time, the Nielsen Report (2014) reduces this vast, complex, and anything-but-uniform group of racialized women to a singular undifferentiated "her," as if all black women in the United States were equivalent. Yet advertisers belie their interest in all black women by addressing only affluent black women, and even then only rarely and often with the most egregious stereotypes. Meanwhile, we do know for a scientific fact that there is only one race of humans. But to suggest that race is merely a social construction irresponsibly ignores the ways that the social construction of a specifically African-American racialized gender has continued to produce unimaginable material horrors that shape the history and contemporary experiences of people circumscribed by a *social* category.

Similarly, Jillian Báez in Chapter 10 describes the construction of the so-called Hispanic market in the late twentieth century, combining vastly different nationalities, ethnicities, and indigenous languages, on the basis of Spanish, the language of the colonizer. Dr. Báez also cites the Nielsen Report (2013), this time encouraging advertisers to target "U.S. Hispanic women, also known as Latinas," for their influence in the marketplace, again often based on offensive stereotypes. Like all the contributors in this volume, Dr. Jenkins and Dr. Báez can't help but participate in the "man-made" categories they wish to undo, categories that reduce people to expectations about race, gender, and class, to name just three identifications.

This paradox of engaging labels to demonstrate their harms and their privileges—not to mention profit potentials—brings up another point about the tension between theory and grassroots identity politics. The theorists—feminist, critical race, queer, trans+, and disability, for example—work to deconstruct the power of names. But "real-world" grassroots identity politics appropriate and recuperate the power of names to advance the movement, the struggle, the cause aiming for social reform. For example, the *raison d'être* of queer theory, emerging out of sexualities studies, is to denaturalize the limits of all names and categories, as in making queer our commonsense beliefs about so-called normal sexuality, gender, and more. However, the 1986 "Silence = Death" poster illustrates the way social recognition based on even problematic identifications can be a matter of life and death. The iconic "Silence = Death" poster—reverse type positioned below a pink triangle on a black background—was, by design, guerrilla advertising, a tactic of last resort for desperate people (Finkelstein 2013). By the mid-1980s, the greater New York City gay community saw its members dying at alarming rates from AIDS-related diseases. At the same time, federal, state, and local governments and agencies mostly ignored not only the sick and dying, along with their loved ones and caregivers, but also the public health threat in the mistaken belief that the epidemic was limited to one undesirable group who did not merit funds, resources, or services. Today, the LGBT+ movement continues to depend on labels to advance the cause, as in "We're here! We're queer! Get used to it!" This early 1990s slogan by ACT UP's Queer Nation provides a teaching opportunity regarding the paradox of identity politics in general, not to mention social movements as an unrecognized, understudied part of advertising history.

Instead the social politics of identities are co-opted into what Wanhsiu Sunny Tsai and Xiaoqi Han in Chapter 12 of this volume call "a plethora of consumer niches," including the LGBT ("lesbian, gay, bisexual, and transgender") designation, another label that lumps together widely divergent and not necessarily analogically comparable identifications. Although gay men and lesbian women are both constituted on the basis of sexuality that is not "hetero," their differences across gender make their experiences of "homo" sexualities quite different, as do race and class within and across the L's, G's, and B's of all genders. Furthermore, sexual orientation is not the same as transsexual and transgender, the "T" in LGBT, which usually although not exclusively refers to gender identity and expression, not sexual erotics. The accretion of ever more specific designations covered by the plus sign or asterisk—Q/ueer, Q/uestioning, I/ntersex, A/sexual, P/ansexual, and so on, for example—makes the category as a single identification even more problematic. However, as a market segment, the LGBT designation has materialized as an economic force, while ignoring the poverty and deprivation of large numbers of people covered under the LGBT label *because* of that label. Studying lesbian and gay consumers, Dr. Tsai and Dr. Xiaoqi write that, although consumer boycotting has a distinguished history in US social movements, minority consumers also might engage in *buy*cotting as a kind of identity politics that rewards brands not only for positive representations of identity groups but also for broader practices of social responsibility beyond one's own identity politics. Thus, the advertising industry and its allied fields actively construct consumer groups likely to purchase on the basis of social identities, for, in the neoliberal First World, consumption itself can be a way to demonstrate one's politics.

INTERSECTIONALITY AND INTERLOCKING IDENTIFICATIONS

In addition to the tensions of engaging the labels we wish to retire in order to be politically visible, there is a second problem of who is included and excluded from such labels. In short, making claims about women always under- or overrepresents some women. The Women's March on January 23, 2017, in many respects stands as a shining example of political coalitions and ally-ship across issues advocacy from reproductive rights and domestic violence to LGBT+ workplace rights and prison reform, to name only some of the groups that participated in solidarity to demonstrate in cities all over the United States and beyond. But the event was not without its controversies of exclusion. Some critiqued all those pink pussy hats because they seemed to exclude trans women by suggesting possession of a vagina as a requirement for membership in womanhood. Some lesbian, black, Chicana, and Muslim women also critiqued straight, white event organizers for assumptions that homophobia, racism, xenophobia, and Islamophobia are somehow not women's issues, despite the fact that lesbian, black, Chicana, and Muslim women not only contributed to the planning and participation that made the Women's March a success but also experience sexism in specifically homophobic, racist, xenophobic, and Islamophobic ways.

To indulge in a little Butlerian (Butler 1990, 2004) word play, if undoing gender troubles our claims about women and men, then intersectionality is the practice of understanding that our gender imaginary exists *because* of racialized class and classed racialization, as well as other identifications that the social order materializes and enforces. As many in this collection have noted, intersectional analysis recognizes that one's experiences of gender do depend on one's other identifications, such as sexuality, for instance. Intersectionality is as much a critique of straight, white, able-bodied, first-world, feminist practice and identity politics as it is a method of analysis developed by Kimberlé Crenshaw (1989, 1991) to understand the ways institutions structure people's experiences pivoting on race, class, and gender. In the present volume, Dr. Báez refers to the "intersectional optic" as a method of accounting for differences in making claims about women. *Interlocking* is a better word than *intersecting,* according to some (e.g., Collins [1990] 2000 and Smith 1986), for understanding, for example, gender as always already racialized and race as always already gendered. Dr. Jenkins (Chapter 5), citing bell hooks (2015), refers to the "imperialist white supremacist capitalist heterosexist patriarchy" to denote the inextricably interlocking functions of Western imperialism, white racism, capitalism, and heteropatriarchy.

Claims about "women" as a caste of people defined by gender are necessarily always provisional on the basis of socioeconomic status or buying power, for one, all woven through sexuality, gender identity and gender expression, race, ethnicity, age, ability, and other identifications. Indeed, analysis of advertising history and practices with regard to gendered disability is conspicuously absent in this volume, an embarrassing lapse for Dr. Kreshel and me. The takeaway here is that any claim on behalf of or about women or men, or gender, necessitates qualification. Without gender, there are no women, but women are specific kinds of women as the result of interlocking identifications.

To my mind, excluding trans women who lack a vagina from womanhood begs questions about the eligibility of trans men *with* vaginas to participate in womanhood. In the month of March, after the 2017 Women's March, Nigerian novelist Chimamanda Ngozi Adichie, of TEDx "We should all be feminists" fame, stepped into controversy by suggesting a distinction between trans women and "natural born women." In her defense, her distinction relied not so much on possession of vaginas as a phenomenological structure of experience. She argued that women reared as women lack access to experiences of gender privilege in the way that women reared as men do. Still, the exclusion chaffed. Many, though not all, transitioned women and men, by the way, prefer to drop the "trans" from their personal identifications since to their minds the point of transitioning is to become one's more authentic self rather than a walking advertisement for identity politics. I teach my students that a woman is anyone who claims to be a woman, which is a fairly safe practice given the time-honored tradition of self-reporting gender on forms and applications, including the US Census and the soon-to-be-defunct Nielsen rating diary.

EQUALITY AND DIFFERENCE

Third, sometimes the change that is warranted is not to make women or any so-called minority group equal to white men or any dominant group, although, in terms of equal rights and protections under the law, that is the change that is legally and ethically, indeed morally, required. However, perhaps, we can recognize that the very standard or practiced custom represented by the dominant group begs critique, and, what is more, a new standard might be the better goal. As long as we live in a society that rewards and enforces heteronormative binary gender, then sometimes people who live as women do merit consideration, such as the fact that women are mostly compelled to be principal caretakers of children, a responsibility generally undervalued and disdained by men because of the assumption that childrearing is women's work, or, put another way, childrearing is somehow emasculating. Moreover, working mothers can find themselves stigmatized as inadequate women if they don't give the impression that childrearing is more important than sacrificing their professional aspirations. Childrearing as women's work represents one of those gendered double standards that hobbles women while men have the privilege to remain oblivious. That extra responsibility for family, whoever ends up doing the job, dictates some accommodation in the workplace. In advertising, the workplace is a white-collar institution originally designed for white men by white men who assumed that white men have access to domestic labor, often not white, which frees white men to focus on their careers. In this way, work and the workplace itself represent a couple of those unnecessarily classed racialized gender "things," quite apart from the human bodies who engage in that white, manly work in such a white, manly workplace. Hence, the origins of anecdotes about successful creative women behaving just like "one of the boys," or, in the case of straight, white, trans man ad creative Chris Edwards (2016), where becoming one of the boys became both career advancement and an epiphany about sexism in the creative department.

I can't help but wonder how the new poster child of the advertising business's progressiveness depends on Edwards's privileged race, class, and gender. Edwards, as a white man, now has the authority to speak credibly "on behalf of" women who experience bias in the creative department. For, as we know, women speaking out about sexism have not been accorded the same trustworthiness as Edwards, who is enjoying additional success on the bully pulpit with publishing a book, doing speaking engagements, and being an expert source for pithy quotes in the trades. I fear this story would not have the same happy ending if Edwards were a trans woman speaking out about sexism. What if Edwards were not white and educated with entrée into the family's ad agency and access to the firm's board meeting where he chose to come out?

It's worth noting here that trans women and especially trans women of color risk higher rates of not just unemployment and poverty, and thus limited access to the insurance-medical-pharmaceutical industrial complex, but also physical violence and murder (Center for American Progress and Movement Advancement Project 2015; Human Rights Campaign 2016; Movement Advancement Project 2016; Office for Victims of Crime 2014). I don't wish to take anything from Edwards's extraordinarily difficult journey; I only wish to point out the ways his journey was differently difficult because of his race, not to mention economic ability to pay for the medical services to transition successfully in the way he desired. Not to belabor the point, but I also wish to point out that today's mainstreamed understanding of "transgender" is not all that radical because it reinforces our beliefs in distinct differences between women and men, and thus does not upset the heteropatriarchal gender system. In contrast, genderqueer or queer theory radically undermines binary heteronormative sex and gender by refusing either–or categories of women/feminine and men/masculine.

To return to my larger point about the gendering of institutions by those who have the power to do so, I'm reminded of Neil French's fateful 2005 public observation about women in creative, which cost him his top creative post at WPP: "Women don't make it to the top because they don't deserve to. They're crap" (Milmo and Book 2005). Dripping with contempt and white, male class privilege, he said that women in creative "wimp out and go suckle something" (Milmo and Brook 2005). The lesson still not learned, just over a decade later, Saatchi and Saatchi Chairman Kevin Roberts publicly humiliated himself when he said "that the debate on gender bias is 'all over' and women lack 'vertical ambition'" (Davies and Obordo 2016). On the eve of his departure from Saatchi and Saatchi, Roberts undermined his own half-hearted apology by reiterating his opinion that gender issues in advertising remain a nonstarter; the "debate is fucking over," he said (*Advertising Age* 2016).

The goal, then, is not for the advertising industry to adjust to the fact that women often end up with more responsibility for the kids, which in turn affects their careers, as if that were some predestined universal order of things. Instead, the goals should be to adjust the workplace, its expectations, and its practices to the reality that some employees, quite apart from their gender identity or gender expression, will have children, parents, not to mention spouses, domestic partners, and lovers to care for at various points in their careers. Perhaps we will be caring for transitioning loved ones. Women are not different in that the workplace must accommodate them and their family responsibilities. No. Rather, the workplace historically has been a privileged place for white men accorded the luxury of not having to worry about domestic labor, paid or unpaid. If advertising were as creative as it likes to believe, it would have solved this problem of gender and so-called work–life balance a long time ago. (I personally find the exhortation to achieve work–life balance objectionable; it's just another assignment for which I might be judged and found lacking.)

So, to return to distinguishing between equality and difference advocacy, some issues require gender equality whereas others require recognition of women's materially different experiences as a result of being required to live as women in an asymmetrical gender order that punishes them for living as women. No one has encapsulated the "dilemma of difference" more succinctly than legal scholar Martha Minow (1990, 20): "when does treating people differently emphasize their differences and stigmatize or hinder them on that basis?" and "when does treating people the same become insensitive to their difference and likely to stigmatize or hinder them on *that* basis?" For students and future "ad grads," much is at stake if we never unpack gender but practice advertising "as if" gender were neutrally ubiquitous, necessary, and, for advertising, lucrative. The ways that feminists think about and articulate the status of intersectional people vary as widely as the issues they address, as the scholars who have contributed to this book make obvious. Taken together, the contributors compose a *Feminism 101* of "brands" of feminist thought from feminist waves as sketchy historical eras to postfeminism as feminist-*not.*

WAVES OF WOMEN'S MOVEMENT

In their chapters, Dara Murray (Chapter 3) and Drs. Lambiase, Bronstein, and Coleman (Chapter 2) employ the feminist waves model as a basic although imperfect pedagogical framework for outlining US feminist history. An intersectional accounting of US feminism sketches approximate and moveable contours around overlapping waves of US women's movements (Golombisky 2012a, 2012b). The first wave flowed from the eighteenth century through the nineteenth century and on into the twentieth century to partially coincide with the second wave, which some might choose to recognize as earlier or later than World War II. Most people, however, associate the US second wave with the civil rights–era version of "women's lib," a period *concurrent* with the third wave if we interpret the third wave not through generations but through mid-century social movements, such as black nationalism, the Chicano movement, the United Farm Workers, Native American rights, and gay rights. Unlike the second wave, however, third-wave feminism survived the 1980s and into the early twenty-first century, to connect with a technology-dependent, social-networked fourth wave, exemplified by black feminists Alicia Garza, Opal Tometi, and Patrisse Cullors, who founded the #BlackLivesMatter movement in 2012.

First Wave

Politically speaking, the crest of the first wave for US white women arrived in roughly 1920 with the Nineteenth Amendment. Viewed through advertising history, as we learn in earlier chapters from Dr. Voss (Chapter 13), Dr. Murray (Chapter 3), and Jeanie Wills (Chapter 14), educated white women working in advertising in the early twentieth century were actively professionalizing white-collar work for white women in the advertising business and allied fields, including consumer goods, government outreach, the press and so-called women's media, and the academy. However, women's workplace issues are generally remembered as located forty to fifty years later during a second wave, sometimes associated with the 1963 Equal Pay Act, requiring equal pay for equal work, and Title VII of the 1964 Civil Rights Act, forbidding discrimination in the workplace on the basis of "race, color, religion, sex, and national origin." But workplace issues do date from the first wave because working-class women by definition and necessity have never had the choice not to work. Women of color, of course, historically have been overrepresented among the poor and working class because of structural racism. Contemporaneous with US women gaining the right to vote, the 1920 Women's Advertising Club of Chicago that Dr. Wills writes about was actively excluding from its membership women already working in advertising clerical jobs *because* they were low-wage, low-status clerical jobs.

Nor has academic advertising thought to catalog the contributions of women of color in histories of advertising. Turn-of-the-twentieth-century women of color such as Josephine St. Pierre Ruffin, Victoria Earle Matthews, and Julia Ringwood Coston, to name a few, were not only important publishers of "colored," "negro," and "Afro-American" women's magazines as well as arbiters of black women's consumer tastes. They were also active in the African-American clubwomen movement and as women's rights advocates (Brown 1988; Kramer 2006; Lyman 2005; Rooks 2005).

Dr. Murray describes early twentieth-century white suffragists employing advertising methods to advance their cause at the same time that advertisers were appropriating the appeal of suffrage among white women to sell products to women. In the meantime, white suffragists for political expedience had abandoned the successful and influential networks of African-American women's clubs, including the National Association of Colored Women's Clubs, which had composed the first-wave white women's political partners since before abolition. In the end, white first-wave suffragists succeeded politically on a reprehensible argument that white men needed white women's votes to offset African-American men's votes after the Fifteenth Amendment was ratified in 1870 and despite the ensuing proliferation of Jim Crow laws thwarting voting rights.

Second–Third Wave

The political crest of the US second wave occurred in the 1970s, after a series of significant legal gains in the 1960s and early 1970s[2] and before the rise of the New Right, or "New *White*" (Golombisky 2006b) of the Reagan administration. The 1980s also became known as Susan Faludi's (1991) era of "backlash" against women's movement, which continued into the new century. But it would be wrong to assume that the waning second wave was giving way to a nascent third wave. Practically speaking, the third wave began with the first critique of the second wave as too white, too economically comfortable, and too straight—homophobic, actually. In 1969, Betty Friedan as president of the National Organization for Women publicly worried that a "lavender menace" of lesbian feminists active in the second wave threatened to undermine mainstream acceptance of women's movement and feminist politics. So once again we find straight, white, economically comfortable feminists betraying their allies for political expedience. The organized response from lesbian feminists such as Rita Mae Brown, for one, was immediate. Like their black feminist contemporaries who faced sexism from the civil rights movement and racism from the women's movement, lesbian feminists faced sexism from the gay rights movement as well as homophobia and heterosexism from the women's movement. However, most of the gains of the second wave could not have been achieved without the sustained, committed activism of lesbian, African-American, Chicana and Latina, and working-class feminists, even as they criticized the movement they actively participated in launching and leading. They *were* the second wave.

In Chapter 6, Juliet Dee documents cavalier attitudes among advertising professionals in the 1970s and 1980s about the growing violence toward women portrayed in advertising, which ad pros justified as harmless expressions of humor and art. Dr. Dee observes how little has changed today in advertising practice when it comes to romanticizing and fetishizing violent and often violently sexual representations of women. But in the 1970s, women's movement was struggling to get the legal system to recognize rape and sexual assault as violence, not private sex, and to give a name to sexual harassment as a form of quid pro quo, and later hostile environment, discrimination illegal at work and school. This narrative is usually remembered through the efforts of white women like Susan Brownmiller (1975) and Catharine MacKinnon. Less acknowledged, however, are the key roles played by women of color in the development of sexual harassment law and policy. If we don't know much about the women of color who spent their careers as advocates and public servants, people such as Patsy Mink and Eleanor Holmes Norton, at least we can find them in a web search. But what of the women of color like Mechelle Vinson who brought the early sexual harassment lawsuits but are not remembered as women of color in a jurisprudence focused on gender, not race? Women of color as plaintiffs endured abuse at school, at work, and at home only to be abused again in courts of law and public opinion before disappearing into obscurity. As many of this volume's contributors have noted, black feminist legal scholar Dr. Crenshaw (1989,

1991) developed intersectional analysis to reveal poor black women's subject positions in a legal system that practices and condones material and symbolic violence against poor women of color because they are poor women of color.

Viewed from Madison Avenue, however, the second wave in many ways mirrored the first wave, including Dr. Murray's "entanglements" between feminists and advertisers. Feminists used advertising techniques to advance the cause, as they criticized the advertising industry for sexism. Advertisers, to sell products and services to women, co-opted feminist slogans about women's rights. But in doing so, advertisers also inadvertently assisted the women's movement by mainstreaming the idea of women's equality. In Chapter 4, Ann Marie Nicolosi describes ads that purport to "empower" women with brands promising straight white women the heterosex appeal advertised as necessary for career success, while other brands offered to "liberate" women with better, more efficient products for the home. Both strategies presume that women wish to be liberated from homemaking to pursue exciting, pleasurable, and profitable white-collar careers. But what about working-class women who wished for opportunities in upwardly mobile white-collar careers? Others might have wished that they had the luxury of staying home to devote time to themselves and their families. This is especially the case for descendants of enslaved people who had neither the privilege of living together or even knowing their family members, nor the right to legal marriage or the freedom to engage in that supposedly feminine pursuit called homemaking in their own households. Women of color often have been excluded from womanhood altogether, first as nonhuman slaves and then as the prerequisite for eugenic racial housecleaning during the first wave, where today's advertising tropes about black women began.

Also like the first wave, during the second wave, feminists, self-proclaimed and accidental, were working in the advertising industry openly and covertly. Politically engaged feminists such as Gloria Steinem who became the public face of second-wave feminism often achieved their fame because of their well-educated media savvy along with their palatable white, feminine, heterosex appeal. In Steinem's case, she joins the pantheon of historically significant ad women on the basis of *Ms.* magazine's fraught relationship with advertising: To survive without advertising or to entertain advertising without sacrificing feminist principles?

As Audre Lorde's (1984) oft-quoted second–third wave essay observed, "The Master's Tools Will Never Dismantle the Master's House." Professor Lorde argued that "this fact is only threatening to those women who still define the master's house as their only source of support" (112). First delivered as a 1979 panel presentation at an academic feminist conference, Professor Lorde's remarks chastise straight, white, well-to-do feminists for failing not only to fulfill their promise of a more inclusive conference but also to notice the absence of "poor women, Black and Third World women, and lesbians" at the conference (Lorde 1984, 110). Most of the essay emphasizes the second wave's ignorance of "differences" among women: "race, sexuality, class, and age" (110), in the senses of lack of knowledge and rudely ignoring.

Radical feminists saw white, economically comfortable, liberal feminists who were working inside the advertising establishment as supported by and supporting the white supremacist capitalist patriarchal system that subordinates women. Florynce "Flo" Kennedy's radical black feminist style was to work outside the system to transform it. An attorney and founding member of the National Organization for Women, Kennedy established the Media Workshop in 1966 to organize activism against racism and sexism in news and advertising. After an advertising agency agreed to confer with her group—because the group was outside on the street picketing the agency—Ms. Kennedy famously said, "When you want to get to the suites, start in the streets" (Martin 2000). Ms. Kennedy and Professor Lorde exemplify the women-of-color feminists who deserve credit for advancing second-wave women's movement even as they critiqued the second wave from a third-wave feminist framework of recognizing differences among women.

On the other side of *Ms.* magazine's advertising insertion orders, it remains difficult to locate the second–third-wave women of color who were working as advertising agency insiders in numbers fewer than even the rare white ad women like "Mad Woman" Jane Maas (2012), "Boss Lady" Jo Foxworth (1978), and "Moving Target" Rena Bartos (1977, 1982). Judy Foster Davis (2016) documents five "Pioneering African-American Women in the Advertising Business" whose careers rose to prominence during the second wave: "Unconventional Advertising Pioneer" Barbara Gardner Proctor, "Tenacious Advertising Trailblazer" Caroline R. Jones, "Transformative Artist" Joel P. Martin, "Marathon Woman" Carol H. Williams, and "Lucrative Woman's Market" G. Joyce Hamer. As Dr. Davis (2016) notes, US advertising history mostly remains unaware of such lapses in its timeline, including, for example, a record of unregulated discriminatory practices that form the advertising industry's structural oppression of women, regardless of race and ethnicity, and nonwhite people of color, regardless of gender.

Third–Fourth Wave

Although the second-wave origins of the third wave lie in recognizing interlocking differences among women, the third wave also has come to be understood as at least partially generational. I like to demonstrate these two currents of the third wave to undergraduates by way of Alice and Rebecca Walker. In the earlier "differences" current of the third wave, Alice Walker's 1983 *In Search of Our Mothers' Gardens: Womanist Prose* functions as a channel marker pointing to the second wave's receding progressive tide before the 1980s rise of neoconservative hostility toward feminists, along with women generally and poor women of color specifically in the 1980s' "undeclared war against American women" (Faludi 1991). Emblematic of the "differences" critique, Alice Walker pointedly differentiated feminism from "Womanism" to resonate with US black women's experience. Preceding Alice Walker's Womanism, 1981 saw the publication of Angela Davis's *Women, Race and Class,* bell hooks's *Ain't I a Woman: Black Women and Feminism,* and Cherríe Moraga and Gloria Anzaldúa's *This Bridge Called My Back: Writings by Radical Women of Color.* In 1982, Gloria T. Hull, Patricia Bell Scott, and Barbara Smith edited *All the Women Are White, All the Blacks Are Men, But Some of Us Are Brave: Black Women's Studies.* These classic texts form the foundations of the third wave's "differences" canon, which continued to grow through the 1980s and 1990s and into the twenty-first century.

But, in 1992, Alice Walker's twenty-two-year-old daughter, Rebecca Walker, wrote "Becoming the Third Wave" for *Ms.* magazine, and in doing so became a third-wave landmark for Generation X–Y–millennial feminists. The postboomer generation of feminists, who benefited from the growth of academic women's studies (including the "differences" canon), continued the "differences" critique while differentiating themselves from their second-wave foremothers. In terms of advertising media, if *Ms.* is synonymous with liberal feminist second-wave media, Christy Haubegger's *Latina* magazine might speak to a pre–social media generational third wave. Haubegger's business plan to address affluent, English-speaking, US Latinas required years of wooing skeptical investors and advertisers to get *Latina*'s first issue to press in 1996, as Dr. Báez notes in this volume (see Chapter 10). If Steinem wavered on *Ms.* magazine's stance toward advertising, Haubegger had to overcome ethnic and class stereotypes of Latina women, despite the advertising industry's own predictions of a growing lucrative US Hispanic "market" waiting to be exploited, as documented by Arlene Dávila (2001).

Creatively, the generational current of third-wave feminists has produced some memorable tactics. On the East Coast, the Guerrilla Girls as "feminist activist artists" (http://www.guerrillagirls.com/our-story/) began in 1985 to shame the New York art scene's exclusion of women. The Guerrilla Girls combine Madison Avenue–style copy and visuals ("Do women have to be naked to get into the Met?") with street-level culture-jamming tactics, including donning gorilla masks to maintain members' anonymity. In fact, the AIDS activists who produced "Silence = Death" credit the Guerrilla Girls as inspiration for how to get "complex messages into smooth one-liners," which then were plastered in public spaces (Finkelstein 2013). In 1995, the Guerrilla Girls published their book *Confessions of the Guerrilla Girls: By the Guerrilla Girls Themselves (Whoever They Really Are),* with a title paralleling David Ogilvy's 1963 *Confessions of an Advertising Man,* which itself paralleled the 1930 *Confessions of a Copy Writer, by a Widely Known New York Advertising Man Who Chooses to Conceal His Identity in Order to Give Unhampered Play to His Pen.*

On the West Coast in Washington State and back East in Washington, DC, the Riot Grrrl movement appropriated and subverted punk rock into feminist art and politics to advance women as rockers along with social reform on issues such as violence against women. The 1995 "Riot Grrrl Manifesto" by the group Bikini Kill calls for "girls" to "take over the means of production." The production and circulation of zines and fan zines is also associated with both Riot Grrrl feminism and the generational third wave. Zines began as hand-drawn, hand-circulated feminist magazines reproduced on copy machines, which evolved into Internet e-zines, which later evolved into blogs and LiveJournal web communities. However, generational third-wave movements such as the Riot Grrrls do not get a pass on the differences critique. The Riot Grrrls movement was mostly white middle to upper middle class (Rosenberg and Garofalo 1998). Moreover, the media-marketplace appropriated and popularized "girl power" (Hains 2014; Kearney 2015; Meehan 2002; Riordan 2001), which has been linked to "commodity feminism/fetishism," an unflattering term invented by Robert Goldman, Deborah Heath, and Sharon Smith (1991, 333) to describe how "advertisers compete at translating women's discourses into stylized commodity signs."

Much less described, however, and perhaps more politically influential, hip-hop feminism also emerged in the 1990s. Joan Morgan (1999) gets credit for naming hip-hop feminism, which refers to a generation of post–civil rights era women of color who grew up with the political and artistic sensibilities of women hip-hop artists during the decade bookended by two Bush administrations invested in rolling back civil rights. Characterized as creative, media-savvy artist-scholars and public intellectuals, hip-hop feminism's twenty-first century next-gen speaks truth to power and functions as public pedagogy amid the backlash racism that arose after Barack Obama became the forty-fourth US president (Durham, Cooper, and Morris 2013). The Crunk Feminist Collective and its 2010 "Manifesto" epitomize this politics, which emerged from and depends on new media. Describing hip-hop feminism, Aisha Durham, Brittney Cooper, and Susana Morris (2013, 731) write, "Today, the blogosphere has become the digital public forum for feminist consciousness-raising, and social media platforms like Twitter, Tumblr, and Facebook have morphed into virtual command centers to mobilize coalitions for grassroots activism." This kind of "social media–based feminist activism" is illustrative of a "fourth wave" (Gill 2016, 613).

Fourth-wave social resistance depends on "connective" social networking to organize, as Drs. Lambiase, Bronstein, and Coleman argue in Chapter 2. In

Chapter 5, Dr. Jenkins makes the point that US black millennial women are new-media trendsetters, including elevating grassroots political movements such as #BlackLivesMatter and #OscarsSoWhite into national conversations about race. At the same time, hip-hop feminists eschew the feminist waves narrative as a white women's story about white women's movement, according to my USF colleague Dr. Aisha Durham. But a historicized waves model can be a useful although imprecise introductory framework for outlining an intersectional interpretation of US feminisms and women's movement seen through the eyes of advertising concerns.

"BRANDS" OF FEMINIST THOUGHT

Likewise, even an introduction to some of the varieties, or brands, if you will, of feminisms is useful for discerning a range of interests in and responses to intersectional women's and gender issues in advertising. Distinctions across forms of feminisms are not firm or stable, either, but rather have legs and travel, and can be usefully combined. Here I offer a necessarily partial and superficial tour of a range of philosophical, theoretical, and political forms of feminist thought.

Black Feminisms

Given the importance of intersectionality (Crenshaw 1989, 1991) to contemporary feminist thought, along with the constancy and continuity of contributions by women of color to US feminist movement, women of color feminisms are a good point of departure. As Dr. Jenkins notes in Chapter 5, Womanism (Walker 1983) is not exactly the same as US black feminism, although they are inextricably related. In 1970, Francis Beal wrote that "to be black and female" is a "double jeopardy," which echoed WEB Dubois's (1903) double consciousness and previewed Deborah King's (1988) multiple jeopardies and multiple consciousnesses. The Combahee River Collective's 1978 "Black Feminist Statement" worked through the history of black feminist thought as well as how its members worked through their own internal disagreements, for example between straight and lesbian black feminists. However, Patricia Hill Collins's ([1990] 2000) explication of "the distinguishing features" of *Black Feminist Thought* remains the most influential. She describes an "oppositional knowledge" (12) born out of US black women's experiences living under what she calls the "matrix of domination" (18): "intersecting oppressions of race, class, gender, sexuality, and nationality" (22). For US black women, this produces a specific epistemology, which Dr. Collins (1986) described as "the outsider within."

African-American women's experiences as racial outsiders in mainstream white social institutions "can be a stimulus to creativity," according to Dr. Collins ([1990] 2000, 289). "On the other hand," she writes, "the commodification of outsider-within status whereby African-American women's value to an organization lies solely in our ability to market a seemingly permanent marginal status can suppress Black women's empowerment" (289). I'm thinking here of the Institute of Advertising Ethics (IAE) and the composition of its thirteen-seat advisory council: Ten of its thirteen members are high-ranking, late-career, or retired white men with impressive titles at well-known organizations. Of the three women on the council, one is a professor. Two of the three women are white, which means that the only person of color on the IAE's advisory council is a black woman: Tiffany R. Warren, the chief diversity officer at Omnicom Group. A cynic might wonder if Warren's role on the council is to connote diversity by her job title and skin color, as if corporate diversity is only the purview of nonwhites. Marilyn Kern-Foxworth (1989, 2004) defined the "acrylic vault" as the tokenism that isolates women of color in highly visible public relations positions without giving them power to influence the organization.

US Third-World and Chicana Feminisms

In writing about US third-world feminism, Chela Sandoval (1991, 2000) powerfully demonstrated that the United States *is* the third world for women of color. In describing the ways women of color respond to historically racist US feminism and women's movement, Dr. Sandoval defined a "differential consciousness" akin to "the clutch of an automobile, the mechanism that permits the driver to select, engage, and disengage gears in a system for the transmission of power" (2000, 57). The differential consciousness is a "tactical subjectivity" for navigating political issues where there are self-interests at stake. Her deployment of the word "third" also upsets binaries and points to unnoticed, unmarked social positionalities residing between dualisms and dichotomies; she writes that "feminists of color exist in the interstices between normalized social categories" (45). Regarding social invisibility, Dr. Hernández cites the "symbolic annihilation" (Tuchman 1978) that women-of-color respondents in her study say they experience; "the omission of both representations of more average women and women-of-color models communicated to participants that they 'did not matter' because they could not see themselves represented in these advertisements" (Chapter 11). Speaking from multiple interlocking oppressions, Chicana and Latina feminists have articulated their social positionalities via metaphors of between-ness, mixed-ness, and hybridity, such as Dr. Anzaldúa's (1987) "queer mixed-race woman in the borderlands," Dr. Sandoval's (1991) "third space interstitial oppositional consciousness," and Emma Pérez's (1999) "decolonial third space feminism" (Golombisky 2015, 406–407).

Radical Feminisms

As Dr. Báez writes in Chapter 10, Chicana and Latina feminists have tended to embrace radical feminism, or what Dr. Sandoval (2000, 55) calls "revolutionary feminist politics" working for "radical transformation" whereby the dominant order is "fundamentally restructured." Jean Kilbourne's is a radical feminist critique of advertising. Dr. Dee's (Chapter 6) discussion of (male sexual) dominance theory in feminist legal studies comes out of radical feminism. Dr. Sandoval (2000, 56) distinguishes between "supremacist" and "separatist" forms of radical feminism. In what I call undergraduate feminist math, women > men = radical feminism, representing the problematic "supremacist" version that merely reverses a binary gender hierarchy. "Separatist" radical feminisms suggest that women are better off segregated in institutions of their own design, such as advertising agencies of, by, and for women only, for example, although intersex and trans+ people complicate separatist practices. *Strategic* essentialism refers to separatist practices that make space for members of marginalized or subordinate groups to raise their own consciousness about their circumstances. For example, the Ohio State University Black Advertising and Strategic Communication Association prepares black students for advertising, public relations, and marketing careers through networking among faculty, professionals, and students.

Cultural Feminisms

The strategic use of separatist practices in radical feminism is not the same as cultural feminism, which locates the origins of gender differences between women and men in the separate gender cultures in which they are reared, as if they have always lived in different worlds. In Chapter 9, Dr. Grow invokes cultural feminism by suggesting women and men self-select in and out of jobs based on their gender-culture backgrounds. In cultural feminism, women ≠ men. Too often, however, cultural feminism's cultural construction of gender slips into biological determinism about natural differences between women and men, to wit, the problematic pop-culture biological essentialism mainstreamed by John Gray's (1992) *Men Are from Mars, Women Are from Venus*.

Liberal Feminisms

Women of color, radical, and cultural feminisms are difference feminisms, as distinguishable from the equality feminism of liberal feminisms. If radical feminism works outside the system to build a new system, liberal feminism works inside the existing system to improve it, although difference feminists are likely to inquire as to who has been granted the privilege of getting inside in the first place. Despite its proclivity to ignore differences that matter, liberal feminism typically has been about removing barriers to access. Liberal feminism is "the equal-rights form" that Dr. Sandoval (2000, 55) critiques as white and economically comfortable. Liberal feminism has been invested in the codification of gender equity law, policy, and regulation. In liberal feminism, women = men, even though men remain the unexamined ideal standard. In Chapter 8 of the present volume, Karen Mallia's critique of creative departments as the "playground of privileged young men" takes a liberal feminist perspective in advocating for equal representation and opportunities for women in advertising creative. Newly awakened feminists, including students, often gravitate to liberal feminism first because it seems to advocate for commonsense equal-rights justice without upsetting taken-for-granted pieties about natural-born differences between women and men. The ad club known as AWNY—Advertising Women of New York—in 2016 rebranded itself as She Runs It, reflecting a liberal feminist approach to the glass ceiling: "When we started over a hundred years ago, we wanted to give more women a seat at the table. Now, we want to see more women at the head of the table" (She Runs It 2016). But to critics, liberal feminism is like demanding an invitation to sit at a table where your presence is unwelcome, the chairs are uncomfortable, the hosts and other guests are hostile, and you'll go hungry because the banquet will only serve rich, white, able-bodied, cisgendered, Anglo, white guys. In other words, opening the door does not change the sexism, racism, homophobia, and country club elitism on the other side of the threshold.

Marxist, Socialist, and Historical Materialist Feminisms

The table analogy segues to Marxist-materialist feminisms by way of a famous Stuart Hall parable: "It is the early 1970's. Picture a room of male marxists around a table, debating the role of feminism in the struggle, deciding that it is, in fact, important. They go do the door, having decided to invite in the feminists. In the meantime, the feminists break through the window and shit on the table" (Lather 1992, 129). Marxist, socialist, and historical materialist feminisms proceed where the men forgot to account for women in the success of capitalist empire. In Marxist and materialist feminisms, women = a class, or rather a *second* class. Materialist feminists examine women's material conditions and assets—or lack thereof.

And so we arrive at the critique of gendered spheres of influence, including the political economy of advertising, with men in the public sphere producing, and women in the domestic private sphere consuming and reproducing.

Private homemaking, housekeeping, and child rearing are mostly unpaid or underpaid women's labor *necessary* for the capitalist system to function. The economic system relies on this workforce but doesn't account for it in economic theories or modeling. Even when those undervalued jobs are performed as paid labor in the public or private sphere, they are low-status, low-pay, pink-collar-ghetto jobs, such as childcare, eldercare, food services, and maid services. Overall, women's paid labor remains undervalued by more than 20 cents on the dollar in the US labor force. For proof, send students to the US Bureau of Labor Statistics (https://www.bls.gov/), which further breaks down the numbers by race and ethnicity, with devastating results.

As far as the advertising and marketing industries are concerned, however, women's primary job is consumption, not production. In Chapter 13 of the present volume, Dr. Voss traces historical linkages among home economics, advertising, and women making careers giving homemakers advice on housekeeping. Her analysis perturbs the myth of a clear boundary between US public and private spheres in the twentieth century—and lays a major guilt trip on Robin Morgan, ironically of *Sisterhood is Powerful* (1970) fame, along with second-wave liberal feminism for the demise of home economics as the educational and occupational categories that Dr. Kreshel and I would recognize from our days as home ec students in that era.

A varietal of Marxist-materialist feminist thought, feminist standpoint theory ranks among the most influential feminist theories (Collins 1997; Harding 1986, 1997; Hartsock 1983, 1997, 1998; Hekman 1997a, 1997b; Smith 1987, 1997). As I write elsewhere, "Early standpoint theory posited that members of the oppressed group have an advantaged viewpoint by understanding the dominant and the subordinate groups' sightlines on reality while the dominant group remains ignorant of all but its own worldview" (Golombisky 2015, 404). Contemporary standpoint theory, however, is understood as requiring reflexive effort; a standpoint is achieved by raising one's consciousnesses regarding one's own positionality in terms of interlocking privileges and oppressions. In Chapter 14 of this volume, Dr. Wills employs standpoint theory to explain the formation of white, middle-class women's ad clubs whose members were highly conscious of their subordinate gender status in the advertising industry. Meanwhile, they were not reflexive about their race and class biases.

Poststructuralist, Postmodern, and Psychoanalytic Feminisms

Dr. Windels has already introduced us to poststructuralist feminism in Chapter 7, interested in the discursive construction of gendered power relations. In poststructuralist feminism, women = Ø outside of language and the symbolic order that constructs women as not-men. Closely aligned with poststructuralism, postmodern feminism also deconstructs universalizing capital "T" truths about gender relations and social power. Related to poststructuralist and postmodern feminisms, is psychoanalytic feminism, on which Laura Mulvey (1975, 1981) built her theory of the scopophilic cinematic male gaze. In psychoanalytic feminism, women = lack because they lack the phallus, thus phallic power. Visual artist Barbara Kruger, who began her career as a graphic designer during the 1960s, is emblematic of the postmodern feminist pastiche sensibility and bricolage aesthetic, exemplified by her piece "You are not yourself," the text graphically superimposed over a kitschy image of a woman's face reflected in a shattered mirror.

Postfeminisms

The other "post" feminism is literally postfeminism. Because postfeminism describes the advertising industry's appropriation of feminist thought in the service of profit, postfeminism ≠ feminism. In Chapter 11, Dr. Hernández addresses postfeminist beauty advertising disguised as health messaging; it seems to "empower" women to be confident about their bodies while reinforcing feelings of inadequacy in terms of race, size, shape, age, and so on, thereby making one's self-improving bodywork a lifelong project of consumption. Postfeminism = antifeminist because of its "double entanglements" with neoconservative and neoliberal discourses that cast collective feminist politics as a quaint anachronism (McRobbie 2004). Another iconic Kruger piece illustrates the feminist critique of postfeminism: "I shop therefore I am." Postfeminism reduces collective feminist social movement into an individual purchasing decision, a process rhetorically positioned as not only necessary for building and communicating one's unique personal identity and politics, but also for demonstrating one's neoliberal good citizenship as a consumer (Gill 2007, 2016; McRobbie 2004; Vavrus 2012).

In their analyses, numbers of the present volume's contributors reference postfeminism and its older sibling commodity feminism. See, for example, Dr. Hernández in Chapter 11; Drs. Lambiase, Bronstein, and Coleman in Chapter 2; Professor Mallia in Chapter 8; Dr. Murray in Chapter 3; and Dr. Nicolosi in Chapter 4. Think about Drs. Tsai and Han's discussion in Chapter 12 of buycotting lesbian and gay consumers who vote their politics via the marketplace. Recall, once again, US Latinx populations lumped together across ascribed and avowed identifications into one vast target market, and yet Dr. Báez's study in Chapter 10 of Chicago-area Latinas finds them gauging their citizenship to being hailed by advertisers in the Althusserian (1972) sense of interpellation. *Voilà,* the neoliberal citizen whose success in the social order lies with individual effort, not collective action.

Transnational Feminisms

Dr. Grow (Chapter 9) argues that the US advertising industry is exporting its sexist version of the advertising agency's creative department around the world. It's not a stretch to argue that we have already exported the entire enterprise of advertising, as we know it. The colonizing proliferation of neoliberal imperialist capitalism leads us at last to international feminisms, including postcolonial, indigenous, and transnational feminisms, and their lack of representation in this volume, although they are covered in our next volume (Golombisky and Kreshel forthcoming). Transnational feminism critiques unbridled enthusiasm for corporatized globalization and its uneven benefits to some at the expense of others. But transnational feminism also employs indigenous worldviews to critique first-world brands of feminisms from the perspectives of women living in colonized and formerly colonized societies and so-called third-world countries. Mostly US women's movements are not troubled to think about Dr. Sandoval's (1991, 2000) US third-world women, let alone women beyond US borders. This is the failure of "market feminism" (Scott 2000), which celebrates capitalism, chastises US feminists for benefiting from capitalism without embracing it, but never critiques the matrix of domination or whom capitalism and market feminism excludes or colonizes. Even when US feminists do consider the world beyond their own front door, all too often they are unreflexive regarding their first-world ideas about women's movement. US and first-world feminists tend not only to presume that they know what is best for second-, third-, and fourth-world women, but also to assume that they will be welcomed as sheroes swooping in to save those poor brown women (Abu-Lughod 2002; Dingo 2012; Mohanty 1984, 2003, 2013; Mohanty, Russo, and Torres 1991). That is one criticism of the Eurocentric universal human rights form of global feminism practiced by development logics. Advertising, like public relations, might not be able "to divorce itself from neoliberal corporatization; nevertheless, the critique must be lodged" (Golombisky 2015, 405).

Taking intersectional analysis seriously, feminist concerns are not just "women's" concerns or even gender concerns regarding workers or consumers. These concerns about inclusion, invisibility, difference, and equity are enmeshed in every aspect of advertising from creative concept to checkout counter. In advertising education, to prepare students to engage advertising as professionals and consumers with a righteous standpoint requires more than a single day or unit of feminist thought. From the transnational to the standpoint, feminist issues are contemporary advertising issues best taught integrated throughout the curriculum.

MAKING GEORGE AND SHIRLEY PROUD

Women and advertising both are globally ubiquitous. But advertising remains one of the most misogynist, heterosexist, racist, and ableist industries, unabashedly so. Even though women represent a majority of the consumers whom advertising targets, the problems of racist, sexist, heterosexist, ableist advertising practices and messages persist in part because women represent such a small percentage of the principals and leaders controlling the industry. In contrast, in undergraduate advertising programs, women represent a majority, and have done so since I was an undergraduate. In the academic literature, most feminists who study advertising are not professors of advertising, and professors of advertising, even those interested in women and diversity, almost never write from feminist philosophical and theoretical foundations, sometimes because doing so would be a professional liability. Neither do we value addressing these issues in advertising classrooms. Thus, there is no tradition of feminist scholarship, research, knowledge, or curriculum in advertising.

Although I began my career, as well as this chapter, with a list of gripes accrued from working in advertising, my experience includes two exceptions worth honoring here. When the late George Lemon hired me at age twenty-two as a fresh-out-of-college "ad grad," he warned me not to "nest" at my desk with a plant, coffee mug, and framed photo. "Update your resume," he said. Then he told me he would be disappointed in me if I didn't exit for a better job within two years. A few jobs later, I went to work for the great Shirley McKneely, where, among other accounts, I worked on Women against Pornography, even though I am a pro-sex or "sex positive" feminist.[3] Shirley made a habit of giving young women unprecedented responsibility, and just as important, giving us the space to make and learn from terrible mistakes. She coached me through some doozies. Each time I confessed some grievous sin, her response was the same: "So what are *you* going to do about it?"

With this modest volume, the contributors hope to initiate a more honest dialogue about intersectional women in the advertising academy and industry. For Peggy and me, this project has been a long time coming. For years we couldn't even get the Advertising Division of the Association for Education in Journalism and Mass Communications to program a proposed panel with the F word in the title. For a long time, we felt like we were the only openly self-proclaimed feminists in academic advertising. Some of our favorite colleagues were hostile in overt and passive-aggressive ways. So Peggy and I have been overwhelmed by the positive support for this project. "Long overdue" is what we hear. Frankly, we have been a bit star-struck by scholars who have so generously written chapters for this project. But where do we go from here?

First, Peggy and I recommend that you head to Volume 2 for a focused examination of advertising content (Golombisky and Kreshel forthcoming). Second, do the research, collect the data. Statistics are persuasive. What happens to all those bright women who are in portfolio schools, for example? Third, as Professor Mallia has suggested in Chapter 8 of this volume, take the cause off campus to our colleagues in the industry. Last, please take these issues back to advertising classrooms and the curriculum. Teach. Empower students with knowledge, including their own vulnerability in the workplace as entry-level individuals but also their strength in numbers via strategic alliances and organizing.

I began writing this chapter optimistic that the country might be ready to elect a woman as president. I end this chapter sobered by a political reality that does require feminists to regroup collectively and connectively, as Drs. Lambiase, Bronstein, and Coleman put it. Going forward, I continue to hope we will be more inclusive and self-reflexive.

NOTES

1. Nonetheless, Dr. Butler (1993b) avers that there is political value to apprehending some kinds of drag performances as hyperbolic theatricality designed to denaturalize heteronormative gender by citing, thus revealing, the artifice of its conventions.

2. In addition to the Equal Pay Act and Title VII of the Civil Rights Act, the Supreme Court in *Reed v. Reed*, 1971, and *Frontiero v. Richardson*, 1973, ruled that women also benefit from the equal protection clauses of the Fourteenth and Fifth Amendments, respectively. Title IX in 1972 extended Title VII's antisexism policies from the workplace to include education, and in 1978 Title VII was extended to protect women against pregnancy discrimination at work. Congress passed protections against discrimination on the basis of disability in 1973 and age in 1978. Congress passed the Equal Rights Amendment in 1972, and the Supreme Court in effect legalized abortion with *Roe v. Wade* in 1973.

3. The late Dorothy "Cookie" Teer connected McKneely Communications to Andrea Dworkin's antipornography work in the 1980s. Teer's papers are housed at the Duke University Library.

REFERENCES

Abu-Lughod, Lila. 2002. "Do Muslim Women Really Need Saving? Anthropological Reflections on Cultural Relativism and Its Others." *American Anthropologist* 104: 783–790.

Advertising Age. 2016. "Saatchi Chairman Kevin Roberts Resigns after Gender Comments." August 3.

Althusser, Louis. 1972. "Ideology and Ideological State Apparatuses." In *Lenin and Philosophy, and Other Essays,* 121–176. Translated by Ben Brewster. New York: Monthly Review Press.

Anzaldúa, Gloria. 1987. *Borderlands/La Frontera: The New Mestiza.* San Francisco: Spinsters/Little Lute.

Bartos, Rena. 1977. "The Moving Target: The Impact of Women's Employment on Consumer Behavior." *The Journal of Marketing* July 1: 31–37.

———. 1982. *The Moving Target: What Every Marketer Should Know about Women.* New York: Free Press.

Beal, Frances. 1970. "Double Jeopardy: To Be Black and Female." In *Sisterhood Is Powerful: An Anthology of Writings from the Women's Liberation Movement,* edited by R. Morgan, 340–353. New York: Random House.

Brown, Hallie Q. 1988. *Homespun Heroines and Other Women of Distinction.* New York: Oxford University Press.

Brownmiller, Susan. 1975. *Against Our Will: Men, Women and Rape.* New York: Simon & Schuster.

Butler, Judith. 1990. *Gender Trouble: Feminism and the Subversion of Identity.* New York: Routledge.

———. 1993a. *Bodies that Matter: On the Discursive Limits of "Sex."* New York: Routledge.

———. 1993b. "Critically Queer." *GLQ* 1: 17–32.

———. 2004. *Undoing Gender.* New York: Routledge.

Carey, James. 1992. *Communication as Culture: Essays on Media and Society.* New York: Routledge.

Center for American Progress and Movement Advancement Project. 2015. *Paying an Unfair Price: The Financial Penalty for Being Transgender in America.* Downloaded April 14, 2017: http://www.lgbtmap.org/unfair-price-transgender.

Collins, Patricia Hill. 1986. "Learning from the Outsider Within: The Sociological Significance of Black Feminist Thought." *Social Problems* 33 (6): 14–32.

———. 1997. "Comment on Hekman's 'Truth and Method: Feminist Standpoint Theory Revisited': Where's the Power?" *Signs* 22: 375–81.

———. (1990). 2000. *Black Feminist Thought: Knowledge, Consciousness, and the Politics of Power.* New York: Routledge.

Combahee River Collective. 1978. "The Combahee River Collective Statement: A Black Feminist Statement." In *Capitalism, Patriarchy, and the Case of Socialist Feminism,* edited by Zillah Eisenstein, 362–72. New York: Monthly Review Press.

Confessions of a Copy Writer, by a Widely Known New York Advertising Man Who Chooses to Conceal His Identity in order to Give Unhampered Play to His Pen. 1930. New York: Dartnell Corporation.

Confessions of the Guerrilla Girls: By the Guerrilla Girls Themselves (Whoever They Really Are). 1995. New York: Harper Perennial.

Crenshaw, Kimberlé. 1989. "Demarginalizing the Intersection of Race and Sex: A Black Feminist Critique of Antidiscrimination Doctrine, Feminist Theory and Antiracist Politics." *University of Chicago Legal Forum* 139–167.

———. 1991. "Mapping the Margins: Intersectionality, Identity Politics, and Violence against Women of Color." *Stanford Law Review* 43: 1241–99.
Crunk Feminist Collective. 2010. "Hip Hop Generation Feminism: A Manifesto," March 1. http://www.crunkfeministcollective.com/2010/03/01/hip-hop-generation-feminism-a-manifesto/.
Dávila, Arlene. 2001. *Latinos Inc.: The Marketing and Making of a People*. Berkeley: University of California Press.
Davis, Angela. 1981. *Women, Race, and Class*. New York: Random House.
Davis, Judy Foster. 2016. *Pioneering African-American Women in the Advertising Business: Biographies of MAD Black Women*. New York: Routledge.
Davis, Rob, and Rachel Obordo. 2016. "Women in Advertising Reveal Rampant Sexism and Macho Culture." *The Guardian,* August.
Dingo, Rebecca. 2012. *Networking Arguments: Rhetoric, Transnational Feminism, and Public Policy Writing*. Pittsburgh: University of Pittsburgh Press.
DuBois, W. E. B. (1903). *The Souls of Black Folk: Essays and Sketches*. Chicago: A. C. McClurg & Co.
Durham, Aisha, Britanny C. Cooper, and Susana M. Morris. 2013. "The Stage Hip-Hop Feminism Built: A New Directions Essay." *Signs,* 38: 721–737.
Edwards, Chris. 2016. *Balls: It Takes Some to Get Some*. Austin, TX: Greenleaf Book Group Press.
Faludi, Susan. 1991. *Backlash: The Undeclared War against American Women*. New York: Anchor/Doubleday.
Fausto-Sterling, Anne. 2012. *Sex/Gender: Biology in a Social World.* New York: Routledge.
Finkelstein, Avram. 2013. "The *Silence = Death* Poster" [guest post]. *LGBT@NYPL,* a New York Public Library Blog for the LGBT Collections, November 22. https://www.nypl.org/blog/2013/11/22/silence-equals-death-poster.
Foxworth, Jo. 1978. *Boss Lady: An Executive Woman Talks about Making It*. New York: Crowell.
Gill, Rosalind. 2007. "Postfeminist Media Culture: Elements of a Sensibility." *European Journal of Cultural Studies* 10: 147–66.
———. 2016. "Post-postfeminism? New Feminist Visibilities in Postfeminist Times." *Feminist Media Studies* 16: 610–30.
Goldman, Robert, Deborah Heath, and Sharon L. Smith. 1991. "Commodity Feminism." *Critical Studies in Mass Communication* 8: 333–351.
Golombisky, Kim. 2006a. "Gendering the Interview: Feminist Reflections on Gender as Performance in Research." *Women's Studies in Communication* 29 (2): 167–92.
———. 2006b. "Reforming Rhetoric: Gender Equity, the American Association of University Women, and the New White." *Iowa Journal of Communication special issue: "Feminist Theories and Practices in Communication"* 38 (2): 101–26.
———. 2012a. "Feminism." *Encyclopedia of Gender in Media,* edited by Mary Kosut, 90–96. Los Angeles: Sage Reference.
———. 2012b. "Feminist Thought for Advancing Women in the Academy." In *Women in Higher Education: The Struggle for Equity,* edited by M. Meyers, 19–38. New York: Hampton Press.

———. 2015. "Renewing the Commitments of Feminist Public Relations Theory from Velvet Ghetto to Social Justice." *Journal of Public Relations Research* 27 (5): 389–415.

———. 2017. "Feminist Methodology." In *Communication Research Methods in Postmodern Culture,* edited by L. Z. Leslie, 2nd ed. New York: Routledge, forthcoming.

Golombisky, Kim, and Peggy J. Kreshel. Forthcoming. *What's the Big Idea: Feminist Perspectives on Advertising*. Lanham, MD: Lexington Press.

Gray, John. 1992. *Men Are from Mars, Women Are from Venus: A Practical Guide for Improving Communication and Getting What You Want in Your Relationships.* New York: HarperCollins.

Hains, Rebecca C. 2014. "The Significance of Chronology in Commodity Feminism: Audience Interpretations of Girl Power Music." *Popular Music and Society* 37: 33–47.

Harding, Sandra. 1986. *The Science Question in Feminism*. Ithaca, NY: Cornell University Press.

———. 1997. "Comment on Hekman's 'Truth and Method: Feminist Standpoint Theory Revisited': Whose Standpoint Needs the Regimes of Truth and Reality?" *Signs* 22: 382–91.

Hartsock, Nancy. 1983. *Money, Sex, and Power: Toward a Feminist Historical Materialism*. Boston: Northeastern University.

———. 1997. "Comment on Hekman's 'Truth and Method: Feminist Standpoint Theory Revisited': Truth or Justice?" *Signs* 22: 367–74.

———. 1998. "The Feminist Standpoint Revisited." In *The Feminist Standpoint Revisited and Other Essays,* edited by Nancy Hartsock, 227–48. Boulder: Westview.

Hekman, Susan. 1997a. "Reply to Hartsock, Collins, Harding, and Smith." *Signs* 22: 399–402.

———. 1997b. "Truth and Method: Feminist Standpoint Theory Revisited." *Signs* 22: 341–65.

hooks, bell. 1981. *Ain't I a Woman: Black Women and Feminism*. New York: South End Press.

———. 2015. *Feminism Is for Everyone: Passionate Politics*. New York: Routledge.

Hull, Gloria T., Patricia Bell Scott, and Barbara Smith, editors. 1982. *All the Women Are White, All the Blacks Are Men, But Some of Us Are Brave: Black Women's Studies*. Old Westbury, NY: The Feminist Press.

Human Rights Campaign. 2016. "Violence against the Transgender Community in 2016." Downloaded April 14, 2017: http://www.hrc.org/resources/violence-against-the-transgender-community-in-2016.

Institute for Advertising Ethics. 2016. "Institute for Advertising Ethics." Downloaded May 24, 2017: https://www.rjionline.org/institute-for-advertising-ethics.

Jamieson, Kathleen Hall. 1995. *Beyond the Double Bind: Women and Leadership*. New York: Oxford University Press.

Kearney, Mary Celeste. 2015. "Sparkle: Luminosity and Post-girl Power Media." *Continuum: Journal of Media & Cultural Studies* 29: 263–73.

Kern-Foxworth, Marilyn. 1989. "An Assessment of Minority Female Roles and Status in Public Relations: Trying to Unlock the Acrylic Vault and Assimilate into the Velvet Ghetto." In *Beyond the Velvet Ghetto,* edited by Elizabeth L. Toth and Carolyn G. Cline, 241–286. San Francisco: IABC Research Foundation.

———. 2004. "Women of Color on the Frontline in Mass Communication Professions." In *Seeking Equity for Women in Journalism and Mass Communication Education: A 30-year Update,* edited Ramona R. Rush, Carol E. Oukrop, and Pamela J. Creedon, 205–22. Mahwah, NJ: Lawrence Erlbaum.

King, Deborah K. 1988. *Multiple Jeopardy, Multiple Consciousness: The Context of a Black Feminist Ideology*. Chicago: University Chicago Press.

Kramer, Steve. 2006. "Uplifting Our 'Downtrodden Sisterhood': Victoria Earle Matthews and New York City's White Rose Mission, 1897–1907." *Journal of American History* 91 (3): 243–66.

Lather, Patti. 1992. "Post-Critical Pedagogies: A Feminist Reading." In *Feminisms and Critical Pedagogy,* edited by Carmen Luke and Jennifer Gore, 120–37. New York: Routledge.

Lyman, Darryl. 2005. Josephine St. Pierre Ruffin. *Great African-American Women,* 3rd ed., 196–97. Middle Village, NY: Jonathan David Company.

Lorde, Audre. 1984. "The Master's Tools Will Never Dismantle the Master's House." *Sister Outsider: Essays and Speeches,* 110–13. Berkeley, CA: Crossing Press.

Maas, Jane. 2012. *Mad Women: The Other Side of Life on Madison Avenue in the '60s and Beyond*. New York: St. Martin's.

Martin, Douglas. 2000. "Flo Kennedy, Feminist, Civil Rights Advocate and Flamboyant Gadfly, Is Dead at 84." *New York Times,* December 23.

McRobbie, Angela. 2004. "Post-Feminism and Popular Culture." *Feminist Media Studies* 4: 255–64.

Meehan, Eileen R. 2002. "Gendering the Commodity Audience: Critical Media Research, Feminism, and Political Economy." In *Sex & Money: Feminism and Political Economy in the Media,* edited by Eileen R. Meehan and Ellen Riordan, 209–22. Minneapolis: University of Minnesota Press.

Milmo, Dan, and Stephen Brook. 2005. "WPP Executive Quits for Calling Women 'Crap' and 'Wimps.'" *The Guardian,* October 22.

Minow, Martha. 1990. *Making All the Difference: Inclusion, Exclusion, and American Law*. Ithaca, NY: Cornell University Press.

Mohanty, Chandra Talpade. 1984. "Under Western Eyes: Feminist Scholarship and Colonial Discourses." *Boundary* 2 (12): 333–358.

———. 2003. "Under Western Eyes Revisited: Feminist Solidarity through Anticapitalist Struggles." *Signs* 28: 499–535.

———. 2013. "Transnational Feminist Crossings: On Neoliberalism and Radical Change." *Signs* 38: 967–91.

Mohanty, Chandra Talpade, Ann Russo, and Lourdes Torres, editors. 1991. *Third World Women and the Politics of Feminism*. Bloomington: Indiana University Press.

Moraga, Cherríe, and Gloria Anzaldúa, editors. 1981. *This Bridge Called My Back: Writings by Radical Women of Color*. New York: Kitchen Table Press.

Morgan, Joan. 1999. *When Chickenheads Come Home to Roost: A Hip-Hop Feminist Breaks It Down.* New York: Simon & Schuster.

Morgan, Robin. 1970. *Sisterhood Is Powerful*. New York: Vintage.
Movement Advancement Project. 2016. *Understanding Issues Facing Transgender Americans*. Downloaded April 14, 2017: www.lgbtmap.org/understanding-issues-facing-transgender-americans.
Mulvey, Laura. 1975. "Visual Pleasure and Narrative Cinema." *Screen,* 16 (3): 6–18.
Mulvey, Laura. 1981. "Afterthoughts on 'Visual Pleasure and Narrative Cinema' Inspired by King Vidor's *Duel in the Sun* (1946). *Framework* 15-16-17: 12–15.
Nielsen Report. 2013. *Latina Power Shift* (Diverse Intelligence Series): 1–24.
———. 2014. "Powerful. Growing. Influential. The African-American Consumer." *Nielsen Consumer Research,* September 25. Accessed October 17, 2106. http://www.nielsen.com/us/en/insights/reports/2014/powerful-growing-influential-the-african-american-consumer.html.
Obeid, Sam(ira), and Sara Crawley (2015). *We Are All Trans*. Talk given at TEDx-USF Fall 2015 conference at the University of South Florida—Tampa Campus. Available at https://www.youtube.com/watch?v=a9_5Wh_T65s.
Office for Victims of Crime. 2014. "Responding to Transgender Victims of Sexual Assault." Office of Justice Programs. Downloaded April 17, 2017: https://www.ovc.gov/pubs/forge/sexual_numbers.html.
Ogilvy, David. 1963. *Confessions of an Advertising Man*. New York: Atheneum.
Pérez, Emma. 1999. *The Decolonial Imaginary: Writing Chicanas into History*. Bloomington: Indiana University Press.
Rakow, Lana. 1986. "Rethinking Gender Research in Communication." *Journal of Communication* 36: 11–26.
Riordan, Ellen. 2001. "Commodified Agents and Empowered Girls: Consuming and Producing Feminism." *Journal of Communication Inquiry* 25: 279–97.
Riviere, Joan. 1929. "Womanliness as a Masquerade." *International Journal of Psychoanalysis* 10: 303–13.
Rooks, Noliwe M. 2005. *Ladies Pages: African American Women's Magazines and the Culture That Made Them*. New Brunswick, NJ: Rutgers University Press.
Rosenberg, Jessica, and Gitano Garofalo. 1998. "Riot Grrrl: Revolutions from Within." *Signs* 23: 812–13.
Rubin, David A. forthcoming 2017. *Intersex Matters: Biomedical Embodiment, Gender Regulation, and Transnational Activism*. Albany: SUNY Press.
Sandoval, Chela. 1991. "U.S. Third World Feminism: The Theory and Method of Oppositional Consciousness in the Postmodern World." *Genders* 10: 1–24.
———. 2000. *Methodology of the Oppressed*. Minneapolis: University of Minnesota Press.
Scott, Linda M. 2000. "Market Feminism: The Case for a Paradigm Shift." In *Marketing and Feminism: Current Issues and Research,* edited by Miriam Catteral, Pauline MacLaran, and Lorna Stevens, 16–38. London: Routledge.
She Runs It. 2016. "We See Women as Leaders." http://sherunsit.org/#stay-connected/.
Smith, Barbara. 1986. *The Combahee River Collective Statement: Black Feminist Organizing in the Seventies and Eighties,* volume 1. New York: Kitchen Table: Women of Color Press.
Smith, Dorothy. 1987. *The Everyday World as Problematic: A Sociology for Women*. Boston: Northeastern University.

———. 1997. "Comment on Hekman's 'Truth and Method: Feminist Standpoint Theory Revisited'" *Signs* 22: 392–98.

Tuchman, Gaye. 1978. "Introduction: The Symbolic Annihilation of Women by the Mass Media." In *Hearth and Home: Images of Women in the Mass Media,* edited by Gaye Tuchman, Arlene Kaplan Daniels, and James Benet, 3–38. New York: Oxford University Press.

U.S. Supreme Court. 1971. *Reed v. Reed* 404 U.S. 71.

U.S. Supreme Court. 1973. *Frontiero v. Richardson* 411 U.S. 677.

U.S. Supreme Court. 1973. *Roe v. Wade* 410 U.S. 113.

Vavrus, Mary Douglas. 2012. "Postfeminist Redux?" *Review of Communication* 12: 224–36.

Walker, Alice. 1983. *In Search of Our Mothers' Gardens*: *Womanist Prose*. San Diego: Harcourt Brace Jovanovich.

Walker, Rebecca. 1992. "Becoming the Third Wave." *Ms. Magazine* 11 (2): 39–41.

West, Candace, and Don Zimmerman. 1987. "Doing Gender." *Gender & Society* 1(2): 125–51.

Index

3% Conference, 6, 13, 23n1, 194
3% Minicon, 195
4A's. See American Association of Advertising Agencies

AAF. See American Advertising Federation
AAUW. See American Association of University Women
ABC (TV network), 9, 109, 123, 124
Abercrombie and Fitch, 46–47, 49
Abzug, Bella, 33
academic research, 348;
on advertising representation, 36–37, 39;
effects research, 41–42, 49;
on magazine advertising content, 41–42;
on sexual stereotyping, 42
Adichie, Chimamanda Ngozi, 344
advertising:
as a career for women, 21, 298–99, 321, 324–25, 327–28;
Chicana/Latina feminist perspectives, 234–36;
critiques of, 8–14;
as culture industry, 156–57;
effects of, 18, 29, 40, 41–42, 49, 85–86, 116, 251;
and feminism, 4–8, 87–89, 361–62;
role of, 2–3;
as social commentary, 161–62;
and "woman's viewpoint", 69, 297, 316–17, 325
Advertising Age (periodical), 77, 92, 93, 177
advertising agencies:
cancelled campaigns, 144–46;
creative departments. See creative departments
gender culture in, 212–14, 345–46. See also creative departments: gender culture in;
homophily in, 184, 189;
Sweden, 211–12, 215
Advertising Careers for Women (Clair and Dignam), 319, 321, 323, 325, 326
Advertising Club News, 316
advertising clubs. See women's advertising clubs
advertising governing boards, 49–50
Advertising Women of New York (AWNY), 298, 317, 318, 319–20, 326, 330
and Dignam, 327–28;
rebranding of, 357.

See also League of Advertising Women of New York
advocacy groups, 194
African American(s):
boycotts by, 115, 118;
discrimination against, 12, 274;
historical account of, 19;
marginalization of, 63, 67–68, 210;
political consumption, 274–75
African American women:
advertising pioneers, 351;
commodification of, 341;
discrimination against, 43;
fashion models, 43;
in Hall of Fame, 12;
life insurance, 95.
See also black women
alcohol, 1, 141–42, 145, 241
Alvesson, Mats, 211, 222
Always (brand), 29, 170;
"Like a Girl" campaign, 46, 162–63, 165, 172, 185–86
American Advertising Federation (AAF), 178
American Association of Advertising Agencies (4A's), 12, 178, 195;
1924 "Standards of Practice", 2
American Association of University Women (AAUW), 305
American Heart Association, 262
American Home Economics Association, 301
America's Next Top Model, 133
Andrews, J. Craig, 112
Anthony, Marc, 235
Anwelt Corporation, 143
Anzaldúa, Gloria, 33, 352
appearance of women:
and feminist magazines, 73–77;
and health magazines, 254–55;
and "modern" woman, 72–73;
and suffragists, 6, 64–65.
See also beauty; fashion
Apple, 277
artistic creation:
as rationale for violence against women, 143, 144
Ash, Theodore E., 320
aspirational advertising, 6, 70, 71–73, 238
athletes of color, 163–64, 165, 169
Atlantic Records, 37
Atwood, Margaret, 35, 47
The Edible Woman, 36, 41
audiences. See consumer audiences
automobiles, 168
Avedon, Richard, 42
awards and award shows, 183, 185–86, 190, 209
AWNY. See Advertising Women of New York
Axe (brand), 30, 170, 171

Badger and Winters (ad agency), 46
Badger, Madonna, 5, 46
Báez, Jillian M., 15, 16, 17, 341, 343, 352, 356, 359
Baker, Jes, 47
Bambach, Laura Jordan, 194
Barbie, 47–48
Bartos, Rena, 351
BBDO (ad agency), 189, 195, 196Beattie, Alison, 187
beauty, 18–19, 30, 61–62, 112;
and "desirable" television audience, 120;
equating health with, 253, 359;
and feminist magazines, 6, 73–77;
femvertising, 29–30, 80;
and humor, 170–71;
and love-your-body discourse, 159–61, 165, 170;
"narcissism as liberation", 98–100;
notion of, 62;
and postfeminism, 79–80, 255–56;
and violence against women, 146–47.
See also fashion
Beer, Amy, 244

Belmont, Alva, 70
beneficiary behavior, 273
Bennett, Lance, 33–34
Berger, John, 137
Beyoncé, 30
black feminism/feminists, 351, 354–55. See also womanism
Black Lives Matter, 118, 347
black women:
as "desirable" audience, 120, 123, 341;
and indistinguishable marketing, 9, 109–10;
marginal status and health, 116;
"strong black women" trope, 116–17, 163;
use of social media, 117–18;
and women of color, 251–52.
See also African American women
Boddewyn, Jean, 42–43
body image:
and advertising, 46–47, 73, 76, 251–52;
advertising effects on, 18, 29, 49, 85–86, 116;
and gendered social norms, 163–66;
love-your-body discourse, 159–61, 165, 170;
and postfeminism, 79–80;
and women of color, 256–57
Bonwit Teller, 98
Bort Carleton, 138, 143
boycotts, 17, 37–38, 272, 285, 342–43
by black women of the Oscars, 117
and diminished consumer choices, 115
and gay rights, 277
motivations for, 273, 275, 283–84
notion of, 272
and social exclusion, 280–85
branded television programming, 117, 119
and indistinguishable advertising, 123–26
Bronson, Mary, 67, 319
Bronstein, Carolyn, 5, 136–37, 149–50, 338–39, 347, 353, 359, 362
Brownmiller, Susan, 32, 135, 349
Brown, Rita Mae, 349
Butler, Judith, 339, 362n1
Butler, William, 37
buycotts, 17, 273, 283–84, 285, 342–43, 359
buying risk, 281, 284, 285–86

Cadwell Davis (ad agency), 38
Cadwell, Franchellie, 38
Calvin Klein, 5, 31, 42
Camay, 72
Cannon, Katie G., 111
Carbine, Pat, 145
career. See professional development
Carlson, Jessica, 213
Carnation (brand), 304
celebrity endorsements, 70, 168–69, 262–63.
See also individual names, e.g. Williams, Serena
Chambers, Jason, 19
Change.org, 47
Charles Morris Price School of Advertising and Journalism, 321
The Chicago Girl (periodical), 327
Chicago Herald, 323
Chicana/Latina feminism, 355–56;
theories, 233–34.
See also Latina(s)
Chick-fil-A, 274
childrearing, 218, 220, 345, 358
Chisholm, Shirley, 32–33
cigarettes, 78–79, 140–41, 142, 233
Clair, Blanche, 323, 325
Clairol, 75
classism, 341;
and early 20th century advertising, 70, 325–26;
and Latina representation, 16, 241–42, 245n7;
and sports, 164;
and suffrage movement, 65;

and women's advertising clubs, 318–19, 330, 348
Coca-Cola, 195, 235
Cohen, Linda, 90
Coleman, Catherine, 5, 338–39, 347, 353, 359, 362
collective action, 32, 35, 45
Collier, Patricia, 304
Collins, Jason, 276
Collins, Patricia Hill, 355;
Black Feminist Thought, 354
The Combahee River Collective: "Black Feminist Statement", 354
commodity feminism, 6–7, 11, 18–19, 29, 77–79, 81, 86, 87–88, 101, 353;
beauty, 98–100;
food products, 97–98;
home appliances, 96–97;
housing, 96;
life insurance, 94–95;
notion of, 77
Commonwealth Edison Electric Shop, 324
communication, 7
and fourth-wave feminism, 34, 35
competitiveness:
amongst creatives, 184, 191
connective action, 33–34, 353–54
conscience behavior, 273, 274
consumer audiences, 7, 14–18, 22;
"desirable", 8–9, 111–12, 113, 117, 236–37, 341;
diminished choices, 114–15;
men as, 166–71, 172;
metrosexual, 170–71;
reception analyses, 256;
stereotypes, 6, 35, 36, 68, 72, 92, 97, 325–26, 329;
vis-à-vis indistinguishable advertising and television, 118–21;
women as 159–66, 172
consumer citizenship, 16–17, 237–43, 244, 359
consumer culture:
and feminism, 77–79, 81;
and identity, 6, 62;
LGBT, 275–77, 342–43;
and stereotyping, 6, 35, 36;
and suffrage, 63–65;
and technology, 75
consumer feminism, 100
consumer mobilization, 115
Consumer's Clinic, 326
consumers' republic, 90–91
contradictions:
beauty and health, 18, 255–56, 260, 261, 266–67;
and weight-loss products, 263–64
Copeland, Misty, 163, 164, 165
Cornell University, 302
corporate advertising, 49–50
corporate social responsibility, 30–31
cosmetics, 75, 77, 98–99.
See also beauty
Cosmo for Latinas (periodical), 237
Cosmopolitan (periodical), 37, 138, 296
Cosmopolitan en Español (periodical), 233
Coston, Julia Ringwood, 348
Courtney, Alice E., 36–37, 42
CoverGirl (brand), 48
covert/masked marketing, 114;
notion of, 112–13;
and television programming, 118–21, 123
Cracker Barrel, 274
Crawford, Mary, 213
Crawley, Sara, 338
Cream of Wheat (brand), 298
creative culture, 179–80;
feminist perspectives, 212–14
creative departments;
"face time", 183–84, 191–92;
gender culture in, 10–14, 156–57, 177–80, 182–90, 196–97;
and meritocracy, 189–90;
sexual language use in, 181;
under-representation of women in, 177–78, 182, 186, 193–96, 207
creative departments in Sweden:

career trajectories in, 217–18;
discrimination in, 219;
facilitating change in, 224–25;
pervasiveness of Western subculture in, 13–14, 208, 216–17, 223, 360;
and work-life balance, 219–20;
work-style behavioral differences, 218–19, 220–23
creative directors, 157, 185;
creative mandate, 148.
See also women creative directors
creatives, 156;
competitiveness amongst, 186, 191;
ideal creative, 190–91;
personality of, 180, 185.
See also women creatives
creative work:
male models of, 190–91;
nature and ways of, 180, 185–86
Credle, Susan, 180, 196
Crenshaw, Kimberlé, 10, 41, 116–17, 136, 343, 349–50
Crocker, Betty, 300, 304–6, 308
The Crunk Feminist Collective, 353
Cullors, Patrisse, 118, 347
cultural feminism, 13–14, 212–13, 217, 219, 224, 356
cultural norms and values;
and gender bias, 218, 219–20;
and gender differences, 212–13, 344–47, 356;
and gender stereotypes, 210–11, 219, 220–23;
of Sweden, 210–12
Cutex, 68

Daniel and Charles (ad agency), 39
Daniels, Lee, 125
Dávila, Arlene, 243, 352
Davis, Angela, 352
Davis, Judy Foster, 351
DDB (ad agency), 195
De Beauvoir, Simone, 100
deceptive advertising, 47, 113–14
DeCourcy, Colleen, 181
Dee, Juliet, 9–10, 349
DeGeneres, Ellen, 48
Demarest, Jack, 100–1
Denny, R. Sue, 141–42
Descente America, 140
dietary cacophony, 262–63
differences:
and feminism, 35–36, 350–52.
See also gender differences
differential consciousness, 355
Digiday (periodical), 181
Dignam, Dorothy, 22, 315, 323, 329–30;
and AWNY, 327–28;
and PCAW, 324–26;
"She's a Stylist in Paris", 327;
"Up the Ladder We Must Go", 327;
and WACC, 323–24;
"Women's Place in Advertising", 327–28
diminished consumer choices, 114–15
discrimination:
of African Americans, 12, 43, 274;
and corporeality, 46–47;
in creative departments, 183, 219;
creditor discrimination, 96;
of racial minorities, 274–75.
See also gender discrimination
dissatisfaction:
with hegemonic depictions of women, 18, 29, 49, 116, 256, 266;
with hypersexualized Latina imagery, 241
dissonance, 261, 266–67
diversity, 23n1;
and "desirable" consumer audiences, 111–12;
in representation, 31;
in workforce, barriers to, 178, 182–83;
in workforce, initiatives for, 195–96
in workforce, lack of, 8, 12, 13–14, 112, 177–78, 179, 184, 189, 196–97;
Dolce and Gabbana, 30–31, 49, 144, 149–50
Dollar Shave Club, 170, 171

dominance theory, 10, 133, 134, 150, 356;
and second-wave feminism, 135–36
Douglas, Susan J., 88, 99, 242, 243
Dove (brand), 170;
Campaign for Real Beauty, 29, 30, 46, 80, 159–61, 163, 185–86, 259–60, 262;
for Men campaign, 168–69
dual-income households, 91–92;
and life insurance, 94–95
Duclos, Rod, 278
Duncan, Margaret Carlisle, 255
Duncan Quinn, 149
Dworkin, Andrea, 135

eating disorders, 18, 29, 40, 116
Ebony (periodical), 95
education:
home economics journalism, 301–3, 337;
and women's advertising clubs, 321, 325, 329
Edwards, Chris, 188–89, 345–46
Elektra, 37
Elliott, Umaara, 118
Empire (TV series), 9, 109, 121, 124–26
employment:
and early 20th century women, 66;
wartime employment, 89–90, 98
empowerment. See commodity feminism
Encore Shoe Corporation, 144–45
Engel, George, 252
enlightened sexism, 242, 243
entitled femininity, 80
equality, 32, 62, 79, 344–47, 350, 362n2;
and differences, 350–52;
and Sweden, 211
Equitable Life & Casualty Insurance Company, 95
Esquire (periodical), 149
Essence (periodical), 233, 238
Estée Lauder, 30, 75
Estefan, Gloria, 235
ethics:
and gender stereotyping, 157;
and indistinguishable marketing, 9, 114–18;
and niche markets, 16–17.
See also womanist ethics
ethnic women's magazines, 15–17, 231–33, 235–36, 237, 241–42, 244, 254, 267
exercise, 263

Facebook, 33, 46, 48, 123, 125, 149
fair trade products, 285–86
false advertising. See deceptive advertising
Famolare, 39, 42, 138, 144, 145, 146
Famolare, Joe, 39, 42, 144
fashion:
beauty ideal, 18–19, 31–32;
black models, 43;
clothing sizes, 46–47;
and indistinguishable advertising, 123–24;
sexism in, 5, 30–31, 42, 46–47, 49;
and suffrage movement, 64–65;
and violence against women, 143–45, 146, 147–50.
See also beauty
FCB (ad agency), 196
Feagin, Joe R., 274
Federal Trade Commission (FTC), 113, 114
feminine hygiene products, 162–63
feminism, 4;
and advertising, 4–8, 87–89, 361–62;
and femininity, 98;
first-wave of, 50n1, 347–48;
fourth-wave of, 33–34, 35, 45–48, 353–54;
and home economics, 301;
interpretations by women of color, 110–11;
and lesbianism, 349;
media's role in spreading, 100–1, 350;
and Ms. magazine, 6, 73–77;

notion of, 62;
second-wave of, 32–33, 34–43, 44, 86, 100–1, 134, 135–36, 295, 306–8, 348–51;
third-wave of, 29, 33, 41, 43–45, 351–53;
waves of, 32, 48, 50n1, 61, 347
feminist(s):
in advertising, 6, 61–62, 69–71, 351
as consumers. See commodity feminism;
and early consumer culture, 6, 63–65;
notion of, 62;
representation of feminism, 73–77;
stereotypes of, 98
feminist activism, 5, 48, 49–50;
and social media, 30–31, 33–34, 35, 45–48, 353–54
feminist audience studies, 233, 252
feminist critique, 5, 29, 36–37, 87–89, 149, 172–73, 359
Feministing.com, 48
feminist media theory, 136–37
feminists of color, 33, 351, 352
femvertising, 29–30, 44
Fernandez, Senaida, 233
Fields, Jill, 88
Finnegan, Margaret, 64
first-wave feminism, 50n1, 347–48
Fletcher, Joyce, 212–13
food and food products, 97–98, 166–67, 262, 300, 302, 303
footwear, 39, 42, 138, 143–45
Fort Sheridan Business Men's Club, 322
fourth-wave feminism, 33–34, 35, 45–48, 353–54
Fox (TV network), 9, 109, 124, 125–26
Foxworth, Jo, 37, 351
Frederick, Christine McCaffey, 6, 65–68, 70, 71, 298, 308, 319–20, 329
Frederick, J. George, 67, 319–20
freelancers, 192
French, Neil, 346
Friedan, Betty, 5, 32, 37, 40–41, 100, 349;
The Feminist Mystique (Friedan), 5, 35–36, 41
FTC. See Federal Trade Commission

Gallop, Cindy, 6, 12, 188, 189, 195, 207
Gardberg, Naomi A., 275, 284
Garner, Jeanette, 100–1
Garolini shoes, 138, 147–49
Garza, Alicia, 118, 347
gender:
notion of, 338–40;
paradoxes of, 341–43
gender bias. See organizational gender bias
gender differences, 13–14;
and cultural norms, 212–13, 344–47, 356;
work-style behavior and traits, 218–19, 220–23
gender discrimination, 177–78, 182, 186, 193, 195, 196–97, 207, 209–10, 211, 219–20, 327–28, 337, 346
gender disparity 12, 13–14, 47;
in creative departments, 156–57, 177–78, 182–83, 186–87, 189–90, 217–18;
and indistinguishable advertising, 115–18
gender representation, 155, 158–59;
exemplars for men, 166–71, 172;
exemplars for women, 159–66, 172
gender roles, 36–37, 218, 219–20, 346–47;
and commodity feminism, 97;
and early 20th century women media producers, 6, 65–71;
and exemplars, 166–67;
"woman's work", 66, 89–90, 98, 345, 358
gender stereotypes/stereotyping, 10, 11, 13, 36–37, 87, 166–67, 172, 185;
challenging, 161–62;

and cultural norms, 210–11, 219, 220–23;
ethical dilemmas, 157
General Foods (firm), 97–98;
Consumer Center, 300
General Hospital (TV series), 134
General Mills, 30, 304, 306
Gentleman's Quarterly, 145
Glamour en Español (periodical), 233
Glass Lion award, 195
Goeppinger, Katherine:
How to Write for Homemakers, 302
Goffman, Erving, 87, 162
Gender Advertisements, 37
Goldman, Robert, 87–88, 353
Golombisky, Kim, 4, 307–8
Gordon, Kat, 6, 194
Gordon, Mary, 5
green products, 285–86
Grow, Jean, 13–14, 44, 340, 356
Gucci, 30
guerrilla advertising, 342, 352
Guerrilla Girls, 352–53
Guess jeans, 138, 146
Guilford, Joy Paul, 180

Hall, Stuart, 156
Hamer, G. Joyce, 351
Han, Xiaoqi, 17, 342–43, 359
Harp, Dustin, 275
hashtag activism, 46;
#betterforit, 30;
#BlackLivesMatter, 118, 347, 354;
#ChimeForChange, 30;
#EmpowerAllBodies, 47;
#FeministHackerBarbie, 48;
#ImNoAngel, 47;
#LikeABoy, 46;
#LikeAGirl, 29, 46;
#LoveTravels, 276;`
#OscarsSoWhite, 118, 354;
#scandalstylethelimited, 124;
#WomenNotObjects, 5, 46
Haubegger, Christy, 15–16, 233, 352
Hawkins, Robert, 37
Hayek, Salma, 241
Hazard, Aline, 295
health, 18;
impact on women of color's self image, 264–65;
messages, 254–55, 261–62, 359;
notion of, 252–53, 258;
"paradoxes of the flesh", 255–56;
"quick fix" messages, 262–64
Heath, Deborah, 87–88, 353
hegemonic masculinity, 155, 166–67, 168, 170–72
Heineken, 1
Henri-Charles Colsenet (HCC) tennis wear, 138, 140
Henson, Taraji P., 124
Herbert, Elizabeth Sweeney, 307
Hermes, Joke, 238
Hernéndez, Leandra H., 18–19, 338–39, 355, 359
heteronormativity, 47, 138, 155, 171–72, 207, 217–18
heterosexuality, 41, 169, 236, 240–41
Heublein/Spirits Club strawberry daiquiri, 138, 145, 146
Hewitt, Nancy, 61
Higgins, E. Tory, 213, 218
hip-hop feminism, 353
Hispanic market, 15–16, 245n1, 341, 352. See also Latina(s); Latinx
historiography:
of advertising, 88, 348;
of feminisms, feminists vis-à-vis advertising, 4–8, 88–89;
of professional development, 19–21, 295–99;
of women's advertising clubs, 314–17
Hobbs, Renee, 40
Hoeflin, Ruth:
Introduction to Home Economics, 295–96
Holtzhausen, Derina, 307–8
home appliances and equipment, 96–97
recommendations by home economists, 299–300
home economics, 20

academic programs, 301–3, 337
advertising career via, 20–21, 296–97, 303–6, 308–9, 358
as career, 295–96
and feminism, 295, 301, 306–8
home appliances and equipment studies, 300, 301
home appliances recommendations, 299–300
radio programs, 295, 304
home economics movement, 66, 72
hooks, bell, 33, 35, 41, 344, 352
Hopkins, Claude:
My Life in Advertising, 326
Hostetter, Helen Pansy, 302–3
housing/home ownership, 96
Huge (ad agency), 190
Hull, Gloria T., 352
Human Rights Campaign:
Buying for Workplace Equality Guide, 277
humor:
as creative rationale for sexism, 155, 170–71, 172;
as creative rationale for violence against women, 139–42;
and women, 214, 222–23
Husted, Marjorie Child, 305–6
hypersexualization, 16, 236, 240–41

IAE. See Institute of Advertising Ethics
IBM, 277
ideal beauty, 18–19, 31–32, 80, 87, 116, 155, 160, 251;
challenging, 161–62;
and social tableaux, 73
ideal woman, 22, 36, 62, 338–39
identity, 338;
and consumer culture, 6, 62;
paradoxes of, 341–43;
political, 6, 63–65;
postidentity, 122
inclusion, 109–10, 111–12, 126–27;
Latinas' perspectives, 239–40
indistinguishable advertising, 8–9, 109–10, 112–14;
and branded television programming, 123–26;
ethical concerns, 9, 114–18, 126–27;
and television, 118–21
Instagram, 33, 124
Institute of Advertising Ethics (IAE):
composition of, 355
interlocking, 343–44
International Chamber of Commerce, 42
International Code of Advertising Principles, 42
interpersonal exclusion, 279
Interpublic (ad agency), 207
intersectionality, 9, 10, 14–19, 41, 50n1, 116–17, 136, 343–44, 360;
gender concerns, 115–16;
and womanist ethics, 110;
and women's advertising clubs, 318–19
In Touch (periodical), 262
Iowa State University, 300, 301, 302
Ivory Liquid soap, 37

Jackson, Michael, 125
Jägermeister, 138, 142
JC Penney Life Insurance Company, 95
Jeffries, Mike, 46
Jell-O Pudding, 97–98
Jenkins, Henry, 113
Jenkins, Joanna L., 341, 344, 354
Jhally, Sut, 40
Jiang, Yuwei, 278
Johnson, Tyrone Reginald, 125
Jones, Caroline R., 351
Jordan, Tom, 195
Joseph, Ralina L., 122
Journalism Quarterly, 302, 303
Journal of Home Economics, 300, 305
Journal of Marketing, 93
J. Walter Thompson Company (JWT), 68–69, 209, 303, 326;
Women's Editorial Department, 69–70, 71

Kansas State University, 301, 302–3
Kennedy, Florynce “Flo”, 351
Kestin, Nancy, 184
Kilbourne, Jean, 39–40, 41, 42, 133, 136, 137, 148, 150, 356
Killing Us Softly (film series), 40, 133, 136
Klos, Lori A., 255
Komisar, Lucy, 36
KOMM (Swedish Association of Communication Agencies), 209, 215
Kraft, 303
Kreshel, Peggy J., 3
Kruger, Barbara, 359

Ladies Home Journal, 100, 299, 319
Lambiase, Jacque, 5, 338–39, 347, 353, 359, 362
Lane Bryant, 170;
  “I’m No Angel” campaign, 47, 161–62, 163
language:
  gendered use of, 181, 214–15
Latina(s), 210, 244n1, 341;
  health to, 256;
  and magazine advertising, 15–17, 231, 232–33;
  magazines oriented to, 235–36, 244
  as markets and audiences, 236–37, 359;
  media literacy of, 239–40, 267;
  representations of, 236, 240–42, 243, 352;
  and visibility, 242–43
Latina (periodical), 15–16, 231, 232–33, 237, 244, 245n6;
  content and messages of, 238–39, 352;
  representations of Latinas, 236, 240–42, 243
Latin music, 235
Latinx, 232, 244n1, 359
  boycott against Taco Bell, 274
  representation in mainstream advertising, 234–35
Lauder, Leonard, 75
Lauper, Cyndi, 77
Lazar, Michelle M., 80
League of Advertising Women of New York, 22, 67, 313–14, 328;
  establishment of, 319–20.
  See also Advertising Women of New York
Lee, Jaehoon, 279–80
LEGO Friends, 47
Leo Burnett (ad agency), 46, 78, 140, 196
lesbianism/lesbians, 36, 50n1, 147
  “lavender menace”, 349
  “lesbian chic”, 43–44
Lévy, Maurice, 209–10
LGBT, 17, 271, 286, 359
  “Silence = Death” project, 342, 352
  and social exclusion implications, 282–86
Libby Glass Company, 298
liberal feminism, 32, 39, 308, 356–57
life insurance, 94–95
The Limited (retailer), 123–24
lingerie, 39, 85–86, 98, 161–62
live trademarks, 304–6
Lockeretz, Sarah, 36–37
Longoria, Eva, 241
Look (periodical), 94
Lopez, Jennifer, 30, 241
Lorde, Audre, 33, 350–51
Loveland, Katherine E., 278
Lux, 68

Maas, Jane, 178, 193, 351
McBride, Mary Margaret:
  How to Be a Successful Advertising Woman, 298
McCalls (periodical), 99
machismo, 168, 169
McJunkin Agency, 324
MacKinnon, Catherine, 135–36, 150, 349
McRobbie, Angela, 79
Macy, 67, 319
Mademoiselle (periodical), 87–88

magazines:
advertising content in, 41;
content control in, 40;
coverage of feminism and feminists, 100–1;
Latina-oriented, 235–36, 244;
mainstream magazines, 18;
and third-wave feminism, 353.
See also Latina (periodical); Ms. (periodical); women's magazines
Maidenform lingerie, 39
male gaze, 137, 161, 236, 241, 243, 359
Mallia, Karen, 13, 357, 359, 362
Mandel, Naomi, 278
Marchand, Roland, 71
Marciano, Paul, 146
marginalization, 43–44;
of African Americans, 63, 67–68, 210;
and boycotts, 275, 284;
of women of color, 29, 37, 43, 254, 349–50;
and women's advertising clubs, 22, 318–19, 330, 348
market feminism, 48–49, 360
market research:
and Latinas, 239–40
Marriott, 276
Marschalk (ad agency), 142
Martinez, Gustavo, 209–10
Martin, Jane J., 318, 330
Martin, Joel P., 351
Martin, Ricky, 235
Marxist feminism, 357
masculinity:
applied to women, 164, 165;
and creativity, 188, 189–90, 213, 214, 219, 223;
hegemonic, 155, 166–67, 168, 170–72;
as selling feature, 168–70, 172;
and violence, 133–34, 136;
viz-à-vis power and control, 166–67
Maser, Wayne, 146
masked marketing. See covert/masked marketing
Massachusetts Institute of Technology, 301
materialist feminism, 357–58
Mattel, 30, 47–48
Matthews, Victoria Earle, 348
Max Factor, 98–100
Maytag, 97
Mead, Nicole R., 278, 279
M. C. Weil (ad agency), 297
media, 18;
and spread of feminism, 100–1;
and minority audiences, 18.
See also magazines; social media; television programming
The Media Education Foundation, 40
media-linking strategies, 112;
and television programming, 121, 123, 126
media literacy, 40;
Latina audiences, 239, 267;
women of color, 263, 264
Men's Advertising League of New York, 319
meritocracy, 189–90
metrosexual consumers, 170–71
millennial blacks, 117–18;
and branded television programming, 124
Miller, Constance, 327
Mink, Patsy, 349
minority consumers;
and political consumption, 274–75;
and social exclusion, 280–81
Minow, Martha, 347
misogyny, 340
Miss Liberty awards (Libbies), 39, 144
Moderna (periodical), 245n6
modern women, 71–73
Molden, Daniel C., 279
moments of entanglement, 63, 80–81;
notion of, 6
Moraga, Cherríe, 33, 352
moral myopia, 10
Morgan, Joan, 353
Morgan, Robin, 20, 32, 295, 308, 358

MPLS MadWomen (advocacy group), 187, 194
Ms. (periodical), 6, 32, 35, 37, 43, 73–77, 95, 145, 351, 352
Mulvey, Laura, 137, 359
Murray, Dara Persis, 5–6, 347, 348, 359

NARB. See National Advertising Review Board
National Airlines (US):
Fly Me campaign, 38
National Advertising Review Board (NARB) (US), 38
National Association of Colored Women's Clubs, 348
National Organization for Women (NOW) (US), 32, 34–35, 349;
1972 study of TV commercials, 87;
Minneapolis-St. Paul chapter's class-action, 306;
Strike for Equality (Aug. 1970), 37–38
National Women's Party (US), 70
native advertising, 9;
and branded television programming, 124, 125–26
Negra, Diane, 79
Nelson, Joyce Kay, 308
neoliberalism, 79, 81, 165–66. See also consumer citizenship
networked activism, 33–34. See also connective action
Newburry, William, 275, 284
New Jersey Citizen Action, 274
Newman, Gary, 124
newspaper women's pages, 296
Newsweek (periodical), 37
Newton, Helmut, 134, 148
New York Magazine, 77
New York Times, 85, 98
NFL, 277
niche markets, 8–9, 15–16, 232, 244;
and ethics, 16–17
Nichols, Synead, 118
Nicolosi, Ann Marie, 6–7, 350, 359
Nielsen, 236–37, 341
Nike, 30, 44, 163–64, 165, 170, 185–86;
boycott of, 272
Nipper, Mads, 47
Nixon, Sean, 12
Norton, Eleanor Holmes, 136, 349
NOW. See National Organization for Women
Nunn Bush brass boot shoes, 138, 143
N. W. Ayer and Son (ad agency), 324, 326

Obama, Barack, 124
Ogilvy, 195
Ogilvy, Davie, 353
Ohio State University Black Advertising and Strategic Communication Association, 356
Omnicom (ad agency), 207
The One Club, 195
online communication. See social media
oppression, 33, 36, 41, 111, 116, 126
organizational culture, 10–14, 22, 156–57, 179–80, 181–82, 183–85;
Sweden, 211–12, 218–19, 220–23
organizational feminism, 213, 217, 218, 220, 224;
organizational gender bias, 13–14, 183, 186, 187–90, 207–8, 346;
and cultural norms, 218, 219–20;
hiring inequity, 184, 189, 210, 217;
pay disparity, 209, 211, 217, 218;
promotional inequity, 217–18
The Oscars (Academy Awards), 118

Paisley, Matilda, 37
Parents Latina (periodical), 237
Parkin, Katherine J., 88
paternity leave, 184–85
pay disparity, 209, 211, 217, 218
PCAW. See Philadelphia Club of Advertising Women
Peñaloza, Lisa, 276
Pennell, Ellen, 304
People en Español (periodical), 235

PepsiCo, 124, 125–26, 195
performative gender, 339–40
personal grooming, 170
Peter Pan International, 85–86
Petty, Ross D., 112
pharmaceuticals, 167
Philadelphia Club of Advertising Women (PCAW), 22, 315, 320–21;
and Dignam, 324–326, 328
Philip Morris (firm), 78, 140–41
Pillsbury, 304
Pingree, Suzanne, 37
Pinkett-Smith, Jada, 118
Pinterest, 124
Playboy (periodical), 37
Playboy Club, 73–74
political consumption, 273–74;
and gay consumers, 275–77;
and racial minorities, 274–75
political economy, 8–9, 357–58
political engagement:
and LGBT, 17, 342;
suffragists, 6, 63–65, 348.
See also boycotts; buycotts
Ponds (brand), 70
poor women, 35, 43, 241, 350
pornography, 135;
and violence against women, 137
Porsche, 168
Possible (ad agency), 190
postfeminism, 6, 45, 88, 122, 359;
and beauty, 79–80;
notion of, 79;
postfeminist advertising paradox, 252, 255–56, 266–67
postracism:
and television programming, 121–23, 124
poststructuralist feminism, 157–58, 358–59
power and control, 166–67, 170
presenteeism, 183–84, 191–92
Printer's Ink (trade publication), 298, 323, 324, 326, 327
Pristeen feminine hygiene spray, 37
Procter & Gamble (P&G), 29, 37–38
Proctor, Barbara Gardner, 351
professional development:
advertising career advocacy, 298–99, 321, 324–25, 327–28;
creative career trajectories, 217–18;
and gender factor, 13, 186–87, 217–18;
historiography of, 19–21;
vis-à-vis home economics, 20–21, 296–97, 301–6, 307, 308–9.
See also women's advertising club(s)
promotional inequity, 217–18
Prudential Life Insurance Company of America, 94–95
psychoanalytic feminism, 359
Publicis (ad agency), 207
Pujols, Albert, 169
Purity campaign, 63, 64

Queen Latifah, 48

racial minority consumers:
and political consumption, 274–75
racism, 36, 110, 209, 210, 341;
early 20th century, 63;
and sports, 164–65;
and white colorblindness, 122
radical feminism, 32, 39, 351, 356;
and rape culture, 135
radio programs:
"The Betty Crocker Cooking School of the Air", 304;
corporate home economics shows, 304;
Famous Women of Yesteryear, 321, 326;
Hazard's Homemakers Program, 295;
Let's Scrap It, 326
Ragaza, Angelo, 31–32
Rakow, Lana, 339
Ramirez, Dania, 48
rape, 31, 135, 144, 149–50

recipe booklets, 299, 300
recruitment practices, 184, 189, 209, 210;
in Sweden, 217, 219
Reebok, 30, 150
refrigerators, 299
regulatory fit theory, 213, 218, 220, 224
Reichard, Raquel, 239
relational-cultural theory, 212–13
representation(s), 87;
of all women, 45–48;
constructed by early 20th century advertising women, 6, 63, 65–71;
of Latinas, 236, 240–42, 243;
notion of, 34;
of "realistic women", 259–60, 261, 266;
of women in 1990s, 43–45;
of women in general interest magazines, 36–37
Resor, Helen Lansdowne, 6, 65–66, 68–71
Resor, Stanley, 68, 69
Revlon, 75
Rhimes, Shonda, 122–23
Ribon, Pamela, 48
Rich, Adrienne, 32
Richards, Bailey Shoemaker, 47
Richards, Ellen Swallow, 301
The Richards Group (Dallas), 115
Richardson, Anna Steese, 326
Riot Grrrl movement, 45, 353
Roberts, Kevin, 346
Rocero, Geena, 276
Rojas, Viviana, 241
Rolling Stones (music band):
Black and Blue album, 134
Rosen, Ruth, 6, 100
Ross, Rick, 150
Roth, Patricia, 305–6
Ruffin, Josephine St. Pierre, 348

Saatchi and Saatchi (ad agency), 196, 346
sadomasochism, 9, 134, 147
Sandberg, Sheryl, 187
Sandoval, Chela, 355–56, 357, 360
Santa Barbara News-Press, 145
Sapient-Nitro, 192
Scandal (TV series), 9, 109, 121–24, 125, 127
Schuppe, Jon, 277
Scott, Joan Wallach, 297, 329
Scott, Linda, 5, 6, 48–49
Scott, Patricia Bell, 352
Sebastian International hair gloss, 138, 147
second-wave of feminism, 32–33, 34–35, 50n1, 348–51;
1960s and 1970s, 35–39;
criticism of, 33, 349;
and dominance theory, 135–36;
and home economics, 295, 306–8, 358;
late 1970s to early 1990s, 39–43;
and media, 100–1
resistance to, 136;
and violence against women, 134.
See also commodity feminism
Segerberg, Alexandra, 33–34
segmentation strategies, 93;
and diminished consumer choices, 115;
and television, 119
Selena (singer), 235, 245n4
Selling Mrs. Consumer (Frederick), 66, 298
separatist feminism, 356
Service Readjustment Act of 1944 (US), 90
Seventeen (periodical), 138
sexism, 29, 30–31, 47, 214–15, 343, 350;
and feminist magazines, 75–76;
food products, 97–98;
and humor, 155, 170–71, 172, 214, 222–23;
impact of, 29;
life insurance, 95;
in magazines, 37, 41
sexual harassment, 135–36, 349
sexual objectification, 5, 42, 71, 253;
and feminist magazine, 75–76;
of Latinas, 236, 240–41, 242;

and violence against women, 136–37;
Woodbury soap ad, 68–69
sexual violence, 37, 134–35, 137–38, 144–45
Shakira (singer), 235
Shape (periodical), 262
SheKnows Media, 29
Shell, 272
She Runs It, 357 .
See also Advertising Women of New York; League of Advertising Women of New York
SheSays (advocacy group), 194
Shields, Brooke, 5, 42
shock value:
as creative rationale for violence against women, 146–49
Shrum, L. J., 279–80
Sidney Frank Importing Company, 142
Sikes, Melvin P., 274
Silva Thins, 37
skincare, 30, 159–61, 163, 168–69
slim/thin body image, 73, 76, 251, 254, 260;
cultural standards of, 253, 259;
equating health with, 253, 263–64;
and women of color, 260–61, 264
Smeesters, Dirk, 278
Smith, Barbara, 352
Smith, Sharon L., 87–88, 353
Smollet, Jussie, 125
Smyth Brothers (Chicago), 138, 147–49
Snapchat, 33
Sobhani, Chaka, 196
social exclusion:
being ignored vs. being rejected forms of, 279–85;
and consumer behavior, 278–80;
and minority consumer behavior, 280–81;
notion of, 278
social invisibility, 212–13, 220, 355
social justice:
and Sweden, 211;
and womanism, 9, 112
social media:
and black millennials, 117–18;
and fashion campaign, 124;
and feminist activism, 30–31, 33–34, 35, 45–48, 149, 353–54;
and television programming, 123.
See also hashtag activism
social tableaux, 71–73
Sorrell, Maurice, 210
Spanish-language media, 245n6;
and class representation, 245n7;
and Latina representation, 241–42
SPARK (Sexualization Protest: Action, Resistance, Knowledge) Movement, 47
Spears, Britney, 125
sportswear, 30, 44, 140, 150, 163–64, 165
Spry Shortening, 304
standpoint theory, 318, 358
Staners, Kate, 196
Steinem, Gloria, 6, 32, 40, 43, 73–74, 75, 76, 350, 352;
"Sex, Lies and Advertising", 40.
See also Ms. (periodical)
stereotypes/stereotyping:
of feminists, 98;
gender. See gender stereotypes/ stereotyping;
of Latinas, 16, 236, 240–41, 352;
sexual, 42;
slim/thin image, 73, 76, 251, 253, 254, 259, 260, 266;
"strong black woman", 116–17, 163;
white women consumer, 6, 35, 36, 68, 72, 92, 97, 325–26, 329
strategic essentialism, 356
Stroh Brewery Company, 138, 141–42
Strong, Danny, 125
suffrage/suffragists, 348;
and early consumer culture, 6, 63–65
Summer's Eve (brand), 115
Sweden:
cultural norms and values, 210–12
Swept Away (retail store: Santa Barbara), 138, 145–46

Swift, Taylor, 48
symbolic annihilation, 137, 253, 254, 261

Taco Bell, 274
Tannen, Deborah, 214, 222
target market, 15–16, 94;
black women, 120–21, 341;
"desirable", 8–9, 111–12, 113, 117, 119–20, 123;
Latina/os, 234–35, 236–37, 244
target media, 17, 18
Tasker, Yvonne, 79
Taylor, Liz, 196
Tecate beer, 241
technology:
and behavioral targeting, 9;
and consumer culture, 75.
See also social media
Telemundo (TV network), 245n6
television commercials:
and violence against women, 138, 141–42
television programming:
impact on audiences, 118–19;
and indistinguishable advertising, 9, 109, 119–21, 127;
and postracism, 121–23;
Spanish-language TV, 241, 245n6–7;
and "strong black woman" trope, 117;
and violence against women, 134, 137–38
temperance movement, 63–64
Temple University, 326
textual determinism, 14–15
thematic analysis, 258
thinness of body. See slim/thin body image
third-wave feminism, 29, 33, 41, 43–45, 50n1, 351–53
The Third Wave: Feminist Perspectives on Racism, 41
"This Ad Insults Women" campaign, 39
Time (periodical), 37
Tometi, Opal, 118, 347
Trahey, Jane, 42
transgender men, 188–89, 345–46
transgender women, 44, 345–46
transmedia storytelling, 113
transnational feminism, 360
Tsai, Wanhsiu Sunny, 17, 277, 342–43, 359
Tuchman, Erving, 137
Tumblr, 149
Turbeville, Deborah, 143
Twitter, 33, 123, 124, 125, 149

UltraViolet (activist group), 150
unconscious bias, 183, 189, 195, 207, 217
Under Armour, 29, 163–64, 165, 170
Unilever, 29, 30, 159–61, 169, 170, 195
United States, 14, 360;
"culture of professionalism", 313
dual-income households, 91–92;
postwar prosperity, 90–91;
third-world and Chicana feminisms, 355–56;
wartime labor, 89–90, 98
United States Department of Agriculture (USDA). Bureau of Home Economists, 299, 302, 303
Univision (TV network), 235, 245n3, 245n6
utilities, 168

Vanderhoof and Sons (ad agency), 324
Van Zoonen, Lisbet, 14
Vergara, Sofia, 48
Viagra, 167
Victoria's Secret Angels, 161, 172
Vinson, Mechelle, 349
violence against women, 9–10, 133–34, 150, 349–50;
cancelled ad campaigns, 144–45;
consumer audience attitudes and behaviors vis-à-vis, 137–38;
creative rationale(s), 10, 133, 134, 138–39;

creative rationale as artistic, 143, 144;
creative rationale as shock value, 146–49;
historical contest, 134–35;
as joke, 139–42;
notion of, 133
Virginia Slims (brand), 78–79, 138, 140–41, 142
Vogue (periodical), 99, 138;
HCC tennis wear advertisement, 140;
"The Story of Ohh", 134
Volkman, Meta, 297
Vonk, Janet, 184
Voss, Kimberly, 20–21, 347, 358

WACC. See Women's Advertising Club of Chicago
Walker, Alice, 110, 351–52
Walker, Rebecca, 352
Walters, Susanna Danuta, 87
Wan, Echo Wen, 278
Warner Bros., 37, 114
Warner-Lambert, 37
Washington, Kerry, 121, 123, 124
WAVAW. See Women Against Violence Against Women
WAVPM. See Women Against Violence in Pornography and Media
weight loss, 262, 266;
"band-aid fix" phenomenon, 262–63;
contradictions in, 263–64
Weil, Mathilde C., 297
Wells, Rich, Greene, Inc., 98–99
West, Candance, 339
Wharton School of Business, 326
Whipple, Thomas, 42
white, middle-class women;
and ideal beauty/woman, 18–19, 22, 31–32, 80, 87, 116, 338–39;
life insurance, 94–95;
as media producers, 63. See also Frederick, Christine; Resor, Helen Lansdowne;
stereotypical consumer, 6, 35, 36, 68, 72, 92, 97, 325–26, 329;
and suffrage, 63–65;
and women's advertising clubs, 322
White Sewing Machine, 298
Wieden, Dan, 12
Williams, Carol H., 12, 351
Williamson, Judith, 87
Willaims, Serena, 163–64, 165
Willard, Frances E., 19–20
Willis, Ellen, 32
Wills, Jeanie E., 21–22, 347, 348, 358
Windels, Kasey, 10–11, 339, 340, 358–59
womanism, 9, 110–11, 112, 126
womanist ethics, 9, 109, 110–11, 126–27, 352;
historical context, 116–17;
principles of, 111–12
women, 208–9
advocacy of advertising as career for, 298–99, 321, 324–25, 327–28;
challenging the "weak" image of, 162–63;
construction of "modern" women, 71–73;
as consumers, 65–66, 71;
as "desirable" television audience, 119–20;
differences amongst, 350–51;
and exemplary advertising, 159–66, 172;
invisibility of, 212–13, 220;
"more complex" women, 92–93;
objectification of. See sexual objectification;
and political consumption, 273;
return to domesticity, 91;
traditional masculinity applied to, 164, 165;
"woman's viewpoint", 69, 297, 316–17, 325;
"woman's work", 66, 89–90, 98, 345, 358.

See also African American women; black women; white, middle-class women; women of color
Women Against Pornography (WAP), 39, 42, 136, 144
Women Against Violence Against Women (WAVAW), 134, 136
Women Against Violence in Pornography and Media (WAVPM), 134, 136
women copywriters:
early 20th century, 67–68, 69–70, 296, 298.
See also Dignam, Dorothy
women creative directors, 187;
increase in number of, 195–96;
under-representation of, 12, 13, 197;
work-life balance of, 192, 193
women creative directors, Swedish:
experiences and perceptions of, 208, 215–17;
and mentoring, 224;
under-representation of, 211
women creatives:
bias against, 13–14, 183, 186, 187–90, 346;
career growth, 186–87;
and mentoring, 188;
"queen bee syndrome", 188, 191;
under-representation of, 177–78, 182, 186, 193, 195, 196–97, 207, 209–10;
work-life balance of, 185, 188, 192–93
women creatives, Swedish, 211;
career trajectories, 217–18;
discrimination against, 219;
work-life balance of, 218, 219–20;
work-style behavior and traits, 218–19, 220–23
women in advertising 5–6, 39, 325–26, 329;
and advertising career advocacy, 297–99;
careers through home economics, 296–97;
history of, 65–71, 297–99, 314–15;
under-representation of, 327–28.
See also Dignam, Dorothy; women copywriters; women creative directors; women creatives
women media producers, 6, 65–71, 74
women of color:
and beauty stereotypes, 260;
as fashion models, 31–32, 43, 161–62;
and gendered social norms, 163–65;
impact of representations of women on, 259–61, 264–65;
interpretation of feminism, 110–11;
interpretation of representations of women, 251–52, 256–57, 258–61, 265–66;
marginalization of, 29, 37, 43, 254, 318–19, 330, 348, 349–50;
media literacy of, 263, 264;
and notion of health, 258;
sexual harassment lawsuits, 135–36, 349;
stereotypes of, 254;
and third-wave feminism, 33, 41, 43, 50n1, 350–51;
and women's advertising clubs, 318–19, 330.
See also African American women; black women; Latina(s)
Women's Advertising Association of the World, 317d
women's advertising club(s), 21–22, 329;
community outreach efforts, 322;
educational efforts of, 321, 325, 329;
and feminist standpoint, 318, 358;
history of, 313–17;
membership in, 22, 318–19, 320–21, 322, 329–30, 348
Women's Advertising Club of Chicago (WACC), 22, 315, 321–22, 348;
and Dignam, 323–24
Women's Day for Latinas (periodical), 237

women's magazines, 232;
  contents and messages, 238;
  health messages, 254–55;
  and ideal American household, 298.
  See also Latina (periodical); Ms. (periodical)
Women's March (Jan, 2017), 343
The Women's Press, 323
Wongdoody (ad agency), 190, 195
Wong, Tracy, 195
Woodbury Soap Company, 68–69
Woodward, Helen:
  The Lady Persuaders, 298–99
workaholism, 184
working–class girls/women, 348, 350;
  and ethnic women's magazines, 16, 241;
  and suffrage movement, 64;
  as wartime labor, 90;
  and women's advertising clubs, 330
workwife, 93
World War II, 89–90, 98
WPP (ad agency), 207, 346

Yang, Jeff, 31–32
Yoplait (brand), 30
YouTube, 33
Yuban Coffee, 68
Yves St. Laurent Opium perfume, 138, 146–47

ZAP award, 39, 42
Zimmerman, Don, 339
Zodiac shoes, 138, 144–45, 146

About the Editors and Contributors

Jillian M. Báez (PhD) is assistant professor of media culture at the College of Staten Island–CUNY. Báez specializes in Latina/o media, audience studies, and transnational feminisms. She received her doctorate from the Institute of Communications Research at the University of Illinois at Urbana-Champaign and her bachelor's degree from Hunter College–CUNY in Media Studies and Black and Puerto Rican Studies. She has published her research in *Critical Studies in Media Communication, Women's Studies Quarterly, Journal of Popular Communication, Centro: Journal of the Center for Puerto Rican Studies,* and several anthologies. Báez is currently completing a book titled *Consuming Latinas: Media Audiences and Citizenship.*

Carolyn Bronstein (PhD) is the Vincent de Paul professor of media studies in the College of Communication at DePaul University. She is the author of *Battling Pornography: The American Feminist Anti-Pornography Movement, 1976–1986,* which won the 2012 Emily Toth Award from the Popular Culture Association/American Culture Association for the Best Single Work in Women's Studies. She is the coeditor of *Porno Chic and the Sex Wars: American Sexual Representation in the 1970s,* published in 2016. Her work on feminism, pornography, contemporary media culture, and representation of women has been featured in academic journals such as *Feminist Media Studies, Camera Obscura, Violence against Women,* and the *Journal of Mass Media Ethics,* and popular venues such as *The Atlantic.*

Catherine A. Coleman (PhD) is associate professor of strategic communication at Texas Christian University. She received her doctorate from the Institute of Communications Research at the University of Illinois at Urbana-Champaign, with a specialization in advertising. Her research examines advertising representation, gender, ethics, consumer culture, and transformative consumer research. She has published in the *Journal of Advertising, Consumption, Markets and Culture, Journal of Popular Culture, Journal of Public Policy and Marketing,* and *Journal of Marketing Management,* among others, and in various edited collections.

Juliet Dee (PhD) is associate professor in the Department of Communication, University of Delaware. She teaches courses in First Amendment law, mass media and culture, broadcast programming, and television production. She has been director of the Legal Studies Program at the University of Delaware, has been an editor of the *Free Speech Yearbook,* and coauthored *Mass Communication Law in a Nutshell* (2014). She received her bachelor's degree from Princeton University, her master's degree from Northwestern University, and her doctorate from Temple University. She has published articles and chapters on First Amendment issues involving controversial artwork funded by the National Endowment for the Arts, copyright infringement, anonymous defamation on the Internet, objectionable lyrics in rock music and hip-hop, media liability for violent content, media liability for classified ads for hit men, the Occupy Wall Street movement, hate speech, intentional infliction of emotional distress, and cyber harassment and cyberbullying.

Kim Golombisky (PhD) is associate professor at the University of South Florida where she is graduate director in the Department of Women's and Gender Studies. A former advertising and public relations professional, she taught mass communications for eighteen years. Her teaching and scholarship focus on feminist media studies and public discourse. Her coauthored graphic design text *White Space Is Not Your Enemy* is in its third edition, with foreign language editions in Russia and China, among others. She has published in *Journal of Public Relations Research, Women's Studies in Communication, Women and Language, Journal of Advertising Education, Journal of Research on Women and Gender,* and *Communication Theory.* She chaired the USF Title IX Committee and the Women's Caucus of the National Communication Association. She earned a Top Feminist Scholar Award from the Organization for Research on Women and Communication, and she has been visiting faculty on diversity at The Poynter Institute. Her consulting clients have included Walt Disney World Resorts, Publix Super Markets, and Progressive Insurance.

Jean M. Grow (PhD) is advertising professor and chair of Strategic Communication at Marquette University. Her research addresses gender and advertising, particularly the lack of women in creative departments and of diversity across the industry. Her work can be found in the *International*

Journal of Advertising and *Advertising and Society Review,* among others. She coauthored *Advertising Creative: Strategy, Copy, and Design.* Prior to joining the academy, Grow worked as an artists' representative. Her clients included Coca-Cola, Kellogg's, and Zenith. She worked with agencies such as DDB, FCB, and Leo Burnett. Grow continues to do consulting, primarily regarding semiotics and ethnography around gender. Her clients include Flamingo International London, The National Hemophilia Foundation, and Nike. You can follow her on her professional blog, https://growculturalgeography.wordpress.com, and her teaching blog, https://ethicalaction.wordpress.com.

Xiaoqi Han (PhD) is associate professor of marketing at the Ancell School of Business, Western Connecticut State University. As a global strategic communications professional, she worked for IBM, China, and Groupe SEB, France, as well as US startup companies such as 321 Experience Consulting. She earned her doctorate in marketing from the University of Cincinnati. Her scholarly interests include consumer information processing, omission neglect, persuasion, consumer inference, consumer biases, and techniques of debiasing. She is particularly interested in exploring the mechanism behind consumers' lack of sensitivity to missing information (omission neglect). Her research appears in the *Journal of Business Research* and *Psychology and Marketing*.

Leandra H. Hernández (PhD) is an associate faculty member of communication in the Department of Arts and Humanities at National University, San Diego. She is a media studies and health communication scholar whose research centers on reproductive rights, prenatal testing, and shared decision-making. She has published in *Communication Research* and her book *Out of Control: Science, the State, Religion, and Institutional Control of Reproduction in the US and South America*, coauthored with Kari Nixon, is forthcoming with Lexington Press. Her writing appeared in *Contexts of the Dark Side of Communication* (2016), *Reality Television: Oddities of Culture* (2014), and *Television, Social Media, and Fan Culture* (2015). She enjoys teaching Latin@ communication studies, popular culture, intercultural communication, and gender and the media.

Joanna L. Jenkins (PhD) is assistant professor of strategic communication in the Cathy Hughes School of Communications at Howard University. A graphic designer by training and creative director by trade, she has extensive professional advertising experience. Today her research interests include the intersection among digital media, advertising, and culture. Some of her writing includes an American Advertising Federation white paper on *A Millennial Perspective on Diversity and Multiculturalism,* her book *The*

Convergence Crisis: An Impending Paradigm Shift in Advertising, and her chapter on "Stereotypes of Black Women and Advertising" in *Black Women and Popular Culture: An Anthology.* She has taught advertising campaigns, copywriting and design, advertising research and marketing, media psychology, visual culture, and graphic design history.

Peggy J. Kreshel (PhD) is associate professor of advertising at the Grady College of Journalism and Mass Communication and an affiliate faculty member of the Institute for Women's Studies at the University of Georgia (UGA). She is a coauthor of *Media Ethics: Cases and Moral Reasoning,* eighth through tenth editions, as well as a contributing author to two other ethics texts. She is active in the American Academy of Advertising and the Association for Education in Journalism and Mass Communication, where the Advertising Division recognized her with the 2011 Outstanding Service Award. At UGA, she is the recipient of the first Richard B. Russell Outstanding Undergraduate Teaching Award and is a member of the UGA Teaching Academy. She developed Grady College's courses in advertising and society, media culture and diversity, and media literacy and social justice. She also teaches feminist media studies, advertising and society, and advertising media planning. Her research focuses on feminist media studies, media culture, pedagogy, ethics and professional culture, and advertising history. Her work appears in the *European Journal of Marketing, Journal of Advertising, Journal of Current Issues in Research in Advertising, Advertising and Society Review, Journal of Advertising Education, Public Relations Review, Journal of Communication, Journal of Communication Inquiry, Journalism Quarterly,* and *Journalism Monographs.*

Jacqueline Lambiase (PhD) serves as professor and department chair of strategic communication in the Bob Schieffer College of Communication at Texas Christian University (TCU) in Fort Worth, Texas. She teaches diversity, writing, ethics, research, and case studies, and she's a core member of both the Women and Gender Studies program and the Critical Race and Ethnic Studies program at TCU. In 2016, she won the Jean-Giles Sims Wise Woman Award for her teaching from TCU students in Women and Gender Studies. Her research focuses on representations of gender and sexuality in media and marketing, on public relations ethics, and on social media, especially related to public-sector communication. She has coauthored and coedited two scholarly collections with Tom Reichert about sexually oriented and gendered images in advertising and marketing. Working on her own and with others, she has published more than thirty book chapters and refereed journal articles in *Journalism and Mass Communication Quarterly, Sexuality and Culture,* and the *Journal of Current Issues and Research in Advertising,* among others.

Karen L. Mallia (MA) is a former copywriter and creative director, now teaching creative leadership, creative strategy, campaigns, and strategic and cause communication at the University of South Carolina. She is a founding contributor of the 3% Conference and an advocate for women's leadership, as well as a former head of the AEJMC advertising division. She founded CreateAthon@USC, launching this pro bono marathon for nonprofits in 2013 and has orchestrated it ever since. Her New York ad agency career included agencies such as Ogilvy; Scali, McCabe, Sloves; and TBWA\Chiat\Day. Her research has been published in *Journal of Advertising Research, Journal of Interactive Advertising, Advertising and Society Review, Journal of Advertising Education, Employee Relations: The International Journal,* and *Advertising Age*. She is currently writing a textbook on leadership in the creative industries.

Dara Persis Murray (PhD) is assistant professor in the Department of Communication and Media, and affiliated faculty in the Women's and Gender Studies Program, at Manhattanville College. Her research addresses consumer, digital, visual, popular, and celebrity cultures, specializing in beauty and the body, popular feminism, gender, race, class, sexuality, and (dis) ability. Murray's work has appeared in *Feminist Media Studies,* the *Journal of Communication Inquiry,* and *Celebrity Studies.* She has also published chapters in *The Routledge Companion to Media and Gender* and *Cyberfeminism 2.0,* as well as pieces in the online academic collaborative *In Media Res.* Before graduate school, she worked in advertising account management at agencies such as BBDO New York and Gotham, Inc. At Manhattanville, she teaches courses in communication theory; advertising, public relations, and culture; gender and media; race and media; and visual culture.

Ann Marie Nicolosi (PhD) is professor of Women's, Gender, and Sexuality Studies at the College of New Jersey, where she teaches courses in Gender, Sexuality, and US History. Her research interests include twentieth-century women's social movements, lesbian history, and media representations of women. She has published in *NWSA Journal, Gender Issues, Transformations: The Journal of Inclusive Scholarship and Pedagogy, Reviews in American History, Journal of Contemporary Criminal Justice,* and *Journal of the Gilded Age and Progressive Era*. Her work also appears in the *Encyclopedia of American Women's History*, and the fifth edition of *Experiencing Race, Class, and Gender in the United States.*

Wanhsiu Sunny Tsai (PhD) is associate professor in the Department of Strategic Communication at the University of Miami. She earned her doctorate in advertising from the University of Texas at Austin. Her research examines the influence of advertising as a cultural institution in capitalist societies. She has investigated gay consumers' response to gay advertising and their political consumerism, women's relationships with advertising representations of beauty, minority consumers' responses to multicultural advertising, consumer engagement on social media, consumer acculturation, and consumer ethnocentrism. Her work appears in *Journal of Advertising, Journal of Interactive Advertising, International Journal of Advertising,* and *Consumption Markets and Culture,* among others. Her coauthored work has won top paper awards from the American Academy of Advertising, the Association for Education in Journalism and Mass Communication, the National Communication Association, and the International Public Relations Research Conference.

Kimberly Wilmot Voss (PhD) is associate professor in the Nicholson School of Communication at the University of Central Florida. She researches the intersection of women and mass communication in the post–World War II years through contemporary women's liberation movements. She is the author of *The Food Section: Newspaper Women and the Culinary Community* (2014) and a coauthor of *Mad Men and Working Women: Feminist Perspectives on Historical Power, Resistance, and Otherness* (2014). In 2014 she won the Service to Food Journalism Award given by the Association of Food Journalists. Her latest book, *Politicking Politely,* about women, journalism, and politics in the 1950s and 1960s, will be published in 2017. She has published more than forty articles about women and mass communication history. Her blog is available at http://www.womenspagehistory.com/.

Jeanie E. Wills (PhD) is assistant professor in the Graham School of Professional Development at the University of Saskatchewan, Saskatoon, Canada. She studies, teaches, and writes about rhetorical perspectives and how they shape communication choices. Currently, she is excavating a variety of academic and historical archives to explore the link between women's professional identities and their membership in women's advertising clubs of the early twentieth century. This project is funded by a Social Sciences Humanities Research Council grant. In addition to work on historical women's professional identity in advertising, she has also published on the rhetorical motives revealed in memoirs written by advertising men in the early twentieth century.

Kasey Windels (PhD) is associate professor in the Manship School of Mass Communication at Louisiana State University. She holds a PhD in advertising from the University of Texas at Austin. Her research focuses on the advertising agency, with special emphasis on creativity and gender in the creative department. Her dissertation was credited with raising awareness of the dearth of female leadership in advertising creative departments and spurring the development of the 3% Conference. Her research has been published in *Creativity Research Journal, Gender in Management, Employee Relations, Journal of Marketing Communications, Journal of Interactive Advertising, Journal of Advertising Education, Journal of Current Issues and Research in Advertising,* and *International Journal of Advertising*. Her work has been reported in *Adweek* and *Advertising Age*.

Lightning Source UK Ltd.
Milton Keynes UK
UKHW011820091119
353137UK00008B/63/P

9 781498 528283